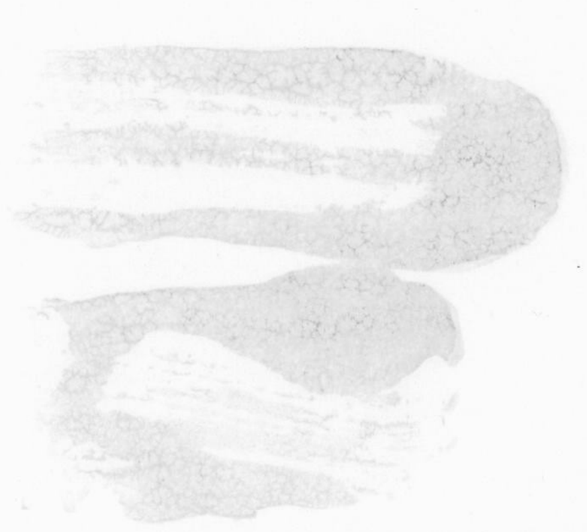

D1116827

CHRISTIAN EXISTENTIALISM

Christian Existentialism

A BERDYAEV ANTHOLOGY

SELECTED AND TRANSLATED

BY

DONALD A. LOWRIE

'God is a subject with whom existential relations exist.'

N. BERDYAEV

Slavery and Freedom, p.24

London

GEORGE ALLEN & UNWIN LTD

RUSKIN HOUSE MUSEUM STREET

FIRST PUBLISHED IN 1965

PRINTED IN GREAT BRITAIN
in 11 point Janson type
BY SIMSON SHAND LTD
LONDON, HERTFORD AND HARLOW

PREFACE

Any attempt to organize Berdyaev's thought is somewhat like trying to discover system in New York's weather. Save for one sketchy classification of all philosophy and philosophers in his *Essay on Eschatological Metaphysics* (in English *The Beginning and the End*), Berdyaev never tried it, himself. His thought leaps from one idea to another, mutually contradictory dicta are not infrequent, as he readily admits, and the broad range of concepts on which he has spoken his mind, make the task of selection and compression into this brief space, one of considerable difficulty. Selection in any case is likely to be subjective, and although it has been guided by counsel from friends of Berdyaev, and I have tried to avoid personal bias, responsibility for this material must be mine.

Quotations included here result from reading Berdyaev's twenty-nine books, hundreds of articles most of them hitherto untranslated, and unpublished material, like the 'Mme K.' letters or Berdyaev's notebooks. About one-fifth of the text appears for the first time in English. In all cases the translation is my own; not all the previous English versions have been uniformly excellent; some have been translations from translations. The present text, good or poor, is at least of fairly uniform quality.

Except for statements which lead to thoughts of his own, the quotations are limited, in principle, to what Berdyaev said for himself, rather than his comments on others. A second volume would be needed to print Berdyaev's consideration of other philosophers, from Plato to Sartre.

With a few exceptions the quotations are presented in chronological order. This sequence does not obtain where another arrangement seemed to offer a more logical and coherent whole. Chronology is important, particularly in the pre-banishment period, where it now seems almost incredible that Berdyaev could have dared say what he did, in the given historical moment.

I acknowledge with thanks the service of three great libraries, the New York Public Library, the Lenin Library in Moscow, and the Leningrad Public Library. Counsel from Paris members of the Berdyaev Society, from Paul B. Anderson, Melvin Arnold, Robert Beach and Serge Levitzsky has been most helpful. For the task of typing twice the amount of text finally included, and aid and counsel all through the five years' work on it, my profound gratitude goes to Helen Ogden Lowrie.

The generous permission to use quotations from books for which they hold English rights by the following publishers is gratefully acknowledged:

The Fate of Man in the Modern World, trans. by Donald A. Lowrie. New York: Morehouse-Barlow; London: S.C.M. Press, 1935.

The Realm of the Spirit and the Realm of Caesar, trans. by Donald A. Lowrie. New York: Harper & Brothers; London: Victor Gollancz, 1952.

The Meaning of the Creative Act, trans. by Donald A. Lowrie. New York: Harper & Brothers; London: Victor Gollancz, 1955.

New York City D.A.L.
August 15, 1964

CONTENTS

EXPLANATORY NOTE ON SOURCES

Pages indicated are those of the Russian originals, except for the three books I had already translated, *The Fate of Man in the Modern World*, *The Meaning of the Creative Act* and *The Realm of Spirit and the Realm of Caesar*. Codes for reference to each title are listed below. Cuts are indicated in the conventional fashion (. . .), and represent the elimination of repetitious phrases, or of sections not essential to the basic thought.

ABBREVIATION	DATE	TITLE
Subjectivism	1901	*Subjectivism and Individualism in Social Philosophy*
Idealism	1903	*Problems of Idealism*
New	1907	*The New Religious Consciousness and Sociality*
Sub Specie	1907	*Sub Specie Aeternitatis*
Crisis	1910	*The Spiritual Crisis of the Intelligentsia*
Philosophy	1911	*The Philosophy of Freedom*
Khomiakoff	1912	*A. S. Khomiakoff*
Russia	1915	*The Spirit of Russia*
M.C.A.	1916	*The Meaning of the Creative Act*
Art	1918	*The Crisis of Art*
Fate of Russia	1918	*The Fate of Russia*
Dostoevsky	1923	*Dostoevsky: An Interpretation*
Meaning	1923	*The Meaning of History*
Inequality	1923	*The Philosophy of Inequality*
End	1924	*The End of Our Time*
Leontieff	1926	*Leontieff*
Freedom	1927-28	*Freedom and the Spirit*
Class War	1931	*Christianity and Class War*
Destiny	1931	*The Destiny of Man*
Solitude	1934	*Solitude and Society*
Fate	1934	*The Fate of Man in the Modern World**
Reality	1937	*The Spirit and Reality*
Origins	1937	*The Origin of Russian Communism*
Slavery	1939	*Slavery and Fredom*
Idea	1946	*The Russian Idea*
Beginning	1947	*The Beginning and the End*
Divine	1947	*The Divine and the Human*
Autobiography	1949	*Dream and Reality*
Spirit and Caesar	1949	*The Realm of Spirit and the Realm of Caesar*
Truth	1953	*Truth and Revelation*

* Quotations are from the 2nd British Edition, 1938.

CHAPTER I

Ten Significant Dates in Berdyaev's Life

I BIRTH

1874

Nicolai Alexandrovitch Berdyaev,[1] the boy who was to become 'one of the greatest philosophers and prophets of our time',[2] was born in 1874 on a broad estate near Kiev, which two years later his father was forced to sell. Those were the times of the shattering economic change in Russian life, resulting from the emancipation of the serfs in 1861. Landholders could no longer maintain their former scale of living, and Berdyaev's father, Alexander Michailovitch Berdyaev, escaped financial disaster by exchanging the family estate for a house and garden in the 'best' section of Kiev. This was home for Nicolai Alexandrovitch until he was twenty-one. His father, one of the rare men of his old family who had not made the army his career, was a difficult, sometimes moody man, widely read in the culture of the past century, and an avowed free-thinker. His mother, descended from a long line of French nobility, was most unlike her husband, loved high society while he loved the country, and was more at home, religiously, in her mother's French Catholic Prayer Book than in official Russian orthodoxy.

Neither parent seems to have known just what to do with Nicolai, born fifteen years after the only other child in the family, his brother Serge. Theirs was not a happy home, unlike most homes of this social class that were filled with guests and gaiety; the boy was much alone, and never had any friends of his own age. As a result, he became a very badly spoiled child who as an adult could say he had never known authority over him. Throughout his life, except for contacts with the police, he did exactly as he pleased, abetted in this by devoted kinfolk. Instead of continuing his military school and entering the 'Pages' Corpus', to which his family's social position entitled him, he chose to study in the university. At an early age, somewhere before he was thirteen, the boy had a sudden 'inner transformation, which changed his whole life' and made him decide to devote himself to philosophy. He had read Hegel and Schopenhauer before he was fourteen, and at seventeen passed an examination in Mill's *Logic* and Kant's *Critique of Pure Reason.* Long before he entered the university in Kiev he knew he would be a philosopher.

II EXILE

1900

University life throughout Russia was astir with the social ferment that culminated in the abortive 1905 revolution. As he had always resisted any authority, the young Berdyaev now turned against the whole social class into which he had been born, maintaining only the minimum permissible of contact with kinfolk, excepting his parents. About the time he entered the university (1894) he took an apartment in town, soon had a group of associates, many of them of the despised Jews from 'the Podol',[3] of whom his parents disapproved, and like most other students was engaged in subterranean political activity, both in and outside the university. Contact with one of these clandestine organizations, a labour union group, gave him a sympathy for the working man, that, although he never did a stroke of manual labour in his life, always remained with him. Despite their inherited distrust of the intelligentsia, this group urged Berdyaev to be their leader. He never had aspired to formal leadership and although he refused this appeal, he rendered signal service to secret revolutionary movements. His family connections made it possible for him to take several trips abroad for contact with revolutionary exiles like Plechanov and Axelrod.

This was the time when marxism, with its 'scientific' answers to all the problems of mankind, had penetrated Russia and was captivating all liberal minds, and young Nicolai Alexandrovitch was inclined to accept. He had some reservations, however, for he could not believe that concepts like truth and justice, for instance, instead of being basic and permanent, were changing according to economic conditions, as orthodox marxism was teaching. But, as he wrote years later, 'At that time I considered Marx a man of genius.' One of his companions in the marxist organization was a fellow student, Anatole Lunacharsky, later the permanent colleague of Lenin. Revolutionary activity was not all secret. On several occasions during Berdyaev's student years, students 'went into the streets' in public demonstrations against the government. Such parades were usually broken up by the police, with some of the participants arrested. If the atmosphere was particularly tense, Cossacks with their terrible whips would intervene, so that participants knew the risks they were taking. Berdyaev was among those arrested in such a demonstration, near the end of his university studies (1897) but was released with a stern warning.

He continued his secret activities, nevertheless, and besides organizing lectures on forbidden political topics, took a responsible part in the clandestine press that provided much of the material for revolutionary effort, right across the Empire. But it was discovered, the police arrested all those mentioned in the address lists they found, and Berdyaev, with about 150 others found himself in prison. Although his family managed to have him released under bail after six weeks, decision in the case of these young revolutionaries was delayed for two years, and it was in May 1900 that Berdyaev and many of his partners in 'crime' were sentenced to three years' exile in the northern province of Vologda.

III BERDYAEV'S FIRST BOOK

1901

Many of the exiles were sent to tiny, primitive villages in the Vologda Province. But Berdyaev, probably because of his family connections, was permitted to live in the city, a town with a good hotel, a theatre and other cultural amenities. He took the best room in the best hotel, and there, with two summer vacations at home to break the term, lived through the next three years. Free from any physical discomfort, Berdyaev found life in Vologda interesting, even exciting. The city was full of intellectual exiles like himself, and they organized a very active 'Union of Exiles', with frequent public meetings and lectures, and the interminable private discussions on all sorts of topics, characteristic of the Russian intellectuals of the period. Nicolai Alexandrovitch was often a speaker, sometimes the chairman at these public meetings. His brilliance and sincerity threatened to win many of his listeners away from orthodox marxism toward the 'idealism' which was already tempering radical marxism in Berdyaev's own thought. Lunacharsky, arriving in Vologda exile later than Berdyaev, was so disturbed by Berdyaev's presentation that he organized a series of lectures of his own, to combat him. Lunacharsky, like dozens of the other exiles, was writing a book. Remizoff, another Vologda exile, reworked his, twenty times and then had to wait until his return from exile to see it in print. But within a year after he arrived in Vologda, Berdyaev saw his first book published.

He had already published several articles, which had attracted some attention to his 'idealistic' ideas. The new book was *Subjectivism and Individualism in Social Philosophy*, a critical essay on Michailovsky. Michailovsky was the accepted leader of a large part of the Russian 'liberal' youth, and for one of them to criticize his book, *The Subjective Method in Sociology*, demanded real courage. Berdyaev's book outraged the marxists, but it impressed many readers by its erudition, worthy of a man twice its author's age.

IV MARRIAGE, MOVE TO ST PETERSBURG

1904

Home again in Kiev after his three years' exile, Berdyaev continued his active participation in the intellectual life of the city. Here he made the acquaintance, which developed into life-long friendship, with a young professor, Serge Bulgakov. Two years earlier Bulgakov had published a marxist book, but Nicolai Alexandrovitch found that Bulgakov had now moved further away from standard marxism than he, himself. Berdyaev stated his own philosophical position at this time (1903) as follows: 'Beginning with my article, "The struggle for Idealism", I finally move from positivism to metaphysical idealism, and . . . change my attitude toward marxism, from which I still retain a series of realistic social ideas, but which I deny as a world-view.' The acceptance of a Christian faith was to come later.

In Kiev also, Berdyaev met the sisters who were to play principal rôles in his life thereafter. Lydia and Eugenie Trusheff, daughters of a leading Kiev attorney, were attracted by the brilliant young lecturer, and the acquaintance depened into friendship which resulted in a marriage. Nicolai Alexandrovitch chose Lydia, beautiful, artistic and socially-minded, as his life-partner. A few years later, after her own marriage and divorce, Eugenie came to live with the Berdyaevs, and remained with them to the end of their lives. Berdyaev's love for Lydia was a profound spiritual devotion, and some of his remarks about it are the most moving of his words.

This same year in the autumn, Berdyaev left Kiev and moved to the Empire's capital, St Petersburg; out of the province to the centre of intellectual life. In the capital the tremendous intellectual renaissance which has aroused the wonder of the world ever since, was beginning its effervescence. Here other thinkers like Frank and Struve were hesitantly moving along the spiritual road Berdyaev and Bulgakov had entered. Life in St Petersburg was an almost feverish round of philosophical and literary discussion groups, one of whose products was a series of artistic and philosophical magazines. Berdyaev and Bulgakov, who had followed him to St Petersburg, joined in editing two of these ephemeral periodicals. Nowhere else in modern times has such a purely intellectual, romantically academic, atmosphere prevailed, refined almost to the point of decadence, as in those years at the turn of the century in St Petersburg. Social and mystical experimentation, month-long disputation over the most abstruse intellectual or spiritual problems combined with a continuous round of parties that turned night into day. The witty, handsome young Berdyaev took an active part in everything.

All this high-tension social and intellectual life was, of course, only for a thin upper layer of society, the gentry and the wealthy intelligentsia. Looking back at it, a half century later, it seems almost incredible that the catastrophic Russo-Japanese war and the precocious 1905 revolution could have attracted almost no attention from the cream of the Empire's intellectual life. These high-powered thinkers were interested in ideas, not people. As Berdyaev once said, the erotic and esthetic predominated over the ethical.

V MOVE TO MOSCOW

1908

It must not be supposed that Berdyaev's life and thought in St Petersburg were occupied only with 'the erotic and esthetic'. Some of the most brilliant thinkers there were deeply concerned with purely spiritual problems. Some, like Merezhkovsky and his wife, Hippius, endeavoured to find solutions outside all tradition; others, like Kartasheff and Frank, were slowly finding their way to a religious, even a Christian position. Almost no one as yet considered entering the Church: in the minds of those thinkers the Russian Church was so completely identified with reaction that a believing Christian would scarcely be considered a member of the intelligentsia.

Gradually the general movement divided into those still interested in politics, despite the government's reaction after the 1905 revolution, and those concerned with things spiritual, art and literature, philosophy and religion. And of this latter section a smaller group turned definitely toward religion, or as Berdyaev always insisted upon calling it, religious philosophy. Led by Bulgakov, whose father had been a parish priest, there was a gradual rapprochement with the Church. This came to its clearest expression in the magazine of which Berdyaev was one of the editors, *Life's Questions*. Shestov, one of Berdyaev's few life-long friends, said, 'On the pages of *Life's Questions* there is unrolled the history of Berdyaev's conversion from a metaphysician to a believing Christian.' Berdyaev's own books and articles of the Petersburg period confirm this statement, as a few quotations will show: 'The dialectic theory of the necessity of social catastrophe is not only non-scientific, logically inept . . . but it is profoundly anti-idealistic.' 'You can talk of dialectic idealism, but not of dialectic materialism.' The marxist theory is 'beneath all criticism'. Even positivism is insufficient: 'Positivism is incapable of . . . recognizing that freedom is above happiness and satisfaction . . . that freedom is God.' These citations from Berdyaev's *Sub Specie Aeternitatis*, a collection of essays he published in 1907, are crowned by one more. Nicolai Alexandrovitch says the group of thinkers to which he belongs wants 'to unite ourselves with the eternally-existing God, to continue the millenial work of His creation'.

All this radical development could not take place without much discussion and disagreement with other equally radical thinkers. After four years in the over-charged atmosphere of the capital, the Berdyaevs moved to Moscow. Nicolai Alexandrovitch wrote that he could no longer endure the 'unhealthy, mystical sentimentality' prevailing in the capital.

In Moscow Berdyaev soon became an active member of a religious-philosophical study group, the Solovieff Society under the leadership of Prince Troubetskoy. The first years in Moscow witnessed Berdyaev's return to Christianity and the Orthodox Church. For the first time in his life he was impressed by the ancient traditions of Russia and the patriarchal life of the venerable city. He began reading the Church fathers, he made pilgrimages to old monasteries. Quite unlike most Russians of his type, Nicolai Alexandrovitch had almost no childhood contacts with the Orthodox Church, its beautiful ritual and its moving music. So that when he wrote that he had 're-entered' the Church, he might have omitted the 're': baptized in infancy, he was always reckoned as a church member, but had never before had real contact with its life. Although he was never a very orthodox Orthodox, Berdyaev remained faithful to his Church, for the rest of his days.

In Moscow, as in St Petersburg, Nicolai Alexandrovitch was only perfuntorily interested in politics. He belonged to a political party out of a sense of duty, but almost none of his writings at this time can be called political.

VI ITALY

1912

Berdyaev wrote less in those Moscow years than later, abroad. There were months when a mood of depression prevented his writing altogether. He continued his active participation in the Solovieff Society with its searching after truth. His own quest was not yet accomplished. Then late in 1912 the Berdyaev family began a year's stay in Italy, most of it in Florence. Here 'he had a sudden new vision of the whole of the world's history, human and divine'. 'The disparate pieces of earlier thinking suddenly fell into an integral pattern.' In what he called an ecstatic climax of creativeness, he wrote *The Meaning of the Creative Act*. For the first time he was presenting his own thought, not comment on the thinking of others. The book contained in embryo at least, most of the ideas he spent the rest of his life developing. It was published in 1916, about a year after his return to Moscow.

Of the basic ideas in *The Meaning of the Creative Act*, one of the most important is Berdyaev's conception of man as co-creator with God. Man must answer God's creative love with creativity of his own. Another idea linked with this is that of the three epochs of history: the Epoch of the Law (Old Testament), the Epoch of Redemption (New Testament) and the Epoch of Creativity. In 1916 Berdyaev felt that the third epoch, that of Spirit, was about to dawn, had perhaps begun in some outstanding personalities. The new creativity would be creativity in the Spirit, in man's becoming divine as a response to the redemptive act of God in becoming man. A third basic idea is that of freedom as primordial, existing before all else. Freedom is one of the basic themes of all of Berdyaev's writing.

The book was denounced as heretical, 'demonic'. Frank called it 'philosophical decadence'. Widely read, it set Berdyaev apart from most of his contemporaries, a situation he occupied throughout his subsequent years. He attained further prominence in 1913 when, after a violent article against the Holy Synod of the Russian Church, he was arrested and charged with blasphemy. Only the outbreak of World War I and the revolution that followed, prevented Berdyaev's spending the remainder of his life in Siberian exile, the automatic penalty for such a crime.

As the war progressed, Nicolai Alexandrovitch's writing took on a patriotic tone. The last of his work published in Russia was a small book, *The Destiny of Russia* (1918). He apparently took no part in any activity connected with the war, however, either military or humanitarian. But he had thought deeply about his country's fate, he resented the incompetence and corruption of the Tsarist régime, and was not surprised when defeat turned into revolution.

VII THE COMMUNIST REVOLUTION

1917

Unlike most Russian liberals, Berdyaev had foreseen that revolution, when it came, would introduce old evils under new names. He had long since broken all contacts with the communist leaders who took over the revolution, and actually appeared to many as a reactionary. This was partly because of his unflinching stand for freedom and the dignity of the individual, and his violent denunciation of the new régime. He called it 'a consistent application to life, of Russian nihilism, atheism and materialism. . . . The denial of all absolute spiritual elements in personal and social life. . . . The bolsheviks are the final Russian nihilists.' This was two months after the communists had seized power. At this distance it seems almost miraculous that after publishing such sentiments, Berdyaev could go on writing for five more years before he was banished.

The Berdyaev family suffered all the hardships of those terrible years in Russia. As 'bourgeois' all three were compelled to work at street-cleaning and other 'socially useful' occupations. They lived through several Moscow winters in unheated rooms, although they were better fed than most because of a special food ration granted for some unknown reason to twenty outstanding intellectuals. Berdyaev continued not only writing, but lecturing in the 'Free Academy of Spiritual Culture' which he organized early in 1919. The only institution of the sort, so alien to communist ideas that the word 'spiritual' was incomprehensible to one police officer who called him in for an explanation, the 'Academy' continued to function as long as Berdyaev was at liberty.

VIII BANISHMENT

1922

Besides the public lectures in the Academy, Berdyaev spoke in other meetings and as a state-employed lecturer in the University of Moscow. Furthermore, there were the weekly 'salons' in the Berdyaev home, where even more freedom of expression about the communist régime was practised, than in his public appearances. All through this period he was writing, producing four books, only one of which was published in Russia.

In 1921 Berdyaev was arrested and held in solitary confinement for six weeks before a midnight interview with Dzerzhinsky, head of the secret police, brought his liberation on condition that he would not leave the city. At his next arrest, in the summer of 1922, he was presented with an order of banishment and forbidden to return to Russia on pain of death. It developed that a group of about twenty intellectuals, among them Berdyaev's friends, Frank and Lossky, with their families was to be deported as 'hopelessly inconvertible to communism'.

Soviet authorities had arranged passage to Germany for this group of about seventy people. For about a year the Berdyaevs (Nicolai Alexandrovitch, his wife, his sister-in-law and her mother) lived in Berlin, enjoying a freedom they had not known for five years. Here Berdyaev organized the Religious-Philosophical Academy, continuing the work of the Moscow Solovieff Society. The speakers were almost all from among the newly arrived exiles, since they did not see eye to eye with the great body of emigrés from Soviet Russia, then centred in Berlin. He continued to write and, after the last years in Russia when his books could not be printed, to publish. His unintended 'best-seller', *The New Middle Ages*, was quickly translated into other languages, and offered him a wide introduction to the thinking world.

Those were the days of the collapse of the German mark, and great privation in Germany. Most Russians moved to Paris, where life was less expensive, and the Berdyaevs did the same, but Nicolai Alexandrovitch never forgot that early German hospitality to the Russian exiles.

IX MOVE TO PARIS

1923

From their arrival in France in late 1923 until his death, Berdyaev lived in a Parisian suburb, Clamart, most of the latter years in a house he owned, thanks to a legacy from an English friend. The house is still maintained, with Berdyaev's study intact, a place of pilgrimage for hundreds, every year, who know and admire his writing. As in the case of the Russian Church, this, Berdyaev's new contact with the west, has left permanent traces in the thought life of the rest of the world. The Religious-Philosophical Academy had moved to Paris with Berdyaev, and its meetings continued until the outbreak of World War II. For nearly a quarter of a century Berdaev lived an active, busy life, lecturing and writing. Fifteen of his most important books were written during this period. All could be published at once, thanks to the YMCA Press in Paris, the oldest publishers of Russian books outside the Soviet Union, of which he became editor-in-chief, retaining this position until his death. Berdyaev's books have now been translated into a dozen languages, including Japanese.

Nicolai Alexandrovitch was frequently invited to lecture to other than Russian audiences, in France and abroad. In 1926 a trip to the Baltics helped him to a new vision of his mission. He often lectured in England, and near the very end of his life obtained the signal honour of a Doctor of Divinity degree from Cambridge, the only university diploma he ever held, since his arrest had closed his career in the University of Kiev before graduation.

Together with the rest of Europe the Berdyaevs suffered privation during World War II. After a hasty removal from Paris at the time of the German invasion in 1940, they returned to Clamart. Although his anti-Hitler articles had been as violent as anything he had written about Russian communists, Berdyaev was not seriously disturbed by the Gestapo, apparently because of some unknown protector high in Nazi circles. The close of the war found him still writing in Clamart, his small library intact, and with four new manuscripts almost ready for the printer.

Lydia died shortly after the end of the war. Her death, Berdyaev wrote, was 'the most poignant and at the same time inwardly significant event' of his life. The house in Clamart now had a vacant chair, but with Eugenie Rapp, the sister-in-law, as housekeeper, life went on almost as usual.

The close of the war brought a peculiarly painful situation for Berdyaev, and for most of the 'homesick million' of Russian emigrés. All through the war they had patriotically shared the losses, and then the victories of Soviet armies, buoyed by the hope that now freedom would come to Russia. Not the least painfully disillusioned was Nicolai Alexandrovitch. Officially invited to return to the Soviet Union he indignantly refused, knowing he would be unable to write and publish there. His fondest hope, to see his homeland again, was not to be realized.

X DEATH

1948

Writing was almost an obsession with Berdyaev. If he were to think of himself in heaven, he said, it would be sitting at his desk. He was seated at his desk when he died, March 23, 1948. His funeral was a true ecumenical observance, Protestant and Catholics joining Orthodox at the services.

Throughout his life in the west Berdyaev had been an active supporter of the ecumenical movement. He believed Orthodoxy had a special rôle to play in bringing together the Christians of the world: his many lectures at meetings of the World Student Christian Federation were in line with this feeling, as were those at the Ecumenical Institute of the World Council of Churches in Switzerland, in 1946. He will be remembered as a world figure in Christianity, as in philosophy.

One of Berdyaev's friends, writing as 'Philippe Sabbant' in a Bulletin of the Berdyaev Society[4] inquires into the reasons for the philosopher's ever-widening influence: 'There are thinkers who attract us solely by the strength of their arguments, the brilliance of their formulae, the harmony of their systems. Their thought asserts itself, independently of the historical climate. But the thought of Berdyaev could come to full value only in the conditions of our world today. . . . Not merely because men are at present more and more caught in the feverish rhythm of a "speeded-up" history, but also because the spiritual values of the past are themselves in question.' After quoting from Berdyaev's *Fate of Man in the Modern World* where he says that the new historical epoch as yet unnamed is really a judgment on the whole of history, rather than a new epoch, Sabant continues: 'For Spengler, the "new epoch" was to be subject to historical contingencies. But Berdyaev has been able to use it to rediscover that liberty which alone is the measure of man.'

In 1937 Berdyaev wrote a summary of his thought for a German publisher. The first paragraph states: 'The centre of my philosophical work is the problem of man. This is why all my philosophy is essentially anthropological. To put the problem of man is to put the problem of freedom, of creativity, of the person, of the spirit and of history. Hence I have been principally concerned with the philosophy of religion, the philosophy of history and with social and ethical philosophy.' The present volume is the first attempt to systematize Berdyaev's thinking in all these fields.

Berdyaev's influence as a philosopher is world-wide, but so is his influence as a prophet, a prophet in the special sense of interpreter of our times, 'sub specie aeternitatis'. Nicolai Alexandrovitch was specially gifted in helping other men see the spiritual problems of today, and of proposing solutions out of personal experience, explanations and solutions the man-in-the-street could understand, and be lifted up. As Sabant says: 'Berdyaev has done more than anyone else in our day, to give back to Christians the true dimensions of the Church. But at the same time he has guided into new ways many for whom, before they met him, God seemed only a "useless hypothesis". For . . . by analysing the contradictions of materialism in the light of today, and also in his profound comprehension of the great social movements of our times, he has spoken in a language all men understood.' F. H. Heinemann calls Berdyaev 'a link between East and West, between Christians of different denominations, between Christians and non-Christians, . . . between philosophy and theology, between the visible and the invisible'.

NOTES

[1] It is the Russian custom to call people by two names, the 'given' name and the patronymic. Nicolai Alexandrovitch means Nicolai, the son of Alexander. All those who knew him used this form.

[2] *The Times*.

[3] The 'Ghetto' of Kiev.

[4] *Bulletin* No. 1, April 1953.

CHAPTER II

What Can We Know?*

*'In philosophy you cannot arrive at being:
you can only proceed from being.'*
DESTINY, p. 3

BEING

What is Being?
A spiritualistic ontology affirms that genuine being, the essence of being, is spirit, and spirit is being, objective being.

But what is being? This is the basic problem of philosophy. We are accustomed to using the concept 'being' as something undoubted and self-evident. But a critique of knowledge puts the question to what degree, in what we call being, are included the products of thought, in what degree the activity of the subject constructs 'being', which then appears to be something primary. In Kant the foundations of the one true metaphysics are laid: the dualism of the order of freedom and that of nature, volontarism, indeterminism, personalism, the doctrine of antinomies, the recognition of another more profound reality behind the world of phenomena. . . .

German idealistic metaphysics never put the problem of man and personality: these were smothered by the impersonal, universal spirit. The universal, the general, conceived otherwise than in Greek philosophy, overcame the individual, the unique, the truly existential. Philosophy of the spirit became the philosophy of objective being. The rational concept of being continued to dominate. . . .

Reality, pp. 8-9

The Ultimate Problem of Being
Being is either community and communion, or company and communication. The idea of complete rationalization and socialization of all spheres of life by means of science is a false and thoroughly anti-Christian idea. Here science is understood as scientism, as the universalization of all degrees and forms of knowledge, which actually have only partial significance. Unity, monism cannot be achieved on the basis of science-like knowledge and the organized forms of society. This would mean attaining unity outside the mystery of human existence, or in a form of

* Sir John Davies.

existence completely outcast in the world, finally objectivized and alienated. The achievement of final unity which will solve all the contradictions and antinomies of human thought and human society, is possible only apophatically, as apophatic knowledge of the Absolute, or communion with God and the Kingdom of God. Up to that moment, with our kataphatic thought about God, in our life in an objectivized society, the dualism remains, the conflict between two elements, contradictions, tragedy. The whole problem lies in this: is the achievement of unity, harmony, communion, thinkable only on some higher level, which is the apophatic, or is it thinkable on the lower kataphatic level, as rationalism, positivism, communism or scientism would have us believe?

Solitude, pp. 63-4

To Have or to Be?

It would be inexact to say of man that he is spirit. But we can say that he has a spirit. Only in God does the difference between 'to have' and 'to be' completely disappear. Man is not yet that which he has. He has reason, but is not reason; he has love, but is not love; he has quality, but he is not quality itself; he has ideas, but he is not idea. The task of realizing human personality lies in this: to be what you have; it is that man should be determined not by what he has but by what he is. To be is reality, realization; to have, to possess something, is only a sign and a symbol.

Reality, p. 147

Being is not Spirit

To think of spirit as being means thinking of it naturalistically, as nature or object, but spirit is not object, it is nature: it is not being. Spirit is subject, act, freedom. The primary act is not being: being is congealed act. The mystics have taught, truly and profoundly, that God is not being, that the limited concept of being is inapplicable to God. God is, but He is not being. 'I am that I am' puts the accent on 'I', rather than 'am'. 'I' is personality, is something preceding 'being', which is the result of thinking in terms of categories. *Personality is prior to being.* This is the basis of personalism.

We must choose between two philosophies, the philosophy which recognizes the primacy of being over freedom, or that which accepts the primacy of freedom over being. This choice cannot be made by thought, alone, it is determined by the integral spirit, i.e. will. Personalism must recognize the primacy of freedom over being. The philosophy of the primacy of being is a person-less philosophy. The system of ontology which recognizes the absolute primacy of being is a system of determinism. Every objectivized intellectual system is a system of determinism. It derives freedom from being, and thus freedom is determined by being, which in the final analysis means that freedom is the child of necessity. Being is revealed as ideal necessity, with no possibility of upsurge: being is whole, absolute unity. But freedom cannot be derived from being: freedom is rooted in nothingness, in bottomlessness, in non-being, if we use ontological terminology. Freedom is without foundations; it is not determined, it is not born of being. There is no such thing as whole, uninterrupted being. Instead, there are upsurges, explosions, abysses, paradoxes, things transcendent. Hence only freedom exists, only personality. The primacy of freedom over being is also the primacy of spirit over being. Being is static: spirit is dynamic. Spirit is not being. We cannot think of spirit intellectually, as of object: spirit is subject and subjectivity: it is freedom and creative act. Dynamism, activity, creativeness—stand over against the intellectual understanding of being. . . .

On his spiritual way, on his road to knowledge, man faces, not being, which is not primary and really means rationalization, but rather truth, as the secret of existence. And man faces, not abstract truth, but Truth as the way and the life. 'I am the truth, the way and the life.' This means that truth is concrete personality, its way and its life; truth is dynamic in the highest degree: it is not given in a final and solidified form. Truth is not dogmatic. It is given only in the creative act. Truth is not being, and being is not truth. Truth is life, the existence of the existing. Only that which exists, exists. Being is only a congealed, hardened portion of life; life which is cast out into 'object-ness'. And the problem of being is inseparably bound up with the problem of God.

Slavery, pp. 65-6, 70

Being and Non-being

Everything compels us to admit the existence not only of being, but of non-being, of the dark abyss preceding the very beginning of the knowledge of being and the distinction between good and evil. This non-being is both lower and higher than being. It would be more exact to say that non-being does not exist, but has existential significance. Dualism, polarization, the conflict of opposing elements, is an existential fact. We should not say that evil is non-being, but rather that the appearance of evil in the world presupposes the existence of non-being, and is inexplicably by a self-contained system of being.

Beginning, pp. 104-5, 107-9, 129

Being and Knowing

Knowledge is essentially active, for man is active. We cannot admit the claim, in the gnosseological contradistinction of knowledge and being, that knowledge merely gives a passive reflection of being, that it is wholly determined by being, as the created world. Something is brought into knowing from free activity. Knowledge is not merely reflection, it is creative transfiguration. And man himself is not consciously active in the creation of the world by the subject. In actuality, the world is not created by the subject, but by God, only; the world is not finished—its completion is left to man. And man must bring into everything his creative freedom and in his knowing continue the world's creation. The world does not enter into me, passively. The world I face depends upon my attention and my imagination, upon the intensity of my thought (this intensity is determined from within, not from without). This means that the present world depends upon the subject as man, as being, as something existant. This means that knowledge is the relation of being to being, a creative act in being. . . .

The riddle and the mystery in the theory of knowledge is still how the object, material and unreasoning, is reflected as knowledge in a subject non-material and endowed with reason. This problem is insoluble, if we are to consider knowledge as reflection of the object in the subject, if we consider being as object, and subject as outside being. . .

How is any mutual relationship possible between subject and object, if the subject is external to being, and being is for him an object? This is the basic problem. Men have tried to solve it by asserting the identity of thinking and being, of subject and object. This returns ontological dignity to thought, to the subject. But it does not make clear what knowledge is. It is not enough to say that thinking is being: one must go further to say what thinking within being means; one must say whether knowledge is a creative act within being, i.e. the self-ignition of light in being, the passage from darkness into light. Knowledge not only throws light on being, it is not only light *on* being but light *in* being. And this means that no being is immanent in knowing, but knowing is immanent in being.

The theory of the identity of being and thinking fails to consider the irrationality of being: it has to deal with being already rationalized. But there is a hidden basis in being. Thinking is not identical with this basis: thinking must illuminate this basis, knowledge must yield light within it. My knowledge faces the dark abyss in being, but it must itself be clear and bright. Knowledge is immanent in being, but it is something which takes place within being, which transcends being; a break through into greater depths, and beyond the limits of all given data. Knowledge adds something, rather than reflecting it. Beyond every given being there lies a being more profound. To move toward a more profound being is to transcend. . . .

For knowledge, existence begins to reveal itself from below, not from above. With Marx as hunger, as economics, with Freud as desire, sex. With Heidegger (more profound), as worry and fear. From above, existence reveals itself as spirit. The supreme mystery of knowledge is that knowledge of material things and objects is possible, when knowledge by its nature is not material. Thomas Aquinas faced this problem as a problem of the intellect. But the problem is solvable only if we recognize that knowledge is existential, that in it the darkness of being is enlightened, that it is capable of taking the objectivized world within the spirit. . .

The knowledge of existence is the accumulation of light and meaning within existence; it is the illumination of being and consequently its renaissance, its hitherto-unknown enrichment. The creative and active character of knowledge is different in the sciences of spirit and from that of the sciences of nature. In the natural sciences the activity of knowing is expressed in objectivization and in the subjection of knowledge to mathematics. In the sciences of spirit the activity of knowing is expressed in a break-through to the meaning of existence. James rightly says that knowledge is an act, not a result. Knowledge is an activity of spirit, and spirit is act. The spirit is active, even when it closes itself off from the world in contemplation, and when it transfigures the world. There are two forms of the spirit's activity. . . .

Knowledge has a conjugal, masculine-feminine character: it is the meeting and union of the two, the possession of the feminine element by masculine sense and meaning. Since an element of pre-existential freedom enters into knowledge, we may say that knowledge has an irrational basis. Those German metaphysicians who had an inoculation of J. Boehme came nearest to an understanding of this irrational basis of knowledge. The active and creative nature of knowledge is expressed in the fact that it is the humanization of being in varying degrees. The recognition that an element of the freedom of the existential subject enters into knowledge, is a type of philosophy which asserts the primacy of freedom over being. *Solitude*, pp. 42-4, 54-5, 65, 67-8, 70-1

THE COSMOS

There is no hierarchical unity of the cosmos, of which personality could be a part. We cannot appeal to nature as a whole because of the disorder of its parts. The whole is in spirit rather than in nature. We may appeal only to God, not to the world-spirit, not to the cosmos as a whole. The idea of a world spirit or a cosmic whole is void of existential significance. The natural sciences, also, do not deal with the world as a whole, with cosmic unity: they know parts of nature and do not favour an optimistic view of the cosmos. Modern physics denies both the cosmos in the sense that word had in antiquity, and the old deterministic materialism. The idea that the world is partial, that there is no such thing as the world as a unified whole—is quite consonant with the revolution in modern physics. A unified whole may be sought only in a spirit which is not alienated away from itself and not objectivized. But then the words take on a different meaning, and do not mean the suppression of the 'partial', the personal, the plural. So too, the teleological concept of the world process contradicts a philosophy of personality and freedom. And not only determinism, the casual explanation of natural phenomena, stands up against objective teleology, but freedom, as well, for objective teleology of the cosmic process clashes with man's freedom, with personality and creativeness, and in reality it means an ideal, spiritualized determinism. The objectivized world is not purposeful, or rather its purpose is only partial; it is immanent in the processes going on in certain portions of the world, but not in the clash and interaction of those parts: it is not in the whole, for there is no whole. The endlessness of the objectivized world cannot be the cosmic whole. *Slavery*, p. 84

Man and the Cosmos

Man's alienation from the inner life of nature quite justly troubles him: he cannot bear the pressure of nature's mechanism: in reality he longs for the return of the cosmos into man. Man's fall away from God brought with it the fall of the cosmos away from man. This is the fallen state of the objectivized world. Man cannot regain the cosmos. . . . Fusion with cosmic life does not liberate personality, but rather dissolves and destroys it. Only the form of the servitude is changed. And this has fateful consequences in social life, in the relations of personality to society. Society takes root in the cosmos, and is considered an organism with a cosmic foundation. And here personality is inevitably subjected to and enslaved by the organic, and in the last analysis the cosmic, whole: man becomes only an organ and all the freedoms connected with his spiritual independence from society and nature are abolished. . . . Man moves in a vicious circle. To break out of that circle requires an act of spirit, not submission to the organic cosmic rhythm, which actually does not exist in objectivized nature. Against the power of the cosmic-organic over man's spirit we must set, not the mechanical and technical, not rationalization, but freedom of the spirit, the element of personality, independent alike of organism and mechanism. By analogy, we must set over against objective theology, not determinism, but freedom. Against man's servitude to society we must set, not reasoned rationalism, although it may be recognized as a good, but spirit, freedom of the spirit, and personality in its spiritual quality, independent of society or nature.

Slavery, pp. 86-7

CONSCIOUSNESS

Consciousness is the way of man, and it lies between the sub-conscious, the elemental, and the super-conscious, the spiritual. Man is a suffering being because he is a dual being, living in both the phenomenal and the noumenal world. On one hand, man is a phenomenon, a thing of nature, subject to the law of this world, and on the other he is a 'thing in itself', a spiritual being, free from the power of this world. Consciousness is an intermediate state, and in this is its duality. But it accomplishes great things, and in it is light. Overcoming the unhappiness of consciousness by means of super-consciousness is not to deny consciousness: the positive results of consciousness enter into super-conciousness. (This is what

Hegel called 'Aufhebung'.) But the structure of the super-conscious corresponds to the noumenal world, just as the structure of consciousness corresponds to the phenomenal world, only not completely or finally; there is always a glimpse of the other, and the possibbility of its breaking through. Consciousness recognizes itself as transcendental to that which would be immanent for super-consciousness. Hence I may say that the transcendent is not something outside me, but rather within.

Beginning, p. 79

The Illusions of Consciousness

Consciousness not only orients us in the midst of this world, not only gives out light, but also creates a great quantity of illusions. There are illusions of primitive consciousness, still very feeble, and with these are connected innumerable illusions, many myths. And there are other illusions of the higher, civilized consciousness. In primitive consciousness there may be less falsehood and more truth than in civilized consciousness. There may be more reality in myth than there is in civilized consciousness. Various societies in which people group themselves, set up a whole series of illusions necessary for their existence and development. These are perhaps the most firm of illusions. Society objectifies human existence, instils in man a kind of awe in the face of his own 'sanctity'. The English sociologist, Kidd, developed the ingenious idea that for their maintenance and prosperity society and social evolution demand belief in holy things which have no relation to the truth. The race instils into the individual illusions of consciousness which are necessary for the race. Schopenhauer also spoke of the illusions of love, which make man a toy of the race. Social illusions take the form of class prejudices which deform consciousness. Hegel has his doctrine of the slyness of reason ('List der Vernunft') in history. As a monist and optimist, he thought the slyness of reason an instrument of the revelation of spirit in history. But in reality this should be a source of bitter pessimism. The race creates illusions, necessary for the social process, for the triumph of the general over the individual, . . . the collective over the personal. And this takes on forms of firm, well established belief, of holy things demanding for themselves idolatrous attitudes.

Beginning, pp. 80-1

SPIRITUAL KNOWLEDGE

Knowing and Being

Gnosseology is an expression of doubt as to the power and justification of philosophical knowledge. It is a bifurcation which undermines the possibility of knowledge. He who has devoted his powers to gnosseology rarely arrives at ontology. He did not take the road that leads to being. The more creative philosophers of modern times, such as Bergson, M. Sheler, Heidegger, are very little concerned with gnosseology. Man has lost the capacity of knowing being, lost his access to being, and in sorrow has begun to get acquainted with knowledge. And so on his whole road of learning, knowledge rather than being, continues to face him. It is impossible to come to being, one can only proceed from it. In using the word 'being', I do not have in mind some definite ontology like that of St Thomas Aquinas, for example, which preceded the critical theory of knowing. I do not believe in the possibility of return to a pre-critical, dogmatic metaphysic. I am speaking of the transition to the object itself, to life itself; of the elimination of the splitting in two, that undermines the power of the act of knowledge. It was inevitable that philosophical knowledge should pass through bifurcation and critical reflex action: such was the way of European philosophy, its inner dramatic destiny. Critical gnosseology itself, which claimed to be above life and being, was a phenomenon of the life of the European cultured man. . . .

No matter how much knowledge has considered itself opposed to life and has doubted the possibility of knowing life, it *is* life at the outset, it is born of life and reflects life's destiny. The primary fact is that knowledge itself is being, and takes place with being. One of the greatest and unjustified prejudices of gnosseology is the belief that over against knowledge stands an object which does not enter into it, an object which must be reflected and expressed in knowledge. If we rise to a spiritual concept of knowledge it becomes clear that knowledge is an action by means of which something happens to being itself: being is clarified. It is not that someone or something comes to know being as something outside himself, but that being comes to know itself and through this knowledge it grows and is clarified. . . .

The basic question of gnosseology is *who* knows, and does he who knows belong to being? How are we to deepen and give meaning to the unavoidable presupposition of knowledge that it is man who knows? Kant and the idealistic theology of knowledge affirm that it is not at all man who knows, since this would mean psychologism and anthropomorphism, i.e. relativism in knowing, and that it is not at all the world which is known, since this would mean naïve realism. *The theory of knowledge which comes from Kant substitutes the problem of transcendental consciousness, the gnosseological subject or the world spirit, divine reason for the problem of man and his capacity to know being.* Even if this theory does not mention transcendental consciousness, it does talk of psychological consciousness. But neither transcendental nor psychological consciousness is man. The theory of knowledge does not want to study man as knower: it leaves the study of man entirely in the hands of psychology or sociology. *But the basic question of knowing is that of the relation between transcendental consciousness or the gnosseological subject, the man, the living and concrete human person.* Kant has inestimable merit in the problem of knowledge, but in reality he decides nothing; he does not eliminate scepticism and relativism, or does so only seemingly. . . . It may be that transcendental consciousness has firm and immovable bases for knowledge, but transcendental consciousness is not man: man is fated to be psychological consciousness which is in the power of relativism. And there is no explanation of how transcendental consciousness takes possession of psychological consciousness, or how the latter can rise to transcendental consciousness. It is of no help to me as a man, as a living, concrete subject, as one who has given himself the daring aim of knowing, that there is such a thing as transcendental consciousness, that in it is *a priori*, that in this ultra-human sphere scepticism and relativism have been conquered from the very beginning. For me it is important to conquer scepticism and relativism in the human sphere, in the man who knows, rather than in the gnosseological subject. I wish to know, myself, and not leave knowing to some gnosseological subject or world-reason: I want knowledge as a creative act of man. The theory of knowledge must become a philosophical anthropology, a doctrine about man, rather than a doctrine of transcendental consciousness and the gnosseological subject. It must not be a psychological or sociological doctrine, but rather an ontological and pneumatological doctrine of man.

Destiny, pp. 3-13

OBJECTIVIZATION

Objectivization is Secondary

The objectivization of the criterion of truth usually means that that is transferred to another's consciousness and conscience, which increases, rather than diminishes the difficulty. The transition from 'I' to God, which means the final conquest of the sin of ego-centrism, is a transition together with other people, but not through others. Others cannot be the source of my relation to God. And it is only on the secondary plane, that is, in social objectivization, that this seems to be otherwise. It is impossible to construct a theory of knowledge which would not itself be knowledge. It is impossible to make knowledge the object of one's research without having the researcher accomplish an act of knowing. Always and everywhere, objectivization which takes place midway on the road to knowledge, and which subjects knowledge to itself, is something secondary, while primal actuality or primal knowing is either before or after objectivization. Man was made the subject, gnosseologically, only in relationship to the object, the objectivized world, and only for that particular objectivization. Aside from this objectivization, aside from this act of facing being which has been transformed into object, the subject is man, personality, a living creature which itself is enfolded in the depths of being. Truth is in the subject, not subject which sets itself up as opposite to objectivization and hence excludes itself from being, but rather in the subject as something which really exists. In the objective, material world there can be neither criterion nor source of truth.

Solitude, pp. 41-2

Objectivization and Knowledge

Can we say that objectified knowledge is in itself defective and sinful, that it is the source of the world's fallen state? To affirm this, would be a great misunderstanding. It is not in knowledge that we should seek sinfulness, defectivness, the fallen state, but always in being itself. Knowledge only knows fallen being in its fallen state. Knowledge as objectivization for which inner existence and the spiritual world are a closed book, is still knowledge, and in this knowledge something is really revealed. Objectivization is inculcation into the fallen world, into a world in fetters, into alienation. . . .

Knowledge of the social world is objectivized knowledge, but this is another degree of objectivization (than mathematical knowledge—DAL) and from this level light may be thrown on the whole process of objectivization, which is inevitably socialization. We shall see that *objectivized knowledge* stands under the sign of society and by this fact it is distinct from knowledge of existence, which stands under the sign of community. Objectivized knowledge in all its levels is withdrawn from the existential subject, that is from man. . . .

Objectivization is rationalization in the same sense that takes the products of thought for realities (for example, substance, universals, etc.). In objectivization and rationalization thought does not transcend to the irrational and individual, that is to existence and the existent. And it is most important to establish two types of knowledge, on one hand, knowledge as objectivization, as rationalization which does not transcend the boundaries of reason, and which can attain only the general, and on the other, knowledge as being, existence, in which the reason transcends to the irrational and individual, as community and communion. These two types of knowledge have always existed in the history of human thought.

Solitude, pp. 58-62

Objectivization and Culture

There are two meanings to objectivization. It means the fallen state of the world, the world's fractionalization and enslavement, in which state existential subjects, personalities, are transformed into things, into objects. But it also means those acts of the subject, of the personal spirit, which are directed toward the establishment of relations and connections in this fallen world. Hence objectivization is linked up with the problem of culture. Here we face the complexity of the whole theme of objectivization.

In objectivization we may find only symbols, but not basic realities. The objective spirit is only a symbol of spirit. The spirit is real. Culture and social life are symbolic. There is never reality in an object: in an object there is only a symbol of reality. Reality itself is always in the subject. . . .

In a certain sense, we may say that the whole visible objective world is only symbolic of the spiritual world. The objectivization of spirit inspires pessimistic thoughts. But the most pessimistic thoughts about the objectivization of spirit in history cannot undermine faith in man and his creative calling. This is only the way of division along which man must pass, his living-out his destiny in which he becomes alienated from himself, in order later to return unto himself. Man passes through an objectivization of spirit in culture, in the state, in national or economic life. *Reality*, pp. 49-54

Objectivization—its Distinguishing Marks

As I understand it, the problem of objectivization has nothing in common with the problem of feeling, or perception, or psychic or physical relationships, or even of the usual relationships of the subjective and the objective. The problem of objectivization is on another line from that of a critique of naïve realism or the defence of idealism. What are the signs of objectivization, of the origin of objective attitudes in the world? We may establish the following signs: (1) the alienation of object from subject; (2) the submergence of the unique and individual, the personal, by the impersonal and universal; (3) the domination of necessity, determination from without, the limitation or suppression of freedom; (4) adaptation to the density and power of the world and of history: adaptation to the average man, the socialization of man and his opinions, which destroy all originality. Over against this we may set community in love and sympathy, the conquest of alienation, personalism, the expression of the personal and individual character of every existing thing; transition into the realm of freedom, determination from within, victory over enslavement to necessity, the predominance of quality over quantity, of creativity over adaptation. This, by the way, is a definition of the distinction between the phenomenal and the noumenal. Both phenomenon and noumen are defined in the process of objectivization. The struggle against the power of objectivization is spiritual revolt of the noumena against phenomena; it is a spiritual revolution. Such a conception of the relationship between the noumenal and the phenomenal is quite different from Platonism, and goes far beyond the dualism of Kant. The noumen is spirit, personality, freedom; it is creative energy acting in this world. . . . *Beginning*, pp. 63-4

Objectivization is only Symbol, not Reality

Objectivization is not true realization, but only symbolization; it produces signs of reality, not reality itself. And this is evident in all of man's creativity, in all products of creativity. The world of noumena, which is the world of creative beings and not the world of ideas, is able to express itself in another world than that of phenomena, but we must not imagine the world of noumena and the world of phenomena as completely isolated and separate from one another. There are no such impassable boundaries, just as there are no impassable boundaries of human consciousness. A break-through of noumena into phenomena is possible, a break-through of the invisible world into the visible, of the world of freedom into that of necessity—with this possibility everything of importance in history is linked up. In the life of the world we have not only phenomena but noumena as well, and their appearance on the scene cannot be called just another phenomenan. The prophets, the men of creative genius, come into this world from the noumenal world—they are ambassadors of Spirit. But this is not a steady evolutionary process; rather, it is an intermittent break-through, a creative process.

Beginning, p. 67

SPIRIT

The World of Spirit

Spirit is the truth of being. *Reality*, p. 57

The Reality of Spirit

Philosophic thought has often naturalized Spirit and introduced it into the hierarchy of the objective world as a higher degree of objectivity. Spirit has been thought of as one among objects, although of a higher order, thus ascribing to spirit a reality like the realities of the objective world. . . . To demonstrate the reality of spirit means showing its objectness. Opponents of the reality of spirit sav that it is only a subjective mental condition. . . .

Not only is spirit not an objective reality, it is not being, as a rational category. Never and nowhere is spirit present as a real object. . . . Spirit is not only another reality than that of . . . objects, but it is a reality in quite another sense. In the terminology of Kant (where, by the way, the word 'spirit' does not occur) we may say that spirit is a reality of freedom, rather than a reality of nature. . . . In the so-called objective world there is no sort of nature, no such thing, such objective reality as may be called spirit. Hence it is so easy to deny the reality of spirit. . . .

The reality of spirit is not objective, not the reality of things, but another sort of reality, incomparably greater and more primary. And this is not to be understood in the sense of abstract spiritualism which contrasts spirit with the realities of mind and body. . . . Spirit is another, higher quality of existence than that of the physical and the mental. The tripartite concept of man as a physical, mental and spiritual being, has eternal significance, and must be retained. But this does not mean that in man there is a spiritual nature along with a mental and physical nature: it means that man's mind and body may enter into another, a higher order of spiritual existence, that man may pass over from the order of nature into the order of freedom, into the realm of meaning, out of the order of discord and strife, into the order of love and unity. . . . Spirit gives meaning to actuality, rather than being itself, another actuality. Spirit is, as it were, the breath of God penetrating man's being and communicating a higher dignity, a higher quality of his existence, inner independence and unity. . . .

The spirit is freedom. It cannot be determined by the world of ideas in the Platonic sense. One of the ways spirit is received into man is its acceptance as an in-breathing, the inspiration of God, which is not the determination characteristic of logical universalism. In spirit man is free. . . .

Spirit, spiritual actuality, is not comparable with the universal laws of reason; it is not of the world of universal ideas, not of the objective world. It is a world comparable to concrete inward humanity, with man's experiencing destiny, human love and death, human tragedy. . . .

The reality of spirit is witnessed by the whole experience of mankind, by all its higher life. Denial of this reality is blindness and deafness to realities, the incapacity to distinguish qualities of being, or incapacity to describe that which is distinguished. Spirit is otherwise real than the world of natural things. This reality is not proven, but evidenced by those who are capable of distinguishing qualities. The reality of spirit lies outside the categorical thinking that has placed its stamp on 'being'. It is inexact to say that spirit is being. Spirit is freedom; spirit is creativity. Spirit has precedence over being, because freedom takes precedence.

Reality, pp. 7-31

Evidences of Spirit

Spirit is a break-through into our heavy-laden world: it is dynamic, creativity, up-surge. Pico della Mirandola says that man's spirit is of a heavenly order, that is, that it does not proceed from the world of nature. . . . By the spirit man is the image and likeness of God. Spirit is the divine element in man. And by the spirit man may rise to the higher spheres of Divinity. Spirit is an integral creative act of man. It is freedom, but freedom is rooted in pre-existential depth. . . . Hence spirit is creativeness, spirit creates new being. . . .

Spirit is of God and to God. By the Spirit man receives everything from God, and by the spirit man gives everything to God, augments the talents given him, creates what has never been. The spirit is from God. It is not, like nature, created by God. Spirit emanates from God, is poured in, or breathed into, man. This is the biblical image. But spirit is not only from God: spirit is also from primary, pre-existential freedom, from the 'Ungrund'. Herein is the basic paradox of spirit: it is an emanation of Divinity, and it may give to Divinity a reply that does not proceed from Divinity. Spirit is not only divine: it is divine-human, divine-worldly: it is freedom in God and freedom from God. It is impossible to work out a concept of this mystery, or to rationalize it: about this only myth and symbol are possible. . . . *Reality*, pp. 32-3

Personality is realized through the victory of the spirit over the chaotic elements of mind and body. Spirit is an active, masculine element: the mind is passive and feminine. Spirit is from the logos: mind is cosmic. Spirit forms mind by means of meaning and truth, gives it freedom from the power of cosmic forces. . . . *Reality*, p. 38

The Mystery of the Spirit

The universal exists, not as something outside personality, but as the higher content of the life of personality, as a super-personal value in personality. God is a person, rather than a universal being. The action of God's Spirit on the spirit of man does not mean the presence of an objective and universal spirit: it means the elimination of the opposition between the personal and the universal, between the subjective and what seems to be objective. Herein is the mystery of the action of the Spirit of God in the world of men. . . .

The final triumph of spirit would mean the fading and disappearance of the objective world as something not genuine, and transition to the plane of the existential, to true existence, transition from symbolization to realization. Such a transition occurs in true love which brings down fire upon the earth. . . . *Reality*, pp. 48, 53

> The spirit seeks eternity: the material knows only the temporal. True achievement is to achieve eternity. *Autobiography*, pp. 42-3

THE SPIRITUAL LIFE

> The spiritual life does not know the measure of figures: it knows only the unique, the one. *Solitude*, p. 158

The Nature of Spiritual Life

The spiritual life is not a reality that exists at the level of physical or psychic actuality, or the actuality of the natural world. It absorbs all actuality into itself, in the consciousness that all actuality is only a symbolization of the spiritual, only a reflection of its situation, its inner events, its way. Spirit is not the opposite of flesh: flesh is the incarnation and the symbol of spirit. Spiritual life is historical, for historical life is life in the concrete, but external historical actuality is only a reflection of spiritual life in time, in separability. Everything external is merely a sign of the inward. Even material is only a symbolization of the inward condition of the spiritual world, rather than a substance existing by itself. Here we are not affirming spiritualism, or some abstract spirituality, but symbolism, concrete spirituality. *Freedom*, Vol. I, pp. 45-6

> Spiritual experience is the supreme reality in man's life: in it the divine is not proven, it is simply shown. *Freedom*, I, p. 36

Spiritual Life needs no Proof: it IS

Perhaps the world does not exist, but my spiritual life does. My experience of the divine is real: it is a manifestation of the reality of the divine; it is irrefutable. The spiritual heights, the tension and ardour of spirit exist, the very reality of the spirit, the manifestation of the spiritual world—are real. And the only significance of assertions that this intensity, this ardour is an illusion and self-deception, is that these are not present in those who think them only illusory. . . . The discovery of reality depends upon the activity of the spirit itself, its intensity and its ardour. We cannot expect spiritual realities to reveal themselves to us, as objects of the natural world are discovered, that these realities will be given us from without, as stones or trees, tables or chairs are given, or as the laws of logic are given. In spiritual life reality is determined by the power of the spirit, itself. *Freedom*, Vol. I, pp. 37-8

> In the spiritual life there is no thought about God, or feeling of Him, but the revelation of God, Himself. *Freedom*, I, p. 54

The Religion of the Spirit

The greatest error of historical Christianity is linked with the fatally limiting idea that the revelation is finished, and that nothing more is to be expected, that the building of the Church is completed and the roof laid on it. Religious discussion centres upon the possibility of new revelation and a new spiritual epoch. All other questions are secondary. The new revelation is not at all a new religion, distinct from Christianity, but rather the fulfilment and completion of the Christian revelation, bringing it to a true universality. This we do not have as yet. But we cannot simply wait for the revelation of the spirit. It depends upon man's creative activity, as well. It is not to be understood as only a new revelation of God to man: it is also the revelation of man to God. This means that it will be a divine-human revelation. In the Spirit, the divisions and contradictions of the divine and the human will be overcome, while the distinction between them will be maintained. This will be the crowning of the mystical dialectic of the divine and the human. It will be also the end of objectivization . . . of naïve realism in understanding the revelation.

The Holy Spirit is the principle uniting God with creation, and in the Spirit the mystery of creation must be made known, a mystery which is both anthropological and cosmological. . . . The opening of a new epoch of the Spirit, which will include higher achievements of spirituality, presupposes a radical change and a new orientation in human consciousness. This will be a revolution of consciousness which hitherto has been considered as something static. The religion of the Spirit will be the religion of man's maturity, leaving behind him his childhood and adolescence. . . .

In the religion of the Spirit, the religion of freedom, everything will appear in a new light: there will be neither authority nor reward: the nightmare of a legalistic conception of Christianity and of eternal punishment will finally disappear. It will be founded, not upon judgment and recompense, but on creative development and transfiguration, on likeness to God. A new anthropology will be made known, and the religious meaning of human creativity will be recognized. Freedom will be perceived as its fundamental principle. The idea of God will be cleansed of its slavish sociomorphism. Some bits of idolatry have remained in the idea of God as self-sufficient. Only the idea of a sacrificial and suffering God, yearning for another, will overcome militant godlessness and atheism. We must express the daring paradox of the knowledge of God: the affirmation of God with my whole being means that God exists; human freedom creates God, and that means that God exists: mine is a divine-human creativeness. . . .

The religion of the Spirit is the expectation that a new human and humane sociality will be revealed, radiating love and charity. It is also the expectation of the revelation of a new relationship between man and the cosmos, of cosmic transfiguration. The process of the decomposition of the cosmos . . . is nearing its end: its final phase will be the decomposition of the atom. All this rests in the eschatological theme, in active eschatologism, and least of all does this mean an optimistic concept of the destiny of history. The discovery of light does not mean a denial of darkness. On the contrary: before the advent of the epoch of Spirit man will have to pass through deepened shadow, through the epoch of night. We are living through the tragic experience of the de-spiritualization and devastation of nature, as it were, the disappearance of the cosmos (the discoveries of physics), the de-spiritualization and devastation of history (Marx and historical materialism), the de-spiritualization and devastation of the mind (Freud and psycho-analysis). The end of the war and revolution has disclosed terrible cruelty: humaneness is vanishing. It is as though the Creator has withdrawn from creation. He is present only incognito (a favourite expression of Kierkegaard). But all this may be understood as a dialectic moment in the revelation of the Spirit, and a new spiritual life. One must die, in order to live again. Man and the world are being crucified. But the final word will belong to the Resurrection.

Divine, pp. 221-4

CHAPTER III

The Eternal Being*

God is completeness toward which man cannot avoid striving. M.C.A., p. 123

CHRIST

Berdyaev's Thought of God

It is very difficult to find a form of expression for the chief idea of my life. Everything I write in this book is linked with the tormenting problematic of spirit. With my type of temperament I take on both an affirmative and a veiled form of my anxious questioning. I ask questions and put problems in the form of assertions. *But in the inward essence my thinking is problematic*, not skeptical, but problematic. For the solution of these problems of the spirit, or that one problem of the relations between man and God, no help can come to me from without. No elder ('staretz'), however deeply spiritual, can help me here. The whole problem is that I must discover what God has concealed from me. God awaits an act of freedom on my part, free creativeness. My freedom and my creativeness are my obedience to the mysterious will of God. God expects greater things and other things from man than are usually thought of when men speak of the will of God. Perhaps we should be studying, not the abstract metaphysics of God, but His concrete psychology.

Only the Language of Spirit can Express God

Christianity came into the world as the complete abolition of idolatry and slavery, as a religion of the spirit and the spiritual life, as a religion of the Holy Trinity, where God reveals himself as a loving Father, as someone near and dear, as attaining the homeland of the spirit. But human nature put the stamp of naturalism on the acceptance and discovery of Christian truth. Even the dogmas of the Christian faith, which are mystical facts and mystical encounters in the spiritual world, were expressed in theological systems in the language of the natural world and of reason adapted to it. But God is life, He is inexpressible in the categories of natural thinking and in no way resembles the realities of the natural, objective world. He is even unthinkable as 'supernatural' for the 'supernatural' is too much like the 'natural'. God is life, and therefore He is revealed only in spiritual life. And the mysteries of Divine life may be expressed only

* Pascal.

in the inward language of spiritual experience, the language of life and of life's way, not in the language of objective nature and of reason.

Freedom, I, pp. 52-3

God is not Limited

We cannot say that God is subject to truth and good as elements ruling over Him, any more than we can say that truth and good are only what God desires. Such an analysis is quite inapplicable to the nature of Divinity, and God can no more be thought of moralistically than despotically. God cannot desire falsehood, evil and ugliness, and this not because He is limited by truth, goodness and beauty, but because He is Truth, Goodness and Beauty, because in Him the freedom and the necessity of Truth, Goodness and Beauty are identical. God cannot desire meaninglessness, because He is Meaning. Meaning is His immanent idea. Wisdom is inherent in God. God cannot desire slavery, because slavery is evil. He can desire only freedom, because freedom is His idea, His purpose for the world. God cannot desire a formal fulfilment of, or subjection to, His will, no matter what this will might be, because God cannot have an obscure will, separate from the idea of God, from Meaning, Truth and Justice, separate from Freedom, without which there is neither Meaning nor Justice. Above all God desires of man freedom—such is the will of God, inseparable from the idea of God, and the will of God must be fulfilled. But to fulfil the will of God, God's idea, I dare not be a slave: I must be free in spirit. I cannot, and I should not, fulfil the will of God as a slave: I must fulfil God's will as one free in spirit, as a spiritual being. We are no longer slaves, but sons, free men, and our freedom was purchased at a great price.

Freedom, I, pp. 217-18

God's Need of Another

God is the Lover, and he cannot and does not wish to exist without the loved one.

Reality, p. 118

Only a mystic-symbolist theology can rise to an esoteric understanding of the mystery of creation as the inner life of the Triune Divinity, as God's need for another, for a friend, for one who loves and is loved, for love realized in the mystery of the Three-in-one, which is equally above and below, in heaven and on earth. The theological and metaphysical doctrine of the absolute immobility of Divinity, of absolute rest in God, is an exoteric and rationalistic doctrine: it indicates the limits of all logical conception of divinity. . . . Absolute rest in God is joined in Him with absolute movement. It is only in our rational consciousness, in our natural world that rest excludes movement and movement makes rest impossible. But the absolute perfection of Divinity unites within itself the absolute maximum of rest with the absolute maximum of movement. For rationalistic thinking movement in God seems to contradict God's perfection; it seems like imperfection and deficiency in Him. But only antinomic thought of God is possible: in God opposites are identical. God's longing for another, for a loved one and that loved one's free answer of love is an indication, not of incompleteness or impairment in the being of God, but rather of the plenteous fullness and perfection of His being. *Freedom*, II, pp. 7-8

The Mystery of the Cross

At the centre of the Christian mystery stands the cross on Golgotha, the suffering and death on the cross of the Son of God, the Saviour of the world. The doctrine of the absolute immobility of Divinity is in contradiction to the mystical fact of the passions of our Lord. Christianity is a religion of a suffering God. Although it is not God the Father who suffers . . . still the suffering of God the Son is suffering in the inner life of the Holy Trinity. *Freedom*, II, p. 9

The God-man and the Man-God

All the complexity of religious life, the meeting and communion of God and man, is linked with the fact that there are two movements, and not one: from God toward man, and from man toward God. If religious life was based upon only the one movement from God toward man, only upon the will of God, and only upon revelation by God, it would be quite simple, the attainment of the purposes of life in the world would be easy, it would be easy to realize the Kingdom of God. Then there would be no world tragedy. But the birth of man in God, man's answer to God, cannot concern God alone; it is man's affair, a matter of man's freedom. By the nature of God as infinite love, by God's purpose in creation, the Kingdom of God cannot be realized without man, without man's participation in creation. Autocracy in heaven is quite as unjust as on earth. The Kingdom of God is the kingdom of Divine-humanity, in it God is finally born in man and man in God, and this is accomplished in the Spirit. *Freedom*, II, pp. 16-17

Man called to aid God

God desires that man should be. God does not wish to be alone. The meaning of existence is the conquest of loneliness, the acquisition of kinship and nearness. This is the essence of religious life and experience. In truth, man is called not only to seek God's aid, to save himself from destruction, but to help God in the realization of God's design for the world. But natural man is incapable of realizing his creative calling, his forces are undermined by sin, his freedom is enfeebled. Man's creative power, man's creative freedom, are restored through redemption in the race of the New Adam in the spiritual man. This creative power, capable of answering God's demand, is finally and fully obtained only in Christ through a new spiritual birth. *Freedom*, II, p. 38

The Psychology of God

It is strange that human thought, and especially theological thought, has never meditated on the psychology of God. Probably such consideration was considered impious. In the traditional theological systems, one of the least understandable items is the psychology of God. Theology has always been constructed from the viewpoint of human psychology. In reality theology has always been more anthropocentric than theocentric, and most of all in the monarchistic concept of God. Can we say that no thought-life, no emotional conditions are inherent in God? The static concept of God as pure act, without potential, self-satisfied, and needing nothing, is a philosophical, Aristotelian, but not a biblical conception of God. The God of the Bible, the God of revelation, is not at all pure act: revealed in Him are an effective and emotional life, the dramatism of every kind of life, inner movement, but this is revealed exoterically. The limitations of man's idea of God are surprising. Men are afraid to ascribe to Him inner tragedy, which characterizes all life, or dynamic, or longing for another, for the birth of man, but they are not in the least afraid to ascribe to Him anger, jealousy, revenge, and other affective conditions which are considered reprehensible in man. There is a great gulf fixed between the conception of man's perfection and that of God. Self-satisfaction, self-sufficiency, stony immobility, pride, the demand for constant submission to Himself—all these are qualities which the Christian faith considers sinful and vicious, but they are quite calmly ascribed to God. *Destiny*, p. 32

Theodicy

> How often men have thought they had to defend God, when actually it was man who needed defence. *Divine*, p. 22

If theodicy is judging God from the viewpoint of our idea of good, it is a false problem. But theodicy is the justification of God, not from the viewpoint of what is good, but from the viewpoint of the origin of the very distinction between good and evil. It is self evident that God is 'beyond good and evil', for this side of good and evil there is our fallen world, not God. God is super-good. But in Him there can be no evil, which lies on this side of the distinction. And when we ask if God is free to desire evil, we are applying to God the categories of our fallen world. We can think of this only apophatically. God is in no way dependent upon good, nor is He bound by good. He himself is Good, as absolute power. But immediately we must admit that He is not good, but super-good, since the category good is inapplicable to Him. There can be no judgment on God, for He is the source of all the values on which such a judgment could be based. God reveals Himself to us as the source of values, as infinite love. And theodicy may judge God only from the viewpoint of that which He has revealed to us about Himself. Theodicy is merely the defence of God from human conceptions of Him, from man's calumny of God. *Destiny*, p. 48

God as a Person

Personality is not the absolute. As the Absolute, God is not a personality. But God as a personality presupposes an 'other', another person: He is love and sacrifice. The person of the Father predicates the persons of the Son and the Holy Spirit. The hypostases of the Holy Trinity are also persons, because they presuppose each other, mutual love, and movement out toward another. In another aspect, the person of God and that of man presuppose each other. Personality exists as the relation between love and sacrifice. It is impossible to think of a personal God in abstract monotheistic terms. A personality, as the Absolute, closed within itself and having need of nothing, cannot exist. Personalist metaphysics and ethics are based on the Christian doctrine of Holy Trinity. The moral life of personality must be understood in the image of Divine Trinity, reflected in the world. Personality predicates the existence of other personalities, and the communion of personalities. . . . *Destiny*, p. 63

God Determines Nothing

It is quite wrong to apply to God, to His relation with the world, the category of causality. This category is applicable only to relationships in the phenomenal world. God is not the cause of the world, any more than he is lord and tsar, or power and might. God determines nothing. When we say that God is the creator of the world we are expressing something boundlessly more mysterious than a causal relationship. In relation to the world God is freedom, rather than necessity or determination. But when we speak of freedom we speak of the supreme mystery. Men have made God into a determining cause, into power and might, just as they have made him lord and tsar. But He resembles none of these: He is quite beyond the limits of such categories. In a certain sense God has less power than a policeman, a soldier or a banker. And we must stop speaking of God and His providence as we speak of the governing of states in this world. This is all a false objectification. Schleiermacher is wrong when he says that the religious feeling is a feeling of dependence. Dependence is an earthly thing. We might have better reason for saying it is a feeling of independence. We may speak of God only by analogy with what is revealed in the depths of spiritual experience.

Truth, pp. 44–5

God is not a Cause

We must note the vast difference between God and Man's idea of Him; between God as subject and God as object. Between God and man stands the human mind, the exteriorization and projection of the limited condition of that mind; objectivization. An objectivized God has been the object of man's slavish worship. But the paradoxical fact is that an objectivized God is a God alienated from man and lording over him, and at the same time a God created by man's limitedness, and reflecting man's limitations. Man becomes the slave of his own exteriorization and objectivization. Feuerbach was right, although his word in no wise solves the problem of God. Man creates God in his own image and likeness, and invests God with both the best and the worst of his own image. But in God and in His relationship to man and to the world there is nothing resembling human social relationships: the base human category of lordship is not applicable to God. God is not the lord and He does not lord it over men. No authority is inherent in God, He has no will to power; He does not demand the slavish worship of a bond-servant. God is freedom; He is the liberator, not the master. God gives a sense of liberty, not of subjection. God is spirit, and spirit knows no such relationship as that of master and slave. We cannot think of God in terms analogous to what takes place in society or in nature. . . .

God can act freely, only in freedom and by means of freedom. *Slavery*, p. 206

God is not the Absolute

The concept of the Absolute is the extreme limit of objectivizing abstract thought. In the Absolute there are no signs of existence, no evidences of life. The Absolute belongs not so much to religious revelation as to religious philosophy and theology: it is the child of thought. The abstract Absolute shares the fate of abstract being which does not differ in any way from non-being. We cannot pray to the Absolute, cannot have dramatic meeting with him. . . . The God of revelation, the God of the Bible is not the Absolute: in Him there is dramatic movement and life, relationship to another, to man and the world. It was by applying Aristotelian philosophy that men transformed the God of the Bible into pure act, and deprived Him of all inner movement, all tragic elements. The Absolute cannot move out of itself and create a world; we cannot ascribe to him movement or change. The 'Gottheit' of Eckhardt and the mystics is not the Absolute, as the ultimate abstraction, but is the ultimate Mystery, and to this no categories are applicable. God is not an absolute monarch: He is a God who suffers with the world and with man; He is crucified Love, the Liberator. And the Liberator appeared, not as authority, but as crucifixion. The Redeemer is the Liberator, not the accounting with God for crimes committed. God reveals Himself as Human-ness. Human-ness is the chief quality of God, not at all omnipotence, omniscience, etc., but humaneness, freedom, love, sacrifice. The concept of God must be freed from distorting, degrading, profane sociomorphism. *Slavery*, pp. 72-3

To possess God is to be boundlessly rich: to consider oneself God is to be boundlessly poor.
Questions of Philosophy and Psychology, No. 1, p. 33, Moscow, 1907

God as Creator

The very complex question remains of the relation between the creative act, in which something new begins to be, and reality. If we define reality as closed and completed being, in which there is no further possibility of change or movement, then we must inevitably deny the possibility of a creative act. There is no creative act except the one in which God created the world. Official theology, which considers itself orthodox, denies that man is a being capable of creativeness. The creature is incapable of creating: only the Creator, who is pure act, has this creative capacity. But if we are to deny the existence of all potentiality in God the Creator, and consequently deny all movement in Him, we are compelled to deny that He has creative power, for the creation of something new is linked with potentiality. But then we must recognize that man the creature is capable of creating, since he has potentiality: he is not actualized to the point of losing all possibility of change and movement. The possibility of performing a creative act, to manifest change and novelty is linked with imperfection. This is a paradox. That which in man manifests the image and likeness of God, and is the most perfect of his qualities, is somehow the result of imperfection, inadequacy, potentiality, of the presence in him of non-being. The doctrine of God as pure act, a being without potentiality, in reality makes the creation of the world meaningless and absurd. The creation of the world and of man in it is something accidental, altogether useless to God. . . . Logical ontology should then deny all possibility of novelty, creativeness, freedom, all of which mean a break-through into the closed system of being. To avoid any misunderstanding, we must say that if we admit the possibility of creativeness in God, and hence the possibility of movement, then we must admit that this creativeness and this movement do not take place in time, as we understand that word.

Beginning, pp. 141-2

God's Creation of the World

The very idea of God's creation of the world must be reconsidered and deepened. As is well known, the idea of creation has always been a difficult one for philosophic thought. The idea was alien to Greek philosophy, as it was to Aristotle, that inspirer of catholic theology. The widely prevalent explanation which says that God created the world for his own glorification (this is the worst explanation) or for the manifestation of his love to something other than himself, is very naïve. And in this connection it was always predicated that God had need of nothing, that he had no need of the world and man, and that the creation was an arbitrary accident. The theologians know very well, although no one knows where they got this knowledge, that God's creative act has no significance within the inner Divine life, that it reveals no movement in Divine life, no sort of enrichment. . . .

Here we come up against the limits of possible human knowledge. But in order that the drama of the creation should not be turned into a comedy, the meaningless play of God with himself, we must admit the idea of uncreated freedom, at least as a border-line idea. Then you may admit, as Father S. Bulgakoff does, that man expressed his consent to his creation. Otherwise this has no meaning. Then it may be admitted that man and the world answer to the call of God, and hence this is not God's answer to himself. *Truth*, pp. 48-9

Can God's Existence Be Proved?

> To solve the question of man is to solve the question of God. *Dostoevsky*, p. 35

Man faces that question of all questions, the question of God. This question is rarely put in its pure and original state: it has become too attached to a scholasticism which stulifies, to verbal philosophy, to the play of concepts. The very persons who have tried to lift up the idea of God have terribly degraded it, imputing to God qualities taken from the realm of Caesar, not from the realm of Spirit. There is no guarantee of God's existence: man can always doubt and deny. God does not force us to recognize Him, as do material objects; He appeals to man's freedom. Belief in God is only an internal meeting with Him in spiritual experience. We must recognize conclusively that all of the traditional proofs of the existence of God, ontological, cosmological, or physico-theological, are not only insolvent: they are quite unnecessary, even harmful. What might be called the anthropological proof is much stronger. It consists in the fact that man is a being belonging to two worlds, and for this reason he is not included completely in this world of necessity: he transcends himself as a being of the empiric, revealing a freedom which does not derive from this world. This does not prove, but it does show, the existence of God, since it reveals the spiritual element in man. Still more important is primal feeling, which cannot be fully expressed. The indubitable result of meditation about God is this: it is impossible to think of God in rational terms, which are always borrowed from this world, which is not at all like God. Only apophatic theology was right: you cannot construct an ontology of God. God is not being, which is always a development of abstract thought. God is not being, God is Spirit. God is not essence, but existence. About God we can speak only in the symbolic language of spiritual experience.

Spirit and Caesar, pp. 35-6

Creation Proves the Existence of a Creator

The being of the world is creature; being which has been and continues to be created. And the stamp of the creative act lies on all created being. A thing created, createdness, speaks of the Creator. Createdness is creativity. The creation of the world is creative development in God, His emergence from solitude; it is all the call of divine love. Creativity presupposes movement and dynamic within divine life. The creative process is carried out in God from all eternity. Only the recognition of created being permits an original creative act in being, an act which produces something new and unprecedented. If everything in being was not created, but had always existed, the very idea of creativity could not have been born in the world. . . . The very idea of creativity is possible only because there is a Creator and because He carried out an original creative act in which that which never was came into being, something which did not proceed from anything which had been before and which neither weakened nor reduced the absolute power of the Creator. . . .

Only a personalist doctrine of the world, for which every being is personal and original, can give meaning to creativity. Such a personalist doctrine recognizes the originality of personality, derived from nothing outside or general, from no other means. God is a concrete personality and therefore a creator: man is a concrete personality and therefore a creator, the whole make-up of being is concrete and personal and hence possesses creative power. The world, through and through, is a hierarchy of living beings, original personalities, capable of creatively increasing being. The process which takes its rise in the substances of the world and their rearrangement is evolution. The process which arises from the internal force of substances, from their personal originality, is creativity.

M.C.A., pp. 128, 135

Only God can Create Persons

Creative philosophy recognizes the dynamic quality of created being. Created being is continuously created—it knows no limits to the creative process; it is not a closed set of data. Created being is through and through personal and plural, i.e. it consists of self-sufficient and creative individual beings. The cosmos is being created; it is not given, it is a task set. But is there a limit to the creativity of created beings? Are they completely like the Creator in His creative powers? There is an eternal and impassable limit which separates human creativity from divine creativity, from the creativity of the Creator. Created beings do not create beings—these are created only by God. Personality is created in God before all worlds. And every attempt on the part of created beings to create beings leads only to the production of an automaton, a dead mechanism. Such an attempt is always demonic—it is black magic. Only God has the power to create living being, personality. *M.C.A.*, pp. 142-3

God as Providence

The mystical doctrine of Providence, considering God to be the Lord and Director of this world, must disturb not only the most refined consciousness, but that less developed, or even little developed. How are we to connect this doctrine with the triumph of evil and suffering in our world? I think this is one of the chief sources of atheism. The usual way out of this difficulty is by means of the doctrine of the Fall of man. But this neither explains nor justifies anything. The power of evil remains unexplained. Men's suffering is disproportionate to their sinfulness. It is not the worse, but the better people, who suffer most. Unexplained also are the periods, both individual and historical, when a man feels that he has been deserted by God. Explaining terrible catastrophes in human life as God's anger and punishment is insufferable. It is terribly difficult to explain and justify the omni-presence of an all-powerful and all-beneficient God in evil, in plague and cholera, in torture-chambers, in the horrors of war, of revolution and counter-revolution. Our concept of the action of divine Providence in this world of evil and suffering needs to be revaluated. Kierkegaard is considerably nearer the truth when he says that God remains in this world incognito. In history we have the conflict of freedom with necessity: but God may exist only in freedom; He is not present in necessity. This leads us to a complete change in the doctrine about Providence. Grace is not a power acting from without: grace is the revelation of the divine in man. There is no conflict between grace and freedom: grace is only transfigured freedom.

Spirit and Caesar, pp. 43-4

God is Spirit

The existence of God is revealed in the existence of spirit in man. And God resembles neither the forces of nature, nor the authority of society or of the state. Here no analogy is valid: all analogy would mean slavish cosmo-morphism and sociomorphism in the understanding of God. God is freedom, and not necessity, not authority over man and the world. What the theologians call grace, placing it alongside human freedom, is this action in man of divine freedom. Christ taught that man is the image and likeness of God, and by that the worth of man, as a free spiritual being, was confirmed: man was not a slave to natural necessity. Freedom is possible only if, beside the realm of Caesar, there exists the realm of Spirit, that is, the Kingdom of God. I repeat. God is not an objective being, to whom rational concepts are applicable: God is Spirit.

Spirit and Caesar, pp. 41-2

God has laid upon man the duty of being free. *Freedom*, p. 44

The Problem of God and of Human Creativity

If we stop to reflect upon the modern forms of godlessness, we will be convinced that the most difficult problem still remains that of the relationship between faith in God and the recognition of man's free creativity. Luther put this question very acutely. There is only one way out of this problem: recognition of the great Truth that God and the divine are incarnate not in domination, lordship, but in freedom; not in authority, but in humanity, in divine-humanity. Then God will be understood, not as a diminution of man's freedom and activity, but rather as the condition which makes these possible. If there is no God then there is no Justice which rises above the injustice of nature and of society: then man is wholly subject to nature and society: he is the slave of natural and social necessity. Faith in God is the charter of man's liberty. Without God, man is subject to the lower world. All the intellectual proofs of the existence of God are bankrupt: they never go beyond the realm of thought. What *is* possible is an inward existential meeting with God. *Truth*, p. 95

Christ

Not only Jesus Christ, but God as well, are in the world incognito: man's freedom is connected with this fact. Herein is the mystery of revelation. *Divine*, p. 24

Christ the New Adam

The revelation of life of Divine-humanity in the Church is closely related to the Christian doctrine of the New Adam, the new human race, which begins with Christ. In the leading forms of church consciousness it is only the old Adam which is recognized, only the natural human race. It seems as though the church had never fully recognized that in Christ and through Christ, man is already a new creature, that in him new power and freedom are manifest. After Christ, original sin no longer has absolute power over man; man and the cosmos no longer belong to the natural order; the break between the natural and the supernatural has been overcome; spiritual life, spiritual creativeness, may now be manifested in the world and in man. And this spiritual life and spiritual creativity which is being made manifest, belongs to the divine-human life of the Church. All the processes of life take place in the Church. In Christ, man received not divine power alone, but human power as well; man became fully man, a spiritual being, a new and eternal Adam. Man is fully revealed only in God-manhood, i.e. in the Church. But this may take place unconsciously: perhaps Goethe was not conscious that everything truly essential in his creativity was taking place within the Church and was a revelation of the Church's life. The conception of Christianity as only a religion of personal salvation compresses and narrows the Church's consciousness; it tends to obscure God-manhood and the Divine-human process of the world.

Freedom, pp. 209-10

On how you think of Christ depends how you think of man. *Freedom* II, p. 39

The Problem of Jesus

The so-called mythological theory, which denies the very fact of the existence of Jesus, has at least this positive value, that it demonstrates the complete hopelessness of science to solve the 'problem of Jesus'. It is true that no historical biography of Jesus can be written, and the Gospels cannot be considered as historical documents. But this only demonstrates that the reality of Jesus Christ is shown by the faith of the Christian community, and outside this circle it is a reality scarcely noticed by history. Historic necessity can never violate faith: faith is an act of freedom. The life of Jesus Christ can never be subjected to historical objectivization: it remains in the sphere of Christian experience, not only personal, but communal, 'soborny' experience. *Truth*, p. 82

THE TRINITY

Unattainable by Logic

Divinity is apprehended, not in categories of reason, but in the revelations of spiritual life. Reason is incapable of developing any sort of logical understanding of the 'Three-in-one-ness' of Divinity. Unenlightened by faith, reason naturally inclines toward monism or dualism, and it is disturbed, even perturbed, by the mythical character of the Christian Trinity: here reason is ready to see polytheism. Only myth or symbol, not concepts, can help us understand the Trinity. But this myth and this symbol reflect and image neither my religious feeling and experience, nor my inner spiritual condition, as the latest symbolists of the subjective-idealistic type would have us believe, but the very depths of being, the profoundest mysteries of real life. Only in the Triune Divinity is there inner life, which escapes comprehension. *Freedom* I, pp. 115-16

Completion Requires Trinity

The Divine mystery play is not completed in Duality: it predicates Trinity. The relation of God to the Other is made perfect in a Third. The lover and the beloved find fullness of life in the realm of love, which is the Third Person. The Kingdom of God, the kingdom of the illumined man and the illumined cosmos, is realized only through the Third Person, the Holy Spirit, in whom the drama is finished, the circle closed. Only in 'Three-in-one-ness' is perfect divine life given: the lover and the beloved establish their kingdom, find final content and completeness for their lives. The Trinity is a holy, a divine number: it means completion, fullness, the conquest of struggle and division. . . . The mystery of Christianity is the mystery of 'two-in-one-ness' (divine-humanity) which finds its solution in 'three-in-one-ness'. Hence the base of Christianity is in the Christological dogma of the divine-human nature of Christ, and the trinitarian dogma of the Holy Trinity. . . . Wherever there is life there is the mystery of 'Three-in-one-ness', the distinction among three hypostases, and the absolute unity of the Three. The Trinity is reflected and symbolized everywhere in the life of man and of the world. In essence, life itself is the distinction among persons and their unity. Fullness of life is 'sobornost', where personality finds its final realization and the fullness of its content. The meeting of one with another is always resolved in a third. The one and the other come to unity, not in duality, but in trinity: in the third (person) they discover their common content, their goal. Being would be in a condition of indifference and non-revelation, if there were only one. It would be hopelessly torn and divided if there were only two. Being discloses its content, and reveals its distinction, while remaining in unity, because there are three. Such is the nature of being, the primal fact of its life. The life of man and of the world is an inner moment of the mystery of the Trinity. *Freedom* II, pp. 19-20

Trinity Predicates a Third Revelation

In the history of religious thought and of human society, an objectivization of God takes place. Kataphatic theology is concerned with an objectivized God. This corresponds to a certain stage in the socialization of Christianity. Apophatic or mystical theology overcomes the limitations of an objectivized conception of God, liberates thought from distorting anthropomorphism and the concept of the relation between God and man in categories of the state or of authority, of judge and punishment. The existential dialectic of the Divine Trinity, like the existential dialectic of the human and the divine, proceeds from the very depths of existence.

The dialectic of the Divine Trinity (three-in-one-ness) predicates an epoch of Triune revelation, which is to say that it leads to admitting the possibility and the necessity of a third revelation. But this means that we must understand the two previous epochs in the light of Trinity (three-in-one-ness), i.e. in the light of the revelation of Spirit, as the final revelation. Only in Spirit is the revelation of Divinity and of Divine-humanity finished and completed. This is the revelation of freedom, of love, and creativity, the revelation of everything God has created. *Divine*, p. 61

CHAPTER IV

God's Latest Image*

'Only in Christ is the problem of man resolved.'
DOSTOEVSKY, p. 53

MAN

To Know Being, Begin with Man

The philosophers have constantly returned to the idea that to solve the mystery of man would mean solving the mystery of being. Know thyself, and through this know the world. All attempts at external perception of the world, without immersion in the depths of man, have produced only a knowledge of the surface of things. . . . The act of man's exclusive self-consciousness of his significance precedes every philosophic perception. This exclusive self-consciousness of man cannot be merely one of the truths of a philosophic knowledge of the world: like an absolute *a priori*, it precedes every philosophic perception of the world, which becomes possible only through this self-consciousness. If man were to consider himself as one of the external, objectivized things of the world, then he could not be an active perceiving subject; by this fact, philosophy has become impossible for him. Anthropology, or more exactly the anthropological consciousness, precedes not only ontology and cosmology, gnosseology and even the philosophy of consciousness—it precedes all philosophy, all knowledge. Man's *consciousness of himself as the centre of the world, bearing within himself the secret of the world, and rising above all the things of the world, is a prerequisite of all philosophy: without it one could not dare to philosophize.* He who knows the world philosophically must rise above all the things of the world: he cannot be one of the things of the world, on a level with other things—he must himself be the world. . . . Man existing as a closed-off individual would have no means of knowing the universe. Such a being would not be of higher order than other separate things in the world, would not overcome this separate condition. The way of anthropology is the only way of knowing the universe, and this way presupposes man's exceptional consciousness of himself. Only in man's sense of himself and in his self-consciousness, are the divine mysteries revealed.

M.C.A., pp. 57-8

* Milton.

The Meeting-Point of Two Worlds

Man is the meeting-point of two worlds. This is attested by the duality in man's consciousness of himself, a duality evident throughout his whole history. Man recognizes that he belongs to two worlds: his nature is dual and, in his consciousness of himself, now one of these natures, now the other, seems to prevail. With equal firmness man founds the most contradictory ideas of himself, equally justified by facts of his nature. Man is conscious at once of his greatness and power and of his worthlessness and weakness, of his imperial freedom and his slavish dependence: he knows himself as the image and likeness of God and as a drop in the ocean of the necessities of nature. With almost equal right we may speak of man's divine origin, and of his development from the lowest forms of nature. With almost equal force of argument the philosophers defend man's original freedom and a complete determinism which leads man into the chain of fateful, natural necessity. Man is one of the phenomena of this world, one of the things caught in the maelstrom of all things of nature: and man passes beyond this world, as the image and likness of absolute being transcends all things of the order of nature. What a strange being—divided and of double meaning, having the form of a king and that of a slave, a being at once free and in chains, powerful and weak, uniting in one being glory and worthlessness, the eternal with the corruptible! . . .

It is almost incomprehensible how a tiny bit of nature, completely dependent upon its irresistible round, should dare to rise against nature and demand his rights as a descendant of another world, as a being with another destiny. *Man's highest consciousness of himself is not explicable by the world of nature and remains a mystery to that world.* . . . Man is not only of this world but of another world; not only of necessity, but of freedom; not only out of nature, but from God. . . .

In his essence, man is a break in the world of nature, he cannot be contained within it. The learned rationalists are compelled to stand in bewilderment before the fact of Christ's self-consciousness, before the inexplicable fact of His divine consciousness of himself. And the learned rationalists should also stand in bewilderment before the fact of man's consciousness of himself, since this consciousness transcends the natural world and cannot be explained by it. There is a deep and very significant anology between Christ's consciousness of Himself and man's consciousness of his own nature. Only the revelation about Christ gives a key to solving the problem of man's consciousness of himself.

M.C.A., pp. 60-2

Man, the Centre of Being

In the world of nature, man does not hold an exceptional place. He is part of the circulation of nature, one of its phenomena, one of its things: he is a tiny, infinitely small, part of the universe. . . . As a purely natural being, man is not the centre of the universe and not its king: he is only one among many and is forced to struggle for his place with an infinite number of beings and powers which are also striving to rise.

But the collapse of naturalistic anthropocentrism, which had naïvely tied man's significance to the natural world, does not mean the collapse of man's highest consciousness of himself as a microcosm. . . . *Man's infinite spirit claims an absolute supernatural anthropocentrism: he knows himself to be the absolute centre—not of a given, closed planetary system, but of the whole of being, of all planes of being, of all worlds.*

Man, the Microcosm

Nature is the organic hierarchy of living beings. The material element in nature is only an incarnation, an objectivization of living beings, of spirits of various hierarchic degrees. And the material element which science so carefully investigates, is not only an incarnation of a living spirit, it is a fettering and enslaving spirit—it bears the stamp of the Fall, of degradation to a lower sphere. Man, the microcosm, belongs to a higher, royal degree in the hierarchy of nature, as a living organism. Man, the microcosm, is responsible for the whole structure of nature and whatever takes place in man affects the whole of nature. Man gives life and spirit to nature, through his creative freedom, and he kills or fetters it through his own servitude and his fall into material necessity. The fall of the highest hierarchial centre of nature carries with it the fall of all nature, of all its lower ranks. The whole of creation groans and weeps and awaits its liberation. The element of death in nature and that evil materialization, into the power of which all the beings of this world have fallen by the force of necessity and can find no way out of their limited condition—all this is the result of man's fall, of an evil shifting of the hierarchial centre of nature. . . . Man becomes a part of the natural world, one of the phenomena of nature, subject to nature's necessity. 'This world', the world of natural necessity, fell with the fall of man, and man will have to renounce the temptations of 'this world' to regain his regnant place in it. And yet fallen man remains a microcosm and contains within himself all the ranks and all the powers of the world. But it was not individual man who fell, it was the all-man, the first Adam, and so not the individual man may rise, but the all-man. The all-man is inseparable from the cosmos and its fate. The liberation and creative upsurge of the all-man is the liberation and creation of the cosmos. The destinies of the microcosm and the macrocosm are inseparable—they rise or fall together. The condition of the one is imprinted upon the other; they mutually penetrate each other. Man cannot escape the cosmos—he can only change or transform it. The cosmos shares the fate of man and hence man shares the fate of the cosmos. Only the man who takes the place in the cosmos prepared for him by his Creator, has the power to transform the cosmos into a new heaven and a new earth. . . . The restoration of man to his former dignity could be accomplished only by the appearance of the absolute Son of God, in the Incarnation.... Man was created the dynamic and creative centre of the universe but, in using his freedom, he followed the fallen angel who had desired to become the centre of the world and lost his royal position, weakened his creative power and fell into an animal-like condition.... The new Adam represents a higher degree of cosmic-creative development than did the First Adam in Eden. The old consciousness that man was supposed to be only a static adjunct to the glory of God, a passive being deprived of knowledge, reflected the fallen state of the fallen angel who wanted to become the ruler of the cosmos. Not man but the fallen angel himself was called to be the adjunct of God's glory. Man, on the contrary, is called to glorify his Creator by creative dynamic in the cosmos. He must leave a state of repose. Adam, reborn through Christ into a new spiritual man, is no longer passive and oppressed and blind, but a clear-seeing creator, the son of God who continues his Father's work. *M.C.A.*, pp. 72-5

Christology, the True Anthropology

Christianity has always taught of the weakness and fall of man, of the sinfulness and weakness of human nature. At the same time, Christian anthropology recognizes the absolute and royal significance of man, since it teaches of the incarnation of God and the divine possibilities in man, the mutual inter-penetration of divine and human natures. *But for some deep reason, hidden in the secret of times and seasons, Christianity never revealed in its fullest what one might venture to call a Christology of man, that is the secret of man's divine nature, a dogma of man, analogous to the dogma of Christ.* Christianity has revealed the nature of the Holy Trinity and the nature of Christ, but very little of the nature of man.... *And yet in Christian revelation the truth about man's divine nature is really only the reverse side of the medal of the truth about Christ's human nature.* The Christology of man is inseparable from that of the Son of God: Christ's self-consciousness is inseparable from that of man. The Christological revelation is also an anthropological revelation. And the task of humanity's religious consciousness is to reveal the Christological consciousness of man.... *Man is not a simple creature, together with other created things, because the only-begotten Son of God, begotten before all worlds and of equal worth with His Father, is not only absolute God but Absolute Man.* Christology is the only true anthropology. Christ, the Absolute Man, appeared on earth and in humanity and hence for ever confirmed a central significance in the universe for man and for the earth. *M.C.A.*, pp. 80-1

Man the Creator

God gave man the gracious aid of Christ's redemption which restored man's fallen nature. Through the redemption, man's creative freedom is restored to him. And the time must come in the world for this creative freedom to be active. Man must create that for which he was redeemed, for which he was created. In man himself, in his terrible and final liberty, the change-over into the religious epoch of creativeness must take place. And it would be a new fall of man if he were to wait and demand that God should make this move for him, that the creative revelation should be accomplished not by man's inner freedom but only by the help of God from outside. . . .

Human nature is creative because it is the image and likeness of God the Creator. That the image and likeness of the Creator cannot fail to be himself a creator is an anthropological truth which was not recognized with sufficient intensity and fullness by former religious epochs. Religious consciousness was full of the mystery of redemption of human nature but the mystery of this to-be-redeemed human nature, itself, was unknown. What is the pre-destination of this redeemed human nature? Within the limits of the religion of redemption, there is no answer to this question. The usual Christian answer, that man's chief end is life in God, cannot satisfy us—it is too general and too formal. Those who give this answer are too much engrossed in the *way* to the final goal. Rest in God is usually thought of as victory over the evil and sin in human nature, as the extinguishing of this nature, as the absorption of the human by the divine. . . . But Christ is God-Man. He redeems and restores *human* nature to its likeness unto God. Human nature which knows itself, knows its independent and free being, must exist eternally only as a creative and creating nature. Human nature finally justifies itself before the Creator not by extinguishing itself but by its own creative expression. Man must absolutely *be*. Human nature, redeemed and saved from evil, has a positive human content and a positive human purpose.

M.C.A., pp. 108-11

Man: His Relation to God

'Man is only a design of God.'

Freedom I, p. 5

We may establish three types of understanding the relationship between God and man. (1) Transcendent dualism subjects human will exteriorly to the will of God; the two natures remain alien, separated, mutually exclusive. (2) Immanent monism metaphysically identifies human will with God's will, denies all independence to human nature, and sees in man only one of the manifestations of the life of divinity. Man is merely a transient moment in the revelation and development of Divinity. (3) The creative, Christian conception: divine-human anthropologism recognizes the independence of two natures, human and Divine, perceives the inter-action of the grace of God and the freedom of man.

Man, as God's 'other', gives a free answer to God's call, revealing his own creative nature.

And within Christianity we may discover three types of comprehension, more or less clearly expressed. The third type of understanding the relation between God and man is the most difficult for rational thought, the most antinomic. And this makes very difficult and burdensome the Christian doctrine of redemption, the Christian conception of world-salvation and deliverance. Here we may note two types of understanding, although they are rarely encountered in a pure state. By means of the organized action of grace, God aids man who lost his freedom in the Fall, to save himself, to conquer sin. In its extreme forms, this conception leads, even, to justifying coercion and compulsion in the work of salvation. But there is another conception of the meaning of the world's life. *God awaits from man a free answer to His call, awaits answering love and creative participation in the conquest of the darkness of non-being.* Man must manifest the greatest activity of his spirit, the greatest exertion of his freedom, to accomplish what God expects of him.

Freedom II, pp. 31-2

What God Expects of Man

God expects of man immeasurably more than is taught in the usual doctrines about redemption and the fulfilment of God's will. Does not God expect man to reveal, in freedom, his creative nature? And has not God concealed from himself what man will reveal in his response to the summons of God? God never forces man, never sets a limit to man's freedom. God's design for man and for the world is that man should give up his powers to God, in freedom and in love, should carry on creative activity in the name of God. God expects man's participation in the work of world-creation, the continuing world-creation, in the victory of being over non-being. He awaits brave needs of creativeness. But what if it is the will of God that man, gifted with creative freedom which bears the mark of the image and likeness of God, should participate in the eighth day of world-creation? What if God awaits from man a feat of free creativeness and demands of man the manifestation of all the powers with which he is endowed? This *is* the will of God, and man must fulfil it. But the mystery of man's creativity, of his creative nature, remains concealed; it is not directly revealed in Holy Writ. If this mystery were revealed and fixed in the holy scriptures, there would be no freedom of creativeness, no feats of creativity: what God expects of man would be impossible. Man's creative calling in the world demands an act of his own self-knowledge, and this act should bring with it an absolute increment in being. *Freedom*, Vol. II, pp. 35-6

The Christian View of Man

The final revelation and confirmation of human personality is possible only in Christianity. Christianity recognizes the eternal significance and the eternal value of man, of the individual human soul and its destiny. The soul of man is more precious than all the kingdoms of the world. The soul contains infinity. Christianity appeared in the world, first of all as a religion of man's salvation for eternity. . . . Only in Christianity can be found the individual, unique and unrepeatable, in his eternal significance. And the unique and unrepeatable visage of every man exists only because there exists the unique and unrepeatable image of Christ the God-man. In Christ and through Christ there is revealed the eternal image of every human being. *Freedom*, Vol. II, pp. 59-60

The Problem of Man in Philosophy

The problem of man, as the centre of being, is pre-eminently a Christian problem. And anthropological philosophy is Christian philosophy. Greek philosophy did not put the problem of man in all its depth and plenitude. It disclosed reasoning man, but man himself had not yet appeared in his full value, as both central and problematic for thought. Man finds himself in being, and he *is* being, even before he knows being. And the possibility of knowing being is determined by what the being of man himself really is. In the make-up, the existential composition, of man's ego, there is that which makes knowing possible. There is such a thing as the transcendent, but it is not at all 'objective', neither is it authoritative: it is immanent in human existence. Not consciousness is primordial, not the subject as over against being, not sensation and perception as separate elements, but integral man, man rooted in the depths of being. But this is not that man who studies psychology and sociology and belongs to the objectivized world: this is the man given in his own inward existence. With the Renaissance, nature began to be revealed and rehabilitated. Man began to know himself as a part of nature and this even appeared to him liberation. Now the time has come to disclose and rehabilitate man, not as a part of nature and of the objectivized world, but as being in itself, outside 'objectness', in his inward existence. Then the problem of knowing, also, will be placed outside the counter-position of subject and object, as the antithesis of knowing and being. *Solitude*, pp. 39-40

Man—Child of God and Child of Freedom

Man is a being dissatisfied with himself and capable of outgrowing himself. The very fact of man's existence is a break in the natural world, and bears witness to the fact that nature cannot be self-sufficient and rests upon supernatural being. As a being belonging to two worlds and capable of overcoming himself, man is a contradictory and paradoxical being, comprehending within himself diametric opposites. With equal right it may be said of man that he is a high or low form of being, strong or weak, free or slavish. The enigmatic and contradictory in man are caused not only by the fact that he is a being which has fallen from the heights, an earthly being, retaining a remembrance of heaven and the shining of heavenly light, but even more profoundly by the fact that originally he is both the child of God and the child of nothingness, of meonic freedom. His roots are in heaven, in God, and in the deepest abyss as well. . . . In principle, man is a novelty in nature. The problem of man is completely insoluble if it is regarded from the viewpoint of nature and only in relationship with nature. We can understand man only in his relation to God. *Destiny*, p. 51

Three New Factors in Modern Man

Three new factors have appeared in the moral life of mankind, factors which are acquiring hitherto unheard-of power. And ethics must reckon, first of all, with these three new factors or tendencies of the spirit. Man has come to love freedom more than ever before, and is demanding freedom with extraordinary insistence. He neither can, nor will he, accept anything otherwise than freely, by way of freedom. Man has become more *sympathetic* than formerly: he cannot stand the cruelties of former times; he has new compassion for every creature, not for men alone, for the very last of men, but for animals and all living things. . . . And man longs to *create*, more than in other times; he wants religious justification and meaning for his creativity. He will no longer tolerate any coercion, external or internal, on his creative instinct. Along with this, we find in modern man other instincts at work: instincts of enslavement and cruelty. . . . But what is new and eternal is this yearning for . . . *freedom*, *sympathy* and *creativity*. *Destiny*, p. 164

Man needs psychosynthesis more than psychoanalysis. *Divine*, p. 165

Man and the Machine

It is no exaggeration to say that the question of technics has become a question of the fate of man and of culture. In a time of little faith, of the weakening not only of the old religious faith, but also of the humanist beliefs of the nineteenth century, the only strong faith of the modern civilized man is his faith in technics, its power and its limitless development. Technics is man's latest love and he is willing to change his own image under the influence of the object of his love. Everything which is happening in the world feeds this new faith of man. Man has desired miracles for his faith, and it seemed that miracles had ceased. And behold technics work veritable miracles. The problem of technics is very disturbing for the Christian conscience: its meaning has not yet been thought out by Christians. The majority consider technics neutral and morally indifferent: that is the business of engineers. It offers perfections in life which can be enjoyed by Christian people. Technics multiply the good things of life. Technics put no spiritual problem. But a minority of

Christians experience technics apocalyptically: they are terrified at its increasing power over human lives; they are ready to see in it the triumph of the spirit of anti-christ, of the beast from the abyss. And both ideas are false. One is the effect of fear, the other puts no problem. . . .

The new actuality of nature with which modern technics faces man is not the product of evolution, but of the inventiveness and creative activity of man himself, not of an organic, but an organizing process. The meaning of the whole technical era lies in this. The domination of technics and of the machine is first of all the transition from organic to organized life, from the vegetable to the constructed. From the viewpoint of organic life, technics means another incarnation, a breaking away from the organic bodies of history, a separation of body and spirit. Technics reveals a new degree of actuality, and this is the work of man, a result of the break-through of spirit into nature and the installation of reason in elemental processes. . . .

Technics have cosmogonic significance: through technics a new cosmos is being created. . . . This is a new category of being. Actually, a machine is neither an organic nor a non-organic body. The appearance on the scene of these new bodies is connected with the difference between the organic and the organized. . . . Man has succeeded in calling into life a new reality. This is proof of man's terrible power, of his royal creative calling in the world. But it is also an indication of his weakness and his tendency toward enslavement. With unusual acuity, the machine puts the problem of man's fate in society and in the cosmos. This is the problem of the relationship between man and nature, the personality and society, spirit to matter, the irrational to the rational. It is surprising that up to now no one has produced a philosophy of technics and the machine, although many books have been written on this subject. . . . The machine is regarded only from outside, only in its social projection. But inwardly it is the theme of a philosophy of human existence, 'Existenzphilosophie'. Can man exist only in the old cosmos, physical and organic, which once seemed to be the eternal order, or can he exist in the new as well, a cosmos as yet unknown? . . . The problem must first be solved in spiritual experience before it is solved in philosophic thought. . . . In the machine epoch, religious life requires more intense spirituality, Christianity becomes more inward and more spiritual, freer from social influence. This is an inevitable process. In the modern world it is very difficult to retain forms of religion determined by national, family or social influences. Religion becomes more personal: it is spiritually determined. This, of course, does not mean religious individualism for the very sobornost and churchliness of religious consciousness is not of a sociological nature.

But in another connection the power of technics may have fateful results for spiritual and religious life. Technics controls and radically alters our attitude toward time. Man, too, is actually capable of controlling time. But the actuality of technics submit man and his inner life to a constantly faster movement of time. In the furious speed of modern civilization, in this race of time, not one instant remains an end in itself. . . . But this conquest of time through speed and haste is also enslavement by time. And this means that technical actuality in regard to time destroys eternity and makes it more and more difficult for man to be related to eternity. Man has no time for eternity. . . . And man faces the problem: will he retain the possibility of moments of contemplation, contemplation of eternity, of God, of truth and beauty? Man unquestionably has an active calling in the world and there is truth in actualism. But man is also a being capable of contemplation, and in contemplation there is an element which determines his 'I'. In contemplation itself, that is in man's relation to God, there is creativeness. Putting this problem convinces us still further that all the ills of modern civilization arise from the lack of conformity between man's organization inherited from other times, and the new technical, mechanized activity from which he cannot escape. Man's spirit cannot endure the speed which modern civilization demands of it. . . . And there will be a terrible struggle between personality and technical society, a struggle between man and the machine. . . .

In ever newer forms is stated the problem of man's liberation, of the spirit's domination of nature and society. This problem can be solved only by a concept which places man above both society and nature, puts the human spirit above all natural or social forces which must submit themselves to it. . . . The way to man's final liberation and the final realization of his calling is the way to the Kingdom of God, which is not only a heavenly kingdom, but also a kingdom of a transfigured earth, a transfigured cosmos. *Put*, No. 38, May 1933

Man Facing the Universe

> Man's fate brings him inevitably either to the Grand Inquisitor or to Christ.
>
> *Dostoevsy*, p. 195

Man finds himself in the world, or is cast out into it, and he stands before the world as before a riddle to be solved. Man's existence depends on the world, and he perishes in the world, from the effect of the world upon him. The world nourishes man and the world destroys him. The milieu into which he has been mysteriously thrust from somewhere else, constantly threatens man and arouses him to struggle. And man sets for himself the extraordinarily daring task of knowing the world and all that may be glimpsed beyond it. Man is a small thing compared with the world, with what he wishes to know. He is terribly small; if you look at him out of the object. And there is nothing more astonishing, more touching or more moving, than these efforts of the human spirit to win through the dark to the light, through meaninglessness to meaning, to break through to freedom from his bondage to necessity. Man measures his strength with the universe and, in the act of knowing, strives to rise above the limitations and the density of the world. He can know light, meaning, freedom, within himself. And even when man recognizes that he is only a creature of the world-milieu and totally dependent upon it, still he lifts himself above it, and finds within himself a higher element than the given world, discovers that he has arrived from another world, another plane. Knowledge would be impossible if man were only nature, if he were not spirit also.

Man—Human-ness

As yet we do not have a genuine religious and metaphysical anthropology. None of the former systems can satisfy us—neither the anthropology of the church fathers, nor that of the scholastics: humanistic anthropology is also unsatisfying. The traditional Christian doctrine of man did not reveal man's creative nature: it was crushed by the consciousness of sin. On the other hand, the concepts of human-ness, humanity, were not pursued to their metaphysical and religious foundations. True human-ness is the god-like, the divine in man. The divine element is not something supernatural, nor is it a special act of grace: it is the spiritual element, as a special reality. Herein lies the paradox of the relationship between the divine and the human. In order fully to be man, man must resemble God. To have a human image, he must have the image of God. By himself man is very little human, he is even inhuman. Not man is humane, but only God. It is God who demands human-ness of man —man himself is not very demanding, in this connection. *Divine*, p. 137

It is often said that the new man must appear. This is Christian terminology. Christianity was the announcement of the appearance of the new Adam, of victory over the old Adam. Man must constantly be made anew, that is he must realize the fullness of his humanity. There is no such thing as completely unchangeable human nature, as Aristotle, St Thomas Aquinas and Kant have held even in a different way, as theology in its dominant forms is claiming, together with many philosophers of the rationalist school. Man changes, he both progresses and moves backward, his consciousness is now broadened, and deepened. . . . But God's intention for man remains always the same. There is the intention of eternal humanity, the fullness of human nature. Man will never he replaced by supermen or by spirits of other hierarchies, the theosophists and occultists think. Man will inherit eternity in his humanity; he is called to life in God; he moves from eternity through time to eternity. The new man may be a creative enrichment and the realization of the fullness of humanity, but he may also be treason to and distortion of the idea of man, may be not a divine-human phenomenon, but a beast-human—that is, a complete denial of humanity.

The new man, also, may be someone standing at the edge of the abyss of non-being, attracted by non-being. In this connection the new tendencies in France are interesting: Sartre, Bataille and Camus. Modern man, wearied by fallen and disintegrating being, seems fatally attracted by non-being. On the very verge of non-being he wants to experience final ecstasy: either in ecstasy of heroism for the sake of nothing, or an ecstasy of creativeness, arising from his own nothingness. . . . Revolutionary social movements may also lead to betrayal of the human. But in the God-man, the Son of God and the son of man, the new man takes his start, the man of new and everlasting humanity. *Divine*, pp. 155 ff

Man and the Cosmos

Man is a natural being: he is bound by many threads to the life of the cosmos; he is dependent on the cycle of cosmic life. Man's body, even, is determined by physics and by chemical processes. He dies, and his physical body is dissolved into the matter and the life of the world. Man lives in a world of nature and has to define his relationship to it. But the mystery of man is that he is not only a natural being, explicable by nature; he is also a personality, that is a spiritual being, bearing in himself the divine image. . . . At the same time, man's relation to the cosmos is defined by the fact that he is a microcosm: he includes within himself the cosmos, or he includes within himself history. Man cannot be only a part of something: he is a whole. Because of the spiritual element in him man is not subject to nature: he is independent, although natural forces may kill him. If man were only a natural and finite being, there would be nothing tragic about death—only the death is tragic of a deathless being, striving toward infinity. Man is part of nature only from without, from the object: from within, from spirit, nature is in him. Hence man's double relation to the cosmos: he is the slave of nature, and nature's king. . . .

We may fix four periods in man's relationship to the cosmos: (1) man's submersion in cosmic life, his dependence on the objective world—human personality has not yet been fully developed—man has not yet conquered nature: his relation toward nature is still in terms of magic and myth (primitive stock-raising and agriculture, slavery); (2) Man is freed from the power of cosmic forces, from the spirits and demons of nature—man struggles by means of ascesis, rather than technics (elementary forms of economics, serfdom); (3) the mechanization of nature, its scientific and technical control, the development of industry in the form of capitalism, the emancipation of labour and its enslavement by exploitation of the means of production, the necessity of selling labour for wages; and (4) the disruption of cosmic order in the discovery of the infinitely great and infinitely small, the formation of a new organization, distinct from the organic, technics and mechanization, the terribly augmented power of man over nature, and his slavery to his own discoveries. These phases in the relationships between man and nature are typological and chronological, although the passage of time plays a certain part. But now, when we have entered the technical age, other terrible themes present themselves. Where once man feared the demons of nature and Christ freed him from demonolatry, now man is in terror before the world-wide mechanization of nature. The power of technics is the final metamorphosis of the realm of Caesar. It no longer demands the sanctification which the realm of Caesar demanded, in the past. This is the last phase of secularization, the dissolution of the centre and the development of various autonomous spheres, where one of them claims totalitarian recognition. Man is now in the grip of one of these autonomous spheres. We may conceive of a fifth period in the relationship between man and nature. In this period will come man's still greater control of the forces of nature, the real emancipation of labour and the workers, technics made subject to spirit. But this requires a spiritual movement in the world, which is the work of freedom.

Spirit and Caesar, pp. 46-8

Man has no 'Natural Rights'

The doctrine of natural laws, recognizing the rights of man, independent of political rights fixed by the state, made a theoretical mistake characteristic of the immature metaphysic of that time. In reality, the inalienable rights of man, which fix the limits of society's authority over him, are fixed not by nature, but by spirit. They are spiritual rather than natural rights: nature establishes no rights whatever. The mistake occurred when they made a revolution in the name of nature; revolution may be made only in the name of spirit: nature, that is the natural instinct in man, created only new forms of slavery. *Spirit and Caesar*, p. 60

Man and Caesar—Authority

Caesar is the eternal symbol of authority, the state, the kingdom of this world. Two basic views are possible, as regards the mutual relationship between Caesar, authority, the state, the kingdom of this world on the one hand, and spirit, man's spiritual life, the Kingdom of God, on the other. . . . Wrong have been the understanding and the interpretation of the Gospel's 'Render unto Caesar that which is Caesar's, and unto God that which is God's' and the words of St Paul: 'There is no power but of God.'

There has been a slavish interpretation of these words. 'Render unto Caesar . . .' does not mean a religious definition of Caesar and his realm; it does not imply evaluation at all. This is merely distinguishing between two different spheres which cannot be combined one with the other. . . . The Apostle Paul's words have no religious meaning whatever: they are purely historical and relative, called forth by the position of Christians in the Roman Empire. St Paul was afraid that Christianity might turn into an anarchistic, revolutionary sect. He wanted to place Christianity into universal history. We must recall, further, that some time later, during the reign of Domitian, the state authority was called the beast from the abyss.

The problem is vastly more complex than those who cite St Paul's words usually think. In the past, Christianity has frequently shown not a little servility to the realm of Caesar. This usually followed a regular formula: any change, revolution or reform, in the realm of Caesar, at first aroused opposition on the part of the Church, condemnation of the novelty as an apparition of the spirit of Antichrist. But when the new power of Caesar became stabilized and confirmed, the Church suddenly noticed that this authority was also from God, and proceeded to sanction it. Thus it turned out that the Church only sanctioned what others had wrought, other forces outside the Church and Christianity, and had no ideal of her own for society and the state. And things were worse when the Church seemed to have her own ideal, in the Christian theocracies of history, because these theocracies were Christian only in name, and in reality they denied freedom. Theocracies were one of the temptations through which Christianity had to pass. This was not limited to theocracy in the mediaeval sense of the word, but included 'Christian' states, which were always Christian only in a symbolic, not a real sense, one which compromised Christianity. The depth of the problem lies in this, that spirit cannot be dependent upon nature and society, nor be determined by them. Spirit is freedom, but in the objectivation of spirit in the course of history, a series of myths were created which were used to confirm the authority of government, such myths as that of sovereignty in the religious sphere, the infallibility of the Pope, or that of a council of bishops. In the life of the state and of society there have been myths: the myth of monarchy, the sovereign power of the monarch, the myth of democracy—the sovereign power of the people (*Volonté générale*), the myth of communism—the sovereign power of the proletariat. Although it has not always been openly acknowledged, all these myths in reality are mystic in their nature, and, as a rule, they have contained not a new understanding of the myth of sovereignty, but the denial of the very idea of sovereignty. Sovereignty belongs to no one: it is only one of the illusions of objectivation.

Spirit and Caesar, pp. 69-71

The Eternal Man

The eternal man, orientated toward eternity and infinity, is at once the eternally new man and an eternal and limitless purpose. The eternal man is not something given once for all: he is not to be comprehended statically. The truly new man is a realization of the eternal man, bearing in himself the image and likeness of God. . . . Hence looking forward to the future involves those parts of the past which were eternal. Man's dignity demands that he shall not become a slave to swift-running time. The new man must be creative, and hence he must look toward the future, toward that which has never been. This is his answer to the call of God. But creativity cannot be identified with work. Work belongs to the kingdom of necessity ('In the sweat of thy brow shalt thou earn thy bread'); it belongs to the realm of Caesar. The dignity of labour must be upheld: hence the central importance of the workers, hence the necessity of ending the exploitation of labour. This is the religious truth of socialism. But creativeness belongs to the purposes of life, to the realm of freedom, which is that of Spirit. We dare not subject the purposes of life, its ends, to life's means: freedom cannot be subjected to necessity: the realm of Spirit cannot be subordinated to that of Caesar. Hence the religious truth in personalism.

Spirit and Caesar, pp. 170-1

PERSONALITY

Personality is changelessness in change, unity in variety. *Slavery*, p. 21

The Riddle of Personality

Man is a riddle in this world, perhaps the supreme riddle. Man is a riddle, not as an animal or a social being, not as part of nature and society, but as a personality. The whole world is nothing, compared with human personality, with man's unique visage, with his unique destiny. Man agonizingly wants to know who he is, whence he came and whither he is going. Even in Greece man wanted to know himself, and in this knowledge saw the key to the riddle of being, the source of philosophical knowledge. Man may know himself from above or from below, from his own light, from the divine element in him, and he may know himself from his darkness, from his elemental-subconscious, from the demonic element within himself. And he may do this because he is a dual and a contradictory being, a being polarized to the highest degree, god-like and beast-like, high and low, free and slave, capable of rising to the heights or of falling, capable of great love and sacrifice or of great cruelty and limitless egotism. *Freedom*, I, p. 19

The Natural and the Spiritual Man

Man is a mixture of the spiritual, the supernatural, with the mental-physical, the natural. Man is the point where two worlds intersect, he belongs to two orders. Here lies the infinite complexity and difficulty of human life. There is the spiritual man and there is the natural man, and one man is both. The spiritual world is manifest in the mental, natural man as his particular qualitativeness. But the natural man does not disappear. Hence in man we do not find the qualitativeness of spiritual life in a pure form. And it is not given to man to rise easily above natural being, or to renounce it. . . . Every man is originally linked with the condition of the whole world, and every one has certain obligations in regard to the world of nature. *Freedom*, I, p. 57

Personality is Spiritual

We cannot think of personality in biological, or psychological, or sociological terms. Personality is spiritual, and presupposes the existence of a spiritual world. The value of personality is a higher hierarchic value, value of the order of spirit. The basic item in a doctrine of personality is the fact that the value of personality predicates the existence of superpersonal values. It is just these superpersonal values that produce the value of personality. Personality is the bearer and the creator of superpersonal values, and only this produces its integrity, its unity and its eternal significance. This is not to be understood as meaning that personality is not a value in itself, and is only a means to super-personal values. . . . This means that the existence of personality presupposes the existence of God; the value of personality presupposes the supreme value of God. If God does not exist, as the source of super-personality values, then personality is valueless, and there remains only the individual, subject to natural and racial life.

Personality is primarily a moral principle; from it the attitude toward all values is determined. Hence the idea of personality is the basis of ethics. An impersonal ethic is 'contradictio in adjecto'. . . . The centre of moral life is in persons, not in relationships. . . . The unity and value of personality do not exist without a spiritual element. The spirit constitutes the personality, brings illumination and transfiguration of the biological individual, makes personality independent of the order of nature. . . . The spiritual element which constitutes personality does not mean a bloodless spiritualism. Only for personality do such things exist as the collision between good and evil or between differing values. Tragedy is always linked with personality, with the awakening and the wrestling of personality. Personality is created by the idea of God and the freedom of man. And the life of personality is not self-preservation, as is the case with the individual, but self-determination and self-development.

Destiny, pp. 61-2

The Person and the Individual

Two processes are at work in the world: the socialization of man, and man's individualization. And in the world there is a constant conflict between man's social-moral consciousness and personal-moral consciousness. From this the distinction arises between law and morality. It is a surprising fact that in the nineteenth and twentieth centuries man has permitted himself to believe that he had received his moral life, his distinction between good and evil, his value—all this from society alone. He was ready to renounce his birthright and the independence of his soul and his conscience. A. Comte, K. Marx, Durkheim all accepted the moral consciousness of the primitive clan as the summit of the moral consciousness of mankind. And they denied personality: they see only the individual correlative to the social collective. Ethics must wage constant spiritual war against that final socialization of man that suppresses freedom of spirit and of conscience. The socialization of ethics is the tyranny of society over the spiritual life of the personality and the freedom of its moral evaluations. . . . *Destiny*, pp. 61-9

Only Personality is Truly Creative

Personality is realized spiritually, not biologically. Ethics is based on personality, and without personality there is no ethics. Human personality, as God's idea, as the image of God, is the centre of ethical consciousness, the supreme value. And human personality is the supreme value, not because it is the bearer of a universally-valid moral law, as Kant thought, but just because it is God's idea, God's image, the bearer of the divine element of life. Hence it is impossible to demean or destroy man by good. A moral act of human personality has not only personal, but social and even cosmic meaning. Moral radiation flows out from human personality and spreads abroad in the world. But human personality always remains the burning centre of the world. Moral life whose subject is society is a life that has cooled, a life of mores and customs, of social opinion. Personality alone is the truly creative and prophetic element in moral life: it forges out new values.

Destiny, p. 144

> Personality cannot be self-satisfying and self-sufficient; something other, higher as well as lower, is necessary for its existence.
> *Slavery*, p. 26

Personality is Integral

From the naturalistic viewpoint personality is a very small, infinitesimally small part of nature; from the sociological viewpoint it is a very small part of society. From the viewpoint of philosophy of existence and a philosophy of spirit, personality cannot be thought of as the partial and individual, in contrast to the general and the universal. This contrast, so characteristic for natural or social life, disappears in personality. The superpersonal builds personality, the 'general' bases the 'partial' on it, and the superpersonal and 'general' never make personality their 'partial' instrument. Here is the mystery of personality, the contrasting elements harnessed together in it. That organic universalism which thinks of personality as part of the world, is wrong. This theory takes a thoroughly unorganic view of personality. All organic theories of society are auto-personalistic and make personality into an organ of the whole. We must understand the relation between the whole and its parts, axiologically, not naturally. Personality is always a whole, not a part, and this whole is given within existence, rather than in the external world of nature. Personality is not object: it cannot be found in the objectified world. We might say that personality is outside the world. For me, meeting a person is meeting a 'thou', not an object. Personality is not an object, a thing: it is not a natural substance, neither is it an objectivization of psychic life, something to be studied by psychological science. And when personality triumphs in the world, there will be no more objectivization. *Solitude*, pp. 148-9

Personality is a Living Contradiction

Personality is distinct from everything partial or sectional in that it may include animal content in itself. Personality realized itself by filling itself with universal content. Nothing partial could do this. Personality is unity in multiplicity, embracing the universe. Hence for the objectivized world personality is a paradox. *Personality is a living contradiction between the personal and the social, between form and content, between the finite and the infinite, between freedom and fate.* Hence personality can not be something given, complete, like an object; it creates itself; it is dynamic. *Solitude*, p. 159

Personality as a Means to an End

Here we approach the problem of the relation between personality and the harmony and order of the whole. Can personality be considered a means to world-order, to the harmony of the whole? This is an ancient, unchristian view which St Augustine adopted, and which then penetrated and distorted Christian thought. For St Augustine, evil exists only in the parts, and vanishes in the order and harmony of the whole. From this viewpoint hell is seen as good and just, the triumph of good, of world order and harmony. But this is nothing other than the final tyranny of the objectivized world over the mystery of inner existence, the domination of the general and racial over the individual and personal. Nothing could be more anti-Christian or anti-human. The idea of world order and harmony is deprived of all moral and spiritual value, which always presupposes relationship to the inner existence of personality. . . . The whole meaning of man's existence is linked with the liberation of his personality from the power of the world, the state, the nation, from abstract ideas and theories; it is in his immediate submission to the living God. And only after this inward and free submission to God, who is not at all 'the general', can human personality define, from within, its attitude toward superpersonal values and real community. . . .

Solitude, p. 163

Personality and Society

The problem of the relationship between personality and society is not only a problem of sociology and social philosophy: it is a basic metaphysical problem, a problem of existential philosophy. We have seen that in the perspective of this problem, the problem of society or community, we may consider all the basic problems of knowledge. Knowledge stands under the sign, either of society, and then it has to do with the world of objectivization, or else of communion, and then the mystery of existence is revealed. What is called intuition is nothing other than communion, the discovery of kinship. The feeling of solitude is quenched only in communion, not in society. Community of men means different attitudes of the personality in society and in communion: in communion, community is a part of personality, its quality: in society, personality is part of community. . . . The realization of personality predicates both community and communion. Personality has social content and vocation, but they are not defined by society, they are defined from within, then move out toward society. Personality remains the supreme value in social life. . . . *Solitude*, p. 165

Personality is Always the Same

Personality is eternal, always remains itself, the unrepeatable, and at the same time, it is always changing, always building, and needs time to attain fulness of existence. Personality is hostile to time as something which brings death: the realization of personality gives birth to time. This is the basic paradox of uniting change and changelessness, time and super-time. Personality presupposes change, the creation of something new; it does not admit a congealed immobility, and yet *at the same time*, while it changes, personality must not betray itself, must be true to its own self. . . . *Solitude*, p. 179

The Aim of Personality

Two conceptions of the meaning of man's existence are in constant collision: one says the aim of man's life is relief from suffering in both time and eternity; the other says that it is qualitative upsurge, the attainment of truth, justice, beauty, i.e. creativity. The quest for salvation may be a heavenly projection of earthly utilitarianism. But of course salvation may be understood as the attainment of fulness and completeness of life. The realization of personality demands fearlessness, victory over the fear of life or death, which is the fruit of utilitarianism, and the quest for prosperity and relief from pain—all this together with freedom and perfection.

Solitude, pp. 47, 148-9, 155-6, 163-5, 168-9, 174, 179, 182-3

Personality Introduces Novelty

If man were not a person, even if not yet developed or even suppressed, even if enfeebled by illness, even if existing in potentiality, he would still be like the other things of the world and there would be nothing extraordinary about him. Personality cannot be contained in the steady uninterrupted process of the world's life: it cannot be a movement in the evolution of the world. The very existence of personality presupposes brokenness which is inexplicable by any kind of uninterruptedness. Man is known alone by biology and sociology, man as a natural or social being, is born of this world and the processes at work in it. But man as a person is not a child of the world, he is of another descent. And this makes man a riddle. Personality is a break-through, a break with this world, the introduction of something new. . . . Man is a person, not by nature, but by spirit. By nature he is only an individual. A person is not a monad, of the hierarchy of monads and subject to it. A person is a microcosm, a whole universae. Only personality can include universal content, can be a potential universe in an individual form. No other reality of the natural or historical world, always characterized as a part, is capable of containing the universal. *The person is not, and it cannot be a part of any sort of whole, even of the enormous whole world.* This is the essential principle, the mystery of personality. . . .

Personality as Subject, not Object

But the person is not a part of the universe: the universe is a part of personality, it is a quality of personality. Such is the paradox of personalism. . . . Personality cannot be known as object, as one among the objects of the world, as a part of the world. This is the way all the anthropological sciences would like to view man, biology, psychology, sociology. In this way man is known only in part, as the existential centre of the world. A person may be known only as subject, in infinite subjectivity, where the mystery of existence lies hidden.

Personality is Self-creative

A person is never a completed datum: it is the task, the ideal, of man. The ideal of man is a perfect unity, the integrity of personality. Personality is a joint effort with itself of creativity. No man can say he is fully a person. Personality is an axiological, an evaluatory, category. Here we encounter the basic paradox of existence of personality. The personality must produce itself, enrich itself, fill itself with universal content, attain unity in integrity, throughout the whole extent of its life. But in order to do this, it must first *be*. . . . Personality is not put together from pieces, it is no aggregate, no mere item; it is primary wholeness. . . .

The Christian Attitude toward Personality

There has always been a dual attitude toward man in Christianity. On the one hand, Christianity seemed to demean man in recognizing him as sinful and fallen, called to humility and obedience. And this is what men find unforgivable in Christianity. But on the other hand, Christianity greatly exalts man, recognizing him as the image and likeness of God, recognizes in him a spiritual element that lifts him above the social and the natural world, recognizes spiritual freedom in him, his independence of the realm of Caesar, believes that God himself became man and thus lifted man to the skies. And on this Christian basis alone can one construct a doctrine of personality, or carry out a personalistic re-valuation of values. A personalistic philosophy must accept the fact that spirit does not generalize, but rather individualizes: it does not construct a world of ideal values, general and non-human, but a world of persons with their qualitative content.

Neither God nor Man is a Means

We cannot say that the super-personal, God, higher than man, is the end, while personality is the means to this end. Man the person cannot be a means for God the person. The doctrine that God created man for His own glory, demeans both man and God. It is astonishing that any doctrine that demeans man, demeans God as well. The relation of personality to personality even to the supreme person, God, can never be thought of as that of end and means. Every person is an end in himself. The end-means relationship exists only in the world of objectivization. . . . Personality is only human when it is divine-human personality.

Personality is only human when it is divine-human. *Slavery*, p. 39

The theologians will argue in fright, that only Jesus Christ was God-man, that man is a creature and can never be god-man. But this argument never gets beyond the limits of theological rationalism. Man may not be God in the sense that Christ was God-man, the Only One. But there is a divine element in man; he has, as it were, two natures; he is the point of intersection of two worlds; he bears an image which is both the image of God and that of man, and it is the image of man in so far as it realizes the image of God.

This truth about man is something beyond dogmatic formulas and is not fully covered by them. . . .

But it is quite impossible to understand this mystery of divine-humanness in the light of a philosophy of identity, monism, immanentism. The expression of this mystery predicates a dualistic moment, an experience of transcendence, a keen sense of the abyss and of overcoming it. The divine is transcendent to man and at the same time it is joined with the human in the divine-human image. Only because of this is it possible that personality free of enslavement to the world, could appear in the world. . . . Man is a symbol, for in him is the sign of something other, and he is a possible sign of something other. The possibility of man's liberation from slavery is linked with this fact. This is the religious basis, a basis existential, spiritually experienced. The truth about divine-humanity is not a dogmatic formula, not a theological doctrine, but an experienced truth, the expression of spiritual experience.

Slavery, pp. 20-2, 24-6, 35, 39-40

Personality is not Nature, but Freedom

The individual is a naturalistic and sociological category. The individual is born in the racial process: he belongs to the world of nature. Personality, however, is a spiritual and ethical category; it is not born of material, it is spiritually created as it realizes God's idea of man. Personality is not nature, but freedom: it is spirit. One might say that personality is not man the phenomenon, but rather man the noumen. . . . We may say of the individual that he is part of the race and of society, but an indivisible part. We cannot think of personality as a part of any whole. It is other-worldly, spiritual. Personality breaks into the natural and social order with the claim that it is an end in itself, supreme value: it claims to be a whole, not a part. . . . But man is a spiritual personality: other forms may or may not be personalities. The total, the whole, the primacy of the whole over its parts—this applies only to personality. The world of nature, society, the state, the nation, etc.—all these are partial, and their claim to totality is an enslaving falsehood arising from the idolatry of man. *Beginning*, p. 125

SOLITUDE

Solitude, a man's being alone, is not alienation from the cosmos. It may be only a symptom of the fact that a personality has outgrown certain conditions under which others live, and its universal content is not yet recognized by the others. The supreme solitude is divine. God, Himself, knows great and anguished solitude. He has the experience of being deserted by the world and by men. Christ was solitary and not understood during His life. Men accepted and understood Christ only after His death on the Cross. Solitude is quite compatible with universality: there may be more of the universal spirit in solitude than in a herded society. Every act of courage, every creative initiative, gives a sense of solitude, of being unrecognized—transcends every given community. And there is always the temptation to overcome this solitude by some sectarian community rather than by the universal community. . . . We must never forget that the religious way moves from the personality to society, from the inward to the outer, toward the cosmos by way of individuality. *M.C.A.*, p. 158

EGOISM

Self-love, egoism, man's chief wound by original sin, hinders our proper appreciation of realities, for at each contact with reality, egoism either attempts to defend itself from pain by means of some fantasy, or else to derive satisfaction, always uncertain, from some other fantasy. Because of egoism one man is exalted while another is humiliated, and neither is appreciated in his reality. Self-love always seeks compensation, and for this purpose does violence to reality. (Adler explains this beautifully.) Out of his egoism man accepts as reality that world of ideas which offer him the greatest compensation, in which his self-love feels the least pain. Man may construct a pessimistic metaphysic for himself because this concept of the world hurts his self-love least. Or, out of egoism, a man may accept a revolutionary world-view because this gives compensation to his self-esteem and in this case realities hurt him less. From egoism, a man joins one or other party, ideological tendency or social group, and sees in them the greatest reality, because this party or tendency or grouping hurts his egoism the least and gives him greater satisfaction. From egoism a man makes friends with some people and quarrels with others, and defines their reality and specific gravity according to whether these people compensate his self-love or cause it pain. This goes so far that sometimes a man loses his faith or becomes a believer, as this defends or compensates his egoism. Egoism constructs its own phantasmagoric world where all realities are confused. And since egoism is a quality of all men in a greater or lesser degree, all men to a greater or lesser degree live in a phantasmagoric world. The conquest of the sin of egoism, the acquisition of spirituality, the revelation in one's self of the image and likeness of God, is a return to the real world, to being. None of the defences and compensations which egoism constructs for itself by means of fantasy really eases the pain; the wound continues to bleed, arrows from all directions pierce the egoistic heart. And the only radical and true cure is the way of spiritual conquest of self-love, i.e. egocentrism, and the acquisition of theocentrism, a spiritually enlightened view of life.

Destiny, pp. 194-5

Egoism is Slavery

Egoists are usually conformists. He who is a slave to self, loses himself. Slavery is opposite to personality, but egoism is the corruption of personality. Man's enslavement to himself is not only enslavement to his lower, animal nature. This is a rude form of egocentrism. But man may be a slave to his higher nature, and this is more important and disturbing. Man is often a slave to his refined ego, something far removed from his animal ego; he is the slave of his higher ideas and feelings, of his talents. And a man may never notice that he makes even the higher values into instruments of his egoistic self-assertion. Fanaticism is just this sort of egoistic self-assertion. The books about the spiritual life tell how humility may become transformed into the greatest pride. There is nothing more hopeless than the pride of the humble. The pharisee is the type of man whose devotion to the law of the good and pure, his exalted idea, has changed into egoistic self-assertion and self-satisfaction. Even sanctity may turn into a form of egoism and self-assertion, and become pseudo-sanctity. An exalted ideal egocentrism always means the setting up of idols and a wrong attitude towards ideas, a substitution of the wrong for the right relationship to the living God. All forms of egoism, from the lowest to the highest, always mean man's enslavement, enslavement to himself and, by this, enslavement to the world about him.

Slavery, p. 111-12

FAITH

> Faith is a unique spiritual experience . . . it cannot enslave philosophy, but only nourish it. *Solitude*, p. 14

Faith is Attained Through Experience

Your characterization of the religious tendencies of modern youth seem to me too diffuse, too indefinite, too much inclined to unite incompatibles. Without sacrifice, without choice and division, no religious life is possible, no religious attainment. Religious truth is not determined by what pleases or does not please modern youth, by what conforms or does not conform to their instincts. The world's vanity cannot be brought into a religious system. Religious consciousness can be neither self-satisfaction nor satisfaction with the world. Rather, everything must be lived out immanently, everything must be part of a man's way, his seeking, the pilgrimage of his spirit toward a higher life. You cannot 'propose' to the younger generation that they believe in the divine Trinity. Belief cannot be imposed on them: it can be only the fruit of life's road and life's experience. And if the words about the Holy Trinity and about Christ the Son of God are still lifeless, you need not feel that you must accept all that as from without.

But I do not believe in the 'Religion of the World' which you say modern youth is seeking. This would be a religion of satisfaction, while every religion is a profound, suffering dissatisfaction with 'the world'. All creativity is dissatisfaction with 'the world', the conquest of 'the world', the fulfilment of the commandment 'love not the world, neither the things that are in the world'. I could wish modern youth to remember and to love Nietzsche and the way of Zarathustra. This is a stern and sacrificial way, an uphill road: it involves a quite special asceticism of the spirit. Sacrifice and asceticism are possible, not only for the sake of one's seeking the commandments of God, but also for the sake of man's higher dignity and his creative calling. Man should not be a slave of the world's vanity; he should be free from various elements of the world, for the sake of his creative and kingly destiny. Man must create both himself and a new world, must transform chaos into cosmos. Egoism can be complete slavery and the loss of one's ego. Ibsen's Peer Gynt was very egotistic. We must hammer out our ego, liberating it from its egoistic chaos. The way of freedom is a hard and rough road: the road of slavery is easy. *From a letter to E. F. Gollerbach*, Sept. 13, 1916

> Miracle should proceed from faith, not faith from miracle. Only then is faith free. *Dostoevsky*, p. 76

Faith is Spiritual, not Mental

The phenomenon of faith in the spiritual life of humanity presupposes a dynamic of consciousness, the possiblity of catastrophic breaking-away of consciousness from our natural world, and of its turning toward another world. You may deny the object of faith, but you cannot deny the fact of faith, in the inner life of man. And this fact, which occupies such a large place in the history of mankind, witnesses to the fact that a change in the structure of consciousness is possible, that our stiff, everyday normal consciousness is not the only one possible. That the religious world is revealed and constructed by a certain direction of our spirit, is no less a fact than that the 'empirical' world is revealed and constructed by another direction of the spirit. Religious experience is no less experience than is 'empirical' experience. Men live under the hypnosis of 'empirical' realities, and their turning to realities of another world is an awakening from this hypnotic sleep. . . . Primitive will always chooses or lays aside, chooses one world and refuses others, rearranges the content of experience. Faith is founded on this primitive spiritual will, not on mental will. It is an event of spiritual rather than mental life. . . . Faith is not compulsion by actuality which is open to ordinary belief. Faith, in the eternal definition of St Paul, is the evidence of things not seen, things outside ourselves which do not in the least compel us to recognize them. Faith is always directed toward the mysterious, hidden, secret world. But knowledge of actuality revealed to the average, normal consciousness, is evidence of things seen. The 'empirical' world about me compels me to recognize it. . . . Faith . . . is a matter of choice and love in freedom.

Freedom, pp. 155-7

Faith is Active

The phenomenon of faith is sometimes described as a condition of man's complete passivity, a silencing and numbing of human nature, as the action of God's grace, alone. This description is specially characteristic of some forms of protestantism and quietist mysticism. But this is not the final truth about the phenomenon of faith. This describes the psychic side of faith—the silencing numbness of the natural, mental man. But behind this is hidden the greatest creative activity of the spiritual man. In the basic life of the spirit, faith predicates man's greatest activity and his greatest creative intensity. The mental man is still; he renounces his natural will. But the inner, spiritual man increases his spiritual activity, his primordial freedom, to supreme intensity. Outward passivity is sometimes only the expression of inward activity. The action of God's grace presupposes the action of man's freedom. Only Calvin's doctrine of predestination in its extreme form denies this action of man's freedom, this two-sidedness, the two natures, of the phenomenon of faith. In the depths of spirit, in the hidden secrets of spiritual life and experience, there is always a meeting and mutual activity, one upon the other, of human and Divine natures. . . . Faith is an act of the freedom of the spirit; without freedom there can be no faith. *Freedom* I, pp. 159-60

Faith and Grace

In the phenomenon of faith is given my freedom, my activity, my choice of love, and this is all mysteriously united with the activity of God's grace, God's love, God's movement toward me. Faith is the acquisition of love. But grace knows no universal validity, in the logical or juridical sense of the word. Grace opens communion of another order. Grace is just the opposite of the logical and juridical. Theophany is given above all in freedom rather than in authority. *Freedom*, I, pp. 165-6

FEAR

Liberation from fear is man's highest spiritual task. *Divine*, p. 85

Fear Creates Phantoms

Fears create a very special world of phantoms. Fear hinders us from distinguishing and perceiving realities. For a man held in the grip of some sort of fear, all life's perspectives are changed. Fear has a big eye, as the proverb says. And since fear in some degree and in some connection is characteristic of all men, we may say that in this sinful world man has a wrong perception of reality in general, that all his perspectives of life are distorted by phantoms. Cowardice, seeking an excuse for fear in everything, always constructs a phantasmagoric world. . . . Fear, and especially fear which turns into cowardice, is a poor way to the knowledge of things, the precision of realities. The highest form of fear, fear of eternal punishment, religious fear, is not at all favourable to knowledge, to purely objective contemplation, to perception of the relationships among realities in the world. And theology, in so far as it is based on the fear of eternal punishment, can never be pure, disinterested knowledge and contemplation. . . . Fear had a place in the origin of religious beliefs. And therefore those who would educate us say that religion sets up a phantasmagoric world, engendered by fears, but also that it is destined to deliver us from fear. Actually, the matter is more complex and more profound. The ancient fear which tormented man, his helplessness and isolation, his search for aid and protection, is a mixture of holy transcendent fear before the mystery of being, before the abyss, and animal fear which controls the sinful world, fear in the narrow sense of the word. And in the history of religious consciousness, including Christianity, animal fear and an unhealthy pathological fear mingle with spiritual fear which I call terror, and spoil the purity of religious faith. Religious faith should turn the sinful man, tormented by the world, toward the discovery of reality and free him from the phantoms born of his fears of the world. *Destiny*, pp. 198-9

The Source of Fear

What is the source of these phantoms; how are we to understand their origin? The evil phantoms which create their world are not like God's creation, do not enter into the purpose of God's creation of the world, God's idea of man. They come from somewhere outside, from some other source. Illness does not come from God: health does. Evil phantoms come out of primordial nothingness and thither they return. 'Nothingness' is always present in man. Evil phantoms come from immemorial, pre-existential, meonic freedom which began to affirm the spirit of non-being in being. And they signify a return to non-being, refusal to participate in God's creative work. In them immemorial freedom is lost and turns into slavery. The evil, phantasmagoric world is a creation of a non-existential, empty, hellish world of endless desire. Thus there is a return to non-being, but to a non-being which has now become evil. Primordial, pre-creation nothingness was not evil: it became evil after the experience of freedom in regard to God's creation of the world, in regard to God's call to participate in it. . . . The evil world of phantoms has its source in the sense of injury and pretention toward God and His world. From this primordial false sense of injury or affront are born envy, selfishness, pride, lust, etc. But a sense of guilt frees a man from phantoms and brings him back to reality, to being. *Destiny*, pp. 200-1

DEATH

> Death is not only the ultimate evil; there is light in death. In death there is the revelation of love. *Autobiography*, p. 366

The Final Evil

The problem of evil rests upon one final antinomy. Evil is death, and death is the final evil. To conquer evil at its root is to pluck out the sting of death. Christ overcame death. And we should freely accept death as the way of life. Death is an inward moment of life. We must die in order to live again. Death is evil, violence done to me by the external, lower world of nature to which I have subjected myself by my own sin and evil, by my falling away from the higher source of life, life eternal. But if I accept death willingly without rebelling against it, death as the inevitable result of sin, then spiritually I conquer death. For me death becomes a moment of the inner mystery of spirit. Viewed spiritually, and from within, death has quite another meaning than it has if viewed without . . . as a fact of the natural world. Having known no sin, Christ freely accepted Golgotha and death. And I must go that same way. Participating in the life and death of Christ, I conquer death. Spiritually, inwardly, mystically, there is no death; death is my way toward life, the way of the crucifixion of sinful life, which leads to life eternal. In communion with the first source of life, I overcome the destructive consequences of death. For the Christian consciousness, death is not only evil, it is good as well. *Freedom* I, p. 270

The Meaning of Death

Death is the most profound and significant fact of life: it lifts the very last of mortals above the greyness and banality of life. And only the fact of death puts the question of life's meaning in all its depth. Life in this world has meaning only because there is death: if there were no death in our world, life would be deprived of meaning. Meaning is linked with ending. And if there were no end, if in our world there was evil and endlessness of life, there would be no meaning to life whatever. Meaning lies beyond the bounds of this closed world, and the discovery of meaning presupposes an ending in this world. . . . And in order fully to comprehend death and to have the right attitude toward it, extraordinary effort and spiritual enlightenment are necessary. We may say that the meaning of man's moral experience throughout his whole life lies in putting him into a position to comprehend death, in bringing him to the proper attitude toward it. *Destiny*, pp. 268-9

Death, the Meaning of Life

Death is not only the meaninglessness of life in this world . . . but a sign out of the depths which indicates a higher meaning of life. Not mean fear, but the profound anguish and terror which death calls forth in us, is what shows us that we belong not alone to things of the surface, but to the depths, not alone to ordinary life in time, but to eternity. But eternity in time not only attracts us, but rouses terror and anguish. This is not only because someone near and dear to us has ceased to be, but even in a greater degree because the abyss between time and eternity has opened before us. The terror and anguish connected with this leap over the abyss is also man's hope, his confidence that final meaning will be revealed and realized. Death is not only man's terror but his hope, as well, although he does not always call it by its right name. The meaning coming from another world casts its burning rays on man in this world and demands his passage through death. Death is not only a biological and psychological fact, but a spiritual phenomenon. The meaning of death is in the fact that eternity is impossible in time, and that the lack of an ending in time is meaningless. *Destiny*, p. 270

In Life We Are in Death

Our life is filled with death and dying. Life is continuous dying, the experience of the end in everything, the constant judgment by eternity on time. Life is a constant struggle with death and the partial dying of the human body and the human mind. The death in our life comes from the impossibility of comprehending plenitude within time and space. . . . In time and space which cannot contain fullness, which condemn us to parting and separation, death always triumphs over life, and death tells us that meaning lies in eternity, in plenitude, that a life in which meaning triumphs will know no parting, no separation, will not know the decline and death of human thoughts and feelings. For us, death occurs not only when we die, but when our dear ones die, also. In life we have an experience of death, although not the final experience. And we cannot be reconciled to death either of man or animals or flowers, trees, things, houses. The essence of life is this striving of all being toward eternity. *Destiny*, pp. 270-1

Death, Resurrection, Immortality

Christianity teaches of the resurrection, of the victory over death for every life, for the whole mortal world, and in this it is infinitely above and more powerful than the Greek doctrine of immortality, which condemned a considerable part of the world to dissolution and death. But the Christian world-view has not revealed the mystery of the origin of the soul. The revelation of the eternal element in the soul means eternity in the past, as well as in the future. That which arises in time cannot inherit a fortune. And if the human soul bears in itself the image and likeness of God, if it is God's idea, then it arises in eternity rather than in time, in the spiritual rather than in the natural world. The Christian consciousness may understand this dynamically, rather than statically, as does Platonism. The struggle for personality, for the realization of God's idea, goes on in eternity, in the spiritual world. And our natural life on earth is only a moment in the process going on in the spiritual world. This leads to the affirmation of pre-existence in the spiritual world, which has nothing to do with reincarnation within earthly reality. Man's appurtenance to the eternal spiritual world does not mean the soul's natural immorality. Our natural world is the arena of struggle for immortality and eternity, i.e. for personality. And in this spiritual struggle the spirit must gain control over the natural elements of body and mind, for their eternal life, for resurrection to eternal life. Christianity does not teach so much of natural immortality which requires no struggle, as it does of resurrection, which predicates the struggle of spiritual, beneficient powers against the powers of death. Resurrection means religious victory over death; it will not give over anything to death and decay, as would abstract spiritualism. The doctrine of resurrection proceeds from the tragic fact of death, and signifies victory over death, something not to be found in any other doctrine of immortality, not in orphism, not in Platonism, not in theosophy. Only Christianity looks death right in the eye, recognizes both death's tragedy and its meaning, but is not reconciled to death, and overcomes it. Immortal and eternal life of human personality is possible and is, not because this is the make-up of the human soul, but because Christ is risen and has conquered the death-dealing powers of the world, because in the cosmic miracle of the Resurrection meaning has conquered meaninglessness. *Destiny*, pp. 277-8

Death and Time

The final problem related to time is the problem of death. Death carries time with it, and death takes place in time. Fear of the future is above all fear of death. Death is an event within life itself, and it is the end of life. But death is the ultimate result of objectivization. Death is an event in time, in the object rather than the subject, and not in his inward existence, where it is only a moment of his inward destiny in eternity.

Solitude, p. 128

Death and Personality

In the beginning man was a slave of nature, then of the state, the nation, the class and finally of technics and organized society. But the realization of personality means overcoming all slavery and having command of everything. Man's final slavery is his slavery to death. And no social order or utopia has known victory over this bondage. But victory over death is at the same time the acceptance of death's mystery. Our attitude toward death is antinomic. The realization of personality is also realization of communion, of social and economic life, the conquest of that solitude which death carries with it. It is just this realization of communion which does not know death. Love is stronger than death. Those who are in the communion of love must part, but with all its tragedy this separation is only external, of the objectivized world: this is death, within, it is the way of life. *Solitude*, pp. 183-4

Man's Fear of Death

With difficulty man endures the fact that in this world he is a mortal being and that everything which happens in him or to him is also mortal. Hence the problem of evil is first of all the problem of death. Victory over evil is victory over death. Evil is death; victory over evil is revivifying life, rebirth to new life. Murder, hatred, revenge, treason, betrayal, vice, slavery—these are death. The divine-human victory over the final enemy, death, is victory over evil. This is the victory of love, freedom and creativity over hatred, slavery and inertia, the victory of personality over impersonality. . . . Death has its positive meaning. . . . Death strikes hardest at the most perfect and individualized organisms. An acute sense of personality means an acute sense of evil. The positive meaning of death is in the fact that its inevitability for every personal being bears witness to the unattainability of infinite aims in life, and of the non-existence of fullness of life within the bounds of this world and this time.

And it is not by chance that in Russian Orthodoxy the chief holiday is the Feast of the Resurrection of Christ. So Orthodoxy understands Christianity. The source of victory over the evil in life in this world is not in death nor in birth, but in resurrection. Experience of the world's evil destroys, but the creative forces of resurrection conquer evil and death. In regard to evil and evil persons, Christian ethics can be only paradoxical. In Christ the God-man and in the divine-human process there is preparing the transfiguration of the whole cosmos. We cannot think ontologically or statistically of evil and of freedom connected with it, but only dynamically, in the language of spiritual-existential experience. *Divine*, pp. 99-122

ASCETICISM

Asceticism and Creativity

In the depths of every true religion and every genuine mystic there is the thirst for overcoming 'the world' as a lower order of being, for victory over 'the world', and hence we have asceticism as a way to this conquest and this victory. Without this ascetic moment, that is the conquest of lower nature for the sake of the higher, conquest of this world for the sake of another world, religious and mystical life is unthinkable. Asceticism, spiritual exercise, is an obligatory formal method for all religious and mystic experience, although the spiritual content of this formal method may be quite varied. . . . Asceticism is only a technique of religious experience, only its formal methodology. No single mystic ever saw in asceticism purpose and content of religious life, for content and purpose are already in another world, the acquisition of divine life. Viewed from outside, from a distance, we see only asceticism, only a technical and formal method, more denial than affirmation. But behind this there lies life in God, development into another life. The ascetic way is negative in its technique, but by its positive content it is return to the bosom of God.

Is there some other religious way, some other religious experience of creative ecstasy? By itself, the way of asceticism is not a creative way, and the ascetic ecstasy of saints and mystics is an ecstasy of return to God, the vision of divine light, rather than the creation of a new world, of life hitherto unseen. The experience of creative ecstasy as a religious way is not revealed in the consciousness of the Church Fathers or in the consciousness of the old mystics. The creative experience, the creative ecstasy, is either denied completely by religious consciousness as 'worldly' and of the passions, or else is merely admitted and permitted. . . . Creative experience is spiritual, in the religious sense of that word. Creativeness is no less spiritual, no less religious, than asceticism. Such a statement of the problem could arise only in our time, in an epoch when the world is passing the divide into a new religious epoch of creativeness. In the religious epoch of the law and the redemption, the religious problem of creativeness was unknown. . . . Creative ecstasy is religious ecstasy: the way of the creative shaking of man's whole being is a religious way. This is a new, as yet unknown, religious consciousness—the consciousness of the creative epoch in the world. . . .

The Gospel commandments 'love not the world' and 'overcome the world' remain valid for ever and can never be revoked. Not to love the world means to be free and to reveal our sonship to God: to cling to this world, however, means being a slave to necessity. Creativeness is not only faithful to this highest commandment of freedom from 'the world', but it is also, by its very nature, a victory over that world in the name of another: it is a revelation of the meaning of the commandment 'love not the world . . .' And 'the world' is burned away in the daring of creative activity, just as in the act of obedience. . . . But there is neither contradiction nor opposition between creativeness and asceticism. Creativeness does not assert what asceticism denies. That world which asceticism denies is denied by creativeness as well: what is affirmed by creativeness is quite another world. Hence the revelation of creativeness lies outside the gospel's denial of 'the world'. Creativeness presupposes an ascetic overcoming of the world—it is positive asceticism. *M.C.A.*, pp. 160-4

The Ascetic Life

The word ascetic may be understood in various senses and may be applied to various spheres of life. First of all, we may use the word askesis in a very wide sense, all-inclusive and formal. But askesis by itself alone does not solve the problems of evil and sin. Literally it means exercise, which may be practised in various spheres of life and for various purposes. Asceticism is a concentration of inner forces and command of oneself. Man needs exercise, he needs self-denial and concentration in order to become master of himself and capable of fulfilling the purpose he has set for himself, be it even something in sport. . . . In this sense a certain amount of asceticism is necessary in everything. Man's dignity is related to this. But man should not be a slave to himself, his lower nature, or to the world around him. Asceticism means man's liberation.

Reality, pp. 66-7

Christian metaphysics are quite distinct and different and hence Christian askesis has a different meaning. This is a very different type of solution for the metaphysical and religious problem of evil. In its pure form, Christian metaphysics consider the word not as essentially evil, but only fallen, sinful. The source of evil lies not in the material, not in some sort of 'nature', but in freedom, in will. Not the many-sided world is evil, not any sort of material substance, but those relationships of the world which have their source in directed will, relationships which assume forms of materialization and bondage to the material. Neither neo-platonism, nor gnosticism nor manicheism understood the problem of freedom. But failure to understand the problem of freedom leads inevitably to the condition where askesis is not the illumination of the lower and its transfiguration into something higher. In this case, askesis means cutting off or destroying the lower. *Reality*, p. 70

The Gospel is not an ascetic book, in the sense in which, later, Christian ascetic books appeared, ascetic instruction for the spiritual life. We have only to compare the Gospels with *Love of Good* ('Philokalia') or *The Imitation of Christ* to sense the enormous difference in style, due to an essential difference in spirit. In the Gospels, God speaks; in the ascetic books, man is speaking. In the Gospels there are elements which might formally be called ascetic, but you will be unable to find ascetic metaphysics related to neo-platonism, for instance. The Gospel is a messianic book: if you wish, a revolutionary-messianic book, but not an ascetic book. *Reality*, p. 72

The Gospel is the good news of the approach of the Kingdom of God and not a revelation of ascetic methods for the salvation of the soul. By itself the Gospel does not found any sort of ascetic school. Asceticism is a school and a method—a long way from perfection and development. But the Gospel speaks of a new birth, a spiritual birth in grace. Here the spirit breaks through into this world: this is not evolution; everything is catastrophic. The thief on the cross in one instant turns to Christ and inherits the Kingdom of God. Publicans and pharisees go first into the heavenly Kingdom. The Gospel is not a book which teaches individual salvation of the soul by means of school or method. It is messianic, oriented toward the Kingdom of God. Herein lies the chief difference. The denial of 'this world' in the Gospels is not so much ascetic denial as it is messianic eschatological. Asceticism is individualistic: the Gospel is social in the religious sense of that word, in the sense that prophecy was social. Here you may fast, live in poverty, sacrifice all this world's goods: but this is not ascetic exercise for the purpose of individual salvation.

Sacrifice still does not mean askesis . . . but the sacrifice of love.

Asceticism was not known in the apostolic church nor in early Christianity. The Christian martyrs were not ascetics. Asceticism arose later. . . . The Gospel does not recommend long-winded prayers, does not teach salvation through prayer in solitude and Christ will not ask about these things on the day of judgment.

In the course of Christian history, asceticism suffered great rebirths and changes and came under non-Christian influences. Monastic asceticism began after the great pagan masses poured into the church, after the empire became Christian, and a terrible lowering of the spiritual level of Christianity impended. Previously, the Christians had represented a spiritual élite standing out against the pagan world, the pagan empire. They were persecuted, and this called forth spiritual concentration and intensity. After Constantine the Great, Christians entered a privileged situation; they no longer faced an external foe who might persecute them. Now it was an inner enemy they had to fight. They had to create a sort of spiritual aristocracy within Christianity which was becoming widespread and vulgar. And so monasticism and monastic askesis appeared, as the centre of a higher and more intense spirituality. Monastic asceticism took the way of greatest resistance, of heroic struggle against nature and its sinful passions, and great were its achievements. Asceticism had its period of youth and flowering. Such was the asceticism of the desert, of Syria and Egypt. The desert had its mirages and deceptions, its demonic visions. Certain manichaean elements crept into Syrian asceticism—not everything in it was truly Gospel quality, but we cannot deny its special kind of greatness. It was one of the most remarkable phenomena in the history of the human spirit. As yet asceticism had not been subjected to legalistic reformation. It was a heroic upsurge in the struggle against, and victory over, a world which lay in evil. *Reality*, pp. 73-4

Inspiration is the breathing of spirit, the spirit's penetration of man; the 'pneuma' is breathed into a man and he becomes as one possessed of the spirit. This is the source of all creativeness. Asceticism may play a large part in relation to inspiration: it can concentrate and direct man's spiritual powers and thus facilitate creative inspiration, but it may also cut off all inspiration by considering it something sinful, and so crush out man's creative energy. And actually, asceticism has more often played this second rôle. The power of Eros inherent in man may be ascetically concentrated, purified and harnessed for creativity—inspiration and creativeness are erotic in nature, but they may be crowded out, dessicated, mortified as something sinful. . . . Man's nature is dried up. With this type of asceticism, God's image is not revealed in man. Patristic literature often states that virtue is made of the same stuff as passion. Every passion is to be crowded out of life by a corresponding virtue. But all too often asceticism quenches—mortifies passion and by this very fact destroys the stuff of virtue also. And there is nothing more repulsive than dried-up, bloodless virtues. *Reality*, p. 85

Only that spiritual asceticism is justified which liberates man and brings him back to real values. Asceticism should restore man his dignity, and not submerge him in a condition of hopeless unworthiness and abjection. In so far as asceticism isolates man and separates him from other people, it turns man more into himself, which really is only transformed ego-centrism. Concentration on one's personal salvation or destruction gives this result. But we need an ascetic life which trains man for social life and for brotherhood. Man has to be in the world, bear its burdens, be creatively active in it, but at the same time be free from the world. Modern men are thrust out into compulsory social living; they are slaves of society and are painfully, terribly lonely in it. And this demands new ascetic methods. Egotistic distortion has given many and varied forms of asceticism. It may even take a shape where man tries to make out of his human relationships a means for his own salvation. . . . Modern man needs askesis, he needs concentration, renunciation, a limitation of his growing requirements which otherwise would condemn him to endless hunger. And this new askesis, like the new spirituality, must now be prepared.
Reality, pp. 87-8

CONSCIENCE

Conscience is the depth of personality where man meets God. *Autobiography*, p. 265

Moral consciousness began with God's question: 'Cain, where is your brother Abel?' It will close with another question of God's: 'Abel, where is your brother Cain?'
Destiny, p. 297

Conscience is God-given
Conscience is that depth of human nature at which it comes in touch with God, where it receives God's message and hears His voice. . . . Conscience is the remembrance, in our sinful life, of God and of life Divine. When, in the most sinful and criminal man, conscience awakes, this means that he remembers about God, and how it is to live a godly life, although he may not express it in these words. Conscience is the organ of reception of religious revelation of truth, of good, of integral truth. It is not a separate side of human nature or a special function; it is the wholeness of man's spiritual nature, its very heart. . . . Conscience is also the source of original primary judgments about the world, and about life. More than this, conscience judges God, or about God, because it

is an organ of the perception of God. Conscience may judge about God only because it is an organ of the perception of God. God acts on man's conscience, awakens his conscience, awakens his memories of a higher world. Conscience is the remembrance of what man is, to what world he belongs by the idea of his creation, by whom he was created, how and why he was created. Conscience is a spiritual, supernatural element in man, and it is not at all of social origin. What is of social origin is rather an obstruction or deformation of conscience. Conscience is that depth of human nature where it has not fallen completely away from God, where it has maintained contact with the Divine world.

Destiny, pp. 179-80

Conscience is Free

A clear conscience is nothing other than freedom from the world. For true freedom of the human spirit is freedom from the world. A conscience enslaved and tempted by the world is no longer an organ for the perception of truth, and it does not judge, but is judged by a conscience more profound and pure. What may be called 'soborny' church conscience, where the perception of truth and judgment upon untruth is accomplished by a sort of collective rather than individual conscience, does not mean that human conscience, before it can stand in purity before God, is conjoined with the conscience of other people or of the world: it means the spiritual-immanent bearing in one's conscience of the common destiny of one's brothers and sisters in the spirit. Sobornost is an immanent quality of a conscience standing before God. The spirit stands before God in free union with other spirits and with the spirit of the world. But its attitude toward other spirits and the spirit of the world, is determined by its own free conscience. *Destiny*, p. 181

GENIUS

All true genius is erotic. *M.C.A.*, p. 201

Marks of Genius

The creative genius is rarely satisfied with what he has created. We may even say that eternal dissatisfaction is one of the marks of genius. The genius's inner fire is never completely transmitted in his works. Perfection of the created object is something other than the creative flame itself. The fate of genius is tragic. Often he is not recognized in his lifetime, he is dissatisfied with himself and he is distorted after his death by the use of the products of his genius for purposes to which he was alien. In creativity, in creative genius, there is something of the prophetic. But there is nothing more tormenting and tragic than the fate of prophets. The voice of God which is heard through them arouses hatred, as an unpleasant and misplaced reminder. Many prophets were stoned to death.

It has been said that genius concentrates in itself, and gives expression to, the spirit of the times. This is a very inaccurate and misleading expression. The genius is a man out of his time, a man unadapted to his time and presenting it with a challenge. But the genius bears in himself the movement of the Spirit, while condemning the falsehood of his time, he visions the coming age. Here genius approaches prophecy. There are various types of genius. He is called a genius who has created the most perfect work. But even the most perfect work falls short of what was in the mind of the creative genius. We must accept the fact that there is a fatal failure in all incarnations of the creative fire, because they are realized in the objective world. Which is higher—St Francis of Assisi, whose very appearance is an expression of religious genius, unique in the whole of Christian history, or the order he founded in which the spirit of St Francis has gone out and the prosaic, everyday has conquered? . . . But the one most terrible creative failure in the history of the world is the failure of Christianity, the work of Christ in the world. All too often the history of Christianity has been the crucifixion of Christ. There is nothing more tragic or sombre than the objectivization in history of the fire which Christ brought down from heaven. . . . The creative failure in this world is sad and tragic, but there is great success in the fact that the results of every truly creative act of man enter into the Kingdom of God. *Beginning*, p. 164ff

CHAPTER V

The Social Animal*

Every society (community) is the realm of Caesar: communion is of the Kingdom of God.
SOLITUDE, p. 178

Society is always a society not alone of the living, but of the dead as well. . . . Not death has the last word, but resurrection. SLAVERY, p. 95

THE SOCIAL ORDER

Societies Are True Organisms

Societies are true organisms, but in your view only masses and atoms exist. You would have liked to pass the whole of history through universal suffrage, and you know in advance that the voting masses do not recognize their own history. Not only could history never be accomplished by universal suffrage; it never would have begun. . . . Neither atoms nor masses would have consented to the sacrifices that are the price which must be paid for history. *Inequality*, p. 33

The 'I' and Society

A Spiritual Problem

Any solution of the social problem that leads to the oppression and enslavement of spirit is illusory and tends towards social corruption. The social question is inevitably a question of the spiritual enlightenment of the masses, without which no sort of justice is possible. In the relationship of ethics to the social question, we meet the tragic conflict between the value of freedom and the value of equality. This conflict is linked to the basic paradox of evil. The evil expressed in social hatred and injustice cannot be destroyed by external or mechanical means. . . . The final conquest of evil is more the task of the church, than of society or the state. But . . . evil must be socially conquered also; but with the sure maintenance of the value of personality and spiritual freedom. That degree of freedom of evil characteristic of bourgeois-capitalist society is just as ethically intolerable, as is the freedom of evil and sinful desire characteristic of a system based on slavery, or turning man, who bears the image and likeness of God, into a thing which may be bought and sold. An awakening of conscience, of a higher moral consciousness, must lead to

* Seneca.

struggle with already crystallized social evil. Regarding the injustice of the bourgeois-capitalist system and the new form of slavery it engenders, the ethical question is specially acute and confused. This system . . . builds itself in freedom and at every attempt to limit the evil in it, its representatives and ideologists scream about infringement of their liberty. The socialists quite justly condemn the falsehood and hypocrisy of these appeals to freedom, which would conceal slavery. But the trouble is that, in the majority of cases, the socialists themselves do not recognize such values as freedom, personality or spirit. Hence, in the conflict between the capitalist and the socialist worlds, ethics cannot finally take either side, although it should see that there is more truth in socialism. . . .

Solitude, pp. 102-4

Social Improvement: a Christian Task

I cannot think that the social order will be changed and improved, will come nearer justice, not by my efforts as a Christian but by those of others, that I, a Christian, must every moment bow to the social order established by others. It is quite evident that Christians, too, must participate creatively in the change, reformation and improvement of the social order. An economy of slavery is not eternal, neither is a capitalist economy, and if there should be a socialist economy, it too will not be everlasting. All these are relative, historical formations. And therefore everyone must face a choice: what he should stand for, what he should build. The responsibility for social construction lies in every one of us. . . . Man is called to creativity in social life, as well as elsewhere. But the Christian ethic demands social idealism, it is against social utopianism and daydreaming. *Destiny*, pp. 242-50

LOVE

True love is . . . the confirmation of immortality. *Dostoevsky*, p. 131

Christian Love

Sexual love, erotic love, is considered as profoundly and absolutely different from general human love, brotherly love, 'Christian' love. Oh, of course it is different! Sexual love knows the secret of two and it is rooted in the polarity of disintegrating elements. 'Christian' love, like humanist love, has become transformed into complete abstraction, bodiless and bloodless, into 'glass love', as Rozanoff has it. Even the holy fathers call us more often to 'harden your hearts', than to love. Christian love has not yet been revealed by humanity in the religion of redemption. The revelation of Christian love demands a creative act. It calls us to another union, 'not of this world', a union of all in a Christian all-humanity, to the union of all in the free Spirit, rather than in the necessity of nature.

Hitherto, Christian humanity has known natural union, union out of adaptation to necessity. . . . In universal, all-human Christian love there should be creative upsurge towards another world, that vision of the human face of every brother by the Spirit in God, which is found in a high degree in erotic love. In true Christian love, not 'glassy' and not abstract, there is a reflected flash of heavenly erotic; it means directing the energy of sex towards all humanity and the whole world. Sexual love overcomes the sinful falling-apart of male and female, in a union of the two which is not of this world. Christian love overcomes the sinful falling apart of all the beings of the world, all parts of the world, in a union of all, that is not of the here and now. *M.C.A.*, pp. 122-3

Sexual Love

Men speak of sex but strangely forget about love. For in truth, sexual love cannot be placed in the category of the family or in the category of asceticism or in that of debauchery. Love is not an ordering of the sexual act for the purpose of begetting children and the social organization of the race; neither is it an ascetic denial of all flesh in sexual life; nor is it unbridled and unlimited indulgence in the sexual act. . . .

The mystery of sex is revealed only in love. But there is no sphere of life where there reigns such inert conservatism and such conditional hypocrisy as in that of sexual love. The most extreme revolutionaries are very often conservative when the question of love arises. The revolutionary consciousness is encountered most rarely in the sphere of sex and love, although here it should be the most radical, I would even say the most religious. The socially minded and learned radicals and revolutionaries think only of the social and physiological ordering of sex—they never go any deeper.

In love there is something aristocratic and creative, something profoundly individual, unracial, something neither canonical nor normative—it surpasses the average-racial consciousness. Love lies in another plane of being than that in which the human race lives and orders its existence. Love lies outside the human race and passes beyond the consciousness of the human race. Love is not necessary to the race, to the perspective of its continuation and ordering. It remains, as it were, at one side. Sexual dissipation is nearer and more comprehensible to the human than love—in a certain sense it is even less dangerous. Man can adjust himself in 'the world' with sexual dissipation—he can even limit and put it into order. Love will submit to no setting in order. In love there is no perspective of adjusting life in 'this world'. In love there is the fatal seed of perdition in 'this world': the tragic loss of youth. Romeo and Juliet, Tristan and Isolde, perished from love, and it was not accident that their love brought death with it. The love of Dante and Beatrice did not permit well-being in 'this world': innate in it was the inescapable tragedy within the boundaries of 'this world'. We cannot theorize about love, nor moralize, nor sociologize, nor even biologize—it is a foreign flower, perishing in the midst of this world. *M.C.A.*, pp. 205-7

'Love Knows No Law'

Love in this world is tragic and admits no careful ordering: it is subject to no norms. Love means failure in this world rather than the well-ordered life. The supreme thing in love, what maintains its mystical sacredness, is its renunciation of all perspective in life, its sacrifice of life. All creativeness demands sacrifice, and so does creative love. . . .

The genuine other-worldly love, the love which creates eternity, excludes the possibility of the sexual act, overcomes it for the sake of another kind of vision. It is well known that to one deeply in love there is sometimes no specific sexual attraction—this is not necessary. And a strong impulse to the sexual act has all too often no connection with real love, sometimes even predicates revulsion. Those truly in love desire absolute union and absolute fusion, spiritual and physical. The sexual act separates: revulsion and murder are at the bottom of it. But love is a creative act, creating a new life, overcoming 'the world', and conquering the race and natural necessity. Personality, unique and unrepeatable, is confirmed in love. Everything impersonal and racial, everything which subjects the individual to natural and social order, is hostile to love, to its unique and unspeakable mystery. . . .

Love is a creative act, but not an act of wilfulness, or of personal profit. The law of love is duty, it is the highest commandment of obedience to love. Obedience to love is higher, more spiritual, than obedience to the family. . . . Love is always cosmic, necessary for the world's harmony, for divine predestination. Hence love should not fear the suffering to which it gives birth. From the cosmic nature of love we must inevitably conclude that unshared, one-sided love is impossible, and so it should be, for love is above people. Unshared love is a fault, a sin against the cosmos, against the harmony of the world, against the androgynous image which is sketched out for us in the divine world-order. And all the strange tragedy of love lies in this tormenting search of the androgynous image, the cosmic harmony. Through sexual love the fullness of man is realized in each of the two participants.

M.C.A., pp. 212-13, 217

Love—Can Convert Evil Passion into Good

Love is a sort of universal energy of life, with the capacity to transform evil passions into creative passion. Even the thirst for knowledge is love in a certain degree: love of the truth, which means philosophy. The same must be said of love of beauty, love of justice. Evil passions become creative through eros. And hence the ethic of creativity is an erotic ethic, as distinct from the ethic of the law. But love reveals itself as a power that transforms evil passions into creative, only when it is a value in itself and is not thought of as a means for saving souls. Love as a good deed, useful for the salvation of one's soul, can never be a source of creativity, a source of life and of life's enlightening. Not only is love a source of creativity, but even love for one's neighbour, love for man, is already creativity: it is the outpouring of a creative energy that is radioactive. Love is the radium of the spiritual world.

Destiny, p. 149

True versus Erotic Love

The mysterious life of sex and of sex-love is a secret of two personalities. No third person and nothing outside can be a judge between them, nor can it vision the reality here manifest. This is the most intimate and individual side of human life, which a person never wishes to expose before others, and sometimes even conceals from himself. Sex life is linked with a sense of shame: in this is revealed its origin in the Fall. The sense of shame and fear of one sex before the other may be overcome either positively, by love, i.e. by the transfiguration of shame, or by depravity, the loss of all sense of shame. And the tragedy of sexual love lies in the fact that the secret, mysterious, intimate feeling between two persons, visible and known only to these two, is profaned and made public in the everyday life of society. It would be normal that, save for the two lovers, no third person, or society itself should know about it. But sexual love has consequences which force it to become part of social custom and subject it to laws, although in reality it does not belong in the sphere of the social. The social community cannot grasp the personal element in sex, but it can comprehend its social element. And therefore sexual love is tragic for personality: it is profaned, given over to the judgment of society; and in it the expectation of personality is lost. Sexual love may be profaned, not only by society but by the person himself, by his sinful passions, inclinations and emotions. Love is both an up-soaring toward eternity, and a letting-down into time, where it is subject to decay and death. There is a mixture of two elements in love: the heavenly and the earthly, the eternal and the temporal, the Heavenly Aphrodite and the Aphrodite of the simple people. . . . Only a mystical love, which overcomes in itself the racial element and is personal to the very depths, can finally escape the social community and liberate itself from the authority of society. Ontologically, only God may be the third person between two lovers, but not society or other people. Only the sinfulness of lovers subjects them to the authority of other people and of society. In its pure essence, in its originality, love is a personal phenomenon. But the family is a social phenomenon. Herein is the inevitable tragedy of love in this world, for genuine love comes into this world from another. Sexual life in the community forms the family.

Destiny, pp. 254-5

Love Must be Real, not Abstract

Much wrong has been done in the name of love—love of God and of man, love of good and love of an idea, especially the love of good and of an idea—when the love of good or of an idea becomes abstract and fanatical, everything is lost: nothing but evil can result. Our love for God must be boundless, but when it is transformed into love for the abstract idea of God, it becomes destructive. Our love of man should know no limit, but when it is changed into abstract love for the idea of man or humanity, it becomes idolatry and it is evil and destructive. The thirst for truth and justice deserves blessedness, but when truth and justice become mere abstract ideas, hostile to everything living, personal and concrete, the results are destructive and evil. We cannot love only the divine in a human personality, only the truth, good or beauty in it, i.e. its content of values: we must love the human as well, love it whatever happens, love and caress the living being itself. At the same time we must remember that human personality can exist only because it contains values, because it is divine, because it is God's image in man. Love is love for the image of God in every man, even the most degraded and sinful. And love for the image of God in man means love not only for the divine element, but the human, as well. We must love, not only the God in man, but the man in God. *Destiny*, pp. 206-7

Love is Both Spiritual and Mental

To understand love as something exclusively spiritual, with no element of the mental in it, is to distort the idea of love. That kind of love would be quite impersonal and inhuman. It contradicts the divine-human concept of love, contained in the Gospels. *Reality*, p. 39

Free Love

A profound and serious bond between a man and a woman, based on true love, is considered by Russian intellectuals as a true marriage, even if it is not consecrated by church or state laws. And on the contrary, a bond sanctified by church law, in the absence of love, where forced by parents with monetary considerations in mind, is considered immoral; it may be masked debauchery. Russians are less legally-minded than western people, for them content is more important than form. Hence free love in the profound and pure sense of the word is a Russian dogma, a dogma of the intelligentsia; it is as much a part of the Russian idea as the denial of capital punishment. Here we cannot come to agreement with the West Europeans, shackled to their legalistic civilization; very specially, we cannot find agreement with official catholics, who have turned Christianity into a religion of law. For us, the man is more important; for them, society and civilization. *Idea*, p. 113

Love of God Comes First

We must love God, first of all. This means that we must not deify and worship anything in the world, people, dear ones, kinfolk, kings—neither ideas nor values, neither humanity nor nature. The meaning of man's life is always in God, rather than in the world: in the spiritual rather than the natural. And from God man receives power to love his fellow-man and all creation with a creative and enlightened love, power to realize justice in the world. The primal source of life is not in man, but in God. Love is defined, not as a relationship of the natural to the supernatural, but as the relation of person to person, the person of man to that of God, the relation of one man to the personality of another. But is it possible to love ideas, values, truth, justice, beauty, science, art, etc.? This is the most difficult question in the entire doctrine of love.

My life is defined not alone by love of living beings, but also by love of higher values, truth, beauty, justice, and there may be a conflict between these two types of love. This is so tragic that we are equally perturbed when living beings are sacrificed for the sake of love of an idea, and when truth and justice are sacrificed for the sake of love of a person. . . . The conflict between love of a living being and love of an idea, between love of a person and love of ideal values such as truth, justice and beauty, cannot be resolved on the basis of abstract idealism. Christianity solves the conflict in principle by its revelation of Divine-humanity, of divine-human love, of love for God and love for men, although the tragic conflict remains and must be lived out in experience and in creativity. Love for ideas and values, for truth, goodness and beauty is only an unrecognized and imperfect expression of love for God, for the divine. We must love God more than our neighbour, more than man, and from this love of God we must draw strength for love of man. *Destiny*, pp. 204-5

Love and Death

Love wants nothing to do with the laws of the objectivized world. It conquers solitude beyond the limits of this objectivized world and hence it is so closely linked with death. And here we see the same duality as everywhere. Connection between the sexes may be realized in society, in social institutions. But then objectivization takes place and true communion is not attained, and consequently solitude is not overcome. But union of the sexes is possible in love, in communion rather than in society, and then solitude is conquered. But this union, by its very fate in the objectivized world, is tragic, and mysteriously related to death. This dualism cannot be resolved within the limits of our world. The process of transcending, as a principle of genuine life, is linked with this dualism: the passage out beyond the world's limits to something higher. To love is to transcend. *Solitude*, pp. 111-12

Love and Personality

Personality is very closely linked with love. Personality is realized through love: by means of love solitude is conquered and communion is achieved. Love presupposes personality: it is the relation of person to person: personality goes out of himself into another personality, comes to know this other personality and confirms it for eternity. . . . Love is dual: it predicates two persons, and not some impersonal identity. And the secret of love is related to the fact that one personality is never exactly identical with another, that the other person is 'Thou'. Hence the secret of love and the secret of personality are inseparably linked together. *Solitude*, p. 180

Man's sexual nature cannot be placed on the same level with other functions of his organism, even the most essential, such as the circulation of the blood. In man's sexuality we perceive the metaphysical roots of his being. Sex is the meeting point of two worlds in the human organism. In this point of sex is hidden the secret of being. We cannot escape from sex. We may leave aside the differentiated function of sex, we may deny or conquer this 'natural' function. But in this case man's sexual function is only transferred—and man still remains a sexual being. . . .

Sex is not only the point of contact of two worlds in man, but also the point of contact between man and the cosmos, microcosmos and macrocosmos. Man is joined with the cosmos first of all by sex. In sex we have the source of man's true connection with the cosmos and of his servile dependence. The categories of sex, male and female, are cosmic categories, not merely anthropological categories. The Christian symbolism of the Logos and the soul of the world, of Christ and His Church, speaks of the cosmic mysticism of male and female, of the cosmic conjugal mystery. Not in man alone, but in the cosmos as well, there is the sexual division into male and female and their sexual union. The spirit of the world, the earth, is feminine in its relation to the Logos —the light-bringing Man—and thirsts for union with the Logos, longs to receive Him within herself. The earth, the bride, awaits her bridegroom, Christ. Nature awaits its ruler, man.

In the world order of things, the masculine is predominantly an anthropological human element: the feminine is a natural, cosmic element. The male, man, is related to the cosmos and to nature through woman; without the feminine element he would be cut off from the spirit of the world, from the mother earth. The woman, aside from connection with the man, would not be a complete person: the dark, natural element, impersonal and subconscious, is too strong in her. . . .

But the world-differentiation into male and female can never finally wipe out the basic genuine bisexuality, the androgynous quality in man —the image and likeness of God in him. In truth neither man nor woman is the image and likeness of God but only the androgyne—the youth-maiden, the integral bisexual man. The differentiation into male and female is a result of the cosmic fall of Adam. Created in the image and likeness of God, the androgyne man falls apart, separates from himself the natural female element, is alienated from the cosmos and falls slave to the power of feminine nature. *M.C.A.*, pp. 180-4

SEX

> Humanity has to pass through the mortal way of the race, and on this road religion must sanctify sex-life and give it spiritual fulness. *M.C.A.*, p. 196

Male and Female: Cosmic Categories

Sex is the source of being; the polarity of sex is the foundation of creation. The sense of being, its intensity and its colouring, has its roots in sex. . . . Sexuality is not a special, differentiated function of the human being. It is diffused throughout man's whole being, penetrates all his cells and determines the whole of his life. . . .

Man, Woman and the Race

> Sex is a cosmic force and may be comprehended only in the cosmic aspect.
> *M.C.A.*, p. 183

Woman is the cosmic universal bearer of the sexual element, of the elemental in sex. The element of sex natural to the genus is a feminine element. The power of the race (genus) over man is realized through woman. This power entered the world of nature and took control of it through the first mother, Eve. Eve is the natural-racial womanliness. The cration of Eve brought the old Adam under the power of race-sexuality, fettered him to the natural world, to 'this world'. 'The world' caught Adam and rules him through sex: Adam is fettered to natural necessity at the point of sexuality. Eve's power over Adam became the power of all nature over him. Man, bound to the birth-giving Eve, became the slave of nature, the slave of a womanliness separate and differentiated from his androgynous image and likeness of God. The attitude of the male man towards womanliness is the root of his attitude towards nature. He can escape neither womanliness nor nature—there is nowhere where he can get away. Deliverance is possible only through the new Adam, who comes into the world through a new womanliness. . . .

Natural sex life is always tragic and hostile to personality. Personality becomes the toy of the genius of race and the irony of the genius of race always accompanies the sexual act. The sexual act is totally impersonal—it is general, and always the same, not only in all men, but also in all animals. In this act there is nothing individual, nothing even specifically human. In the sexual act personality is always caught in the power of the non-personal element of race, the element which makes the human world akin to the world of beasts. . . .

Race is the source of the death of personality—race is the source of birth-giving life. The Greeks knew that Hades and Dionysios were the same god—they felt the mystic connection between death and birth. This is why in the very depths of the sexual act, in sexual union, there lurks a deathly anguish. In the birth-giving life of sex there is a foreboding of death. That which gives birth to life carries with it death as well. The joy of sexual union is always a poisoned joy. This deadly poison of sex has always been felt to be sin. In the sexual act there is always the anguish of the shattered hopes of personality, the treasonable surrender of the eternal to the temporal. In the sexual union of this world not only is something born but something always dies. In the depths of the sexual act there is revealed the mystical nearness and relationship between birth and death. *M.C.A.*, pp. 190-5

Love, Marriage and Divorce

> True love is always love for another—
> lechery is love for one's self.
>
> *Dostoevsky*, p. 125

The ethics of sex are, more than anything else, in the power of social custom. And here the most intimate phase of personality, quite incomprehensible from outside, about which a man is ashamed to speak to anyone, is the most highly organized and regulated, socially. This is because the consequence of intimate sex-life is the birth of children, the continuation of the human race, i.e. the intimate and personal; the quite non-social has social results. Therefore there is an especially tragic conflict between personality and society in the life of sex, the fatal conflict of personal and social destinies. . . . There is no sphere of life into which so much hypocrisy has crept, and in consideration about which as much cowardice has been evidenced. It is in their judgments about sex-life that people are most insincere and cowardly, and most terrorized by society.

The first thing to note is that social custom is concerned with the life of sex only as a physiological, and not as a social fact. As a physiological fact, sex-life results either in procreation and the satisfactory continuation of the race, or in debauchery and racial degeneracy. As a fact of social life, sex-life results in the formation of the family, that is organized in the interests of, and in agreement with, society. But for social custom the phenomenon of erotic love, true love between man and woman, is inapprehensible. . . . True love is not social, but extra-social, with no connection with either society or the race. . . . It is surprising that Christian literature and the church fathers never noticed the problem of love and never said anything interesting about its real meaning. . . . In essence, the treatises of St Augustine and others about sex and marriage are concerned with organizing the life of the race, and very much resemble treatises on cattle-breeding. In these treatises personal love and personal fate are altogether absent. No one says a word about the phenomenon of love, so completely distinct from the phenomenon of the physiological satisfaction of sexual impulse or of the social organization of the life of the family and the race.

Although for Christian thought sex life has remained exclusively a social and physiological fact, and has been referred to the life of the race, rather to personality, the Christian Church established the sacrament of marriage. A sacrament is always related to intimate personal life. And on this score the greatest tragedy has arisen in the Christian world. Personal life has been sacrificed to the race and society. In the very nature of the sacrament of marriage there is an insoluble problem, and a lack of correlation with the other sacraments. We cannot understand in what the material of the marriage sacrament consists. The Church performs the sacrament of marriage, uniting the fates of two people, with any man and woman who externally and formally appear free, and who externally and formally express their consent to be married. . . . The Church has no means of knowing whether one or the other partner loves someone else, is not already inwardly joined with another. And under these conditions marriage is all-too-often a formal rite, void of spiritual content, but of fateful consequence in peoples' lives. . . .

The denial of divorce, which the Catholic Church maintains with such stubbornness, is one of the greatest cruelties in the life of people who are compelled to live in falsehood, in hypocrisy, in constraint, in the profanation of the most intimate of human feelings. Marriage as a sacrament, mystical in its content, is eternal and indissoluble. This is unquestionable truth. But the majority of human marriages have no mystical sense, and no relation to eternity. Christian thought should recognize this. . . . The denial of divorce is . . . a legalistic conception of Christianity. . . .

Marriage is a sacrament, but only that marriage whose content is love, love with ontological reality, not transient attraction or falling-in-love. The sacrament of marriage is an ontological, not a social sacrament. But then the basic quality of a true marriage and genuine love is freedom. Any social coercion or compulsion deprives a union of man and woman of all sacramental or mystical meaning: this is present only in true love. But love is not to be discerned and defined socially: it is undiscernible, not only by the State, but by the Church as a social organization. . . . This is why marriage and the family based neither on love nor on freedom, should be recognized as institutions of social-legal and economic nature. The only love that is holy, sacramental and mystical, is ontological love, unique and eternal, leading to the Kingdom of God. . . .

The family is connected with social custom and is subject to its laws. All too often the family chills love. But it would be a mistake to think that there is no depth in the family and lightly to deny it any spiritual meaning. This meaning is not only in the fact that in our ordinary world love is brought into the form of a family: its highest sense is in the fact that the family is mutual burden-bearing, a school of sacrifice. Its seriousness is in its being the communion of souls facing the sufferings and terrors of life. It is two-sided, as is almost everything in our fallen world. It not only lightens suffering and burdens but produces countless new sufferings and burdens. It not only liberates a person spiritually, but spiritually enslaves him, and creates tragic conflicts with man's calling and with his spiritual life. Hence a person must sometimes follow the Gospel precept and leave his father and mother, his wife or husband. . . .

The Ethics of Sex

> Sex is the meeting-point of two worlds in the human organism. *M.C.A.*, p. 18

Christianity set forth the cult of virginity, and connected this with the cult of the Virgin Mary. This is the one truly profound and Christian attitude toward sex. The teaching about marriage and the family has always been opportunistic and adapted to everyday social life. Virginity was linked with the person, marriage with the race, the family with society. Once having recognized procreation as the sole purpose and justification of marriage, Christianity linked this meaning and this purpose with the physical sex-relationship, but this is accompanied by the loss of virginity, which Christianity condemns, metaphysically, and which it considers a lower condition than virginity. . . . The continuation of the human race presupposes loss of virginity and wholeness, the enslavement of the person and the spirit to the person-less element of race, to the material. This fact . . . is specially catastrophic for woman, called to continue the human race: it points out the profound baseness in sex, shows man's fall in sexual life. But the meaning of love, its idea and principle, is victory over the fallen life of sex. . . . Love is the restoration of the personal element in sex, not the natural element, but the spiritual.. . . . But in its meaning and essential idea love is something quite other than sexual desire, it has no necessary relation to physiological attraction, and may even offer release from it. Hence the spiritual meaning of conjugal union can be only in love, in the personal love of two beings, in a longing for union in one androgynic image. . . . Love must overcome the old flesh of sex, and reveal a new flesh, where union will not mean loss of virginity, but rather its realization, that is wholeness. Only at this ardent point can the world's transfiguration begin.

Destiny, pp. 250-60

The Sex Instinct Divides

Man is a social creature, i.e. a half-man, partial, un-whole, yearning for completion, wholeness. Sex cuts a deep gash in the 'I', which is bi-sexual An integral and complete 'I' would be male-female, androgyne. The conquest of loneliness in communion is first of all the conquest of sexual loneliness, exit from the solitude of sex, union in sexual wholeness. The very fact of the existence of sex is seclusion, loneliness and languor, longing to enter into another. But the physical union of the sexes, though it stops physical yearning, does not by itself conquer loneliness; afterward the sense of loneliness may be more acute. . . . As a biological and social fact, sex life casts the 'I' out into the objectivized world. But in the objectivized world loneliness is not conquered, it is only blunted. The biological union of the sexes, their social union in the institution of the family, do not finally conquer loneliness and human yearning. . . . There is a regular demonic in sex. This is developed both in the external manifestations of sex and in its suppression. There is something death dealing and destructive in the demonic of sex. . . . Love is the conquest of loneliness, it is going out of self into another, the reflection of another in oneself and of self in the other. Love is primarily personalistic communion of person with person. Friendship is also personalistic, and in it is an element of the erotic. There is a profound and indissoluble connection between personality and love. The 'I' becomes a personality through love. Only in love is there true union of one with another, and the true conquest of loneliness. . . . The final conquest of loneliness is thinkable in the attainment of an integral androgynic image. But an androgynic image means the transfiguration of nature. *Solitude*, pp. 110-12

The Sexual is Impersonal, the Erotic, Personal

Sex is the impersonal in man, the power of the general, the racial: only love can be personal. Not sexuality, but the erotic, is personal. . . . Sex infringes upon the dignity of personality, makes it the sport of impersonal forces and demeans man. Hence the sense of shame connected with sex. This sense of shame grows with the growth of the personality, and personal consciousness. The racial life of sex makes a person the means for the procreation of other persons, and personal satisfaction turns out to be an illusion, necessary for the life of the race, but not for the person himself. But when sex finds an outlet, aside from procreation of the coming generation, it easily turns into debauchery and painfully impairs the person's integrity. . . .

These are sexual conflicts: they arise before erotic conflicts appear: these latter relate to a higher sphere of human existence. Love-eros is in conflict with the faceless life of sex beneath, and above with objectivized marriage, the life of the family as a social institution. Man knows slavery to sex and slavery to the family, and both are the results of objectivization, the objectivization of sex, and the objectivization of love in social custom. . . . Disorganized sex, given over to the power of natural impulses, may mean the disintegration of the person, the ruin of a man. But socially organized sex, subject to limitations and censorship, produces new forms of enslavement. *Slavery*, pp. 192-3

Sex and Love (eros)

We must not confuse the sexual with the erotic: these are elements which intermingle, but are distinct from each other. The union of sexes is a biological, animal element, the family, a social element connected with procreation; love is a personal and metaphysical element. For the first there should be established an ascesis limiting or even completely eliminating it; for the second, free comradeship and brotherhood: for the third, no norms are possible, for love is free, mystical, unrepeatable, and individual in its nature, not subject to earthly law, sometimes demanding free sacrifice. *Divine*, p. 147

The Family—a Secular Institution

By its very nature the family has always been, is now and always will be, a positivistic, secular institution of good order, a biological and sociological ordering of the life of the race. . . . No other phenomenon in human life can be so successfully explained by economic materialism as the family. In this sphere sociological materialism won its greatest victory. The family is first of all an economic unit and its connection with sex is always indirect rather than direct. And the connection of the family with love is much more tenuous. Man's sexual life was never held within the limits of any form of the family, it always flooded over all boundaries. But in the process of racial self-protection and the ordering of humanity it was necessary to work out forms of adaptation and limitation. . . . A legalized, normal form of sex had to be developed as an inevitable adaptation to the given condition of being. . . . *The family was born of necessity and not of freedom.*

Religiously the family is completely Old Testament, in the law which convicts of sin. The family is obedience to the results of sin, adaptation to the necessity of the race. The family is always an acceptance of the inevitableness of the procreative sexual act, an adaptation to the necessities which result from it, the moral redemption of the sexual act by acceptance of the yoke of sex. The basis of the family is fallen sex, the unconquered differentiated act of sexual life, the lost integrity of sex, loss of chastity. . . . The whole *pathos* of the family is born of the sexual act and any other union of man and woman is not recognized as family, is not considered justified. . . .

The moralists of the family are ready to justify the sin of sex as the bearing of a burden and as obedience. . . . The moralists of the family do not know what to do with the fact of the union of men and women outside the sexual act; they do not know how to evaluate such union.

To them one of three cases is necessary: the procreative sex-life of the family, debauched sex-life, or the ascetic absence of any sexual life at all. And it is most surprising that in the usual ideology of the family, be it religious or positivist, the attitude towards that very sexual act on which the whole ideology is based remains unexplained. Orthodox and Catholics alike do not believe that men can completely overcome the sexual act, just as they do not believe that men can completely abstain from eating meat. Is the sexual act something good and justified in itself, or is it good and justified only as a means, as an instrument of procreation? At this central point of the problem of sex and the family there has been heaped up a mountain of hypocrisy. The moral *pathos* of the begetting of children which prudishly scorns the sexual act is essentially hypocritical: from both the religious and the moral viewpoint, the *pathetic* attitude towards procreation should be transferred to the sexual act itself. If the begetting of children is divine, then so is the act on which it depends. . . .

In the profound mystic of its substance, the New Testament denies the family. . . . A genuinely 'Christian family' is no more possible than a 'Christian state'. The family is a racial institute; it is putting the race in order. . . . Like the law of the state, the law of the family is essentially Old Testament, pre-Christian, but the New Testament justifies it as obedience to the Old Testament subjection to the law, obedience to the results of sin. The Christian family is merely a disinfection of the sexual sin, which renders it harmless. *M.C.A.*, pp. 207-12

The Christian Family

The Christian family, the Christian ordering of racial sex life is merely an inevitable compromise with the world, only obedience to the consequences of sin. In this Christian ordering of sex, this adaptation to race, there has not yet appeared the revelation of the mystery in sex. In Christianity only the ascetic denial of the sex life of the old Adam is truly profound and truly religious. . . . The old race, the old sex, remain in the Old Testament and in paganism. The whole of natural sex life with its limited laws carries on, on the Old Testament, pre-Christian level. Whatever is *personal* in sex is already on the level of the New Testament, for the New Testament is above all a revelation about personality. The confirmation of the non-racial in sex life is the beginning of the revelation of the new sex. This will be positively revealed only when the nature of love is revealed, the essence of the erotic.

M.C.A., p. 197

Marriage—the Family—Monogamy

Marriage is a sacrament, but only that marriage whose content is love, love of ontological reality, rather than mere being in love or simply feeling mutual attraction. But then the basic quality of a true marriage and genuine love is freedom. All social constraint or pressure deprives the union of two people of all sacramental or mystical meaning, meaning present only in love; but love is not socially perceptible or definable. This is true not alone for the state, but for the church as a social organization.

This is why marriage and the family, based neither on love nor on freedom, must be recognized as social, legal and economic in nature, defined by the laws of the social community and in principle distinct from the sacrament of marriage. They must be recognized as neither holy nor mystical in their nature. Only that love is holy, sacramental and mystical which is truly ontological, unique and eternal, which leads to the Kingdom of God. It is a phenomenon of quite another order from the physiological life of sex or the social life of the family. And this mystical, holy meaning of love is not revealed in the thought of the church. This revelation belongs to creative ethics, distinct from ethics of the social comunity. . . .

The spiritual liberation from enslavement to sexual lust which degrades man's worth, the sublimation of subconscious sexual attraction, is the basic fundamental requirement of ethics. This spiritual liberation is not achieved by negative asceticism alone: it presupposes creative direction of sexual energy. True love is the most powerful means against sexual lust, that source of enslavement and degradation. To attain chastity through love is to attain integrity, to conquer the sinfulness of sex and the lack of wholeness. *Destiny*, pp. 253-4

The Family in Christianity

Christianity rightly justifies and sanctifies marriage and the family for the sinful human race, and it spiritualizes and renders harmless the life of fallen sex. But it says nothing about the transfiguration of sex, the appearance of a new sex. Like much else, this remains mysterious in Christianity. The sanctity of motherhood has cosmic significance, but does not solve the problem. The abyss between racial, birth-giving love and mystical love, oriented toward eternity, produces an antinomy in Christian thinking. . . . This is the result of the fact that in Christianity the anthropological consciousness is not fully developed. Like much else in man's creative life, love remains without reasoned meaning, unsanctified, uncanonical, as though it were outside the law and condemned in the world to a tragic fate. The Christian teaching about marriage and the family, like Christian teaching about authority and the state, has profound meaning for the sinful natural world, for the racial element where man carries on, living out the consequences of sin. But this does not even touch the problem of the meaning of love, whose nature is not related to physiological attraction, nor to child-bearing, nor to the good social ordering of the human race. By its very nature, love occupies the same place as mysticism. It is aristocratic, spiritual, and cannot be translated into the language of the intellectual and spiritual organization of human life. *Freedom*, II, pp. 27-8

LABOUR

Labour: its Freedom

A new form of the enslavement of labour is arising in the modern authoritarian states, based upon a dictated world-view. This is a surprising process. The social milieu becomes more unified, but in this very unification personality is more heavily oppressed than in a more differentiated society. Instead of the living personality of the worker, his welfare, the rights of labour, we see proclaimed as the supreme value the power and well-being of the state, the social collective. The means of production, instead of being given to the producers, as Marx demanded, are turned over to the fascist or communist state. The State is recognized as the subject, while man becomes the object. This is the extreme form of the objectivization of human existence: man is emptied of every inner value. The process of socializing economic life, a process not only just but necessary, now becomes a process of socializing integral humanity, that is, the subjection of man to society, in the most secret and intimate spheres of his being.

But this process is just the reverse of that needed to produce a true brotherhood of man, the communion of personalities, of 'me' and 'thee'. All men become the objects of organization. The crisis through which mankind is passing, the denial of liberty is the denial of man himself. For the truly justified process of reducing mankind to a level may proceed in two directions: it may proclaim the dignity, the value and the liberty of every individual because in him there is seen the image of God, or the existence of this image may be denied, and with it all freedom and value of the individual man. . . . We may conceive either a general aristocratization of human society, or a general democratization which would mean lowering the level of all human qualities. At the moment the process is evidently moving in the latter direction, and hence the problem of society is above all the problem of man.

Fate, pp. 54-5

A New Christian Approach to Labour

How are we to free labour from the satanic feelings which Marx thought had messianic significance? The minds of workmen are poisoned by these satanic feelings. The usual preachment of Christian virtues, of love, humility and forgiveness are not only powerless and without positive results, but they may sound like empty rhetoric, like hypocrisy and insincerity, like a disguised attempt to weaken and disarm labour in its struggle. . . . The task which Christians are facing here is extraordinarily serious and responsible. Words must be found, which have freshness, youth, creative energy. Such words have not yet been discovered. The traditional preachment of humility sounds false when it demands humility in the face of social evil. It is extraordinarily difficult to approach the spirit of the worker with the truth of Christianity, contaminated as that spirit is by the poisons produced by capitalism and the class struggle. If Christianity is to touch the worker, it must be organically related in his mind with ideas in which he sees social truth, and it must deny ideas in which the worker sees social untruth.

Class War, p. 132

The Christian Attitude toward Work

The Greco-Roman world of antiquity scorned work, considered it fit for slaves, and unhallowed by anything. That world was based on aristocracy: even its democracy was aristocratic. And this ancient aristocratic principle prevented the greatest of Greek philosophers, Plato and Aristotle, from understanding the evil and injustice of slavery. When the stoics began to recognize the injustice of slavery, and the truth that all men are brothers and equals began to reveal itself to them, this was the beginning of the dissolution and fall of the aristocratic culture of antiquity. Christianity brought with it a radical change in regard to work. Respect for work and workers is of Christian origin. Ethically contempt for work was overcome on Christian grounds. As a man, Jesus Christ was a carpenter. . . . But the positive idea of the values of qualitatively aristocratic creative work remained over from the Greco-Roman world, and had to be brought into agreement with the biblical-Christian idea of the holy and ascetic significance of work, and the equality of all men before God. From these premises we may establish the following principles of an ethical relationship toward work. A person must transform every sort of work into redemption, and at the same time strive for creative work, even if it be on a low hierarchical level. But society should strive for the liberation of work, and the creation of less difficult and unpleasant conditions of work: society should recognize man's right to work, which is his right to bread, his right to life itself. But to have more freedom and joy in work does not mean a greater specialization of a person in his work, but rather greater individualization. The socialization of labour resulting from every-day social life is taking place in a bourgeois-capitalist society, just as it did in another way in a society based on slavery. And socialism wants to extend this socialization. Of course work is social and is carried on in society. But from the ethical viewpoint we should strive for greater individualization of work which is in its nature social. And this partial desocialization does not mean making the person anti-social, for he is called to social life and social action. But it does mean that the person realizes the freedom of his spirit, and in his actions and his judgments he makes original decisions, based on his own sources, and not on the pressure of social custom. It is just in society that the person should manifest his original, i.e. his own inborn conscience. . . . The liberation of labour means the liberation of the person from the oppressing phantoms of the bourgeois-capitalist world, from the oppressive authority of social custom.

However, this ethical aim is only partially realizable. For the tragic conflict of personality with society cannot finally be eliminated within the limits of our sinful world. This tragic conflict is not to be understood as the person's hostility toward society, as an anti-social attitude. Ontologically, personality is social, and that partial desocialization which is its liberation from the yoke of social custom is its way toward realizing its cosmic and social calling, resulting from freedom of the spirit. Society should be a working society, and only a working society where work of various qualitative degrees, right up to higher spiritual creativity, forms a hierarchical whole, can be justified, ethically and religiously.

Destiny, pp. 332-3

Aristocracy

Aristocracy is not a class in the modern sense of the word, because it is of an inherited race or caste, a strain developed through the centuries, blue-blood. It is quite impossible to define aristocracy in regard to derivation: it is defined above all in regard to one's ancestors, and the inheritance received from them, biological, psychological, or social. Social class war destroys aristocracy. The only war aristocracy can endure is that of races, nationalities or states: aristocracy is formed here. But it cannot endure the war of social classes. It has no place in the marxist system.

Class War, p. 11

Personal Aristocracy

The realization of personality is an aristocratic task. Personalism includes the aristocratic principle. But this aristocratic principle has no connection with the aristocratic organization of society, with social aristocracy. Social aristocracy is racial, inherited, received from one's ancestors, has nothing to do with personal qualities. Here we are speaking of personal aristocracy, the aristocracy of personal qualities, related to man's inward existence, rather than his social objectivization, man's personal worth, real, not symbolic, a function of his personal qualities and gifts. Collective racial dignity is symbolic, not real: it is inherited from the past; from one's ancestors: it is related to qualities of the nation or the class. There is truth in democracy in so far as it affirms the worth of every man. Its error is in extreme forms of objectivization of human existence.

Solitude, pp. 177-8

True Aristocracy

I believe in the genuine aristocracy of personality, in the existence of genius, of great men, who are ever conscious of the duty of service, who feel the need not only of rising above the mass but of coming down to it. But I do not believe in group aristocracy, based on social selection.

Nothing is more repulsive than the scorn of the popular masses by people who consider themselves the élite. *Slavery*, p. 18

Inequality, Basis of Cosmic Order

Inequality is the basis of all cosmic order and harmony, the justification of the very existence of human personality, and the source of every creative movement in the world. Every birth of light in darkness is the beginning of inequality. Every creative movement is the beginning of inequality, and uplift, the emergence of quality from the quality-less mass. The birth of God, itself, is inequality. From inequality the world and the cosmos came into being. From inequality man, too, was born. Absolute equality would have left being in an unrevealed condition, in indifference, i.e. in non-being. . . . The revolutionary demand for return to equality in non-being arose from unwillingness to bear the sacrifice and suffering, through which the road to a higher life leads us. This is a most terrible reaction, the denial of meaning in the whole creative process in the world. The pathos of revolution is a pathos of reaction. The demand for a forced levelling, which comes out of the lower levels of chaotic darkness, is an attempt to destroy the hierarchic, cosmic order which was formed by the creative birth of light in darkness, an attempt to destroy human personality itself as a stage in hierarchy, as born of inequality. *Inequality*, p. 44

'BOURGEOISITY'

The evil in human life is most disturbing and painful, not when it strikes one in the eye, but when it is partly concealed by falsehood and deceit, when it tempts man by the pretence of being 'good'. The greater part of the evil in the world history takes the form of 'the good'. And this 'good' all too often turns out to be evil. Even Christian 'good' has been this sort of 'evil'. This Christian 'good' has included phariseeism, legalism, hypocrisy, exalted rhetoric and the crystallization of 'good' into bourgeoisity. Bourgeoisity is a spiritual category only in the sense that it is denial of spirit, the deceitful transformation of spirit into something just the opposite. The whole history of the world has a fatal tendency to settle into the realm of the bourgeois, to hedge itself in, in the spirit of the bourgeois. Christianity means the cessation of the creative movement of spirit, the quenching of the spirit's fire. Bourgeoisity uses the creative movement of the spirit: there is not a single great symbol of the past which it has not used for its own purposes. Bourgeoisity does not believe in the world of the unseen and will not accept the risks which accompany the joining of one's fate with that world. Bourgeoisity does believe in the world of visible things, attaches its fate only to this world, works to build and strengthen the visible world, only. It has made Christianity into a guarded, visible thing. Bourgeoisity is afraid of anything that does not offer a guarantee, anything which may be problematic. The bourgeois is always afraid that something may disturb his guaranteed and peaceful existence. A special sort of spirituality has been worked out for the bourgeois, although this spirituality is anything but spiritual. A great amount of literature, drenched in rose-water or oil from the church lamps, has been written to reassure the bourgeois. The kingdom of the bourgeois is the kingdom of the world. Everything gravitates toward this kingdom by some universal law of gravitation. And all the revolutionary movements of the world, are drawn toward this kingdom. This has happened most notably with Christianity; herein lies the tragedy in its fate The values of the spiritual and of spirituality have been used to strengthen and protect the kingdom of the bourgeois. Spirituality has been used both because men were afraid, and in order to make others afraid. The normal, legalistic order of life, from which all spirit has fled, has been called spiritual. . . . All the revolutionary movements of the world, although in their origins they were anti-bourgeois, once they had overthrown the old kingdom of bourgeoisity, proceeded to set up a new kingdom of bourgeoisity. The French revolution created the bourgeois capitalistic world, and the socialist and communist revolution will in its turn set up a new realm of bourgeoisity. *Reality*, pp. 104-5

The Bourgeois

The bourgeois in the metaphysical sense of the word, is a man who firmly believes only in the world of visible things, things which compel him to recognize them, a man who wants to assure himself a firm place in the world. He is a slave of the visible world and of the hierarchy of social order which has established itself in that world. He esteems others, not for what they are but for what they have. The bourgeois is a citizen of this world, a king of the earth. The idea has entered his mind that his mission is to become a king of the earth. The aristocrat might conquer the earth: with his sword he aided the organization of kingdoms, but he could never become a king of the earth, a citizen of that world: there are limits which he could not transgress. The bourgeois is deeply rooted in this world and is content with it as the basis of his ordered life. He has little feeling of the world's vanity, the magnificence of the world's goods. The bourgeois takes economic power very seriously, and often worships it quite unselfishly. The bourgeois lives in the finite: he hears the attraction of the infinite. True, he accepts the idea of the infinite growth of economic power, but that is the only infinity he will accept: he hides from spiritual infinity behind the infiniteness of the order of life he has set for himself. He recognizes the infinity of the increase of prosperity, of organized life, but this simply fetters him to finiteness. The bourgeois is a being who will not transcend himself. The transcendental hinders him from establishing himself on the earth. The bourgeois may be 'a believer', a 'religious' man, and he even appeals to 'belief' and 'religion' in order to maintain his place in the world. But the 'religion' of the bourgeois is always a religion of the finite, a religion imprisoned in the finite: it always covers up all spiritual infinity. The bourgeois is an individualist, specially as concern property or money, but he is an anti-personalist; the idea of personality is foreign to his thought. In reality the bourgeois is a collectivist: his consciousness, his conscience, his judgments are all socialized: he is a man of the group. His interests are individual, but his conscience is collective. *Slavery*, pp. 151-2

The Bourgeois is a Slave

The bourgeois is an individual, sometimes a very swollen individual, but he is not a personality. He may become a personality in so far as he overcomes his bourgeoisity. The essence of bourgeoisity is the impersonal. All social classes tend to move into this atmosphere: the aristocrat, the proletarian, even a member of the intelligentsia—all may become bourgeois. The bourgeois cannot overcome his bourgeoisity: he is always a slave. He is a slave of his property and his money, slave of his will to enrichment, slave to bourgeois social opinion, to social position; he is a slave of those slaves whom he at once exploits. . . . The bourgeois establishes a realm of things and he is governed by them. He has done terribly much for the dizzy development of technics, and he is governed by technics which he uses for the enslavement of other men.

Slavery, p. 153

Some Positive Values in the Bourgeois

It would be unjust to say that the bourgeois is always a selfish man, who thinks only of his own profit. A bourgeois man may be neither selfish nor egoistic: he may have an unselfish love for the bourgeois spirit, or even an unselfish love for money and for gain. Max Weber has adequately shown that in the first stages of capitalism it was characterized by what he calls an 'Innerweltliche Askese'. The bourgeois may be an ascetic and not at all interested in the pleasures and comforts of life; he may be a man of ideas. And it is also untrue to say that the life of the bourgeois is a happy one. The sages of the whole world and of all ages have told us that riches and money do not produce happiness. This has become almost proverbial. For me it is more important to say that the bourgeois is himself a slave and that he makes slaves of others. The impersonal force in whose grasp both bourgeois and proletarian find themselves, enslaves them, a force which casts human existence out into objectness. The bourgeois may be very virtuous; he may be, and usually is, an observer of all the norms of life. But mastery demoralizes the bourgeois. Every ruling class becomes demoralized.

Slavery, p. 156

RACE

White versus Non-white

One more force must be noted which has now entered history and threatens the stability of European culture. The peoples of the East, the 'coloured' races, now wish to take an active part in history; to be subjects instead of objects. The end of Europe's monopoly of culture is approaching. The reaction of East upon West, which, it would seem, had been discontinued since the Renaissance, is renewed. Along with the bursting forth of militant nationalism we see the universalization of mankind. . . . The attitude of the Christian nations of the West toward the non-Christian nations of the East has been anything but Christian. The resultant unpleasant associations have seriously compromised Christianity in the whole world. A few missionaries have demonstrated true heroism and sanctity, but in general it has not been a Christian face or attitude which the West has shown toward the races of the East. And we now have to pay for that mistake. Europe, in so far as she remains Christian, must adopt a Christian attitude toward the East, not that of the exploiter. The white race can no longer play the rôle of a superior civilizing agent to the coloured races. The peoples of the East, Japanese, Chinese, Indians have begun to adopt Western civilization; they have become materialists, have learned Nationalism from the West. And only in a very small measure have they accepted the light of Christian truth. Thus great human masses, vastly outnumbering those of Europe, have actively entered history, and entered at the moment when they have acquired the worst phases of European civilization. All this makes the world-crisis all the more acute and opens really frightful perspectives to our vision. We have entered a period of decadence and anarchy, and at the same time men were never so possessed by the idea of organization, planning, compulsory unity, state absolutism, as now. The roots of all this must be sought in the plane of the spiritual, in the crisis of Christianity and of religious consciousness in general, in the decline of spirituality. And only a new spirituality, which has not yet defined itself as an historical force, can bring real recovery. *Fate*, pp. 105-6

Racialism: Hebrew, not Christian

Racialism is a purely Hebrew ideology. The only classic example in history of the racialist ideal is that afforded by the Jews. It was the Jewish race which strove for racial purity, opposed mixed marriages and all sorts of mingling with others, strove to remain a world closed to outsiders. Judaism gave religious significance to blood-relationship and bound up inseparably the religious element with that of Nationalism. The Messianic consciousness of any people is always an evidence of the Jewish spirit. Exclusiveness, the loyalty to one's own things and people only, is one of the prime qualities of Judaism. Thus the anti-Semite may well be accused of Jewish practice and spirit. It is just we non-Jews who should be far from all racialism, exclusive Nationalism, all Messianism. . . .

Even if, in the world of Judaism, there is some justification for racialism, it has no basis at all in Christianity. . . . The ancient religious conflict between Christianity and Judaism, a real conflict by the way, has taken such a turn in our difficult and uncertain times, that militant anti-Judaism turns out to be anti-Christianity. Truly Christian anti-Judaism is directed, not against the Bible or the Old Testament, but against the Talmudic-rabbinic Judaism which developed after the Jews' refusal to accept Christ. But when religious anti-Judaism becomes racialist anti-Semitism, it inevitably turns into anti-Christianity, for the human origins of Christianity are Hebrew. It is proper for orthodox Jews to be racalists: they may be at enmity with 'Aryan' Christians. But it is impossible, it is forbidden, for a true Christian to be a racialist and to hate the Jews. This is one of the advantages of Christianity.

Fate, pp. 98-9

CAPITAL PUNISHMENT

Capital punishment is the ancient instinct of blood-vengeance and human sacrifice, which has taken on the legal forms of a civilized state. If wars and duels are not murder, since man goes to war not only to kill but to die, and always risks his own life, capital punishment is pure murder. Men will tell you that in capital punishment there is no moral subject, such as the person who commits murder. It is not a person who causes the execution, not a man, but that 'cold monster' the state. That is, there is no hating and revenging personality. Capital punishment is defended on the basis that it is quite apart from human impulse and affects, that it simply and coldly expresses the social instinct of self-preservation of a society. This is true only in that capital punishment is absolutely inhuman. In the 'cold monster', the state which executes quite without anger or passion, it is still the instincts, feeling and thoughts of living people, which are in action. And the instincts of revenge and terror of a whole people are acting in and approving of capital punishment. The institution of capital punishment bears witness to the moral feelings and the moral consciousness of a people and its rulers. It is no use claiming that in capital punishment a completely cold non-personalism is attained, that here the law, separate and objective, alone is in action. The very 'coldness' of the death penalty is the greatest accusation against it, the most horrible thing about it. The execution makes no sacrifice, does not risk death. Herein is the baseness of capital punishment. And who is the killer? Not the executioner who chops off a head, who is himself a victim of the institution, since he must deny the image and likeness of God in man. The real killer is the whole nation which demands and approves the death sentence. Here we have the brightest example of how the state can transgress all bounds, for the life of a man does not belong to the state; it belongs to God. The final decision of a man's fate, the final judgment on personality does not belong to the state. The state cannot and should not know the hour of a man's death; this is a supreme mystery, which demands an attitude of reverence. In capital punishment the state does violence to God, to Divine Providence. It is the same as any other murder. *Destiny*, pp. 221-2

Capital Punishment

No man can be the incarnation and personification of evil, the evil in him is always only partial. Therefore there can never be a final judgment on anyone. This puts limits on the very principle of punishment. A man may commit a crime, but man as an integral personality cannot be a criminal: we cannot treat him as the incarnation of crime: he remains a personality: in him is still the image of God. And the person who commits a crime does not belong wholly and finally to the state or to society. The person is a citizen of the Kingdom of God, not that of Caesar, and the judgments and verdicts of Caesar's kingdom about him are partial rather than final. Hence personalism is definite and finally opposed to capital punishment. *Slavery*, pp. 49-50

From Khomiakoff to Solovieff our best thinkers have rejected capital punishment, and Russian criminal legislation rejected it also. We may be proud of this before the peoples of the West which by instinct and by principle are more inclined toward capital punishment. In his epistle to the Serbs Khomiakoff wrote: 'Do not punish the criminal by death. He can no longer protect himself and it is shameful for a manly people to kill a defenceless person, while for a Christian it is sinful to deprive a man of the possibility of repentance. Here in the Russian land capital punishment was long ago abolished and now it is something repulsive to all of us, and in general it is not permitted by the ordinary processes of criminal courts. This attitude of mercy is the glory of the Orthodox Slavonic race. Cruelty and punishment appear here under the influence of the Tartars and Germans, but the last traces of this will soon have disappeared completely.' (*Khomiakoff Collected Works*, Vol. I, p. 402.) Capital punishment in the form of terror was accepted by just those Russian revolutionaries . . . for whom it was a means of wiping out evil and implanting good. Capital punishment became the basis of Russian justice after the enthronement of the communists. The necessity of killing in war, which no one denies, is not capital punishment.

Put, No. 4, June-July 1921

COMMUNICATION

Communication and Communion

But the 'I' is not content with communication with other 'I's in society and the state, in social institutions, communications by means of conditioned signs: it strives for communion with other 'I's, for entrance into genuine existence. All conditional communication relates to the world of objectivization, it is communication with objects. But the bursting-out toward communion is movement beyond objectivization toward true existence. The symbolization of communication is linked with varying degrees of objectivization. Communion predicates mutuality: one-sided communion is impossible. Unrequited love is not communion. In communion not only 'I' is active, but 'thou', as well. Only symbolic communication is possible with an object, and this does not have to be a mutual affair. Communion is possible only with an 'I' who is 'thou' for me, and this demands mutuality, i.e. the activity of 'thou'. Communion is possible only on the plane of existence, not on that of objectivization.

Solitude, pp. 102-3

Communication versus Communion

The objectivized and socialized world, the world of mass and quantity, of 'Das Man' and 'Es', is a fallen world, which does not know communion. In this world communication is established without communion, without intuition or love. In no single stage of communication does this world know the union of one human soul with another. In this world both the Church and religious togetherness take on the nature of objectified and socialized communication. And in this world the Church may be both a communication and a society. This is a secondary, a reflected world, rather than primary, and in it communication is possible only thanks to symbols. Objectivized and socialized communications are symbolic, rather than realistic. *Solitude*, p. 170

Friendship

The 'I' tries to conquer loneliness in a number of ways, by means of knowledge, in the life of sex and love, of friendship, in social life, in moral acts, by means of art, etc. It would be wrong to say that by these means loneliness is never quite overcome, but neither can we say that it is completely conquered. For in all these ways objectivization takes place, and the 'I' meets not another 'I', or a 'thou' in inward communion, but with an object, with society. Loneliness is not always of the same quality: there are different forms and degrees of loneliness. It is noteworthy that quarrels, conflicts, even hatred, are social phenomena which often weaken or lessen loneliness. . . .

The 'I' has a profound need to be truly reflected in another, to have the confirmation of his own 'I' in another; the 'I' longs to be heard and discerned. Narcissism is a more profound phenomenon than is often thought; it is bound up with the very existence of 'I'. The 'I' looks into a mirror or wishes to see his reflection in water, in order to confirm his own existence in another. Actually, 'I' is not desiring to be reflected in the mirror or the water, but in the other 'I' in 'thou', in communion. The 'I' longs to be finally recognized, confirmed, by some other 'I' in the world (not an object); he wants this other to perceive him in beauty, to listen to him, to reflect him, as in a mirror. *Solitude*, pp. 88-9

Friendship with Nature

It is a mistake to think that communion, which conquers loneliness, is possible only between persons, only in human friendship. It is possible with the world of animals, even with the vegetable and mineral worlds: these have their own inner existence. Friendship is possible with the ocean, with a mountain, a wood, a field, a river. So it was with St Francis. The most striking example of true communion, overcoming loneliness, is that of a man with his dog: dogs are true friends, often better than other men. At this point man's reconciliation with alienated, objectivized nature takes place; in nature man meets not an object, but a subject, a friend. Men's relationship with dogs has metaphysical significance, for here the break through objects to genuine existence takes place.
Solitude, p. 104

ANIMALS

It is a mistake to think that communion, which conquers solitude, is possible only between persons, only in human friendship. It is possible with the animal world, even with the vegetable and mineral, which have their own interior existence. Friendship is possible with nature, with the ocean, with a mountain, with the woods, the fields, with a river. It was like this with St Francis. The most surprising example of true communion which eliminates solitude is the communion of the human 'I' with dogs who become real friends, often better friends than other humans. At this point man's reconciliation with alienated, objectivized nature occurs; in nature a man meets, not an object, but a subject, a friend. Man's relationship to dogs has a metaphysical significance, since here there occurs a break-through via object into genuine existence. *Solitude*, p. 104

The use of machines replaces the terrible exploitation, in the past, of both men and animals. This exploitation has hindered true communion. Perhaps in the technical epoch it will be possible more strongly to feel and realize the possibility of communion with animals, which eliminates loneliness. A dog may be 'thou' to my 'I', and not an object. Here we have the possibility of discovering something new. *Solitude*, p. 172

After painful illness our dear Muri died. I experienced Muri's suffering before his death as the suffering of all creation. Through him I felt myself united to the whole of creation awaiting deliverance. . . . I very rarely weep, but when Muri died, I wept bitterly. And the death of such a charming one of God's creatures, was for me the experience of death in general, the death of those ones loves. I demanded for myself eternal life with Muri. *Autobiography*, p. 362

CHAPTER VI

The Mother of all the Arts*

'Philosophical knowledge is a spiritual act, where not only the intellect is active, but the whole of man's spiritual power, his emotions and his will.'
SOLITUDE, p. 16

PHILOSOPHY

Philosophy and Life

Much has been written about 'the idealists'. Polemic against 'the idealists' is almost the only spiritual food which for several years some journals have been spreading before their readers. Some budding writers have gained a certain publicity by these polemics. 'The idealists' have provided themes for their opponents, have put them up against questions at which they never would have arrived by their own thinking, have transformed them almost into philosophers and esthetes. And all this only to uproot the hated and dangerous 'idealism'. The marxism represented in our magazines bears visible signs of decadence, the cry of a drowning man grasping a straw. Among such straws are empiriocriticism, socially-harmless and vulgarized nietzscheanism and all those purely verbal hymns of life. Once upon a time there was a great and glorious doctrine, and we were all held under its hypnotic power. This was classic marxism: creative power was moving in it. But marxism, which was born in a special historic epoch, now already past, has grown old and feeble and can no longer play a rôle in creating spiritual culture for our time. The Epigones of this doctrine are trying to patch its old clothes, but with quite unsuitable cloth, which does not match. . . .

Idealism has been suspected and even accused of being reactionary: reactionary from both the scientific-educational and the social political standpoints. I shall concentrate my answer on these two points. From our religious-philosophic viewpoint, do we consider scientific enlightenment and the process of liberation necessary? This evidently arouses great doubts, for our intelligentsia has an attitude of religious veneration toward science and politics.

On the first point we shall not tarry long: it is a very elementary, simple and almost boring question. No one, ever, has attacked science. The idealists make a sharp distinction between the realm of scientific

* Cicèro.

knowledge and that of philosophy and religion. . . . We limit the competence of science only when it mixes into what is not its business, when it attempts to solve religious and philosophic questions. But we would be just as negative toward the philosophic or religious solution of scientific questions. . . . Our reaction is not against science, but against rationalism, against positivism: encroachment upon the fullness and integrity of man's nature. It is almost awkward to repeat for the thousandth time that science cannot set up a world-view, cannot be a religion, cannot create values or be a guide to life, that outside the scientific-rationalistic knowledge of one small reason there lies infinity which the positivists and in general all rationalists neither can see nor want to see. From such limitation of its competence, science can only gain. . . .

Our critics operate very uncritically and wilfully with the concepts 'freedom', 'personality', 'progress', etc. . . .

What is 'personality'? What is 'freedom'? Our positivist critics know that freedom is a lovely and attractive thing, that one must struggle for personality: they know even better that we have no freedom, and that personality is oppressed and throttled. These are all good feelings, but positivism in all its shades and forms is powerless to give a basis to personality and freedom, or to lead us to a philosophy of liberation, to a world-view of liberation. Personality and freedom should be not alone the aim and result of struggle, but the subject of struggle. . . . Personality can rise against something outside itself which oppresses it, only in its quality of a free being which possesses creative energy. Otherwise *what* would rise up? *Who* would struggle? Human personality, that metaphysical spirit, inwardly free, may be bound, enslaved or oppressed, but it possesses absolute value, though its worth may be ridiculed. But only a free being, not a bit of matter, an accidental drop in the ocean of necessity, can struggle against oppression and enslavement. . . .

In winning freedom for itself and for others, the inwardly free personality realizes his predestination in the world, sets upon it his creative seal, defends his right to self-determination by his own freedom alone, his inner creative power coming up against the world which is forced upon him. And that un-free object which the positivists call man, cannot set himself up against anything, any exterior pressure, any non-freedom; he cannot bring into this shackled and slavish world any creative or resisting element. Only a free spiritual being whose roots go down to the bottomless depths of existence, can strive for final freedom, is able to fight for it: an un-free piece of nature would remain in slavery to the end of the ages. . . .

There are two ways: one is that of the love of man, which wants to make men happy, to calm and organize them, to build comfortable housing for their neighbours where they will forget their irrational and tragic freedom, will renounce their right to absolute, supra-mundane truth. This is the way of the Grand Inquisitor. It leads to the ant-hill where there will be neither freedom nor personality. The other is the way of the love of God which wants to liberate men, puts truth and super-human values above prosperity and the ordering of life. This is the way of Him who came with words of boundless freedom, and was a reminder that God and freedom and truth are above the well-being and tranquility of men. And we must choose either the philanthropic way of well-being or the God-loving way of freedom. . . .

The position of 'idealism' in the historic moment we are now living through in Russia is very difficult and very responsible. We see the profound subterranean basis for the social ferment which has affected Russian society in all its layers, and we clearly recognize that we are concerned with the very existence of a great people, with the question whether we shall go the way of creativity and consequently of freedom, or the way of denial, the quenching of the spirit and of slavery. . . .

I see the difficulty and the responsibility of our situation in the fact that we cannot and must not yield purpose for the sake of means, give up our right to all the fullness of our spiritual experience and striving. We do not want to borrow anything from the theory and practice of the Grand Inquisitor, who with one hand opened the door to human happiness, and with the other closed forever the door to freedom. We need relative, outward, social freedom for freedom absolute, and inward and mystical. We need the social guarantee of the inalienable right of personality, not for the comfortable ordering of life, but for the revelation of religious truth, which now we are hindered from doing, by two opposing factions. The hour is near when political objections to religious-philosophical seeking and assertion will finally lose all meaning, when the whole shameful poverty of these objections will be revealed. That will be an hour of the social renewal of our fatherland, the hour of its liberation. We must be ready for this historic crisis not only as social beings, but as those sent from another world. *The New Way*, No. 11, 1907

Philosophy Must be Active

Philosophic knowledge cannot be only a passive, obedient reflection of being, of the world, of actuality—it must be an active, creative overcoming of actuality and a transfiguration of the world. . . .

In the creative, knowing act of philosophy there is an upsurge towards another being, another world, daring to approach the ultimate mystery. Philosophic knowledge does not stand over against being as something opposite to it and outside itself. This is an error of abstract rationalism. Philosophic knowledge is in being itself, since the knower is in being—it is a special quality of being and a special function of universal life. Knowledge is a function of the growth of being. It is the sun's ray which penetrates to the inner depth of being. A passive, obedient philosophy of necessity always considers necessity as truth and, with a certain moral *pathos*, demands humility before it.

Obedience to necessity (of nature or of categories) is understood as intellectual honesty and conscientiousness. Men believe that the criteria of truth are intellectual and that truth is accepted positively by the intellect, that knowledge of truth is honest and conscientious obedience. They doubt everything else but believe firmly in this. If truth lies in this, that the world is necessity and not freedom, that there is no meaning in the world, then it is dishonest and conscienceless to turn away from this truth and invent non-existent freedom and meaning, to recognize as truth whatever you will. And all the efforts of our spirit along the line of least resistance, the line of the given world, all the passive obedience of the spirit, speak for the assumption that there is neither freedom nor meaning in the world, that that towards which the spirit strives is non-existent. The *pathos* of obedience to necessity, to the world as it is, is transformed into the *pathos* of truth. The passive philosophy of necessity may be a sad and hopeless, but yet a true, philosophy, not thought out according to our desire. *M.C.A.*, pp. 42-3

In philosophy intuition is the ultimate: logic, the penultimate. *M.C.A.*, p. 38

Discursive Thought versus Intuition

In philosophy, as in art, creative intuition is not arbitrariness or wilfulness. But we dare not trust every intuition. The intuition of philosophical knowledge is bound up with the truly-existent, with the meaning of being, and its creative nature does not mean that the existing is formed only in perception. In creative knowledge the existing only develops into higher forms, it only grows and increases. Can intuition be based on and justified by discursive thought? Can the intuition of philosophy be subject to the judgment of science? This would mean the grounding and justification of freedom by necessity, of creativeness by conformity, the limitless existence of the world by its limited condition. This would be seeking a safe shelter in the compulsoriness of discursive thought, in the necessary firmness of science—it would mean the withering of creative daring in knowledge. Men wish to assert themselves and their intercourse with one another on the basis of a minimum of the compulsory data which is necessary both in the material and in the form of knowledge. Whence has come this confidence that discursive thought is more universally valid than intuition? From reducing to a minimum the level of spiritual communion. Discursive thought is always the realm of the middle, never either the end or the beginning. The end and the beginning are always implicit in intuition. In discursive thought, taken by itself, there is always an inevitable necessity, a forcible compulsion, an inexorableness—a vicious circle. Left to itself, discursive thought falls into the power of an evil infinity, a bad plurality. Here there is no resolving end, as there was no beginning; the source is not visible. Discursive thought is a formal, automatic apparatus, brought into action by forces which lie outside it. In the final analysis, discursive thought is only an instrument of intuition; it is intuition which makes all beginnings and all endings. Discursive thought is an apparatus beautifully adapted to operations on the given world which is forced upon us; in it there is the necessity of adaptation to the necessity of the given world. Only by as much as men have lowered their spiritual communion to a dull medium level do they seek exclusive support and the basis for their knowledge in the middle way of discursive thought; they see in necessity the justification of knowing. A more elevated spiritual communion, communion in freedom and from within freedom rather than in necessity and within necessity, should also recognize in philosophic knowledge the self-justification of creative intuition. . . . When there is no spiritual communion responsibility is assumed only for the middle course of discursive thought, only for conformity to necessity in knowledge. Understanding it thus, it becomes clear that philosophical intuition seems less universally valid than scientific discursive thought, only because of the reduction to a minimum of spiritual community, of community in consciousness. In actuality, intuition is a sympathetic living-into the world, entering into the essence of the world, and hence it presupposes oecumenicity (*sobornost*)—being and acting together. For Christian communion, for the churches' consciousness, the truths about the Trinity and the divine-human nature of Christ are no less all-obligatory than the truths of mathematics and the laws of physics.

M.C.A., pp. 34-5

Philosophy Must be Free

No matter how knowledge sets itself up as opposite to life, or how it doubts the possibility of knowing life, it is itself life, from the very outset: it is born of life, and it reflects life's destinies. Gnosseological reflection, too, mirrors those destinies. This is the experience of every life, and life's experience cannot be simply stricken out without leaving a trace: it can only be gotten rid of and overcome by fuller experience of which previous experience is necessarily a fact. Contrasting knowledge with being, as something opposite to it, is the result of something already secondary, not primary: it is the product of reflection. It is a primary fact that knowledge itself is being and proceeds from being. . . .

The fate of philosophical knowledge is tragic. It is difficult for philosophy to defend its own freedom and independence. The freedom and originality of philosophical knowledge has always been threatened, and often from two directly opposite sides. If at present philosophy is dependent upon science, once it was dependent upon religion. Philosophy is in constant danger of enslavement, now by religion, now by science, and she finds it difficult to maintain her own place, to hold to her own way. . . . Both religion and science may fertilize philosophical knowledge from within, but they must not be some external authority for it. Men have demanded that philosophy be conformable to the theological formulations of faith, that it conform to science, even to mathematical physics. Philosophy had only a brief moment of breathing the air of freedom, after freeing itself from the oppressive power of theology, when it fell into even deeper slavery to autocratic and despotic science.

But refusing philosophy's enslavement to alien spheres does not mean that it closes itself within itself and breaks away from life. If the philosopher believes in religious revelation, he cannot but nourish his knowledge from it. But revelation is not an external authority for his philosophic knowledge: it is an internal fact; it is philosophical experience. Revelation is immanent to philosophical knowledge, as an inner light. Philosophy is human: philosophical knowledge is human knowledge: it always contains an element of human freedom. It is not revelation, but man's free perceptional reaction to revelation. If the philosopher is a Christian and believes in Christ, he should not try to make his philosophy conform to Orthodox, catholic or protestant theology, but he may acquire the mind of Christ, and that makes his philosophy quite different than if he did not possess the mind of Christ. . . .

Philosophical knowledge must commune with the primal source of life, and from this draw its perceptional experience. Knowledge is initiation into the mysteries of being, into the miracle-plays of life. It is light which blazes out from being and within being as well. Knowledge cannot create being from within itself, from concepts, as Hegel would have it. Religious revelation means that being reveals itself to the knower. How can he be deaf and blind to this, and affirm what is contrary to that which is revealed to him, autonomy of philosophical knowledge? *Destiny*, pp. 4-7

Philosophy Between Religion and Science

Truly, the position of the philosopher is tragic. Almost no one loves him. Through the whole history of culture we can trace hostility to philosophy, and this from various angles. Philosophy is the most unprotected phase of culture. Men are constantly doubting the very possibility of philosophy, and every philosopher is compelled to begin by defending philosophy and justifying its possibility and its productive value. Philosophy is attacked both from above and from below: both religion and science are hostile to it. It has none of what is known as social prestige. The philosopher does not give the impression of one who is fulfilling the 'social command'. . . .

The first and most powerful assault which philosophy had to withstand came from religion, and this continues to our day, since, notwithstanding Comte, religion is an eternal function of man's spirit. This collision between philosophy and religion causes the tragedy of the philosopher. The collision of philosophy with science is less tragic. The keenness of the conflict between philosophy and religion stems from the fact that religion has its perceptional expression, its zone, in theology. Philosophy has always put and solved the same problems as theology. Hence theology always restrained the philosophers, often persecuted or even burned them. And this was true, not only in the Christian world. The struggle of the Arab moslem theologians against philosophy is well known. The poisoning of Socrates, the burning of Giordano Bruno, Descartes' exile to Holland, Spinoza's ex-communication from the synagogue—all these bear witness to the persecutions and tortures inflicted upon philosophy by representatives of religion. And the philosophers had to defend themselves by the practice of a doctrine of dual truth. But the source of this persecution is not in the nature of religion as such, but in its social objectivization. *Solitude*, pp. 5-7

Philosophy and Religion

Philosophy has always fought against popular religious beliefs, against the mythological elements in religion, against tradition. Philosophy begins by struggle against myth, and finishes by return to myth as the crown of philosophical knowledge. . . . No true philosopher will ever refuse to put and solve questions with which religion is busied, and which theology considers its sole province. There is also a prophetic element in philosophy and it is not by accident that it is sometimes proposed to divide philosophy into scientific and prophetic. It is prophetic philosophy which gets into trouble with religion and theology. Scientific philosophy might be neutral. The true philosopher, conscious of his vocation, desires not only knowledge of the world, but its alteration, its improvement, the world's transfiguration. It cannot be otherwise if philosophy is first of all the teaching about the meaning of human existence, of human destiny. Philosophy has always claimed to be not only love of wisdom, but wisdom itself. And to refuse wisdom is to refuse philosophy and put science in its place. The philosopher is first of all the knower, but his knowing is integral: it includes all phases of human existence, and inevitably teaches about ways of realizing its meaning. . . . Philosophy has always been a break-through out of this meaningless, empirical world that crowds and compels us from every side, to the world of meaning, to the world beyond. . . .

In the conflict between religion and philosophy, religion is right when philosophy claims to replace religion in the matter of salvation and the attainment of eternal life. But truth is on the side of philosophy when it asserts its right to a knowledge higher than that given by the naïve perceptual elements of religion. Here philosophy may have purifying value for religion, freeing it from objectivization and the naturalization of religious truth. The living God to whom man prays, is the God of Abraham, Isaac and Jacob, not the God of the philosophers, not the Absolute. But this problem is more complex than it appeared to Pascal, for the God of Abraham, Isaac and Jacob is not only the true, living, personal God, but also the God of a primitive, pastoral tribe with its limited knowledge and its particular social life. He who awakes to knowledge always experiences a conflict with those who slumber in traditional forms. Philosophy cannot endure the herd.

Solitude, pp. 9-10, 21

> Philosophy should be oriented not alone to scientific knowledge, but to religious knowledge as well. *Divine*, p. 7

Philosophy and Theology

Not philosophy alone, but theology also, is a perceptual act of man. Theology is not revelation: it is thoroughly human, rather than divine. And theology is not an individual, but a collective, socially-organized perceptual reaction to revelation. Out of organized collectivity comes the pathos of orthodoxy. Here we have the conflict between philosophy and theology, between individual and collective thought. Knowledge is not revelation, but revelation may be of enormous importance for knowledge. . . .

Theology always includes some sort of philosophy: it is philosophy, legalized by the religious collective, and this is specially true of Christian theology. The theology of all the church fathers included a large dose of philosophy. Eastern patristics was infused with Platonism, and without the categories of Greek philosophy would never have been able to develop Christian dogmatics. Western scholasticism was infused with Aristotelian thought, and without the categories of Aristotelian philosophy would never have been able to develop even the catholic doctrine of the eucharist (substance and accidence). . . . It is just the philosophical elements in theology, which have taken dogmatic form, which rise against the freedom of philosophical knowledge. . . .

[Modern] philosophy becomes freer because it breaks the connection of Christianity with certain forms of philosophy. But the theologians, who represent religion on the territory of knowledge, do not want to recognize this liberation of Christian knowledge, do not want to recognize that Christianity now becomes immanent to human thought and knowledge. This immanence always troubles the representatives of religion. In actuality philosophy, like science, may have a purifying influence on religion, may free it from non-religious elements which have grown together with it, from backward forms of knowledge and outdated social forms. . . .

Objectivized naturalism always thinks of all forms of being in material images. We find this in theology, where it plays a determinant rôle. God is represented as object and is known as things and objects of the natural world are known. But my existence can touch the existence of God only because He is not object, and does not belong to the objectivized world, and only because I may belong to Him. . . . *Solitude*, pp. 58-9

Philosophy Must be Subjective

Can philosophy be anything but personal and subjective? Can we identify truth with objectivity and impersonality? . . . We must start with a decisive break between truth and objectivity. Philosophy cannot be other than personal, even when it is trying to be objective. The mark of the philosopher's personality lies on every philosophy of any importance. The philosophy of St Augustine, of Pascal, of Schopenhauer and Kierkegaard and Nietzsche was personal. Not less so was the philosophy of Plato, Plotinus, Spinoza, of Fichte and Hegel. We see the personal quality of philosophy in the choice of problems, the selection of one of the two types of philosophy of which we spoke earlier, in the prevailing intuition, in the direction of attention, in the man's general spiritual experience. Philosophy can be only mine, although this does not mean that I am shut up within my own philosophy. True philosophy, that really discovers something, is not that which investigates objects, but that which is tormented about the meaning of life and of personal destiny. Philosophy begins with this. It cannot be said too often that the knower is not some world-spirit or world-reason, not an impersonal subject, or 'consciousness in general', but I, the given, concrete man, the person. And the basic problem of knowledge is that of my personal, human knowledge. We do not need a critique of pure reason as much as we need a critique of the concrete, human, individual, personal reason. All creative thinking is personal, and here this does not mean something closed or limited. The beams of light flow out from one source but they are received into each person separately. We cannot believe the philosophers who say their thinking is free from all emotionalism. The most 'objective', 'impersonal' philosophers know by means of emotion. Descartes arrived at his 'cogito ergo sum' by way of emotion and he experienced this discovery in an emotional ecstacy. That he was convinced of his own existence by his thinking, does not mean that he arrived at this point by pure thought. In this case 'thought' for him was passionate emotion.

Spinoza's 'ethics', despite its geometric method, is suffused with emotion. The 'Amor Dei Intellectualis' bears the mark of passionate emotion. Intellectualism itself may be personal emotion. Even 'objectivity' may be only a name for a personal ruling passion. In one sense the philosophy of Hegel is no less subjective than that of Nietzsche. Only philosophy that is quite unoriginal and uncreative ever remains 'objective' and impersonal. . . .

We must break with the prejudicial idea that 'personal' and 'subjective' mean closing oneself in, incapacity to go out into the broad life of the world, something opposite to communion with the divine. On the contrary, it is the 'impersonal' and 'objective' that signify cloisteredness and the impossibility of breaking out. The 'personal' nature of knowing must not be confused with the 'egocentric' nature of knowing. 'Egocentricism' is just the cloisteredness and impossibility of breaking out, mentioned above; it is fixation on self, original sin. The 'personal', on the other hand, is the way to God, for only the person is the image and likeness of God. It is always the person who knows and philosophizes. Philosopical knowledge is always empirical in the sense that it is connected with personal experience, with its breadth and richness. The whole, living man philosophizes. Philosophy is personal and human. Man cannot be eliminated from philosophy. The perceiving philosopher is immersed in being; he exists before he knows being and existence, and upon this depends the quality of his knowledge. He knows being because he himself is being. *Solitude*, pp. 27-9

Types of Philosophy

There are many possible ways of classifying types of philosophy. But the distinction between two types carries down through all the history of philosophy, and this dualism of elements is manifest in the solution of philosophy's basic problems. And there is no visible, objective reason for choice between these different types: the choice merely bears witness to the personal nature of philosophy. I would note these two types in the following problems: (1) The primacy of freedom over being, or the primacy of being over freedom; this is the first and most important. (2) The primacy of the existential subject over the objectified world, or the reverse. (3) Dualism or monism. (4) Voluntarism or intellectualism. (5) Dynamism or statism. (6) Creative activism or passive contemplativity. (7) Personalism or impersonalism. (8) Anthropologism or cosmism. (9) Philosophy of spirit or naturalism. These elements may be differently combined in different philosophical systems. I choose unquestionably a philosophy where the primacy of freedom over being is affirmed, the primacy of the existential subject over the objectivized world, dualism, voluntarism, dynamism, creative activism, personalism, anthropologism, the philosophy of the spirit. The dualism of freedom and necessity, spirit and nature, the subject and society, the individual and the general, seems to me basic and definitive. But this is a tragic philosophy. The tragedy results from the primacy of freedom over being. Only the assertion of the reverse, the primacy of being over freedom, is without tragedy. The source of the tragic in philosophical knowledge is in the impossibility of attaining being by means of objectivization, of community by means of socialization, in the eternal conflict of 'I' with 'object'. This is also related to the difference between a philosophy of human existence on many planes or a philosophy of one plane of existence. *Solitude*, pp. 25-6

> The philosopher is a man in love with knowledge. *Beginning*, p. 45

Berdyaev About His Philosophy

As I began this book I cast a glance backward and felt the need to explain, to myself as well as others, my mental and spiritual way, to understand the seeming contradictions in my thought during the years. The book is about man's slavery and freedom, and much of it relates to social philosophy, but it contains my integral philosophical world-view: at its base is placed a philosophy of personalism. This is the fruit of a long philosophical way of search for the truth, a long struggle to reassess values. In my philosophy there has been not only a desire to know the world, but this desire has always been accompanied by the desire to change the world. In both my thought and my feeling I have always desired that this given world be the solid and final reality. To what degree is the thought expressed in this book true to the thoughts in my previous works? In what sense can we speak of the development of a thinker's thought? Is this development a matter of steady, uninterrupted process, or does it pass through crises and self-contradiction? In what sense can it be said that my thought has developed, and what changes have taken place in it? Some philosophers arrive early at a system to which they remain faithful all their lives. Others reflect the struggles of the spirit in their philosophy, and one can discover various stages of their thought. In our stormy historical time, an epoch of great spiritual crises, a philosopher who is not to remain a man of the study and of books cannot but participate in the spiritual struggle. I have never been a philosopher of the academic type, and never wanted philosophy to be something abstract and distant from life. Although I have always read a great deal, the source of my thought is not in books. As a matter of fact, I have never been able to understand a given book, except as I brought it into contact with my own life experience. By the way, I think that true philosophy has always been struggle. This was true of Plato, Plotinus, Descartes, Spinoza, Kant, Fichte, Hegel. My thought has always been of the existential type. The contradictions which may be found in my thinking are contradictions of spiritual struggle, contradictions in existence itself, which cannot be disguised by any apparent logical unity. Genuine unity of thought, closely related to unity of personality, is existential, not logical unity. . . .

Recognizing the superiority of personality means metaphysical inequality, distinction, refusal to accept confusion, the assertion of quality against the power of quantity. But this metaphysical, qualitative inequality does not mean social or class inequality. Freedom which does not know pity becomes demonic. Man must not only rise up: he must also descend. As the result of a long spiritual and mental experience, I have come to recognize with special clarity that no human person, even of the least of men, which bears in itself the image of higher being, can ever be a means for anything else, that it has an existential centre within itself, and that it has a right not alone to that life that is denied by modern civilization, but also to the possession of the universal content of life. This is the truth in the Gospels, although as yet insufficiently revealed. . . .

It is easier to understand my thought out of Kant and Schopenhauer than out of Hegel and Schelling. And actually Kant and Schopenhauer were of great importance at the outset of my spiritual way. I am not a school-philosopher and never belonged to any school. Schopenhauer was the first philosopher whom I profoundly received into myself. Even as a boy, I read philosophical books. Although in my earlier years I was close to Kantianism. I never shared the philosophy of Kant, or of Schopenhauer either, in any complete fashion. I even fought with Kant. But there are certain definite ideas which in one or another form have persisted all along my philosophic way. The dualism of Kant, his distinction between the realm of freedom and that of nature, his doctrine of mentally perceivable freedom, his voluntarism, his view of the world of phenomena as distinct from that of the real world which he unfortunately called the world of things in themselves—all these are specially close to me. And Schopenhauer's distinction between will and representation, his doctrine of the objectivization of will in the world of nature, which creates something not truly the world, Schopenhauer's materialism—all these remain close to my own thinking. . . .

In my very early years, while I was practically still a boy, I learned very much from Leo Tolstoy. My very early conviction that injustice lies at the base of civilization, that there is original sin in history, that all the society about me was built on falsehood and injustice, are connected with Tolstoy. I was never an adept of the Tolstoyan doctrine, and actually never liked Tolstoyans very well, but Tolstoy's revolt against false greatness and the false sanctities of history, against the falsity of all human social relations, sunk deep into my being. Even today, after this long way of thought, I can still recognize in myself these first evaluations of social and historical actuality, this freedom from binding social traditions, from the moral prejudices of well-thinking people, this repugnance for violence, both 'left' and 'right'. . . .

In Western Europe I saw clearly how the anti-communist front is moved by bourgeois-capitalist interests, or has a fascist colour. The circle of my thinking in social philosophy closed up. I returned to that truth of socialism which I had confessed in my youth, but now on the basis of ideas and beliefs borne out in the whole course of my life. I call this personalistic socialism, which differs radically from the dominant metaphysic of socialism, based on the primacy of society over personality. Personalistic socialism proceeds from the primacy of personality over society. This is the social projection of personalism, in which I have become more and more confirmed. . . .

The philosophy of this book is consciously personal: here I say about man, the world and God only what I have seen and experienced: here the concrete man is philosophizing, rather than world-reason or the world-spirit. *Slavery*, pp. 9-18

I define my philosophy as a philosophy of the subject, of the spirit, a philosophy of freedom, dualist-pluralist, a creative-dynamic philosophy, as personalistic and eschatological. Up to the present philosophy has been eschatological in only a small degree: eschatology has been related only to the religious sphere. But eschatology may and must have its epistemological and metaphysical expression, and I am striving for that expression.

Beginning, p. 53

KNOWING

Knowledge

Knowledge is struggle, not passive reflection. *Beginning*, p. 14

The Nature of Knowing

Is knowledge a creative act, or is it obedience, adaptation to necessity? Critical gnosseology demands of man's creative nature perceptive submission and humility. It even adds to its demand an ethical meaning, as though it desired man's ascetic self-limitation. Critical gnosseology gives a flavour of ascetic obedience to knowledge itself. And there is doubtless a strong admixture of moralism in this gnosseology. This type of gnosseology knows perception only as obedience, not as creativity. By its most profound nature, perception cannot be only an obedient reflection of reality, an adaptation to the data at hand; it is also an active transfiguration, giving meaning to being, the triumph in being of the world-reason, the sunlight within being. But critical gnosseology orients itself exclusively by science, i.e. by knowing as an adaptation to the given world, as submission to necessity. But gnosseology itself reveals itself only as obedience to science—as obedience to obedience. And the partial truth of this gnosseology of science claims to be the whole truth. . . .

The perceptive solution of the problem of creativity is possible only to the creative perceptive act. Creativity is known only by creativity, like knows like. Knowledge as obedience has nothing to say about creativity. Hence the nature of all creativity is unknown to science or the doctrine about science that is gnosseology. And this means that creativity neither demands nor permits a gnosseological justification or foundation. In no case can creativity be obedient to gnosseology. Man's creative nature is comprehensible only to creative knowledge, as one of the expressions of that same nature. Creative knowledge is an existential act, an act of ascension into being. Hence creative knowledge cannot be opposed to being and being cannot be killed in the creative act. Knowing is not outside being and cannot be considered as opposed to it: it is in the depths of being itself: it is activity within being. Knowledge is the sunlight which causes being to develop. Knowledge is creative development, the growth of being in the sun. *M.C.A.*, pp. 123-4

Knowing is not only Rational, but Emotional

It is evidence of prejudice to think that knowledge is always rational and that the irrational is not knowledge. We know much more by means of our feelings, than by means of our intellect. It is remarkable that knowledge is aided not only by love and sympathy, but sometimes by hatred and hostility. The heart is the central organ of integral human existence. This is, first of all, a Christian truth. That whole phase of knowledge which evaluates, determines values, is emotional, of the heart. And in philosophic knowledge evaluation plays an important part. Without evaluation, Meaning cannot be known. And the knowledge of Meaning is of the heart, above all. In philosophic knowledge the integral existence of man is known. And hence faith inevitably enters into knowledge. Faith enters into all philosophic knowledge, even the most rationalized. This was true of Descartes, of Spinoza, of Hegel. And that is one of the reasons for the insolvency of the idea of 'scientific' philosophy. 'Scientific' philosophy is philosophy devoid of the philosophic gift or calling. It was invented for those to whom nothing can be said, philosophically. It is the product of democratization, a child of the democratic age, in which philosophy feels crowded. So-called scientism is incapable of proving the very fact of science, the very possibility of man's knowing, for the very posing of that question takes us beyond the limits of science. For scientism everything is object: even a subject is only one among objects. Philosophy is possible only in case it is a special way of philosophical knowing, apart from the scientific. 'Scientific' philosophy is a denial of the primogeniture of philosophy. And it is no denial of reason to recognize emotional knowledge, knowledge through a sense of value, through love and sympathy. We are concerned with restoring the integrity of reason itself, which in the Middle Ages, despite the intellectualism of the scholastics, was more integral than now, since the intellect was often made the equivalent of the spirit. Philosophy should not deny reason, but should reveal its contradictions and immanently disclose its limits. In this regard, Kant's doctrine of antinomies maintains its leading rôle. But the criteria of truth are not in reason, or in intellect, but in the integral spirit. The heart and the conscience remain the supreme organs for evaluation and for knowing the meaning of things. Philosophy is not a science, not even a science of existing things, but is the creative perception by the spirit of the meaning of human existence. But this presupposes that the knowing philosopher bears in himself the experience of the contradictions in human life, and that his very tragedy is the way of knowledge. The philosopher who does not know that tragedy is impoverished and impaired in his knowledge. . . .

The process of knowing is not the passive reception of things, not only the action of the object upon the subject; it is inevitably active, it is the interpretation, the giving of meaning to what comes from the object; it always means the establishment of resemblance and commensurability between the knower and the known. This is above all true in regard to the knowledge of God. Knowing is humanization in the profound ontological sense of the word. And there are various degrees of this humanization. The maximum of humanization is in religious knowledge. This is linked with the fact that man is the image and likeness of God, and it means that God includes within Himself the image and likeness of man, pure humanness. Next comes philosophical knowledge, which is also humanization, the knowledge of the mystery of being in man and through man, the knowledge of the meaning of existence, commensurate with man's existence and man's history. The minimum of humanization takes place in scientific knowledge, especially in the physical and mathematical sciences. In modern physics we are witnessing the dehumanization of science. It seems to pass completely out of the human world, even out of the physical world to which man is accustomed. But the physicists fail to notice that the very success of their efforts at dehumanizing physics puts the question of the power of human knowledge. This very power of man's knowledge revealed in the bewildering successes of physics, is man's power in face of the secrets of nature, it is humanization. And this brings us to the fact that knowledge, all knowledge, is steeped in human existence, is at the same time a revelation of the power of man as an integral being and that this power is revealed even in the contradictions and conflicts, in the very tragedy of the philosopher and of philosophy. Three elements are active in knowing: man himself, God, and nature. In knowledge these three are inter-active: human culture, God's grace and nature's necessity.... *Solitude*, pp. 16-19

In knowing, as in every creative activity, man may take two positions. He may stand before being and before God, and then primary and original knowing takes place, genuine philosophy. In this situation man is given intuition and revelation. But then he is least protected from society. Or man may be facing other men, society. And then his philosophic knowledge and religious revelation are subject to social adjustment and social objectivization. In this case he is best protected socially. And this social protection is often purchased at the price of his conscience and his consciousness being deformed by socially useful falsehood. . . .

The Subject is Active in Knowing

We cannot admit the complete passivity of the subject in knowing. The subject cannot be simply a mirror reflecting the object. And the object cannot enter the subject as one enters the open door of a room. This kind of realism cannot be consistent; it cannot be carried out to the logical end. If the subject were completely passive in knowing, and knowledge were the passive reflection of the object, we could not understand how a material thing, in its quality of object, is transformed into the subject in knowing, how it is transformed into an intellectual and spiritual event. The subject is active in knowing by the very fact that he possesses the capacity of transforming the most material thing into an intellectual event. Knowledge reveals meaning behind meaninglessness, order behind disorder, the cosmos behind chaos. And all this is linked with the activity of thought. . . . *Solitude*, pp. 66-7

Knowing is not a Simple Reflection of Being

In the gnosseological contrast between knowledge and being, it is inadmissible that knowledge simply reflects being, passively, is altogether defined by being, as the created world. Something of free activity is brought into knowing. Knowledge is not merely reflection (of an image); it is creative transfiguration. And this is not to be understood as Kant and Fichte understood it. They held that the subject (transcendental consciousness, 'I') somehow creates the world, but here there is no element of human freedom, nothing human at all. Here man himself is not knowingly active in the subject's creation of a world. In reality, the world is not created by the subject, but by God, but it is unfinished and the finishing process is turned over to man. And man must bring his creative freedom into everything, and in knowledge itself continue the process of world-creation. The world does not enter into me passively. The world I face depends on my attention and imagination, on the intensity of my consciousness. (This intensity is determined from within, not from without.) This means that the present world depends on the subject, as man, as being, as something which exists. This means that knowledge is the relationship of being to being, a creative act in being.

Solitude, pp. 42-3

Knowledge is Creative

Knowledge is active and creative because the existential subject brings into knowledge the element of freedom, not determined by any object, or by known being, freedom which is before being, primordial. In knowledge freedom is conjoined with the Logos. The Logos is from God, while freedom is from the abyss, it is pre-existent to being. Knowledge is not only the reflection of being in me, as knower; it is also inevitably the creative reaction upon being of my enlightened freedom, which means a change of being. In knowledge, freedom is enlightened by the Logos. In knowledge, freedom is connected not only with the Logos, but with Eros as well. Knowledge completely separate from love is transformed into the will to power, and in this is a demonic element. Without love, everything, even faith, is transformed into the demonic, just as everything becomes demonic without freedom. *Solitude*, p. 70

Philosophical Knowledge

Philosophical knowledge is knowing truth, rather than being. Knowing truth is an uprising of the spirit to truth, a spiritual uprising and entrance into truth. But there is a social side to knowledge which is not usually given sufficient attention. Knowledge is a form of communication and communion among men. But knowledge consists first of all, not of the knower's facing others, but facing truth, that primal reality which philosophers have loved to call 'being'. Man's knowledge, and specially philosophical knowledge, depends on men's spiritual condition, on the capacity of their minds, and here the form of their community and their intercourse plays a large part. Philosophical knowledge has a personal quality, and the more personal it is, the more significant.

Beginning, p. 43

Philosophical knowledge predicates a primordial, existential act, before all rationalization, and it is measured by the depth and breadth of that act. Philosophical knowledge may be passion or mourning or rapture or painful striving for the meaning of life. This was the case with Spinoza. 'Amor intellectualis Dei' is a perceptional passion. Intellectual passionlessness is a false invention and pretence. The results of knowing are accepted emotionally: the very primordial intuition is, above all, emotional. There is such a thing as emotional thinking but only in pure abstractions can the emotional element be separated from the intellectual. Passion, emotional intensity, is determined by meeting reality, contact with life at the beginning. Only thinking which is plunged into itself, without any movement outside, can be completely passionless, void of all emotional tension. Hegel's concepts are full of passions. There is no reality without the subject's creative attitude toward it.

Beginning, pp. 68-9

Knowing is Conditioned by the Whole of Life

Since knowing is a part of life, reason a function of life, the phenomenon itself, the object of knowing (objectivization) is conditioned by the whole of life, by feeling, passions, the illnesses of spirit. Life at its source, the depth of existence (noumenal), defines the structure of consciousness, and how the world appears to us depends on this structure. If consciousness changed, the world would appear differently. But such a change presupposes a change in the nature of life itself, of the very element of life. We cannot characterize elemental life as primarily intellect—this is a Greek viewpoint. To a great degree it is passion, noumenal passion, preceding even the distinction between good and evil. The buddhist 'sympathy', Christian love, Schopenhauer's will to life. Nietzsche's will to power, are noumenal. For most people the real world, 'actuality' (that which acts upon them) is made identical with the limits of average, normal consciousness: that is, with consciousness which is already both objectivized and objectifying. . . . It's not only primordial intuition that is socialized; a rationalized consciousness is subject to the process of socialization. Knowledge and the very apprehension of the world depend upon social relations among men, on the degree of their communion. The realm of objectivization is a social realm, set up for the average, mass man, for everybody, for 'Das Man'. The objectivity of apprehension and representation is social in character. One might say that a man apprehends a certain picture of the world, depending on the form of his social relationships. Therefore there are special worlds revealing themselves for confessions, nationalities, professions or social classes. Here there is a bit of truth in the class-ideology of Marxism, but its expression is philosophically unsound. The only genuine creative inspiration is when a man is moved by spirit rather than society, when he is determined from within, not from without, when he is independent of social suggestion and social imitation. *Beginning*, pp. 69-70

FREEDOM

Freedom is not a right, but an obligation.
Spirit and Caesar, p. 106

The Origin of Freedom

That inward, profound and mysterious energy which creates life is revealed through spiritual causality. Here the opposition between freedom and causality disappears; in the determination of events and the production of life there is no longer anything external. In the spiritual life cause acts from within; there is self-determination; the mysterious connection of world life is revealed; the inner nucleus of being, normally hidden by the symbols of the world of nature, is disclosed. Freedom of the spirit which itself gives birth to consequences, which creates life, is revealed to us a bottomlessness, baselessness, as a force from out the boundless deep. We cannot feel a base, a foundation for freedom, nowhere can we find some solid element which determines freedom from within. Freedom of the spirit is a bottomless well. Our substantial nature could not be the basis of freedom. On the contrary, all nature is born of freedom. Freedom proceeds not from nature, but from God's idea and from the abyss which preceded being. Freedom is rooted in 'nothingness'. The act of freedom is primordial and completely irrational. To understand an act of freedom rationally is to make it resemble the phenomena of nature. The determined world, that of physical and psychical causality, is a secondary world . . . the child of necessity, as very many thinkers hold, but necessity is the result of freedom, the consequence of a certain directed movement of freedom. . . . *Freedom* I, pp. 183-4

Freedom and Being

We have to choose between two philosophies, the philosophy which recognizes the primacy of being over freedom, and that which recognizes the primacy of freedom over being. We cannot make this choice by thought alone, but by the integral spirit, that is by the will. Personalism must recognize the primacy of freedom over being. A philosophy of the primacy of being is a philosophy of the impersonal. An ontological system recognizing the absolute primacy of being is a system of determinism. Every objectivized intellectual system is one of determinism. It derives freedom from being; it appears that freedom is determined by being, which in the last analysis means that freedom is the child of necessity. Being is thus ideal necessity, with no possibility of outburst; it is complete and absolute unity. But freedom cannot be derived from being; it is rooted in nothingness, in non-being, if we are to use ontological terminology. Freedom is baseless, neither determined by nor born of being. There is no such thing as continuous, uninterrupted being. There are break-throughs, separations, abysses, paradoxes, there are transcendencies. Therefore freedom exists, and personality. *Slavery*, p. 65

Freedom is Hard to Define

. . . the problem of the mutual relation between freedom and being. The question is more profound than the traditional question of the relation between freedom and necessity. From a consistent ontological viewpoint, freedom appears as subject to, and determined by, being. Does being have primacy over freedom, or vice-versa? Is not the final secret of being in this, that freedom is primary, and precedes being? And this may be the reason why all ontologists are so unsatisfactory, so unbearably rational, so steeped in the concept, which is applicable only to the world of phenomena. . . .

Actually, freedom cannot be the object of knowledge: but it is just in freedom that we come into contact with the primary entity, and freedom is more authentic than being. Being is secondary: it is the product of objectivization; it is born of abstract thought. Freedom is more primary than being: it cannot be determined by our being; it is bottomless, foundationless. In determination, in rationalization, that is to say in objectivization, freedom disappears. That is why it is so difficult to define freedom, it is afraid of definition. . . .

In any case, the sphere of existential freedom is distinctly different from the sphere of objectivized and determined nature. Freedom is not only man's freedom, but man's fate as well. This fated freedom is the most mysterious phenomenon of human existence. The Fate, on which Greek tragedy was based, derives from primary freedom. The tragedy in the Christian world is tragedy of freedom, rather than of fate. It is the kind of tragedy which we find in Dostoevsky. *Truth*, pp. 55-6

Two Freedoms

There are two freedoms: divine and diabolic. The freedom of the first Adam could not be diabolic freedom, because divine freedom in its positive content could not be revealed in the seven-day creation. Adam's freedom was the first stamp of man's likeness to the Creator. And even in paralysing sin there was still a sign of man's power. The fall of the first man, Adam, had positive meaning and justification, as a moment in the revelation of creativity, preparing for the appearance of the Absolute Man. . . .

The freedom of Adam the first man had to be destroyed in his experience of good and evil; it had to be swallowed up by necessity so that the true and higher freedom might be revealed through the Absolute Man, Christ. The fall of the first Adam was a necessary cosmic moment in the revelation of the new Adam. This was the way to a higher completeness by means of a falling-apart. In Christianity the experience of sin is peripheral, exoteric. The deep experience of resisting God, of being deceived by God as an inward way of falling apart and division in divine life is esoteric. . . .

In Adam's fall, freedom was reborn into necessity which was subject to the fallen angel. But this was still no final loss of freedom. Final loss of freedom and final enslavement are possible only in that epoch of creation where there is already the revelation of the Absolute Man, Christ, and when the Antichrist, a false image and caricature of the Absolute Man, tempts man by the blessed condition of non-being. *M.C.A.*, pp. 148-9

St Augustine speaks of two freedoms, 'libertas minor' and 'libertas major'. And in truth we see at once that freedom has two different meanings. By freedom is meant either the primordial, irrational freedom which precedes good and evil and determines choice between them, or the final, reasonable freedom, freedom in good and truth, which is to say that freedom is understood both as the starting point and the way, and also as the end and the aim. Socrates and the Greeks recognized only the second sort of freedom, freedom given by reason, truth and good. And the Gospel 'know the truth and the truth shall make you free' speaks of the second freedom, freedom in truth and derived from truth. When we say that a man has attained true freedom, having conquered the lower elements in himself, and subjected them to a higher spiritual element or to truth and good, we are thinking of this second freedom. . . . This is the freedom toward which man moves, the summit and crown of life, the end of all his striving, the freedom which ought to be, which comes from the triumph of the higher elements of life. But there is another freedom, the freedom from which man proceeds, by which he chooses his way and accepts truth and good, themselves. There is freedom as the mysterious source of life, as primordial experience, as the abyss which lies deeper than being itself, and out of which being is determined. . . .

The true, higher freedom is possible only in Christ and through Christ. But Christ must be freely accepted; an act of freedom of the spirit must bring us to Christ. Christ needs our freedom in accepting Him. Christ desired man's free love. Christ can never compel man to anything; His countenance is always turned toward our freedom. God accepts only free men. God awaits man's free love. Man expects from God freedom, he expects that Divine truth will liberate him. But from man God also expects freedom; he awaits man's free answer to His call. True freedom is what God demands of me, not what I demand of God. Man's freedom is based on this profundity, freedom grounded in his boundless depths. Truth gives us the higher freedom. But freedom is needed in the very acceptance of truth. Truth can force or compel no one; it cannot force freedom on man. It is not enough to accept Truth or God; the acceptance must be free. Freedom cannot be the result of compulsion, even of the compulsion of God. It is useless to expect freedom from an organized, harmonized, perfected order of living: this very order must be the result of freedom. Salvation comes from the Truth which gives us freedom, but compulsory salvation is impossible and unnecessary. Man's salvation cannot be achieved without man's freedom. Salvation is man's liberation in Truth, in God. But man's liberation cannot be accomplished by compulsion, without the freedom of man himself. When freedom is affirmed in Truth, in God, that is the second freedom as the only freedom, this affirms God's freedom, rather than that of man. *Freedom* I, pp. 185-7

The Dialectic of the Two Freedoms

Freedom is dynamic. It has its own destiny. And it is possible to understand freedom inwardly only if we fathom its tragic dialectic. We have noted the existence of two freedoms, freedom in two different senses. And either of these, the first or the second freedom, has its fateful dialectic, in which freedom turns into its opposite, into necessity and slavery. The fate of freedom is truly tragic and its tragedy is that of human life. The first primordial, irrational and bottomless freedom by itself offers no guarantee that man will pass by the way of good and come to God, that Truth will conquer in his life, that the final and highest freedom will triumph in the world. . . . The first freedom may lead by the way of disagreement and anger, the way of self-assertion by one part of being against another, by the way of the ruin of the spiritual world, i.e. by the way of evil. The first freedom is easily reborn into evil freedom, and evil freedom is fatally reborn into necessity and slavery. The first freedom has not received the grace of love, is not enlightened by the inner light of Truth. When freedom precipitates man into the world of disagreement and self-affirmation, man falls under the power of natural necessity; he becomes the slave of lower elements. Out of its own depths freedom gives birth to this slavery and necessity. . . . We know by experience that the anarchy of our passions and of the lower divisive elements in ourselves enslaves us, deprives us of freedom of spirit, subjects us to the necessity of our lower nature. The danger of anarchy lies in wait for the first freedom, if it is left to itself. . . . The dialectic of the first freedom gives rise to the tragedy of the world-process and there is no way of escape out of it, either through this freedom or through the necessity it engenders. Is there a way out in the second freedom?

The second freedom, taken by itself, also has its fateful destiny. It has its own irresistible inner dialectic. And it is always threatened by the danger of transition into its opposite, into necessity and slavery. Taken without the first freedom, the second leads to compulsion and force in truth and good, to forced virtue, i.e. to a denial of freedom of spirit, to a tyrannical organization of human life. If the first freedom gives birth to anarchy in which it perishes, the second engenders an authoritarian order of life, theocratic or socialistic, where freedom of the spirit and of conscience is destroyed without a trace. The authoritarian type of society is born of the second freedom, taken abstractly. Human life, individual and social, is compulsorily organized into subjection to truth and good. Whether this truth and good are theocratic, in the sense of papal or imperial theocracy, or communist, freedom of spirit and of conscience is denied in either case; no possibility remains, of free choice of truth or good. . . .

We can see no way out of this tragedy of freedom: freedom is doomed to destruction: in the depths of freedom itself is hid the poison which will destroy it. The dialectic of both first and second freedoms takes place in a world already fallen from its spiritual centre. And the most fearful thing is that Christianity itself has constantly been tempted on the score of freedom (pelegianism, Augustine, Jansenism, Calvinism, the church's denial of freedom of conscience). The tragedy of the world-process is that of freedom: it is born of the inner dynamic of freedom, of its capacity of changing into its opposite. *Freedom* I, pp. 185-97

The Third Freedom

There is no natural way out of the tragedy of freedom. No naturalistic metaphysic can indicate a way of escape from that tragedy of freedom in which it destroys itself. The natural man moves from the first to the second freedom and back again, but both here and there an inner poison destroys his freedom. The conflict between freedom and necessity cannot be eliminated. From its own depths freedom gives birth to necessity. . . . How are we to overcome the poison in freedom without limiting it by some force from without? How liberate freedom from the evil it engenders, without destroying freedom itself? This is a world-problem which finds a solution only in the coming of Christ. Only the appearance on earth of the New Adam, the Spiritual Man, finds a way out of the tragedy of freedom, eliminates the conflict between freedom and necessity. The Son of God descends into 'nothingness', that is into primordial freedom. Only the Spiritual Man, the New Adam, extracts the poison from freedom without destroying freedom itself. This is something unattainable in the race of the old Adam, where the elimination of evil in freedom encroaches upon freedom itself. In Christ a third freedom is revealed, which comprehends the other two. The grace of Christ is an elimination of freedom from within without any force or compulsion from without. The truth of Christ, which makes us free, does not force or compel anyone; it is not like the truths of this world which forcibly organize spirit and deprive it of freedom. The light of Christ enlightens the irrational darkness of freedom, without limiting it from without. The grace of Christ is the elimination of evil freedom and good necessity.

The secret of Christianity, as a religion of divine-humanity, is just this secret of freedom. Rationalistic metaphysical systems are unable to explain or justify the two natures, divine and human; they cannot understand the uniting of two freedoms. Too many doctrines of freedom err in a monophysite deviation; they teach about God's freedom, but the freedom of man escapes their view. Only the Christian revelation reconciles the two: only the religion of the God-man and of Divine-humanity combines God's freedom with that of man. Redemption is the deliverance of man's freedom from the evil which destroys it, deliverance not by means of necessity or compulsion, but by grace. Grace is a force acting from within, rather than from without, acting within human freedom itself. And therefore the Christian doctrine of grace is a true doctrine of freedom. . . . *The source of man's freedom is in God, not God the Father but God the Son; but the Son is not only God, but man, absolute man, eternal man.* The freedom of the Son is that in which and by which a free answer to God is possible, a free turning to God. The freedom of the Son is also the source of freedom for the whole human race, since the human race is not only that of the natural Adam, but of the spiritual Adam, Christ. . . .

Through Christ man receives freedom, inwardly joined with grace. This grace does no violence to man's freedom; it comes to man from without. In the grace which comes from the Son, in Christ the God-man, it is not only God's energy which acts, but human energy as well, the energy of the Absolute Man, eternal energy, heavenly humanity. Grace acts as a third freedom, the freedom of a heavenly, spiritual human-ness. The mystery of grace in Christianity and its inner unity with freedom is still the same mystery of divine-humanity, of the unity of two natures. Grace proceeds not only from the Divine nature of Christ, but from human nature, from its heavenly human-ness. Here man's freedom, the third freedom, is active and is enlightened. The third freedom is freedom joined with grace, with gracious love. What takes place in time, on the earth, also takes place in heaven, in eternity. Esoterically the incarnation takes place on earth, in the process of time, but exoterically it takes place in heaven, in eternity, on the spiritual plane. This is a mystery-play of the spirit in which the Son is eternally born of the Father. Grace is the realm of the Third Hypostasis, it is the grace of the Holy Spirit. In the realm of the Holy Spirit there is no opposition between the freedom of God and that of man, between freedom and grace. Grace is active within freedom. *Freedom*, I, pp. 197-204

He truly loves freedom who affirms it for his fellows. *Spirit and Caesar*, p. 111

Freedom of the Spirit

The question of freedom is not at all that of freedom of the will, as this is usually stated in naturalistic, psychological or pedagogical-moralistic usage. It is rather a question of the very basic foundation of being, of life. The very perception of being depends on freedom, and freedom precedes being. . . . Philosophical tendencies and religious doctrines separate over this question. The problem of freedom of the spirit is put in all its depth of acuity by Dostoevsky. And of course what troubled Dostoevsky was not the academic question of freedom of the will, but an incommensurably more profound problem. . . . Dostoevsky's Grand Inquisitor says to Christ: 'You desired man's free love, that he should freely follow after You, reduced and captivated by You.' This is not a differential putting of the question of free-will: this is an integral question of freedom of the spirit. Here freedom is the integral atmosphere of spiritual life, its ultimate foundation. A special quality of the feeling for, and the understanding of life, is linked with freedom. Christianity predicates a spirit of freedom and freedom of the spirit. Outside this spiritual atmosphere of freedom, Christianity does not exist, it is devoid of all meaning. . . . Outside Christianity there is no freedom, outside Christianity determinism always wins the victory. Freedom of the spirit is not a natural condition of man as a natural being, just as immortality is not his natural condition. Freedom of the spirit is a new spiritual birth, the revelation of the spiritual man. Freedom is disclosed only in spiritual experience, in spiritual life. The source of freedom is not in the mind and still less in the body of man, not in man's natural being which is always subject to natural law and limited on all sides by external determining forces, but in spirit, in the acquiring of spiritual life. Freedom is entrance into another order of being, the spiritual rather than the natural order of being. There is a classic definition of freedom which is indisputably true, but gives no positive attainment of the secret of freedom. Freedom is self-determination from within, from the depths, and the opposite of all determination from without, which is necessity. Hegel defined freedom thus: *Freiheit ist bei sich selbst zu sein.* Self-determination from within is determination from the depths of spirit, from spiritual forces, rather than out of forces of external nature, or out of my own nature. In freedom my self-determination is not from without, from a nature akin to mine, or even from my own nature, but from within my own spiritual life, out of my own spiritual energy: I am within my own native spiritual world. *Freedom*, I, pp. 174-80

Freedom Demands Struggle

Freedom needs resistance and struggle. This is why we are faced with the determined everyday world where processes are going on in time, and the future seems inexorable. Man is burdened and bound. He both strives toward freedom and fears it. The paradox of liberation lies in the fact that to maintain freedom and struggle from freedom, it is somehow necessary to be free, to have freedom in oneself. He who is a slave to the depths of his being does not know the word freedom and hence cannot struggle for it. The ancient taboos surround man on every side, cramp his moral life. And to liberate himself from their power, man must first feel himself inwardly free, and only then can he struggle externally for freedom. The inward conquest of enslavement is the basic task of moral living. And this means conquest of enslavement to the past as well as to the future, conquest of enslavement to the external world and enslavement to oneself, to one's lower self. To arouse man's creative energy means inward liberation, and this is accompanied by a sense of freedom. Creativity is the way of liberation. . . . Man's liberation is not only *from* something, but *for* something. And this *for* is man's creativity.

Destiny, p. 158

Freedom is Aristocratic

The problem of freedom in its social applications is complicated by the fact that the average man of the masses does not very greatly value freedom. And a mass-revolutionary movement does not strive for freedom, at all. In order that man should struggle for freedom, freedom must already be in him, that is that inwardly he is not a slave. Demagogy, always used to move the masses, deprives people of their freedom: it is psychological compulsion. It is not easy to govern the masses which have actively entered history. In reality, freedom is aristocratic, not democratic. With sorrow we must recognize the fact that freedom is dear only to those men who think creatively. It is not very necessary to those who do not value thinking. In the so-called democracies, based on the principle of popular sovereignty, a considerable proportion of the people are those who have not yet become conscious of themselves as free beings, bearing within themselves the dignity of freedom. Education to freedom is something still ahead of us, and this will not be achieved in a hurry. . . . There is always the danger that in the name of freedom, men begin to deny it. Dictators and tyrants refuse freedom to others, but love it for themselves, and always insist upon it for their fellow travellers and those who are connected with them. But he truly loves freedom who affirms it for his fellows.

Spirit and Caesar, pp. 110-11

Nothing has meaning for me without my freedom. *Put*, No. 49

The Paradox of the Creator and the Creature

It must be admitted that in the antinomies of Creator and creature, freedom is a paradox which cannot find place in any category. Both the monistic and the dualistic concepts of the relationship between God and the creature lead to a denial of the creature's freedom. Man is not free if he is only a . . . particle of Divinity, and man is not free if he is endowed with freedom by God the Creator and includes within himself nothing of the divine, and he is not free if evil proceeds from an evil God, from material upon which he becomes dependent. All these viewpoints turn out to be dangerous for man's freedom. The Christian doctrine of grace was an attempt to save Christian freedom. Man was not free when God defined his attitude toward him as Creator of the world, but he was free when God defined his attitude toward him by sending him grace. Man freely accepts or refuses grace, but grace does not force him. But even the doctrine of grace suffered a rebirth, after which it enters into conflict with freedom. If grace acts upon man without any participation of man's freedom, we get the doctrine of predestination. Here the only possible escape is to recognize that freedom is uncreated, that it is rooted in nothingness. . . . It is difficult to bring man's freedom into agreement with the existence of God and it is equally difficult to bring man's freedom into agreement with a denial of God and the recognition only of non-divine nature. N. Hartmann's ideal values, quite powerless and hanging in the air, do not help here. If man is an exclusively natural being, it is incomprehensible whence he takes his freedom. The paradox lies in this, that man's freedom, without which there is neither creativity nor moral living, is not from God, and not from created nature. But this means that freedom is not created and at the same time is not divine freedom. The recognition of divine freedom does not help one bit in solving the question about man's freedom. The powerless nature of human freedom and the non-human character of grace form an insoluble paradox. The mystery of Christ the God-man is a solution of this paradox of freedom and grace, but it cannot be subject to rationalization. Theology rationalized this mystery and by so doing deprived it of meaning rather than giving meaning to it. Only in Christ the God-man is the paradox resolved of the relation of creature and Creator. And this is the essence of Christianity. *Destiny*, pp. 38-9

> Truly there is nothing more torturing and
> unbearable for man, than freedom.
>
> *Dostoevsky*, p. 205

Freedom and Creativity

Creativity is inexplicable: creativity is the mystery of freedom. The mystery of freedom is immeasurably deep and inexplicable. Just as deep and inexplicable is the mystery of creativity. Those who would deny the possibility of creation (creativity) out of nothing must inevitably place creativity in a certain determined order and by this very fact must deny the freedom of creativity. In creative freedom there is an inexplicable and mysterious power to create out of nothing, undetermined, adding energy to the existing circulation of energy in the world. . . . Creativity is something which proceeds from within, out of immeasurable and inexplicable depths, not from without, not from the world's necessity. The very desire to make the creative act understandable, to find a basis for it, is failure to comprehend it. To comprehend the creative act means to recognize that it is inexplicable and without foundation. The desire to rationalize creativity is related to the desire to rationalize freedom. Those who recognize freedom and do not desire determinism have also tried to rationalize freedom. But a rationalization of freedom is itself determinism, since this denies the boundless mystery of freedom. Freedom is the ultimate: it cannot be derived from anything: it cannot be made the equivalent of anything. Freedom is the baseless foundation of being: it is deeper than all being. We cannot penetrate to a rationally-perceived base for freedom. Freedom is a well of immeasurable depth

M.C.A., pp. 144-5

The Freedom of the Eighth Day

True freedom is an expression of the cosmic (as opposed to the chaotic) condition of the universe its hierachic harmony, the inward unitedness of all its parts. The cosmic is always free; in it there is no obligatory necessity, no burden or pressure, no materialization of one of its parts for another. In the cosmos everything is alive, nothing is inert or overburdened, nothing compels by its material consistence. Every time that man's living spirit encounters the resistance of heavy and lifeless material bodies, he feels the fall of the all-man and the strife and alienation which were born of it. The lower ranks of being were deadened, made burdensome, materialized by the fall of the all-man and by the strife and enmity engendered by that fall. The obligatory 'materiality' of being is born of man himself. It is the result of man's loss of his hierarchic position in the universe, his inward estrangement from the lower orders of the cosmic hierarchy, the result of dualizing being. . . . People who are near to us in spirit are the least obligatory for us, and we feel them to be the most alive of all things because they are nearest to us, dear to us, joined with us. Love burns up all necessity and gives freedom. *Love is the content of freedom—love is the freedom of the new Adam, the freedom of the eighth day of creation.* The world is bewitched by evil and can be released from the spell only by love. The world's necessity is enchantment; the world's material 'obligatoriness' is letting evil take the lead; it is an illusory being, born of dissension. The inert, heavy and oppresive material of the world can be released from bewitchment, can be unfettered, made alive, only by the power of the unifying love which the Absolute man, the new Adam, brings with him into the world. Love is creativeness.

God expects from man the highest freedom, the freedom of the eighth day of creation. This, God's expectation, lays on man a great responsibility. *The final, ultimate freedom, the daring of freedom and the burden of freedom, is the virtue of religious maturity.* To arrive at religious maturity means to know final freedom. The immaturity of Christian consciousness has hitherto made impossible a knowledge of man's ultimate freedom. Christianity has always been a training, a guardianship of the immature. And hence Christianity has not yet revealed itself in fullness, as an experience of freedom. The religion of freedom is a religion of apocalyptic times. Only the final time will know the final freedom. Christianity, . . . as a religion of the fear of temptation for the immature, is being deformed and is becoming torpid. But only a religion of freedom, a religion of daring and not of fear, can answer to man's present age, to the times and seasons of today. We can no longer refuse the time of freedom: Christian men are now too old, not only ripe but over-ripe for that. At the end of the Christian path there dawns the consciousness that God expects from man such a revelation of freedom as will contain even what God Himself has not foreseen. God justifies the mystery of freedom, having by His might and power set a limit to His own foreseeing. . . . Freedom is not a right: it is an obligation. Freedom is a religious virtue. He who is not free, the slave, cannot enter the kingdom of God: he is not a son of God; he is subject to lower spheres. There is a freedom which corresponds to the world's creative epoch. Before that there was only a freedom of the law and the redemption. *M.C.A.*, pp.150-1, 158-9

Uncreated Freedom

Revelation has somehow become crossed with theological interpretation which always includes one or another philosophy, even if subconsciously. The problems of the origin of evil, of freedom, etc., having their source in spiritual experience, belong in their intellectual solutions to the sphere of religious philosophy. Here also belongs what I have to say about uncreated freedom. That freedom by means of which men have tried to explain the Fall and the origin of evil, is always freedom not only for good but for evil as well. Freedom cannot be understood as the choice between good and evil, since the very distinction between the two is a result of the Fall. Pristine freedom and the origin of evil are ultimate mysteries and in the sphere of thought and knowledge we have to do with what in philosophic terminology is called ultimate concepts. But such is the dialectic of these problems. If God endows man with freedom, He knows that this is freedom, not only for good but for evil also. It remains incomprehensible why freedom for good should be ascribed to God and freedom for evil exclusively to man. We are faced with the impenetrable mystery of the origin of evil, if it is given by God. . . . This is an ultimate mystery which theology has tried to rationalize. It is impossible to ascribe to God his foreseeing of that evil which has its source outside being and outside the world He has created. . . . You cannot think about this, you can speak of it only mythologically, only in symbols. The Fall, also, cannot be understood rationally: it is a myth, which does not at all mean the opposite of reality. The creation of the world may be interpreted as a struggle against non-being, which meets resistance in the dark element of non-being. Freedom for good and evil, proceeding from non-being, are unconquerable in the original act of the world's creation by God the Father, but it is conquerable by God the Son, descending to the depths of non-being, conquerable not by force, but by sacrifice and love. *Put*, No. 48, July-Sept. 1935

Freedom is Primal

The philosophy of freedom begins with a free act before which there is not, nor can there be, existence, being. If we were to begin with being as the basis, and recognize this primacy of being over freedom, then everything, including freedom, is determined by being. But a determined freedom is not freedom at all. Another type of philosophy, however, is possible, which asserts the primacy of freedom, of the creative act, over being. And only this second type is favourable to freedom. But rational definition of freedom is impossible. Bergson also recognized this. Of the two types of metaphysics, the intellectual and the voluntary, the former is always unfavourable, and the latter favourable, to freedom. But voluntary metaphysics, taken by itself, is not yet a philosophy of freedom. What we must decisively affirm is this, that freedom is spirit, and not being. What has been known as essence or substance is a product of the original existential act. Greek intellectual thinking was unfavourable to freedom. Good was determined by reason. The primacy and reign of reason do not recognize freedom.

Spirit and Caesar, p. 109

CREATIVITY

God created such an astoundingly exalted image of himself, that in God's very creation there is justified the limitless audacity of man's creative act, of man's creative freedom. *M.C.A.*, p. 138

Creativity is not in the New Testament

There is not one word in the Gospel about creativeness: by no amount of sophism can we derive from the Gospel creative challenges and imperatives. The Good News of redemption from sin and of salvation from evil could not reveal the mystery of creativeness and show the way to creativity. The Gospel aspect of Christ, as God sacrificing Himself for the sins of the world, does not go so far as to reveal the creative mystery of man.... The revelation about creativeness cannot be directly derived from the revelation about redemption. Man's creative activity has no holy scriptures: its ways are not revealed to man from above. In the holy scriptures which reveal to man the will of God, man always finds absolute truth, but it is another kind of truth and about something other. In creativeness, man is, as it were, left to himself, alone, and has no direct aid from on high. And in this fact the great wisdom of God is evident.

A justification of creativity through distortion of the Gospels is not revealed to us, but something else is, instead. We feel the *holy authority of the Gospel's silence about creativeness.* This absolute silence of Holy Scripture about man's creative activity is divinely wise. And to discern the all-wise meaning of this silence is to discern the mystery of man; it is an act of man's highest self-consciousness. . . . The man who still lives wholly in the religious epoch of the law and the redemption is not conscious of his creative nature; he wishes to create according to the law and for redemption, seeks creativity as obedience. *If the ways of creativeness were indicated and justified in the Holy Scriptures, then creativeness would be obedience, which is to say that there would be no creativeness.*... The fact that the mystery and the ways of creativeness are not revealed in Holy Scripture is an evidence of the all-wise esoteric of Christianity. By its very nature the secret of creativeness is esoteric, it is not open for all to see but rather concealed. Only the law and the redemption can be revealed from on high. Creativeness is something mysterious and hidden. The revelation of creativeness does not come from above but rather from below—it is an anthropological, not a theological, revelation. God revealed His will to sinful man in the law and granted man the grace of redemption, sending into the world His Only Son. *And God awaits from man an anthropological revelation of creativity; in the name of man's god-like freedom, God has hidden from him the ways of creativeness and the justification of creativeness.*

M.C.A., pp. 96-9

The Mark of God-Manhood

The Creator's idea of man is sublime and beautiful. So sublime and so beautiful is the divine idea of man that creative freedom, the free power to reveal himself in creative action, is placed within man as a seal and sign of his likeness to God, as a mark of the Creator's image. *The compulsory revelation of creativeness as a law, as an indication of the way to go, would contradict God's idea of man, God's desire to see in man the creator, reflecting His own divine nature.* . . . Christ would not have been God-man if human nature is merely passive, unfree, and reveals nothing from within itself. For truly the God-man is a revelation not only of divine but of human greatness, and predicates faith not only in God but in man as well. In the spirit of man, all the mystical events of the life of Christ are accomplished. Man's likeness to God in His Only Son is already the everlasting basis for man's independent and free nature, capable of creative revelation. . . . Herein lies hidden the great mystery of man. And there can be no divine revelation of this secret; it is inevitably hidden. The creative secret is both hidden from man and revealed by man. This is an esoteric mystery of divine revelation and of Holy Scripture. God the Creator, by an act of His almighty and omniscient will, created man—His own image and likeness, a being free and gifted with creative power, called to be lord of creation. This is an inner process in God. By an act of His almighty and omniscient power the Creator willed to limit His own foresight of what the creative freedom of man would reveal since such foreknowledge would have done violence to and limited man's freedom in creation. The Creator does not wish to know what the anthropological revelation will be. Herein we see the great and sublime wisdom of God in the work of creation. God wisely concealed from man His will that man should be called to be a free and daring creator and concealed from Himself what man would create in his free courageous action. . . . *The world has not yet seen a religious epoch of creativeness.* The world knows only the religious epochs of the Old Testament law and New Testament redemption. The world has lived in either religious obedience or sinful disobedience. And in the world one cannot create by obedience alone. Whatever has been called creativeness, no matter how great or valuable it was, was only a hint at true creativeness, only a sign, a preparatory stage. Man's whole history has been accompanied by creative impulses but his creative nature was rendered powerless by cosmic fall, by its being plunged into the lower spheres of being. *M.C.A.*, pp. 99-101

Creativity and Gnosseology

The creative act does not come under the jurisdiction of gnosseology, with its endless reflection. The creative act exists immediately in being: it is the self-revelation of the powers of being. The creative act justifies but is not itself justified; it is based upon itself and requires no foundation upon something outside itself. Man's consciousness of himself as a creative being is a primary, rather than a derived consciousness. And man should proceed from this consciousness of the creative act within himself: this is a revolutionary consciousness in man which cannot be arrived at by means of either logic or evolution. This, man's consciousness of himself as a creator, does not result from any doctrine about man: it precedes all science and all philosophy; it is before, rather than after, all gnosseology. Man's creative act is accomplished on a plane of being over which the competence of science does not extend and hence even gnosseological science has no bearing upon it. To justify or to deny man's consciousness of himself as a creator, by means of gnosseology, is neither possible nor desirable. Creativeness as a religious experience does not know any dualistic division into subject and object.

M.C.A., p. 113

Creativity is Theurgic

True creativeness is theurgy, God-activity, activity together with God. But it is important that we understand that the problem of theurgy is not a problem of Christian creativity, of Christian culture. In the strict sense of the word, there can be no Christian creativity, and Christian culture is impossible. *We face the problem of Christian being rather than Christian culture, the problem of transforming culture into being, science and art into a new heaven and a new earth.* There never was a truly Christian culture. Culture was created outside Christianity; its only deep connection with Christianity was in the fact that in culture obedience to the results of sin were so strongly evident and sin was redeemed by the tragic difference between the creative idea and its results. And in his culture, beginning with technics and economics and ending with the sciences and the arts, man, as it were, sought redemption from his sin, but his creativity was not theurgic. In the sweat of his brow man creates culture but cannot attain what is necessary for his creative nature. What man needs is a new heaven and a new earth, the transition of the creative act into another kind of being. This is the way of theurgic creativity.

M.C.A., pp. 126-7

Only he who is free, creates.

M.C.A., p.144

Creativity and Sanctity

The thought of the Church Fathers was concerned with the ways of saving souls, rather than the ways of creativity. The thought of the Church gave inner religious sanction to that condition of the human spirit known as sanctity, but did not give this sanction to the condition known as genius. Holiness is anthropological; it is a higher attainment of human nature, its illumination and deification. . . . But is the way of holiness the only religious way for man, the only religious attainment? Can it be said that all man's creativity which is not directly in the way of sanctity is permitted only because of the sinfulness of man's nature, but has not positive religious justification? This is a tormenting question within Christian consciousness, and the fact that it has not been answered tears human life apart and renders an important part of it unsanctified. The way of genius, the way of creative inspiration remains secular, worldly, not sacred, not sanctified. The religious meaning of genius, like the higher manifestation of man's creativity, remains unrevealed. For Christian consciousness what is the meaning of the existence, along with saints, those wrestlers of the spirit, with those who are saving their souls, of geniuses, poets, artists, philosophers, scholars, reformers, inventors, of people concerned primarily with creativity? One cannot brush aside this question by saying that Christianity does not deny science, philosophy, art, social life, etc. This question is immeasurably more profound: it touches the very depths of the metaphysics of Christianity, its dogmatic consciousness. Is creative inspiration a positive spiritual experience, the manifestation of man's positive calling? Does God await creativity, creative audacity, from man? Creativity cannot be merely tolerated, cannot be constantly excusing itself; it must be positively justified, religiously. Creativity is religiously justified and given meaning, if in his creative inspiration, his creative upsurge, man is answering God's Challenge. God's demand that man participate in God's creativity.

Destiny, pp. 60-3

Creativity is the supreme mystery of life, the mystery of the appearance of something new, hitherto unknown, derived from nothing, proceeding from nothing, born of nothing other. . . .

Freedom, determined by nothing else, gives the answer to God's call to creative activity, but it gives this answer together with the gift, the genius received from God at the time of creation, and with the materials which exist in the created world. Man's creation of something from nothing must be understood as his creativity out of freedom. In every creative intention there is an element of man's primary freedom, undetermined by anything other, bottomless, freedom which does not proceed out of God, but which proceeds to Him. The call of God is addressed to this abyss and out of it the answer is awaited. This abyss of freedom is in all creativity, but creative construction is so complex that it is not easy to detect this primary element in it. The creative act is also the interaction of grace and freedom, going out from God to man and from man to God. And the creative act may be described chiefly, now in terms of freedom, now in terms of grace, the grace of possession and inspiration. But inspiration is impossible without freedom. . . .

Every creator must be free: he cannot stand compulsion. *Spirit and Caesar*, p. 96

Creativity, not Development, is True Life

True life is creativity, not development: it is the freedom for creative acts, for creative fire, rather than necessity and the heaviness of congealing self-perfection. And this truth has special significance in moral life. Moral living should be constant creativity, free and ardent: the eternal youth and virginity of the spirit. It should rest upon primary intuitions, in which man is free from life's confinement and stratification, things which paralyse the freedom of his moral judgments. But in actuality it is difficult to break through to this youthfulness of the spirit. And a great part of moral judgments and acts do not derive from this primary source. And the ethic of creativity is not an ethic of development; rather, it is an ethic of the youthfulness and virginity of spirit, an ethic whose source is the ardent first source of life, the element of freedom....

Creativity Means Increase

The Gospels constantly speak of fruit which seed falling on good ground should produce, of talents entrusted to a man which should be returned with interest. Here Christ in parables is speaking of man's creativity, his creative calling. Christ condemned the burying of a talent in the earth, i.e. the lack of creativeness. The whole of St Paul's teaching about various gifts is teaching about man's creative calling. Gifts are from God, and they indicate a call to creativity. And these gifts are various: each man is called to creative service according to his special gift. Hence it cannot be said, as is so often the case, that nothing about creativity is said in the Scriptures, in the Gospels. There is word of creativity, but we must know how to read, we must divine what God wishes and expects from man. Creativity is always increase, supplement, the production of something new in the world. . . .

All Creativity is Individual

The ethic of creativity is distinct from the ethic of the law and the norms in the fact that a moral problem is individual and unrepeatable. The problems of life cannot be solved by the automatic application of universally-valid norms. We cannot say that under the same conditions one must act in one certain way, everywhere and always. This cannot be said, first of all, because conditions are never exactly the same. We might state the maxim conversely: man must act individually and solve the moral problems of life individually, must manifest his creativity in the moral acts of his life, never for a moment becoming a moral automaton. Facing the problems life presents to him, man must be an inventor and a discoverer in the field of morals. . . .

Destiny, pp. 135-8, 140-1, 152-3

Creativity and Time

Ontologically, there is no such thing as the past, just as there is no such thing as the future. Our attitude toward time changes completely, depending on creativity. If in Heidegger's thought worry gives time to being, creativity can liberate being from the power of time. The products of creativity extend downward and are found to be assigned to some particular segment of time, past, present or future; but the creative act itself escapes time and liberates man's existence from it.

Solitude, p. 126

Creativity under God

You love poetry, but you do not understand that great creativity—yes all true creativity, is impossible in one's own name: one can create only in the name of God. Creativity has two contrasting parents: it is born of poverty and impairment, and of riches and a superfluity of power. When the natural man creates, not for God but for himself, he creates non-being. In genuine creativity, in the creative ecstasy, there is more resignation than in humility, more thought of God than of oneself. Creativity is always sacrificial. Creativity that does not pass by the way of sacrifice, is emptiness. *Letters to Mme K.*, p. 11

Materialism

The spiritual world cannot be the result of something which has nothing in common with spirit. This is a radical falsehood. The lower can never create something higher; material cannot create spirit; meaningless cannot give birth to meaning; the world cannot produce God. Spirit is the beginning, not the end. For this reason I am an aristocrat by conviction (not in the social, but in the spiritual sense of the word). I can never accept the idea that quantity creates quality, that darkness and evil can beget light and good. *Letters to Mme K.*, p. 6

Materialism Cannot Know 'Exploitation'

Like all communists, you talk of the exploitation and oppression of the worker. And it is true, exploitation exists. But you forget that in materialism and atheism the very concept of exploitation does not exist. If man is material, as communism teaches, then the power of the strong is both natural and lawful. In the struggle for existence, it is the better and stronger who come out victorious. Hence the 'kulaks' and exploiters are ruling by virtue of natural necessity and are therefore the best among men. *Letters to Mme K.*, p. 18

HUMANISM

Humanism is the reign of the middle-of-the-road. *Dostoevsky*, p. 60

Humanism's Deification of Man Degrades Him

Humanism does not know man as the image and likeness of God, since it does not wish to know God: it does not know man as a free spirit, because it is in the grasp of natural necessity. Hence humanism can deify only the natural man, only man as an empirical fact, as a drop in the sea of nature which has subjectively set itself up as a final purpose. If the patristic consciousness, while having a Christology, lacks a corresponding anthropology, humanistic consciousness has no Christology to correspond with its anthropology. . . . The *pathos* of all humanism lies in its affirmation of man as the highest and the final, as God, and in its denial of the superhuman. But once you have denied God and deified man, man falls to a level lower than the human, since man remains at the height of his dignity only as image and likeness of a higher divine being; he is true man only when he has sonship with God. Man cannot be only a father, the father of his children, of future human generations; he must also be a son, he must be a descendant—must have roots which go down into absolute being and eternity. Humanism denied man this sonship, renounced his descendence, renounced man's freedom and his guilt, renounced man's dignity. Humanism undertook to abolish everything difficult or problematic or tragic in man, in order to establish man better on the earth and make him happy. But man's well-being and happiness on the earth, if it turns away from the ineluctable tragedy of human life, is a denial of man as belonging to two worlds, as participating not only in the natural kingdom of necessity, but also in the supernatural kingdom of freedom. *M.C.A.*, pp. 86-9

EXISTENTIALISM

Existential Philosophy

Existential philosophy is the expression (expressionism) of my personal fate, but my fate must express the fate both of the world and of man. This is not moving over from the individual to the general, but the intuitive revelation of the universal in the individual. Philosophy, metaphysics, are not a reflection of objective realities, but a change within human existence, the discovery of the meaning of existence. Metaphysics is the *expression* of existence. The world looks different to different men, depending on whether a man is engaged in economic work, political struggle, intellectual or artistic creativity, or religious contemplation. And man really understands something, only when his thought is penetrated by his feeling and when his whole being comes into movement. But what is known as 'being' is determined, not by thought, or knowledge, or idea, but by the integral subject, i.e. by feeling and will and the whole direction of the spirit. By this each person creates a different world. Truth is created in the subject, and not given objectively from without. . . . We cannot come to existence, we can only proceed from it. Truth is an act of freedom, it is created. *Divine*, pp. 8-9

Existentialism

Existentialism may be variously defined, but the most important definition, it seems to me, is that it is a philosophy which does not accept objectivizing knowledge. Existence cannot be the object of knowledge. Objectivization means alienation, depersonalization, the loss of freedom, submission to the general, knowledge by means of concept. Almost the whole history of philosophical thought has stood under the sign of objectivization, although this was differently expressed in different types of philosophy. Empiricism also bore the mark of objectivization, just as did the most extreme form of rationalism. This objectivization we may also discover in the newer forms of pragmatism and that life-philosophy which always has a hint of the biological about it. And in so far as Heidegger and Sartre wish to construct an ontology using the rational apparatus of understanding, they are caught in the grip of objectivizing knowledge and have not broken with the tradition which comes down from Parmenides. . . . Kierkegaard recognized as existential only knowledge in the subjective, but not in the objective; in the individual, but not in the general. In this he was a pioneer. Jaspers has remained most faithful to Kierkegaard. Kierkegaard turned toward subjectivity in his effort to express his own unrepeatable, individual experience. His significance lies in this. But he never managed to get completely outside the differentiation between subject and object; he maintained this distinction, placing himself on the side of the subject. Another definition of existential philosophy is that it is an expressionist philosophy, that is, it wants to express the existentiality of the known, rather than abstraction from this existentiality, as objectivizing philosophy would do. In this sense we may discover, in all the great philosophers, an element of existentialism, behind the process of objectivization. Existence (Existenz) is not essence, not substance, but rather a free act. Existenz holds primacy over essence. In this sense existential philosophy is akin to every philosophy of act or of freedom. In reality, Kant's sphere of freedom is Existenz, although he himself failed to make this clear. The depth of Existenz is freedom. We find this both in Jaspers who allies himself with Kant, and also in Sartre who has little in common with Kant. What takes place in the existential sphere is outside causal relationship. Causal relationship exists only in the sphere of objectivization. Hence we cannot say, for example, that God is the cause of the world. Between God and man there cannot exist a causal relationship. God determines nothing. God is not a power 'outside of' or 'over' anything. Hence the traditional concept of the relation between freedom and grace in this form is out-of-date: it remains in the sphere of objectivization. Actually, everything lies in the existential sphere, in which there is no objectivity at all. We must plunge to the depths of subjectivity in order to escape the very antithesis between subject and object. Heidegger and Sartre remain in the sphere of an objectivized world, the world of things, and this is the source of their pessimism. With Heidegger 'Dasein' exists only as it is cast out into the world and there experiences 'Angst', worry, hopelessness, death, as the inevitable result of its finiteness. Even though Sartre recognizes the existence of freedom outside the world, this does not help. This is connected with the denial of the primal reality of spiritual experience. The only metaphysics which existential philosophy can recognize is the symbolism of spiritual experience. Jaspers has the same idea, but in another form, because he has no spiritual experience in the real sense of the word. *Truth*, pp. 3-5

EVOLUTION

Evolution is Objectivization

Bergson's expression 'creative evolution' must be considered a misunderstanding of terms. Evolutionism is completely in the power of determinism and of causal relationships. In evolution, as it is understood by naturalistic evolutionism, a real novelty cannot arise, since there is no creative act. And a creative act is always traceable back to freedom and it interrupts the chain of causal relationship. The evolutionary theory is applicable only to the results of creative acts, but it does not accept the idea of an active subject of development. Evolution is objectivization.

Beginning, p. 142

Evolution is a Shallow Thing

We have to have a dual attitude toward the change which is always going on in the world. Life is change, and there is no life without novelty. But change may be betrayal (a play on words, DAL). The realization of human personality presupposes change and novelty, but it also presupposes changelessness, without which there can be no personality. In the development of his personality, man must be true to himself, must not betray himself, must maintain his own visage, which is predestined for eternity. In life it is necessary to combine change and novelty with fidelity.

I have already said that recognition of the basic fact of development in life does not require an evolutionary theory in the style of Darwin, Spencer or Haeckel. That kind of evolutionism is out of date, both scientifically and philosophically. Nineteenth-century evolutionism was a form of naturalistic determinism, and never was able to explain the source of evolution. It would talk of the results of evolution, of the forms of change, but not of its sources or causes. For nineteenth-century evolutionism, the subject of development, the inward factor of development, does not exist. In actuality, evolutionism is a conservative theory and denies creativity in the world; it recognizes only the rearrangement of already-existing parts of the world. . . . Evolution is only the expression, on one plane, the horizontal, of creative acts which are accomplished on the vertical line and in the depths. *Divine*, pp. 68-9

PROGRESS

Progress is movement from what is, to what should be. *Sub Specie*, p. 27

Progress or Development?

We quite justly criticize the theory of progress, seeing in it a false religion that is a substitute for Christianity. But we should remember that the idea of progress is of religious, even Christian origin, that it is only a secularization and distortion of the Christian messianic idea, of the Christian search for and expectation of the Kingdom of God. The idea of progress is a theological and religious idea, presupposing an absolute purpose and meaning for universal history. Put on the basis of positivism, this idea actually loses all meaning and becomes contradictory. In positivism, one can speak only of evolution, devoid of purpose and meaning. But progress predicates spirit values that are above it and determine its meaning. This is a truth long established and elemental. But it is not sufficiently taken into account that the very idea of progress, i.e. movement toward an absolute, supreme purpose of the historical process, became possible only thanks to Christianity, that it never could have arisen on the ground of the Hellenic mind. History moves toward its central and absolute event, the coming of Christ, and thence it moves from Christ to the final, completing event of universal history, the Second Coming. This determines the existence of epochs in universal history, of spiritual progress in history. This causes the inward, spiritual dynamic of history. The world's history is not an external evolution, devoid of meaning, the rearrangement of elements in the world, where no absolute meanings or values are revealed: there is a dynamic of meaning in the world's history, the Logos, determining inner movement. Christianity is messianic and eschatological, i.e. dynamic, progressive, in the profound spiritual sense of that word. . . .

Even the Church of Christ is the product of development: it developed from the original eschatological idea of the Kingdom of God. In the development and disclosure of Christianity there have been stages and periods. . . . The absolute truth of Christianity is not in the least disturbed by this fact. And there is no reason to deny that there may be further development and revelation of Christianity in the world. Enormous potential riches are inherent in the Christian revelation and they may become actual in the world, may be revealed in history. Every word in the Gospels is only a seed, only the start of an endless process of development. If Christianity in the past was dynamic in the highest degree, then it may be just as dynamic in the future. Cessation of the dynamic of development, is merely a sign of spiritual enfeeblement, ossification. There may and there should be, dogmatic development in the Church. Cardinal Newman and Vladimir Solovieff insisted on this convincingly. Not all problems have been solved. Christianity has not been completed, and it will not be, until the end of time: this will be the coming of the Kingdom of God. But when we seek the Kingdom of God, move toward it, we are in a state of development and we can not be static. . . .

Creative development, creative movement in the world, is not only possible, but inevitable, because man bears in himself the image of the Creator, of His freedom and creative power. There occurs the creative revelation of what is potentially inherent in the depth of freedom, of spirit. This is development of quite another order than that taught by Darwin, Spencer and Haeckel, this is not naturalistic evolution, but development or disclosure out of spirit. . . .

A Christian renaissance can be linked with a feeling of creative youth, not conservative age. It is difficult to frighten the modern mind into anything: it has passed through the ultimate temptations of the deification of man, through the religion of humanism, marxism, Nietzscheanism, socialism and anarchism, through estheticism and occultism. For the modern mind, to come to God, to Christ, is not conservation, but spiritual revolution. The soul comes to God, to Christ, out of the depths—out of bottomless freedom. This movement of the modern spirit was shown us by the genius of Dostoevsky. . . . We cannot stop spiritual development: we must pass through it.

Freedom, II, pp. 158-83

Progress versus Evolution

We must note the distinction between evolution and progress. Evolution is a naturalistic category, while progress is a spiritual category: it predicates evaluation from the viewpoint of a principle higher than the natural process of change. The idea of progress is of Christian origin: it was born in the Christian messianic expectation, in awaiting the Kingdom of God as the culmination of history. The idea of progress has eschatological content. But in the thought of the nineteenth century the idea of progress became secularized and naturalized: it became subject to tattered time. In the world of objectivization progress makes the present a means to the future, the present generation a means to the next: it carries death as well as life. In the world of nature and of history, birth is pregnant with death. The eschatological idea of the resurrection of the dead and the transfiguration of the whole world and all humanity is quite foreign to progress, subject as it is to the objective, definitive world. Therefore it has been considered possible to speak of the law of progress, of the necessity of progress. Actually, there is no such law. Progress presupposes creative freedom. In this world there is no such thing as progress along a direct rising curve. There is progress only as regards parts or groups of phenomena, but not as regards the whole. . . .

Beginning, p. 146

Progress is not a Straight Line

You confess the most banal rationalistic theory of progress—the idea that man can completely rationalize his life, and subject it to reason. This is the rationalism proclaimed by the French philosophy of enlightenment of the eighteenth century, deepened by Hegel and inherited by Marx, which has become superficially stupid in his followers. I do not love optimism: I consider it a mockery of unbearable human suffering. Even the blessedness of the future, if it is attainable, cannot redeem the suffering and injustice of the past. The question of progress is very complex. I do not deny progress, but it is not a straight, ascending line. Good increases, but so does new evil. Just now there is an enormous regress in moral consciousness, in regard to mankind, to murder, capital punishment, cruelty. The consciousness of the eighteenth and nineteenth centuries was higher. I trust that you are not excluding Soviet Russia from your list of 'totalitarian' states. This is the worst form of a totalitarian state, altogether fascist. This is a military, police, bureaucratic state, dogmatically supporting itself on the masses.

When you say there are various 'goods' and 'evils' and that everyone has his own 'God' you are reproducing the usual argument of sceptics against any sort of faith. There is only one reply to this: leave the world of scepticism, where everything is doubted, divided into two, and enter that world where there is one God, where 'good' and 'evil' are realities of being, rather than human thoughts and feelings.

Letters to Mme K., pp. 30-1

TRUTH

Truth . . . is the creative transfiguration of reality. *Truth*, p. 4

There is nothing higher than the search for, and the love of, Truth.

Spirit and Caesar, p. 29

Truth is Meaning

Truth is revealed only by the creative activity of the spirit; outside this, truth is incomprehensible and unattainable. The absolute reply of the Gospel: 'I am the Truth' has also absolute philosophical and gnosseological meaning. The Absolute Man is Truth. Truth is not that which is, that which is forced upon us as a given condition, as necessity. Truth is not the duplication, the repetition of being in the knower. *Truth is comprehension and liberation of being, it presupposes the creative act of the knower within being; Truth is meaning and may not deny meaning. To deny meaning in the world means to deny truth, to recognize nothing but darkness. Truth makes us free. To deny freedom is to deny truth.*

M.C.A., p. 43

Truth, the one integral truth, is God, and to perceive Truth, is to enter divine life.

Spirit and Caesar, p. 29

Knowing Truth

It must be said, first of all, that truth is not the conformity, in the knower, of reality objectively given. No one has ever explained how the reality of being may become the ideality of perception. When I say 'this is a table', this is a sort of partial truth, but there is neither correspondence nor equivalence between that table and my statement that it is a table. This modest knowledge of 'table' has pragmatic significance, first of all. There are degrees of perception of the truth, depending on the degree of community among people, and what they have in common with the world as a whole. But on the other hand, truth is not the agreement of reason with itself and its own universally valid laws. *The* truth, on which all partial truths must be made dependent, is not abstractly reasonable, but spiritual. But spirit lies beyond a rationalized opposition between subject and object. Truth does not mean staying within some closed ideas, in an inescapable circle of consciousness: truth is an unlocking—a revealing. Truth is not objective, but rather trans-subjective. . . .

The knowledge of truth is not a developing of rational concepts, but first of all an evaluation. Truth is the light of the Logos, lighted within being itself, if we use the traditional terminology, or in the depths of existence, or of life itself. This one complete Truth is divided into a multitude of truths. A sphere of knowledge lighted by one ray of light (such as a given science) may deny the source of light, the Logos-Sun. But it could never be lighted save for this one source of light. . . .

Spirit and Caesar, pp. 17-20

Truth is Disclosed, not Proven

Whence came this firm conviction that the truth is that which is most completely proven? Who knows but that proof is an obstacle of necessity encountered in the way of knowing the truth? Creative philosophy must free itself from the tempting power of proof, must fulfil the act of renouncing this safe adaptation to necessity. In science that which is most completely proved is the most completely adapted to the world's necessity, for better orientation in it. Hence the force of demonstration in the logic of the sciences. In philosophy, the most true, the most creative, that which bursts out through necessity to freedom, out of meaninglessness to meaning, may be the least provable. There is no logic of proof in philosophy. . . . In philosophy, what had been proved would not be creative knowledge: it would only be adaptation. In philosophic knowledge it is the creative intuition which is convincing, not the demonstrable evidence of discursive thought. In philosophy truth is shown and formulated, not proven nor grounded in reason. . . . Demonstration lies always in the middle, neither at the beginning nor at the end, and hence there can be no proof of initial or final truths. In essence, demonstration never proves any truth, since it presupposes the acceptance of certain truths by intuition. In the middle you may prove any sort of lie. Proof is only the technique of the logical apparatus and has no relation to truth. . . . Proof is necessary only for those who love differences, who have differing intuitions. You offer proof only to the enemies of your beloved truth, not to its friends. *M.C.A.*, pp. 48-9

Of Falsehood and Truth

Up to the present, ethics has given insufficient attention to the monstrous and colossal rôle played by falsehood, in moral and spiritual life. And we are speaking, here, not of that falsehood which is considered a manifestation of evil, but that which is affirmed in the interest of good. Man will not believe that good may be affirmed and maintained without the help of evil. Good is the end, while falsehood is a means. . . . The whole life of mankind, and perhaps especially the life of that portion of mankind known as Christian, is permeated with falsehood. Falsehood has attained almost dogmatic significance. I am speaking here not of the external mendacity which catches the eye and is easy to pass judgment on. I am speaking of that inward, secret tendency to lying, to oneself and to God, which eludes man's attention and in men's minds takes on the quality of good. There is such a thing as falsehood which is considered a moral and religious duty. And the man who denies this falsehood is considered a trouble-maker. We have a social accumulation of lies which have been made into social norms. This is linked with the very most fundamental bases of moral apprehension and moral judgment, with the absence of what I would call the primogeniture of moral acts. This conventional, almost socially organized falsehood accumulates in the family, in the social order, in the party, in ideological tendencies, in the various religious confessions, in nationality, in the state—in all social groupings. And this conventional falsehood is a means of self-protection for these groups: because the truth might lead to their dissolution. The conventional falsehood of socially-organized groups (and here I include ideological tendencies and schools) deprives a man of freedom of moral apprehension and moral judgment. Moral judgment is effected not by the person standing in freedom before God, but by the family, the class, the party, the nationality, the confession, etc. . . . Our conscience is clogged and roiled not only because of original sin, but also because we belong to various social formations which, for their own self-protection, consider falsehood more useful than truth. How much conventional falsehood piles up in the life of a family! And this is considered the basis of their existence and self-maintenance. How much true feeling is concealed, how much false feeling is expressed, how conventionally false are the relations between parents and children, between men and their wives! Pretence takes on the quality of a family virtue. How much we accumulate in our subconscious, which is never consciously expressed, or expressed in some quite unconscious form! . . .

Scholars have a superstitious fear of science and are all too often its slaves rather than its masters. Their freedom of judgment is obstructed and muddied. There is a conditioned social opinion of scientism, very tyrannical, which throttles judgment and deprives it of freedom. The conventional falsehood in the judgments of representatives of one nationality about representatives of another are all too well known. The same is true of representatives of different social classes: here through the centuries falsehood has accumulated, which in the class or national consciousness becomes normal and is considered good. . . . Men have even dared to transform the Christian revelation into conventional rhetoric, and this has given rise to doubt of its truthfulness. So-called 'public opinion' is based on conventional lies, and employs falsehood as a means of influence. Every social mode is a conventional lie. Falsehood is recognized as useful to support and organize human living together, and fulfils a social function. Herein is the tragedy of the problem of falsehood: pragmatically, falsehood justifies itself; while truth and right often appear dangerous and harmful. The very noblest ideas may take on the nature of conventional falsehood. There is a conventionally-false rhetoric of love, of justice, of science: there is a conventionally rhetorical attitude toward even the idea of God. And so, from the depths of human nature a protest rises against conventional lies and rhetoric, against false idealization in the name of pure truth, for the sake of reality. And there is awakening a thirst for ontological truthfulness and reality, a break-through toward what I would call *original and virginal conscience*. Sometimes this takes the form of a return to nature from the falsehood of civilization, but in reality this is a return to God. Only a pure, original and free conscience can stand before God: only its judgments are original. The desire for originality is not the wish to be different, not to resemble anyone else, but only the desire to draw one's judgment from the fountain head. *Destiny*, pp. 172-5

Truth May Be Dangerous

The view of pragmatism, that truth is what is useful for life, is quite erroneous. Truth may be dangerous to everyday life. Christian truth might even become very dangerous—might cause the collapse of nations and civilizations. Hence pure Christian truth has been distorted and adapted to man's everyday life; the work of Christ has been corrected, as Dostoevsky's Grand Inquisitor says. But if we believe in the power of Truth unto salvation, this is in quite another sense. It is in relation to Truth that division is made between what is God's and what is Caesar's, between spirit and the world. *Spirit and Caesar*, p. 21

Truth is not an Objective Reality

'I am the way, the truth and the life'—what does this mean? This means that truth is not exclusively of an intellectual or perceptional nature, that it must be comprehended integrally: it is existential. This also means that truth is not given to man ready made, as a thing, an objective reality, but that man acquires it by his way and his life. Truth predicates movement, movement toward infinity. Truth can not be understood dogmatically, as in a catechism. Truth is dynamic rather than static. Truth is fullness which is not given in completed form. . . .

The reason why Jesus did not reply to Pilate's question, 'What is truth?' is related to this. He was Truth, but Truth which is to be divined and discovered through the whole course of history. Truth is surely not knowledge which conforms to some reality which is outside man. The knowledge of truth is not identical with objectivity. The knowledge of truth is not objectivization, i.e. alienation and loss of warmth. Truth is primary, rather than secondary, i.e. it is not conformity with something else. In the final depth Truth is God and God is Truth. . . . Truth is not reality, neither is it conformity with reality, its *logos;* it is the supreme quality and value of reality. . . . Truth may pass judgment on God, but only because Truth is God in purity and majesty, as distinct from a God who has been reduced and deformed by human concepts. Truth is not something given objectively, but rather a creative achievement. It is creative discovery, rather than the reflected knowledge of an object or of being. Truth . . . is the creative transfiguration of reality. The intellectual world, the world of purely intellectual knowledge, is in reality an abstract, to a significant degree a fictive world. Truth is the alteration, the transfiguration, of given reality. *Truth*, pp. 13-14

> Truth is given, not for deposit in some safe place, but for realization in the fullness of life, and for development.
>
> *Put*, No. 49, p. 81

> Pure truth could burst the world apart.
>
> *Reality*, p. 57

Truth is spiritual, and it is not at all useful for the objectified world, for objectified society; it is harmful. Truth can burst the world apart. The pure truth of the Christian revelation, proceeding as it does, not from the object-world, might lead to the end of the world. But this truth was objectivized and socialized, adapted to make it good for common social usage, and only because of this, historic Christianity became possible. But original and authentic Christianity, based upon truth which had been neither objectivized nor socialized, would be a personalistic revolution in the world. Even in the Gospels the purity of the revelation of the spirit is clouded by the human social milieu, by human language, human limitations. The spirit can never express itself fully in its historic products: it is symbolized more than it can be fully realized. . . . The truly holy is only in spirit: it is not to be found in nature, nor in history, nor in society, even in the society known as the Church.

Reality, pp. 51-2

> I have always thought . . . that truth serves
> no one and nothing: we must serve truth.
>
> *Slavery*, p. 14

Truth is not Socially Useful

The objectivization of truth in the Church led to a false sacralization and to the mistaken recognition of certain things as holy. This objectivization, under the influence of large numbers, organized great masses of humanity and undertook to organize and strengthen both society and the state on spiritual bases. The objectivization of spirit in the life of societies and of states is caught in the useful error of thinking that society or the state or civilization may have Truth as their bulwark, that Truth can be useful in the business of human organization. This has been the pragmatic conception of Truth, which believed that Truth and usefulness are coincident. But this is an illusion arising from objectivization, from the adaptation of Spirit to the fallen state of the world. . . . Truth is spiritually revolutionary; so is spirit, although in a different way from that in which revolution is applied to politics. And objectivization weakens or even completely destroys this destructive, anarchic quality of truth, which is spirit, since spirit is the truth of being. Therefore the work of Christ was corrected and adapted to the level of millions upon millions of men. (Dostoevsky's 'Grand Inquisitor'.) And the fate of the world and of man is tragic as the result of this radical dualism of truth and utility, of the subjective, personal spirit and the objective, general spirit, the dualism of existence and objectivization. Truth is given only in the subjective spirit, and it is existential. *Reality*, pp. 56-7

The Philosophical Search for Truth

The aim of philosophical knowledge is not in the knowledge of being, of the reflection of actuality in the known, but in knowledge of the truth, in the discovery of meaning, in giving reasoned meaning to actuality. Hence philosophic knowledge is not passive reflection, but active upsurge, a victory in the struggle with the meaninglessness of the actual world. I wish to know, not actuality, but the truth about actuality. And I may learn what this truth is, only because in me, the knowing subject, there is a source of truth and because I may communicate with this truth. That I am sitting at a desk and writing with a pen on paper, is not truth—this is sensual perception and the affirmation of fact. The question of truth is put by my writing. In the object there is no grain of truth: truth is only in the subject. Truth is related not to the world of phenomena, but to the noumenal, ideal world. Truth is relationship, but this is not at all the relationship between subject and object, it is not the reflection of object in subject. We cannot understand truth in the spirit of gnosseological realism, or in any case if this is realism, it is of a quite different sort. Truth has two meanings: there is truth as knowledge of reality, and truth as reality itself. Truth is not only idea, value, but that which exists, the existent. 'I am the Truth.' Truth is not the thing which exists, but the meaning, the Logos of what exists. . . . Truth is a creative act of spirit in which meaning is born. Truth is something higher than the actuality which holds us in compulsion, higher than the real world, but God is higher than truth; better, God is truth. . . . Truth is spiritual, it is in the spirit and is the spirit's conquest over the spiritless objectivity of the world, the world of things. Spirit is not an epiphenomenon of something else: everything is an epiphenomenon of spirit. Truth is the awakening of spirit in man, his communion with spirit. . . . Is it Truth with a capital letter, or with a small letter? This demands explanation. All the small particles of truth receive their light from the great integral Truth—all rays of light proceed from the sun. . . . *Beginning*, p. 48

Where shall we seek criteria of truth? All too often men seek these criteria in what is lower than truth, in the objective world with its compulsions, seek criteria for spirit in the material world. And they fall into a vicious circle. Discursive thought can provide no criteria for final truth: it is only at the half-way mark, and knows neither the beginning nor the end. Every proof rests upon the unproven, the postulate, the created. There is risk, and no guarantee. The very search for guarantee is wrong and really means subjecting the higher to the lower. Freedom of the spirit knows no guarantees. The sole criterion of truth is truth itself, the light which streams out from it. All other criteria exist only for the every-day, objective world, for social communication. I never prove truth to myself. I am only obliged to prove it to others, I recognize that I live in two worlds—in the primary existential world where communion with Truth is possible, and in a secondary objectivized world where Truth is demonstrated, where it is fractioned into a multitude of truths, because of adaptation to the world's fallen state. *Beginning*, p. 49-50

Truth is not so much liberation and salvation in this world, as it is liberation and salvation from this world. Full acceptance of the truth of the Gospel, consent to its actual realization, would lead to the destruction of states, civilizations, societies organized according to the laws of this world—to the end of this world which in every way is opposite to Gospel Truth: therefore men and nations have corrected the Gospel, filled it with 'truths' of this world which were really pragmatic, because they were false and adapted to falsehood. The recognition and the confession of the Truth is connected, not with usefulness and profit, but with risk and danger. . . . *Beginning*, p. 50-1

Supreme Truth is eschatological, and by this it eases the falsehood of pragmatism, the lie of an optimistic cult of life. Truth is not of the world, but of the spirit: it is known only in transcending the objective world. Truth is the end of this objective world, it demands our consent to this end. Such is the Truth of Christianity, freed of its social adaptations and deformations. . . .

Knowledge seeks Truth and truths; it strives for purification of everything which shadows or distorts the process of knowing, for the self-purification of the subject. But the knower may know the world's falsehood, how the world is roiled and soiled; knowledge may be a revelation of the truth about falsehood. And the proclamation of the Truth is the end of the world of lies. In every genuine act of knowing, the end of the world is begun. . . .

There will be a new day, in which truth will be revealed to all men, all will pass through this shattering experience not only the living, but even more so the dead. But in this our eon, in this objectivized object-world, general philosophy or common sense reveal, not truth, but a socialization of truth necessary and useful for the life of society. . . . The objectivized world which is quite uncritically considered the 'objective' world is conditioned transcendentally and socially. It is an error to think that truth is revealed to social consciousness. Truth is revealed to spiritual consciousness, bordering on the super-conscious. The spirit is freedom, creative uplift, personality, love. *Beginning*, p. 72

Truth: Absolute or Conditional?

We live in a time when men neither love nor seek the truth. In ever greater measure, truth is being replaced by the will to power, by what is useful or valuable to special interests. This lack of love for the truth appears not only in nihilistic or sceptic attitudes toward it, but in substituting for it some sort of faith or dogmatic doctrine in whose name falsehood is permitted, falsehood which is considered not evil, but good. . . . Falsehood is affirmed as some holy duty for the sake of higher purposes. Evil is justified in the name of good. . . . The views of truth held by the empiricists and the positivists were vague and contradictory, but in reality even they recognized its undoubtability, as well as did the opposing philosophic tendencies, for which truth was absolute. Doubt of the old concept of truth began with pragmatic philosophy, but in a form neither radical nor permanent. . . . The dialectic lie, widely practised by Marxists, is justified by dialectic materialism, which, in flat contradiction to its philosophical bases, is finally hailed as truth absolute. And to this truth revealed by Marxism we find a dogmatic attitude resembling that of the Catholic Church to its dogmas. But

Marxist philosophy, which is a philosophy of the practical, considers truth as a weapon for the struggle of the revolutionary proletariat, for whom truth is something different than for the bourgeois classes, even when they are dealing with the truths of natural science.

Spirit and Caesar, pp. 13-14

Truth Develops

The dogmatic affirmation of immovable, completed Truth is a supreme error. This we find in the dogmatics of both catholicism and marxism. Nietzsche refused to accept a so-called 'objective' Truth, Truth universally valid just because of its objectivity. Truth is subjective; it is individual, and universal in its individuality. . . . The universal validity of Truth concerns only its socialized phase, the communication of Truth to others. Truth is quality, and therefore it is aristocratic as is every quality. It is quite wrong to say that only that which is obligatory is Truth. Truth may be revealed to one person only and be refused by the rest of the world: it may be prophetic, and a prophet is always lonely.

At the same time, Truth does not exist specially for a cultured élite: this is just as false as the democratic debasement of the quality of Truth. All men are called to communion with Truth: it exists for the whole world. But it is revealed only under certain spiritual, intellectual and cultural conditions. When Truth as it is being revealed is socialized and applied to the average man, to the human mass, its quality is lowered, its depth disappears for the sake of accessibility to all men. This has always happened in the historic churches. This is what I call sociomorphism in regard to God. The Truth about Spirit and spirituality presupposes a certain spiritual condition, a certain level of spirituality. Without this condition, Truth becomes stiff, static, even ossified, as we often see in religious life. . . .

Truth is not objective, ordinary reality, reflected in the knower and entering into him from outside, but rather the enlightenment, the transfiguration of reality: it is the introduction into the world's data of a quality, which was not there before truth was revealed and known. Truth is not conformity with what we call being, but rather the kindling of a light within being. I am in darkness and seek the light; I do not yet know truth but I seek it. But by this very fact I affirm the existence of Truth and light, existence in another sense than the existence of the world's realities. My seeking is already the dawning light, and truth already beginning to reveal itself. *Truth*, pp. 14-16

Truth did not begin with me.
The New Religious Consciousness, 1907

A Firm Criterion for Truth

When people who are completely submerged in objectivization, and consequently in authoritarianism, ask where is there a firm criterion for truth, I refuse to answer. From this point of view, truth is always doubtful, infirm, problematic. Accepting truth is always a risk; there is no guarantee and there should be none. We find this risk in every act of faith, which is the disclosure of things unseen. Only the acceptance of things visible, of the so-called objective world, is without risk. Spirit always presupposes risk, from the viewpoint of the objective world which has us under compulsion. That absence of risk, which men often affirm in urging the acceptance of the Christian faith, which has taken the form of organized orthodoxy, is of a sociological rather than a spiritual nature, and is motivated by the desire to guide human spirits. This is specially clear in the concept of the more socially organized Catholic Church.

We cannot accept as truth that which has always been accepted by all men: this is a quantitative and numerical criterion. . . . Knowledge of truth is attained by the totality of man's spiritual powers, not by the intellectual alone. And this is determined by the fact that truth is spiritual and is life in the Spirit. . . . The discovery of Truth is a free act of the will, not alone an intellectual act; it is the turning of man's whole being toward creative values. The criterion lies in this very act of the Spirit. There is no criterion of truth outside the witness of truth itself, and it is wrong to seek absolute guarantees, which always demean the truth. Such is the consciousness of man, at the border-line between two worlds. *Truth*, pp. 30-1

CHAPTER VII

The First Philosophy*

'The end of time will not be in the future, but on another plane.' SOLITUDE, p. 141

TIME

Time and Creativity

The problem of time, along with that of freedom, is a radical and most tormenting metaphysical problem. . . . Creativity is unquestionably related to time. It is usually held that creativity presupposes time, since the prospective of a future is necessary for creativity, and creativity presupposes a change in time. Actually, it would be more true to say that movement, change, creativity, give birth to time. Thus we discover the dual nature of time. It is the source of both hope and fear and torment. The charm of the future is due to the fact that the future may be altered, and in some degree depends upon us. We can do nothing about the past; we may only remember it, either with gratitude and respect, or with repentance and indignation. The future may bring us the realization of our desires, our hopes, our dreams. But the future, too, inspires fear in us, tears us with worry about the unknown. . . . In time everything appears determined and necessary, and in our feeling of the future we anticipate this finality; history sometimes seems to us like portending fate. But the free creative act is accomplished outside the power of time, for there is no predetermination in it: it proceeds out of that depth of being which is not subject to time; it is a break-through from another order of being. . . . The creative act means going out from time: it is accomplished in the realm of freedom, not that of necessity. In essence it is the opposite of the worry which our fear of time produces. And if man's whole life could become one creative act, time would be no more; neither would there be the future, as a part of time, there would be movement outside time, in extra-temporal being. There would be no predetermination, no necessity, no oppressive laws. There would be the lifting of the spirit. *Destiny*, pp. 156-7

Time and Eternity

Time exists because there is activity, creativeness, transition from non-being to being, but this activity and creativeness are incomplete, not

* Aristotle.

whole, not in eternity. Time is the result of the change of what is passing, into realities, into existent things. It is not true that change to realities is conditioned by time. Therefore time may be conquered. Time is a fallen thing, the time of our world is the result of a fall that took place in existence. Fallen time is a product of objectivization in which everything became object, external, i.e. everything became incomplete, disunited, fettered and bound. We cannot say that all things are in time. This is a naïve view. Time is only the condition of things. Another condition of things would lead to the quenching of time. The duality of time, its double meaning for human existence, is linked with the fact that time is the result of things new, never previously existent, while at the same time, it is the produce of cleavage, of the loss of wholeness, the product of worry and fear. . . .

Present and Past

The problem of the relationship between past and present, is expressed in two ways. How to make the evil, sinful, painful past as though it had not been, and how to make the dear, kind, beautiful past, which has died and ceased to exist—how to make this continue its existence. Here the relationship to the past is interwoven with relationship to the future. The problem of the future has become basic for both philosophy and for art. It always was basic for religion, and specially for Christianity. The mysteries of repentance and the forgiveness of sins, the mysteries of death and resurrection, of the end of the Apocalypse, are mysteries of time, of the past, the future, the eternal. . . .

Time and Freedom

The good thing about the future is that freedom is associated with it, that the future may be actively created. In regard to the future this is the conquest of the determinism that is connected with the past. But we must discover freedom in regard to the past, as well, the possibility of the transmutation of time. In religious thought, this is the problem of the Resurrection. . . . This is victory over death-dealing time. *Le temps retrouvé* can be only victory over the illness of time, not movement toward past or future. Time that has recovered from its illness is eternity. And all creative activity, all creation of something new, should be directed not toward the future with its fear and worry and its incapacity to conquer determinism, but toward eternity. This is the reverse of movement to hasten time. It differs from the speeding-up of time, connected with technics and from sorrow and melancholy, connected with the passive and emotional experience of death-dealing time. This is the victory of the spirit.

Time and Technics

Time is measured mathematically by figures, clocks and calendars. This is another kind of time than the time of man's fate. But man's fate is cast abroad in the world and objectified. Therefore it is subject to mathematically enduring time, to clocks and the calendar. Only in the spirit does time cease to be measured by numbers. . . . We are witnessing a mad speeding-up of time, and man's life is subject to this constantly swifter time. Each moment lacks value and completeness in itself, we cannot stop on it, it must be succeeded as quickly as possible by the next moment. . . . The 'I' has no time to think of itself as the free creator of the future. It is carried away by the mad current of time. This is, as it were, a new eon of time. Speed, created by technics and mechanization is destructive for the 'I', for its unity and concentration. . . . A full-value, indestructible moment is the moment of contemplation, not content to be a means to the next moment: it is communion with eternity. 'I' presupposes activity; there can be no 'I' without activity and creativeness: this is part of its constituent indications. But 'I' also presupposes contemplation, without this there is no concentration, profundity or wholeness of the 'I'; it is alienated in its activity, and objectified, i.e. it falls away from its own existence. Contemplation is just as necessary for making the 'I' into a personality, as is creative activity. . . .

Time and Eschatology

In the final analysis, time becomes an eschatological problem. The Christian viewpoint, in contrast to the Hindu or Greek, recognizes a meaning for time. The meaning of time is the meaning of history, my history and that of the world. Existence is in eternity, but as Jaspers truly says, time is the meaning of existence. Christianity intensified time extraordinarily, narrowed it to one point, from which the results of every act are extended through all eternity. . . . This intensification of time indicates the possibility within a moment of time, of passing out toward eternity, toward events with eternal, and not merely temporal, meaning. But responsibility throughout all time, and eternity for what was done or what happened in one bit of time, even if this bit were our whole life from birth to death, is of course a great injustice. In no bit of time, taken apart from the rest, has man the experience or knowledge, the sufficiently wide horizon, to make him consciously responsible, not for time, but for eternity. Responsibility forever, for one moment of time, exists only if that moment is not a sector of time, but communion with eternity.

Solitude, pp. 118-37

Time and History

The philosophy of history puts the problem of the relationship of history to time, to freedom, to personality. History occurs in time. But historical time differs from cosmic time. Movement in historical time is not in a circle; it is in a line, moving ahead. This movement aims at a goal. But just in historical times the goal is unattainable, and an evil endlessness is revealed. The only way out is a break-through of the transcendental. Immanently, history may aim at the establishment of a perfectly rationalized and mechanized society. But I do not want this: I want the Kingdom of God, that comes unseen. *Divine*, pp. 214-15

> If there is no eternity, there is nothing whatever. *Autobiography*, p. 41

ETERNITY

> Eternity is not infinite time, time measureable quantitatively: but a quality which transcends time.
>
> From an article in the *Philosophers' Lexicon*, Berlin, 1937

Eternal Life

The question of immortality and of eternal life has been a basic religious problem for me. And I could never understand people who comprehend and accept the perspective of their life without solving this problem. Nothing is more pitiful than consolation derived from the idea of the progress of humanity and the happiness of future generations. The consolation of world-harmony as frequently offered to personality, always revolted me. Here I am very close to Dostoevsky and am ready to stand by not only Ivan Karamazof, but by the 'man in the cellar'. Nothing 'general' can comfort the 'individual' man in his unhappy fate. Progress itself is acceptable only if it is effected, not alone for future generations, but for me, as well.

I have never felt any special fear of death, and have really not given it much thought. I am not among those possessed by the fear of death, as was Leo Tolstoy, for instance. For me, only the question of the death of those near and dear to me has been tormenting. But victory over death has always seemed to me to be the basic problem of life. I have considered death an event more profound than birth. I recall Rozanov's contrast of the religion of birth with the religion of death, and I vote against Rozanov. To confess a religion of death (this was what he considered Christianity) means to confess a religion of life, life eternal, life which has overcome death. If we are to imagine a perfect eternal life, divine life, your loved ones will not be there, you yourself will disappear in it—then this perfect life is devoid of all meaning. Meaning must be commensurate with my own destiny. Objectivized meaning has no meaning for me. Meaning can be only in subjectivity; meaning in objectivity is merely a mockery of meaning. . .

The problem of eternal destiny faces every man, every living thing, and every objectivization of it is false. If God does not exist, if there is no higher sphere of freedom, eternal and genuine life, if there is no deliverance from the world's necessity, there is no reason to treasure this world and our frail life within it. . . .

Only Christianity rightly affirms the immortality of the whole man, of all humanity, with the exception of the results of sin and evil corruptibility. Christianity is unique in its consistent personalism. Man's soul is more precious than all the kingdoms of the world; the fate of the person comes before everything else. We do not find such personalism in theosophy, for instance, where one personality is separated into its cosmic elements and then reunited in another person. But Christianity does not deny the tragedy of death; it recognizes that man passes through a discontinuance of the integrity of personality. But this is not an optimistic evolutionary view of death. I deny reincarnation on one plane, that is the reincarnation of souls on this earthly plane, since I see here a contradiction to the idea of the integrity of personality. But I recognize multi-plane reincarnation, reincarnation on another spiritual plane, as well as pre-existence on a spiritual plane. The final fate of man cannot be determined only in the brief time of his earthly life.

Autobiography, pp. 317-21

MYSTICISM

Mysticism is Both the Depth and the Height of Spiritual Life —Mysticism Defined

Through all human history, mysticism has revealed the world of the inner man in contrast to the world of the outward man. In various forms these mystical revelations of the inward man have always taught of man's microcosmic quality. The mystical experience has revealed the cosmos within man, the whole immense universe. Mysticism is in profound contrast to every kind of closed-in individualism, isolated from cosmic life: it is in contrast to all psychologism. Mystical submersion in oneself always means going out of oneself, a breaking-through beyond the boundaries. All mysticism teaches that the depths of man are more than human, that in them there lurks a mysterious contact with God and with the world. The man who is described in psychology is, after all, the outward rather than the inner man. The inward man is spiritual rather than intellectual. The mystical element is spiritual: it is more profound and more primordial than the intellectual element. In the course of history, phenomena which belonged to the spiritual or astral plane of man have also been called mystical: mysticism was not yet sufficiently separated from magic. But in the strict, differentiated, absolute meaning of the word, only that may be called mystical which relates to the spiritual plane. *M.C.A.*, p. 296

Mysticism is not Subjective

Mysticism is not some refined psychologism, not an irrational spiritual experience, and not simply the music of the souls. And the Christian religion justly revolts against this idea of mysticism. . . . In mystical experience, man always goes out of his closed spiritual world and comes into contact with the spiritual first principles of being, with divine actuality. In contradiction of those Protestants who like to ascribe to mysticism an individualistic character and to identify it with religious individualism, it must be said that mysticism is the conquest of individualism and an escape from an individualistic condition. . . . Mysticism is intimately secret, but not individualistic. . . . We must insist that mysticism is not a subjective condition: it is an escape from the very contrast between the subjective and the objective. Mysticism is not subjective romanticism. It is not an illusive subjective experience. Mysticism is realistic in the highest degree, sober in its acquaintance with and revelation of realities. Only he is the true mystic who sees realities and distinguishes them from phantoms. *Freedom*, II, pp. 74-5

Mysticism and the Church

Mysticism presents a great problem to the Christian world: where mysticism begins, there is the end of the realm of dogmatic clarity, of general validity. The relationships between mysticism and the Church are very complex. The Church, both Catholic and Orthodox never disavowed mysticism, but was always afraid of it, and always suspicious toward mystical tendencies. . . . While denying the mystical quality of Christianity, they attempt to render mysticism harmless by establishing officially permitted forms of it. There is an official, Church mysticism, both Orthodox and Catholic. But there always remains an enormous sphere of Christian mysticism which is either considered suspect, or definitely condemned. This mysticism of the gnostic type always at odds with theology and disturbing the established hierarchical interdependence of various spheres, is as well mysticism as that of the prophetic type. *Freedom*, II, pp. 87-8

Two Types of Mysticism

We may distinguish separate forms of mysticism. There is mysticism as a way of spiritual perfection, of spiritual ascent, of approaching God, and there is mysticism as knowledge of the secrets of being, of divine mysteries. In the mysticism officially recognized by the Church, the first type invariably prevails. The ascetic-moral moment, the factor of purification, dominates. This type of mysticism teaches above all, renunciation of 'the world', and concentration on God. But there is also gnostic mysticism, and in the course of its history it has given the world great creative geniuses. We have only to name Plotinus, Kabbala, Eckhardt, Jacob Boehme. What are we to do with them? . . . Theology has always been jealous of mystical gnosis and considered it spurious knowledge. And so one of the greatest gifts with which man was endowed from on high, was condemned. German mysticism, one of the supreme phenomena in the history of the human spirit, was gnostic: in it was revealed a spiritual knowledge, the attainment of God's mysteries, outside the established distinction between metaphysics and theology. The history of the human spirit, of human culture, bears witness to the fact that the gift of mystical gnosis, of mystical contemplation of the mysteries of being, is a special gift, not at all identical with sainthood. Jacob Boehme had the gift of mystical gnosis in incomparably greater measure than St Francis, or St Dominic, greater than St Thomas Aquinas, although he was a philosopher. And if St Seraphim had the gift of mystical contemplation of the mysteries of cosmic life, this was the result, not of his attainment of sanctity, but of a very special charism.

Freedom, II, pp. 90-1

Catholic and Orthodox Mysticism

The difference between Orthodox and Catholic mysticism is to be sought first, in their differing spiritual experience in the sphere of mysticism. In its depths, the whole Christian world is one. And both Orthodox and Catholic mysticisms are Christian. But these two worlds have moved by different paths toward the same goal, and have developed two spiritual types. Orthodox mysticism is the acquisition of the Holy Spirit—a mysticism of the Holy Spirit. In it human nature is transfigured and illumined from within. This is a mysticism of the heart, as the centre of spiritual life. The mind must rely upon the heart—only then is spiritual integrity achieved. Christ enters the heart, and by this 'christ-ization' of the heart the whole human nature is changed: man becomes a new creature. . . . Orthodox mysticism looks toward the transfiguration of the creature. It presupposes severe ascetic living, heroic struggle against the old Adam. But Orthodox mysticism is light and joyful; to it is revealed the mystery of God's creation. The grace of the Holy Spirit is acquired by means of humility, rather than by suffering.

Catholic mysticism is more Christ-centred, and more anthropological. It is primarily a eucharistic mysticism. In Catholicism in general we find a certain 'subordinationalism' in the understanding of the nature of the Holy Spirit. Here the Holy Spirit is often identified with grace. Catholic mysticism is imitation of Christ, experiencing the Lord's suffering. Hence the stigma—impossible in Orthodoxy. . . . In the (Catholic) mystical way, its classical form, three stages are established: the via purgativa, the via illuminativa, the via unitiva. . . . In the mystical life there is inevitable passage through what St John of the Cross calls the 'nuit obscure', night of feeling, of reason, death to the world. Orthodox mysticism knows nothing of this 'dark night' as a special, separate condition on the mystical road. . . . In Catholic mysticism, in the lives of

Catholic saints, there is an ecstasy of suffering and sacrifice, often to the length of self-torture. One cannot deny the peculiar greatness of Catholic-mysticism, its depth and its essentially Christian character, but its type is other than ours, and more anthropological.

The classic examples of Russian Orthodox mysticism are to be found in St Seraphim of Sarov, and in that little book by an unknown author which charms us by its naïve simplicity, *The Tales of a Wanderer*. The practice of mental prayer, of the 'Jesus prayer' lies at the centre of Orthodox mysticism. In this prayer, Jesus penetrates our heart and our whole nature is illumined. This prayer ('Lord Jesus Christ, Son of God, have mercy on me, a sinner') is a method of mystical concentration. Catholic mysticism, passing through various stages, through 'dark night', attains 'union divine', union with God. The orthodox way is different. . . . In the 'Jesus prayer' Jesus himself is present. In the name of God is contained God's energy which overflows into man, enters into him and changes his nature. The Name has an ontological, and in a special sense, a magic significance.

The New Mysticism

We are entering an epoch of a new spirituality, that will correspond to the new form of mysticism. It will no longer be possible to argue against a heightened spiritual and mystical life that human nature is sinful and that sin must first be overcome. An external, everyday Christianity will no longer be possible. A heightened spiritual and mystical life is the road to the victory over sin. And the world is entering a catastrophic period of choice and division, when these will be required of all Christians, an uplifting and intensification of their inner lives. The external, everyday, moderate Christianity is breaking up. But eternal, inward, mystical Christianity is becoming stronger and better established. And within mysticism itself a 'paraclete' type is beginning to predominate. The epoch of new spirituality in Christianity, can only be an epoch of a great and hitherto unheard of manifestation of the Holy Spirit.

Freedom, II, pp. 111-12

Mysticism versus Theology

The eternal conflict between mysticism and theology is largely due to the fact that they speak different languages. And one cannot be translated into the other. When men try to translate the mystical experience into the language of theology, mysticism is immediately accused of heresy. The language of mysticism is paradoxical: it is not a language of concepts, it is not cogitation subject to the law of identity. On the other hand, the language of theology always strives, although unsuccessfully, to be a rationalized language that does not admit contradictions. This is why it is so difficult to express mysticism in the language of theology or of abstract metaphysics: distortion always results. . . .

The mystical experience signifies the overcoming of everything that is creature. And for this conquest there is no corresponding concept in theology. To theology this looks like pantheism, when it is something quite other, dynamic instead of static, theologically inexpressible. . . .

We may establish three conditions for Christian mysticism, three marks or signs of it: personality, freedom, love. Any Christian mysticism which lacks one of these marks is imperfect. It is a deviation.

Reality, pp. 115-27

The New Mysticism

The world is moving through darkness toward a new spirituality and a new mysticism. In it there will be no more of the ascetic world-view which turned away from the pluralities and the individualities of the world. In it ascesis will be merely a method and the means to purification. Although addressed to the world and to men, the new mysticism will not consider this objectivized world as final reality. It will be at once more involved with the world, and more free from it. This is a process of spiritual deepening. The prophetic-messianic element will be strong in the new mysticism, and in it will be revealed a true gnosis which will avoid the cosmic temptations of the ancient gnostics. And all the tormenting contradictions and divisions will be resolved in the new mysticism, which will be deeper than religions, and ought to unite them. At the same time this will be the victory over false forms of social mysticism, the victory of the realm of Spirit over that of Caesar.

Spirit and Caesar, pp. 181-2

MYTH

Religious philosophy is always steeped in myth and cannot escape myth without abolishing both itself and its task. . . . At the basis of Christian philosophy, no matter how much it operates with concepts, lies the great central myth of humanity, the myth of Redemption and the Redeemer. The driest scholastic theology and metaphysics are nourished by religious myths. Pure abstract metaphysics, completely free of myth is the death of living knowledge, a breaking-away from being, a stoppage of nourishment. Living knowledge is mythological. We must recognize this, consciously, at the same time having clearly in mind just what myth is. Myth is a reality incomparably greater than knowledge. It is time we stopped identifying myth with the inventions and illusions of the primitive mind, something just the opposite of reality; as we use the words myth and mythical in our ordinary speech. But in myth there is hidden the greatest reality, the basic phenomena of the spiritual life. The mythmaking life of peoples is real spiritual life, more real than the life of abstract concepts or rational thinking. Myth is always concrete and, better than rational thinking, it reflects life. The nature of myth is connected with the nature of symbol. Myth is a concrete story, imprinted in the memory of a people, in folk creativity, in its language, of the basic phenomena of spiritual life, symbolized and reflected in the natural world: the very first reality is grounded in the spiritual world and reaches down to mysterious depths. But the symbols and signs, the imaging and reflection of these first realities are given in the world of nature. Myth represents the supernatural in the natural, the superperceptive in the perceptive, the life of the spirit in that of the flesh. Myth is the symbolic bond between two worlds.

Freedom, I, pp. 111-12

SYMBOLISM

> . . . Knowledge of Divinity is an endless movement of the spirit. But a mystery always remains, which can never be plumbed to the bottom. And this is expressed in symbol: it cannot be expressed in concepts. *Freedom*, I, p. 105

Symbol and Symbolism

Man has a great need for the holy, not alone in heaven, but here on earth, need for the evidence, the perceptibility of spirit. The most varied things have been considered holy—the state, the nation, the family, property, society, culture and civilization. This always means that the spirit is objectivized and passes over into these formations. Socialization is always symbolization. The holy in this world is not a holy reality, but the symbolization of holy reality. Socialization was not the realization of the holy, but its symbolization. The holy was symbolized in anointed hierarchical order, in material objects sprinkled with holy water. Socialization is . . . not a manifestation of human spirituality. In it spirit is objectivized in signs and symbols. There is a vast difference between thinking that anointed orders and consecrated objects are holy, and thinking that the human subject, his creativity, freedom, love, justice, knowledge, spiritual beauty, etc., are holy. The former is symbolic, the latter realistic. In the former, spirit is objectified; in the latter, spirit is revealed in its very existence. *Reality*, pp. 60-1

The Meaning of Symbolism

'Symbol' in Greek means both 'sign' and 'union'. Symbol and symbolization predicate the existence of two worlds, two orders of being. If there is only one world, one order of being, symbol has no place. Symbol tells us that the meaning of one world lies in another, that signs of meaning are given from this other world. Symbol tells us, not only that another world exists, that being is not all-included in our world, but that connection between the two is possible, the union of one with the other; that these two worlds are not finally separate. Symbol both sets the limits of these two worlds and joins them. By itself our natural, empirical world has no meaning or significance; it receives these from another world, the world of spirit, as a symbol of that world. . . . Everything which has meaning and importance in our life is only a sign, a symbol of another world. . . . In the world of nature, and in natural life, closed in themselves it is impossible to discover meaningful connection or significance. . . . In the life of man, as a bit of the natural world, it is impossible to discover the logos, and even man's reason is only an adaptation to the whirlpool of the natural world. Thought oriented totally to the closed-in-itself, natural, world is often struck by the meaninglessness, the accidentality, the unimportance of being. Such thinking is repressed, and unable to put meaning into the darkness of the natural world which surrounds man on every side, where no signs are visible of another world, a world of meaning. But man is measurelessly significant and meaningful, as an image and likeness of divine being, as a symbol of Divinity. . . . We cannot prove the existence of meaning in the life of the world, meaning cannot be deduced by reason and from the contemplation of the natural world. . . . The meaningfulness of the processes of nature is doubtful. We may discover meaning only by living it in spiritual experience, only by turning our thought toward the spiritual world. *Freedom*, I, pp. 88-90

Where the competence of understanding ceases, there the symbol enters into its right.
Freedom, I, p. 105

Christ as Symbol

The birth into this world of the Son of God, his life, his death on the cross and his resurrection, are a symbol unique in its significance, a central, absolute symbol of events in the spiritual world, in mysterious spiritual life. This symbol liberates us from, rather than enslaving us to, the power of the world. The fact that God's Son lived in natural flesh is the source of our hope that natural flesh may be conquered in its nightmare realism, may be illuminated by another world, and transformed into spiritual flesh. All the flesh of the world is a symbol of spirit, the reflection, the image, the sign of another reality, of something boundlessly more distant and more profound. . . . The illumination of the flesh revealed in the earthly life of the Son of God is a sign of movement taking place in the world of the spirit. . . .

Everything that happens in the upper world, takes place in the lower. Even the Divine Trinity is repeated everywhere in our world. Depth presupposes superficiality and exteriorality, the inner presupposes outer, the different presupposes the duality of the inner life. The world, nature, history—these are only a way of the spirit, only a moment in its inner, mysterious life. The life of the spirit is my life, but also life in general, both divine life and the life of the whole world. In the life of the spirit, on my spiritual way, I am cast forth into the objectivized world, the world of symbols, and then I return to my inner self, to the depths, to primary life and reality. Thus the miracle play of life is accomplished.

Freedom, I, pp. 88-129

HISTORY

Not only am I in conflict with history . . . I am responsible for it: it is my way and my experience. *Notebook*

History needed man as her material, but never recognized him as her purpose.

Fate, p. 23

The Meaning of History

The history of the world and of mankind has meaning only if it ends. Endless history would be meaningless. Even if continual progress should be revealed in endless history, it still would be inacceptable because this would mean that everything which has lived, is now living or is called to live in the future, every living generation would be turned into a means for future generations, and this *ad infinitum*. Everything present becomes a means for the future. Endless progress, an endless process, means the triumph of death. Only the resurrection of everything which has lived can give meaning to the world's historic process, a meaning commensurate with the fate of personality. Any meaning which is not commensurate with the fate of personality, with my fate, and has no significance for it, is meaningless. If the universal meaning is not at the same time personal meaning as well, then it has no meaning. I cannot live in the 'great whole'; the 'great whole' must live in me. I must reveal it in myself. If God existed, and this meant nothing for me and for my eternal destiny, this would be just as though God did not exist at all. . . .

My life is meaningless if it is finished by death. And even the values which may fill this life cannot save it from meaninglessness. But my life would be just as devoid of meaning if it were endless life in this objectivized world: it would not be eternal life into which all the creative achievements of beings enter. Meaning lies beyond the boundaries of history, beyond the limits of personal and world-history.

Beginning, pp. 198-9

The Paradox of Time and the End of Time

The metaphysical and gnosseological meaning of the end of the world and of history marks the end of objective being, the elimination of objectivization. It also means the elimination of the counter-distinction between subject and object. . . . The end also means the victory of existential time over historic and cosmic time. Only in existential time, measured by the tension and intensity of the condition of the subject, can the way be opened out into eternity. We cannot think of the end in historic or cosmic time; here it is caught in the power of an evil endlessness. This is related to the basic antinomy of the end. From the philosophical viewpoint, the paradox of time makes an interpretation of the Apocalypse, as a book about the end, very difficult. We cannot think of the end of the world in historic time, within history, i.e. we cannot objectivize the end. And on the other hand we cannot think of the end of the world quite outside history, as an event wholly beyond history. This is another antinomy of the Kantian type. Time will be no more—the objectivized time of this world. But the end of time cannot be in time. Everything takes place not in the future, which is a torn-off part of our time, and this means that this all takes place in existential time. This is transition from the objectivity of existence to the subjectivity of existence—transition to spirituality. Man as a 'noumen' is at the beginning and man as a 'noumen' is at the end. But he lives out his destiny in a world of phenomena. What we call the end, projecting it into the outward sphere, is the existential experience of contact with the noumenal, the noumenal in its conflict with the phenomenal. This is not an experience of development; rather, it is an experience of shock, of catastrophe in both personal and historical existence. In view of the objectivity of the world, of the fallen state of man's existence, the end is thought of as a 'fatum' weighing down on the sinful world and on sinful men, and this means first of all the last judgment. The end holds an inevitable moment of the judgment of conscience, which is, as it were, the voice of God within man. But the end brings also the beginning of the Kingdom of God. . . . *Beginning*, pp. 200-1

Positive or Negative Results of History

The historic process is accompanied by a whole list of failures, and within the bounds of history the theme of history is insoluble: that theme is the Kingdom of God. And we face the question: will there be any sort of positive result of history, or only negative? In other words the question is: will men's creative acts be reckoned in eternal life, will they enter the Kingdom of God? To deny positive results of history for super-history is to deny all meaning for history; to deny the significance of human creativity for the realization of the future of the Kingdom of God is to deny the god-like worth of man. The failure of human creativity is linked with the objectivization of all products of creativity. But creativity itself passes out beyond the bounds of objectivization and is turned toward a new life, to the Kingdom of God. . . . We must remember that we are speaking of a new eon, of the epoch of Spirit, the epoch of the Paraclete, and here our categories are not applicable. The Kingdom of God, which we cannot think of as either order or disorder, not as necessity nor wilfulness, must be here on earth, although at the same time it is a heavenly kingdom. God can be all in all, only eschatologically, only in the Kingdom of God, and not in the kingdoms of this world. Only in Christ's second coming, in the form of the Coming Christ, will the fullness of man's perfection be revealed, and into this perfection and this fullness will enter all of man's creative acts.

Beginning, pp. 215-16

Philosophy of History

The world may be considered from two viewpoints: for one the world is first of all cosmos; for the other the world is first of all history. For the ancient Greeks the world was cosmos: for the ancient Hebrews the world was history. Greeks and Jews lived in different times; not *at*, but *in* different times. The view of the world as cosmos is cosmocentric. This is the dispute as to whether man is to be comprehended from the cosmos, or the cosmos from man. Is human history a subordinate part of the cosmic process, or the cosmic process a subordinate part of human history? Is the meaning of human existence revealed in the maelstrom of cosmic life or in the events of history? This is also the quarrel between the static and the dynamic world-views; the concept of the world first of all in space, versus the concept of the world primarily in time. Actuality is always historic—there is no other. And so-called 'nature' has its history in time. So do the stars in the sky and the crust of our globe. But nature may be understood as cosmic infinity into which our human history has stumbled, and then there are no events of significant meaning in it. But it may be understood as belonging in human history, as a preparatory part of it, and then it takes on meaning and significance. A philosophy of history could never have arisen among the Greeks, because of their cosmic-centric concept of the world. For them the golden age was in the past, and out of this came their gift for creating myths. They had no great hope, oriented toward the future. A philosophy of history could arise only in connection with a messianic-eschatological consciousness, which Israel and the Persians who influenced her, had; with their intense expectation of a great event in the future—the appearance of the Messiah, that is the incarnation of Meaning, the Logos in history. We may say that messianism constructs the historic. The philosophy of history has Iranian-Hebrew-Christian sources. The nineteenth-century doctrine of progress, despite its un-christian exterior, has the same sources in messianic expectation. There has been much doubt even denial of the possibility of a philosophy of history. And certainly it is impossible to construct a purely scientific philosophy of history. We live within historic time. History is not yet ended and we do not know what sort of history awaits in the future. . . . Can history be revealed before its close? A philosophy of history was possible, and could exist just because it always included a prophetic element passing the boundaries of scientific knowledge. There can be no other philosophy of history than the prophetic. . . . The messianic-prophetic character of the philosophy of history is determined by the fact that the meaning of history depends upon the unknown future, that it is knowledge not only of what is no more, but also of what is not yet, . . . prophecy not alone of the future, but of the past, as well. *Beginning*, pp. 171 ff

My thought, concerned with the beginning and the ending, can admit only one possible type of metaphysics—meta-history. Everything existential is history, dynamic, fate—man is history; the world is history; God is history, completing the drama. The philosophy which I would like to express is a dramatic philosophy of fate, of existence in time which passes over into eternity; of time which moves toward its end. And that end is not death, but transfiguration. Therefore we should consider everything from the viewpoint of the philosophy of history. And this philosophy of history can be only 'prophetic philosophy, unravelling the mystery of what is to come'. *Divine*, pp. 7-8

Man in History

Man is an historic being; he comes to self-realization in history; he can neither cast aside the burden of history, nor free himself from responsibility for it. Man cannot escape history. And man cannot abdicate his God-like worth and dignity, cannot consent to being turned into a means for the merciless and inhuman process of history. History is not a phenomenon of nature: man creates history and we may think he creates it for himself. But history has been criminal, it has realized itself in violence and blood, and has never shown any inclination to spare man; history has trampled man underfoot. Hegel's sly reason has been used by men and nations to realize their own purposes. For Hegel this higher purpose was the final triumph of the world-spirit, its self-realization and of its freedom. Everything partial or individual is only a means for the triumph of the general, the universal. The founding of empires, wars and revolutions, by means of which the purposes of history were realized, have always been the triumph of the general and universal, the crowding and crushing of everything partial and individual. This has been characteristic of the founding of all states as well as of their destruction. And the economic development of human societies, whose purpose is the satisfaction of the material needs of men, on which the very possibility of their existence depends—this development is concerned with the general, rather than the individual; man is only a unit of statistics. Capitalist society is a brilliant example of this, and communist society may become another. . . .

History is a terrible tragedy. In it everything becomes distorted, even all great ideas. In history revelation, too, has been distorted. History is objectivation, a creative vertical movement in which historic causality has always been discontinuous, movement which then is objectivized on the horizontal. But the objectivation of spirit which takes place in history is an act of my spirit. And I cannot escape the two elements of the antinomy: I both accept history as my way, the way of all men, and in indignation I unmask revolt against it. My fate is bound up with the fate of the world: I cannot separate the two. The world has taken the road of objectivizing existence and I am thrust into that process: I am responsible for it. I cannot put upon others the responsibility for this, setting myself apart as unsoiled by the dirt of history. History has put on me its ineradicable seal. And at the same time I am a free spirit, a personality bearing in myself not only the image of the world, but the image of God. Herein lies the difficulty and the tragedy of my situation. I must somehow maintain my freedom in a realm of necessity. . . .

I am History

History does me violence, and has no concern for me, whatever. This is one of its aspects. But history is also my history: it happened to me. If man includes the cosmos in himself, we may say all the more positively that he includes history within himself. In my spiritual depths, in the transcendental man, the contrast is eliminated. The history of ancient Israel, of Egypt and Persia and Babylon, of Greece and Rome, of the Middle Ages and the Renaissance—all this is my history, and only because of this can I understand it. This is my road, my quest and my temptation, my falling and my uprising. If for me, all this were only objectivation and objectiveness, in which everything is received only from without, I should not be able to understand a bit of it. The Russian revolution happened to me, also; I am responsible for it; it is simply my way and my experience. I must never pose as a man who considers that he has always been in the right, and that others have been in the wrong and in falsehood. I must never consider anything as completely outside myself. I am responsible for the act of Cain. History is alien to me, as objectivation, as estrangement, and still very near to me: it is mine. And within the limits of our world we cannot escape this contradiction.

Truth, pp. 66-7

CHAPTER VIII
A Handmaid to Religion*

There is nothing more evil than the determination to create good, no matter what the cost.
SPIRIT AND CAESAR, p. 94

GOOD

Good and Beauty
Good should not be thought of in teleological terms, but in terms of energy. In good what is most important is creative energy realized, rather than an ideal, normative aim. Man struggles for the good, not because he has consciously accepted the purpose of struggle for the good, but because he is good, virtuous, that is, he has within himself the creative energy of good. The source of action, not the aim, is important. . . . The good and the moral life are a way in which the starting point and the finish coincide; this is radiant creative energy. Ontologically and cosmologically, we should think of the ultimate purpose of being as beauty, rather than good. Perfect, full and harmonious being is beauty. Plato defined beauty as the splendour of good. Beauty is the realization of the good in nature, and the 'love of good' means the 'love of beauty'. A teleological ethic is legalistic and normative: good is the purpose of life, i.e. the norm, the law which we should fulfil. Teleological ethics always shows a lack of imagination, for it thinks of life's purpose as fulfilling the norm of what ought to be, rather than as an image, the product of the creative energy of life. Moral life should be formed, not according to purpose and norm, but by creative emanation. Beauty is an image of creative energy, radiating throughout the whole world and transfiguring the world. Teleological ethics, based on the idea of good as absolute aim, is hostile to freedom, whereas creative and energetic ethics is an ethic of freedom. Beauty is transfigured creation; good is creation fettered by the law which condemns sin. *Destiny*, p. 155

Beauty versus Goodness
The true transfiguration and illumination of human nature is the attainment of beauty, goodness. When good is accomplished really, rather than symbolically and legalistically, it is beauty. The highest aim is the beauty of creation rather than good, which always bears the stamp of

* Bacon.

the law. Beauty will save the world; that is, beauty *is* the salvation of the world. The transfiguration of the world is just this attainment of beauty. Paradise, the Kingdom of God—these are beauty. In art we are given only symbols of beauty. In reality beauty is given only in the religious transfiguration of created things. Beauty is God's idea of created things, of man, of the world. *Destiny*, p. 266

EVIL

> We can give reasoned meaning to evil only if we accept the principle of development in divine life. *M.C.A.*, p. 150

The Source of Evil

The problem which torments me, and which I consider basic, is the problem of the origin of evil and responsibility for evil. It is difficult to be reconciled to the thought that God is responsible for evil. Everything is in the hands of God, God is active everywhere, God uses even evil for good purposes; no one, nothing is free in relation to God. Out of this concept Calvin made the consequent and radical deductions about predestination. Does God act in evil and by means of evil? If this is true, then responsibility for the evil and the suffering in the world lies on God. If not then there exists some freedom from, and in relation to, God. And this limits the unique authority of God, as it were makes God powerless in relation to the freedom of evil. (I understand all the limitations of the language used here.) This is the most tormenting of problems and it admits of no comfortable and optimistic solution. It amazed Dostoevsky. Most of the theodicies, from St Augustine to Leibnitz, are not only unsatisfactory but directly offensive in regard both to God and to man.

Of course we may take the purely agnostic viewpoint and admit that here we have to do with the ultimate mystery which it is impossible to comprehend rationally. This viewpoint is better than a rational theodicy, but neither in theology nor in metaphysics was it ever maintained to the end, and finally theories were constructed, which are offensive to a sensitive conscience. Many teachers of the Church, as is well known, have taught that evil is non-being. But if we think this through to the end, we have to admit that the sources of evil lie outside being which is altogether under an all-powerful God, i.e. in an existential and uncreated freedom. This is only a philosophical interpretation, a philosophical expression of the ultimate mystery related with freedom and evil. This is the source of the tragic sense of the world, of the world-comprehension. We are led to this both by our experience of the world's evil and suffering and by the experience of creativity, the creation of something new in the world. The escape from evil is in the suffering of

God himself, that is in Christ. Not in God the All-mighty, but in God the Redeemer, the God of sacrificial love. I think that herein lies the essence of Christianity.

God is always active in the world and this gracious action can never resemble human judgment, with its cruelty, its lack of attention to the human person, its mercilessness. But God's action in the world is unusually complex and for us incomprehensible, because of its relationship to man's freedom and to the dark elements in the world. This action can never be action from without, or violence. And God's judgment on the world itself seems merciless just because God respects human freedom and does not wish to use force. *Put*, No. 46, 1935, pp. 33-4

The rationalistic mind of modern man thinks the chief hindrance to belief in God, the chief argument for atheism, is the existence of evil, and the sorrow and suffering it causes in the world. It is difficult to reconcile the existence of God, the all-good and almighty Providence, with the existence of evil, so strong and powerful in our world. This has become the classical and only serious argument. People lose their belief in God and in divine purpose in the world, because they encounter triumphant evil, because they sense the meaninglessness of the suffering born of evil. But belief in God and belief in gods arose in the history of human consciousness, just because mankind experienced great suffering and felt the need of freeing itself from the power of evil. If there were no evil affecting our world, mankind would be satisfied with the natural world as it is. A world of nature free of all evil and suffering would become man's only god. If there were no evil and the suffering it causes, there would be no sense of the need of deliverance. Life's suffering and torment which witness to the existence of evil are a great religious school through which mankind must pass. Life in a world which knew no evil, which was free of suffering and torment, would lead to self-satisfaction and self-sufficiency. The existence of evil is not only a difficulty for our belief in God, but also a proof of God's existence, proof that our world is not the only and final world. The experience of evil turns man toward another world, calls forth a holy satisfaction with that world. . . .

The secret of evil is the secret of freedom. Without our understanding of freedom the irrational fact of the existence of evil in God's world cannot be understood. At the basis of the world lies irrational freedom, in the very depths of the abyss. And out of these depths pour the dark currents of life. This abyss hides all sorts of possibilities. This bottomless darkness of being, pre-existent before all good and all evil, cannot be rationalized, fully and completely: it always hides the possibility of the outflow of new, unilluminated energies. The light of the Logos conquers darkness, cosmic order conquers chaos, but without the abyss of darkness and chaos, without endless death, there is no life, no freedom, no meaning of the process which is taking place. Freedom is founded in the dark abyss, in nothingness, but without freedom there is no meaning. Freedom gives birth to evil as well as good. Therefore evil does not deny the existence of meaning, but rather confirms it. Freedom is not created, because it is not nature; freedom existed before the world began, it is rooted in immemorial nothingness. God is almighty over being, but not over nothingness, or over freedom. And this is why evil exists. . .

The inward dialectic of freedom from within its depths, gives birth to evil. The source of evil as well as of all life, lies in the earliest, irrational freedom in infinite potentiality. Primordial freedom gave birth to evil on the very highest hierarchical stage of being. In freedom, a spirit which stood on the highest hierarchical stage of being, fell away from God, committed an act of self-assertion in spiritual pride, and from him the hierarchy of being was spoiled and perverted. The first appearance of evil occurred on the heights of spirit, not in the depths of the material. Primordial evil is spiritual in nature and it took place in the spiritual world. The base evil which fetters us to the material world, is a secondary produce of spiritual evil. . . . For the Christian consciousness, the problem of evil is joined with the problem of freedom, and hence they cannot understand the appearance of evil. The understanding of the mystery of evil through the mystery of freedom is a super-rational understanding; for reason it presents an antinomy. The source of evil is not in God, and not in positive being on a level with God, but in bottomless, irrational freedom in pure possibility and potency based in the dark abyss which preceded all positive definition of being, which lies deeper than all being: it is not born of an ontological source. The possibility of evil is hidden in that dark base of being which hides all possibilities. The abyss (Boehme's 'Ungrund') is not evil: it is the source of all life, every actualization in being; in it are hidden the possibilities of both good and evil. A primordial, irrational mystery, the abyss lies at the base of the world's life. And no system of logic can completely cover this irrational mystery of life. *Freedom*, I, pp. 230-9

Evil is inexplicable without freedom. Evil is the child of freedom. *Dostoevsky*, p. 88

The Struggle against Evil

Because of man's sinful nature conflict with evil gives rise to new evil. It is very difficult for a man who is struggling with evil to remain uninfected by it, himself. History is full of evil born of the struggle against evil, be it conservative or revolutionary. And the attitude toward evil should be not an evil, but an enlightened attitude. Toward the devil himself, one should have gentlemanly, noble, attitude. The devil rejoices when he succeeds in rousing evil, that is devilish, attitudes toward himself. He wins a victory when we fight him in evil, diabolic ways. The devil has inspired men with the deceitful idea that they may fight evil with evil. . . . Imperceptibly, the means of conflict take the place of its aims. What seems to a man the struggle against evil takes the place of good, itself, for him. The state is called to fight evil and to put a limit to the manifestation of evil in the world. But the state can very easily become self-sufficient, and change into a self-sufficient purpose. The means by which the state fights evil may themselves become evil; may become evil means. So it is, always and everywhere.

We should see evil first, in ourselves, rather than in others. And truly spiritual intention implies that we should believe more in the power of good than in the power of evil, believe in God more than in the devil. By this the power of good in the world is augmented by good feelings, and that of evil by evil feelings. And men seem only faintly conscious of this elementary principle of spiritual hygiene. Anger against good is not alone in destructive effect on man's spiritual world; anger against evil does the same. . . .

The attractiveness of evil is a snare and a delusion, and we should direct all our spiritual powers toward revealing this fact. The devil is talentless, empty, dull. Evil is non-being. And non-being is the ultimate in dullness, emptiness and powerlessness. The experience of evil in its final stages always reveal this: at the end, nothing but non-being and emptiness awaits. When in your struggle with evil, you imagine it to be strong and tempting, but forbidden and terrible, you do not win final and radical victory over it. Evil which is viewed as strong and tempting is evil unconquered and unconquerable. Only a consciousness of the complete nothingness and the absolute dullness of evil overcomes it and tears up its roots. At the end of its realization, no single evil passion has being. Every evil consumes itself, reveals its own emptiness, in its immanent development. Evil is a world of phantoms. . . .

May I say to myself: I will take the way of evil in order to enrich my consciousness, to attain still greater good? When I begin to think of evil as a positive way to good, a positive method of knowing truth, I am lost. I am powerless to unmask its falsity, darkness and emptiness. The experience of evil can be a way to good form, only in case that in this experience I recognize and unmask the falsehood, nullity and non-existentiality of evil and refuse it as a means of enrichment for my soul. . . . Not evil itself enriches the soul, for non-being can offer no riches; what gives enrichment is the immanent unmasking of evil's emptiness, the suffering which burns up evil, the tragedy we live through, the light glimpsed through darkness. . . . Evil is not the way to good, but only the experience of recognizing and unmasking its non-being. We have to recognize, however, without fearing the paradox, that evil has a positive meaning. The meaning of evil is linked with freedom. Without it, no theodicy is possible. Otherwise we would have to admit that God's creation of the world was a failure. The forced innocence of Eden could not last: it was worthless, and to it there can be no return. Man and the world pass through free suffering, free knowledge, and freely they move toward God and the Kingdom of God.

Freedom, I, pp. 261-8

The Paradox of Evil

The paradox of evil lies in this, that evil is meaningless, a falling away from Meaning, a mockery of Meaning, and at the same time evil must have some positive meaning, if the final word in being belongs to Meaning, that is to God. There is no escape from this paradox by the acceptance of one or the other affirmation, so diametrically opposed. We must recognize both the fact that evil is meaningless and the fact that it has a meaning. Rationalized theology, which considers itself orthodox, has found no way out of this difficulty. If evil is pure senselessness, a violation and mockery of the world's Meaning, and if it is crowned with eternal hell, then the hellish meaninglessness is part of God's plan, and the creation of the world was a failure. If, on the other hand, evil has positive meaning and eternal hell will not be its result, if it will somehow be positively reckoned into paradise then conflict with evil becomes difficult, and evil is transformed into an unrealized form of good. Men have attempted to escape from this difficulty by means of the doctrine of creative freedom, of the freedom of the will, in its traditional form. But as we have seen, this simply pushes the difficulty over on to the source of freedom. The positive meaning of evil lies in the fact that it is a trial of freedom, and that freedom, the creature's highest dignity, predicates the possibility of evil. Man is not satisfied with a paradise-life, not knowing evil, which means not knowing freedom, for man bears in himself the image and likeness of God. Man desires a paradise-life in which he would experience freedom to the fullest. But the experience of freedom produces evil and hence this life which has experienced freedom, is a paradise which has known the positive meaning of evil. Freedom has its source in the abyss of pre-being, and the darkness which proceeds from this source must be enlightened and transfigured by divine light, by the Logos. The genesis of evil thus brings us to recognize its positive meaning, which will be reckoned in the life of paradise, and to a ceaseless struggle against, and condemnation of it. The positive meaning of evil lies only in the enrichment of life which comes from ceaseless struggle against it, and triumph over it. But this struggle and this conquest do not mean that evil is to be crowded off into some special order of being: evil must be actually and finally overcome: it must be illumined and transfigured. This is a special paradox of ethics, with both an exoteric and an esoteric side. Ethics passes inevitably into eschatology, and is there resolved. Theosis is the final word, but it is attained by means of man's freedom and creativeness, which enriches even the divine life itself.

We may formulate the basic proposition of ethics, thus: act as though you had heard God's voice and are called to participate in His work by free and creative deeds; reveal in yourself a clean and original conscience, discipline your personality, struggle against evil within you and about you, but not in a way to crowd evil and evil men into hell, and set up a realm of hell, but rather really to conquer evil and forward the illumination and creative transfiguration of evil men. *Destiny*, pp. 317-18

Evil and Suffering

Evil appears in the world in two ways: the dark, evil will of those who crucify, and the innocent suffering of those who are crucified. Evil is the cause of injustice, untruth and suffering and the endurance of these is also evil. Herein lies the boundless difficulty of any attempt to understand, even partially, the action of Divine Providence in the world. A rationalistic understanding of Divine Providence would lead inevitably to a denial of evil, in the last analysis, to the viewpoint of Job's comforters. A rational theodicy, such as that of Leibnitz, for example, leads to an atheist revolt, to a denial of God. Whereas the mystery of the cross, the crucifixion of God himself, was for the Jews a temptation and for the Greeks foolishness. The world lies in evil: it is a fallen world, the result of original sin. In such a world it is hopeless to seek for rational and moral purpose. In this world there is evil which cannot lead to good, there is the suffering of the innocent, the tragic fate of the just, of the righteous; in this world the prophets are stoned to death and the evil unjust, the oppressors, those who crucify their betters, triumph. In this world there is the suffering of innocent children, of innocent animals. In this world death triumphs, that ultimate in evil and suffering. Is God's Providence active in this world? This is reason's question, baffled by the mystery of love. Suffering is a mystery. The mystery of suffering lies in this, that it may be changed into redemption. . . . *Reality*, pp. 94-5

Evil

But the source of evil is not in knowledge of the world of phenomena, the 'natural' world, not in the gnosseological subject itself which has produced 'objective' science, but rather in the existential condition of man and the world, in alienation, in the loss of freedom. Even scientific knowledge has liberating significance in this world, and becomes an enslaving force only when it is transformed into scientism.

Beginning, p. 65

A Christian Solution

A rational solution of the problem of evil is just as difficult as the solution of the problem of freedom. With good reason we may affirm that evil has no positive being, and that it attracts us only with what it steals from good. Yet evil not only exists, but prevails in the world. What may be called non-being has existential significance, although it would be wrong to say that it exists. One of the attempts to solve the problem of evil and bring it into agreement with a possible theodicy, consisted in the idea that evil exists only in parts, that the whole is only good. This was the thought St Augustine, of Leibnitz, really of most of the theodicies, for they admit that God uses evil for the purposes of good. But this kind of doctrine is based on the denial of the unconditional significance of every personality, and it is characteristic rather of the morals of antiquity, than of Christian morals. Here the esthetic viewpoint prevails over the ethical. . . .

Here is a paradox of the conflict with evil men: good men become evil for the conflict, and do not believe in other methods of conflict than evil ones. Kindness arouses a disdainful attitude and seems uninteresting and vapid. The men of struggle think that anger is more intelligent than kindness. The problem here is that, in actuality, it is impossible to realize good ends. . . . One must be in good and radiate good. Only the Gospel overcomes this transformation of conflict with evil into new evil, as it recognizes in the condemnation of sinners a new sin. . . .

Evil is above all a loss of integrity, a breaking away from the spiritual centre and the formation of autonomous parts which begin to have an independent existence. Good, on the other hand, is inner integrity in mass, unity, the subjection of mental and physical life to the spiritual. . . .

It is not by chance that in Russian orthodoxy the greatest feast-day is that of Christ's Resurrection. This is the way Christianity is understood. The source of victory over the evil of life in this world is neither death nor birth-giving, but resurrection. Experience of the world's evil is destructive, but the creative forces of the resurrection conquer evil and death. As regards evil and evil men, Christian ethics can be only paradoxical. In Christ the God-man, and in the divine-human process, the transfiguration of the whole cosmos is preparing. *Divine*, pp. 107-22

THE DEVIL

> No one ever proposes evil ends: evil is always disguised as good, and detracts from the good. *Spirit and Caesar*, p. 87

The myth about the Fall is a symbolic story of events in the world of spirit. Here, in pictures taken from our natural world, man and the devil are presented as external realities. But in the spiritual world there is no such exteriorality—the interior hierarchy of being has quite another structure from that of the natural world: in it everything is inward, everything is included in itself. And hence in the spiritual world the devil as a higher order of the hierarchy of spirits, and man as the centre and lord of creation are inwardly one within the other and are included, one within the other. The devil is also a reality of man's spiritual world, and appears as something exterior only in images of the natural world. The devil is a reality, but not of the order of nature, we cannot think of him naïvely, realistically. The devil is not an independent source of evil being, he is only the manifestation of irrational freedom at the summit of the spiritual. *Freedom*, I, p. 236

The Devil is Neutral

Man would like to escape from the tormenting problem of evil, and by this escape he would conceal his betrayal of God. We might even say that the devil is neutral. It is an error to think that the devil is the polar opposite of God. The polar opposite of God is God, again, the other face of God: the two extremes meet. But the devil, the prince of this world, hides himself in the neutral. The belief in demons and in the devil has played an enormous rôle in religious life in general, and particularly in Christian life. This was one of the attempted solutions of the problem of evil. When the devil is recognized as the source of evil, what happens is an objectivization of the inward drama of the human soul. The devil is an existential reality, but not at all the sort of objective, substantive reality as are the realities of the world of nature; this is a reality of spiritual experience, of the way along which man passes. The idea of the devil has been much misused, socially: it has been used to frighten people, and the realm of the devil has been enlarged to huge dimensions, with ever new areas added to his dominion. Thus a regular spiritual reign of terror has been set up. And the liberation of the spirit from the demons who torment it, is possible only in a purified spiritual religion. *Divine*, p. 111

> Evil is of an inner metaphysical nature,
> rather than external or social.
>
> *Dostoevsky*, p. 91

ETHICS

Ethics Must be Practical

Ethics should be not only theoretical but practical: ethics should challenge us to the moral transfiguration of life, not only to the appropriation of values, but to the revaluation of values. And this means that there is inevitably a prophetic element in ethics. Ethics should reveal a clear conscience, unsullied by social everydayness: it should be a critique of clear conscience. Ethics is axiology, a doctrine of meaning and of values. But meaning and value are not given passively and objectively, they are created. The doctrine of values must be classed with the higher values.... The supreme value should be a force radiating beneficial, transfiguring energy. Ethics not only teaches secret values, is not only axiology, it also teaches of values as power, of supreme good as power and the source of all power; it is also ontology. And hence it cannot be only normative, for norm by itself is powerless. Ethics deals not with powerless norms and laws, hanging in the air, but with real moral energies and with qualities which possess power. . . . Ethics includes everything which concerns man's freedom, that is with distinctions and evaluations produced in freedom. A free moral act may be accomplished in regard not alone to so-called moral life, but to the whole of man's life. And a moral act accomplished in regard to life as a whole, to all its values, is linked with the fullness of the spiritual life of man. Ethics is a knowledge of spirit, rather than of nature: to ethics belongs only that which is connected with spiritual freedom, rather than with natural necessity. The ways of knowing the spiritual world are different from those of knowing the world of nature. There is a scientific element in ethics; it employs the material of history, culture, sociology, mythology, psychology, etc. But ethics is a philosophical discipline, with all the singularity of philosophical, as distinct from scientific, knowledge. Ethics cannot but be prophetic. And, most important, ethics cannot but be personal. . . . The social ethics of the nineteenth and twentieth centuries, which consider the life of society as the source of moral distinctions and values, and affirm that good and evil are social in nature, quite evidently are turning in a vicious circle. The social cannot be the supreme value and ultimate sum of human life. If the social origin of the distinction between good and evil could be demonstrated, the problem of ethical valuation would not be solved, or even touched. The task of philosophical ethics is not in a knowledge of the origin and development of moral ideas of good and evil, but in knowledge of good and evil themselves. We are interested in the ontology of good and evil, not in how people understand them. . . . The concepts of good and evil incarnate in customs, depend on society, on the social whole, but good and evil themselves do not; on the contrary, society depends upon good and evil, upon their ontology. You may say that my knowledge of good itself leads to my idea of good which forms a part of the general concept and idea of good. This is the usual argument of relativism. My concepts of good may be mistaken, and as such they are relative. But there is no sense in developing concepts and ideas of good which do not exist, any more than knowledge without an object, unrelated to any reality. Ethical evaluation inevitably predicates ethical realism; it presupposes that good exists and is not merely imagined by me. And society can never be substituted for good.

Destiny, pp. 19-20, 24

The Ethic of the Law

The ethic of the law is pre-Christian, not only Old Testament and Judaic, but pagan, primitively social, and within Christianity itself Aristotelian, stoic, pelagian and Thomist (for the greater part). And at the same time the ethic of the law is an eternal element, recognized by the Christian world, as well, since in this world sin and evil are not conquered. We cannot think of the ethic of the law exclusively in terms of time: it co-exists with the ethic of redemption and the ethic of creativity. Both the ethics and the metaphysics of the law have had a complex development in the history of Christianity. Christianity is the revelation of grace and the Christian ethic is that of redemption, rather than of the law, the ethic of beneficient power. But in a world of law Christianity became heavy, and was reborn. Christianity itself was interpreted in a legalistic way. Thus official catholic theology is to a very great degree legalistic. Even the Gospels were distorted by a legalistic interpretation. . . . Even the idea of grace was interpreted legalistically. Men were frightened by the teachings of St Paul, and limited and softened them. Semi-pelagian, rationalistic and legalistic elements made their way into church consciousness itself. In the history of Christianity there has been a constant struggle between elements of grace, super-legalistic, elements of spiritual renaissance, with legalistic, juridical and rationalistic elements. Legalistic ethics have their deep and ancient roots in human society; they hark back to primitive clans with their totemistic cults, back to primitive taboos. The ethic of the law is primarily social, in contrast to the personal ethics of redemption and creativeness. The fall subjected man to the conscience of society. Society becomes the bearer and conserver of the moral law. And those sociologists who teach of the social origin of the ethical, certainly see some sort of truth. But they do not see the original source of this truth and its profound meaning. First of all, the ethic of the law means that the subject of moral evaluation is society, not the personality, that society establishes moral prohibitions, taboos, laws and norms, which the person must obey, under pain of social ostracism and punishment. The ethic of the law cannot be individual and personal; it never penetrates into the intimate depths of a person's moral life and experience and wrestling. It exaggerates evil as this concerns human personality, by fixing prohibitions and punishment. And it minimizes the evil of social and world-life; it is optimistic. Social ethics builds an optimistic doctrine of the power of moral law, of freedom of the will, of punishment of offenders: moral law, they say, is confirmed by the justice that reigns in the world. The ethic of the law is at once human in the highest degree, adapted to human needs and demands to the human level, and also in the highest degree inhuman, merciless toward human personality, toward individual destiny and man's intimate life. *Destiny*, pp. 92-4

Christianity and the Law

Christ not only denounced the legalism of the Pharisees, but said He was come not to destroy the law, but to fulfil it: here is the whole paradox of the Christian attitude toward the law. The Gospel overcomes and abolishes the ethic of law and replaces it by another, the higher and nobler ethic of love and freedom. But it does not permit the external and mechanical denial and abolition of the law. Christianity opens the way to the Kingdom of God, where there is no longer any law. But as always, the law denounces sin, and the law must be fulfilled by a world which lies in sin. The sinner needs salvation, and salvation comes not from the law, but from the Saviour: salvation is achieved, not by the law but by redemption. But the lower sphere of the law still remains, and for this sphere the law remains in force. And the social life of Christian humanity remains in the power of the law almost as much as the life of a primitive clan, worshipping a totem. . . . The ethic of the law was primarily social: the Christian ethic is more individual than social; for it the human soul is worth more than all the kingdoms of this world. This situation makes terrible difficulties for the ethic of the law, which treasures the kingdom of the world above everything else. And for men of the law, Christianity must seem like anarchy. . . . But man's life, his freedom and rights cannot depend altogether on the spiritual condition of other people, of society or the authorities. Man's life, his rights and his freedom must be protected if the spiritual condition of others, of society or the authorities is not very elevated, or not sufficiently enlightened by grace. A society which thinks to base itself on grace alone, does not want to recognize law, will be a despotic society. Thus communist society is also founded exclusively on grace, rather than law, although it is a dark sort of grace, rather than Christian. The result is tyranny, the opposite of theocracy. And we face this paradox: the law does not know the living, concrete, unique personality, does not enter into its intimate life, but the law protects that personality from encroachment or violence on the part of other personalities, protects it regardless of the spiritual condition of these others. Herein lies the great and eternal truth of the law and of justice. *Destiny*, pp. 107-9

The Gospel Ethic

We have seen what a great change in moral evaluations was accomplished by the Gospel; the most radical revaluation of values the world has ever known. Everything becomes unusual, with no resemblance to what the world holds dear and by which it lives. The world is compelled to refuse not only its evil but its good as well. Do not resist evil by force. But the world thinks it good to use force in resisting evil. . . . He who takes the sword shall perish by the sword: but the world defends its existence by the sword. The spirit of freedom poured out in the Gospel frightened the world, and seems to be destructive. The Gospel and the world are poles apart and completely incompatible. The Kingdom of Christ is not of this world: how is it to be brought into the world? Men have been trying to do this for nearly 2,000 years. Christ came not to condemn, but to save. But the world loves judgment and needs judgment, and has a poor understanding of salvation, although this is what it needs the most. The Gospel's absolute revelation does not fit into any social or historical form: these are always relative and temporary. The truth of spiritual life is not commensurate with natural life. There never was and there never can be such things as a Christian state, a Christian economy, Christian science, a Christian way of living, for in the Kingdom of God and in perfect, divine life there is no state, no economy, no family, no science, nothing which stands under the sign of law. Even the church in its historical incarnations became infected by the state and accepted its use of force; it came under the order of law. But the Gospel revelation of the Kingdom of God, all unobserved, secretly, inwardly, brought a change into all spheres of life, altered the very structure of the human spirit, roused new emotions. The Kingdom of God comes unobserved. And whenever it has come too noticeably, it has always been falsehood and fraud. The beneficient power flowing out from the Gospel revelation frees men from the fear, egoism, love of power which torment them, from the lusts of life which know no appeasement. But many of life's basic problems are not solved by the Gospel directly, but only in a veiled form. And the solution of constantly new tasks is left to man himself, to his freedom. The Gospel teaches not so much the solution of life's problems, as it does the healing and regeneration of the tissue of the soul.

Destiny, pp. 132-4

MORALITY

Morality is Innate in Man

We all know very well that pleasure is a plus and suffering a minus; we also know that happiness is a dream of man—but all this has little to do with ethics. Pleasure may be ugly and immoral, happiness may cause us shame, while suffering may be morally valuable and heroic. The aim of ethics is not men's empirical happiness but their *ideal moral perfection.* Therefore, in opposition to hedonists of all shades, I recognize as necessary the following psychological premise to ethics: morality is an independent *quality* of the human spirit: it is not to be derived from such non-ethical concepts as pleasure or happiness; happiness itself is subject to *moral* judgment, and the judgment defines the quality of happiness in recognizing it as worthy or unworthy of man's moral nature.

Idealism, p. 5

Christian Morality: Bourgeois?

Hitherto, the traditional morals of the Christian world have not been creative. Christian morals were either still the Old Testament law which, like the Christian state, denounced sin, or obedience to the results of sin, a redemptive obedience. The creative New Testament morals of evangelic love have not been revealed in the Christian world—they have only been rarely glimpsed, like lightning flashes, in the lives of such chosen spirits as St Francis. Christianity was oriented towards the world as a religion of obedience rather than a religion of love. . . . Christianity, as the revelation of grace, freedom and love, is something other than a set of morals under the law: in it there is neither utilitarianism nor general validity. But the Christian world is infected with the utilitarian morals of adaptation, with the criteria of usefulness and good order for this over-burdened world. The official morals of the Christian world are through and through adapted to this world, to its heaviness, to lowered forms of intercourse in this world. These are the morals of utilitarian fear. They deny the seraphic nature of man, man's natural divinity. . . . *Under the sign of submission to the world's heaviness, Christian morals justify the world as it is, a world lying in sin.* This morality is impregnated with the *pathos* of small acts and modest situations: it is afraid of great, heroic, broad-winged action. And the lack of wings has been raised almost to the rank of religious heroism. A modest moral professionalism is sanctioned: let each sit modestly in his own place and patiently do his own small job. It is not good to rise too high above the world's evil and distortion. . . . Here we have the source of inertia and reaction on the ground of a certain sort of religious democratism. This type of morality has no love for the heights; it is hostile to any aristocratic spirit. The dominant morality connected with Christian consciousness is permeated, through and through, by a bourgeois-democratic adaptation to the conditions of the world. . . . All 'practical' morality is essentially bourgeois—even Christian everyday morality is bourgeois; while in the pure morality of the Gospels there is no trace of this practical, everyday morality, no hint of the bourgeois. Was the morality of St Francis the dominant Christian morality of the time? Men have always held the morality of the Gospels as inadaptable to life, with its concern for a good situation and for security. And the Christian world has accepted a non-Christian, bourgeois morality as useful for living and justified by submission to the consequences of sin. . . .

The whole of Christian history is full of the duality of the pre-Christian morality of the race and the Christian morality of personality. On the Christian morality of personality it would have been impossible to construct any worldly, racial or social order. The whole Christian morality of personality was based on ascetic sacrifice of this world for the sake of another. And all worldly order has rested on the basically bourgeois, extra-Christian morality of the race. *M.C.A.*, pp. 251-6

Christian Morality is Aristocratic

Christian morality is not slavishly plebian but rather aristocratically-noble, the morality of the sons of God, with their primogeniture, their high birth and their high calling. Christianity is the religion of the strong in spirit, not the weak. . . . True Christian morality lays on man, who has become a son of God, free responsibility for his own fate and for the fate of the world, makes it impossible for the sons of God to feel slavish, plebian, ignoble resentment against fate, against life and against other people. The experience of free guilt is an experience of power; the experience of slavish resentment is an experience of weakness. He who is counted in the kingdom of the sons of God is free. And he who longs to redeem his guilt and his sin longs for power out of power, rather than longing for weakness out of weakness: he will participate in the salvation of the world. . . .

The religion of Christ is the religion of man's highest powers—it is the very opposite of all weakness or depression in man. Christianity is a way of the revelation in every man of the Man Absolute. But in the world-epoch of the redemption the Absolute Man is revealed in his sacrificial aspect, and Christian morality is sacrificial. The true *pathos* of Christian morality is in readiness to sacrifice. Readiness to sacrifice is always noble, always aristocratic. . . . But in Christianity sacrifice is never for the sake of human well-being, for the sake of the bourgeois virtues, but rather in the name of God and for the sake of creative values. . . . Christian morality is a morality of values, of the creative heightening of life, rather than a morality of altruistic distribution. Christianity is a religion of love rather than of altruism. Christianity does not permit a lowering of quality for the sake of quantity—it is wholly in quality, i.e. in aristocratic value.

M.C.A., pp. 256-61

Tragedy and Paradox in Moral Life

When we face concrete problems of ethics, we must begin by understanding that our difficulty in solving them is linked with the tragic and paradoxical nature of moral life. And this tragic element lies not in the opposition between good and evil, between the divine and the diabolic, but above all in the clash of one good with another, one value with another value—the conflict between love for God and love for man, love for one's fatherland and love for one's neighbour, love for science and art and pity for man, etc. A moral value in the narrow sense of the word, conflicts with a perceptive or an aesthetic value, a value of personal life conflicts with a super-personal, historical value. . . . A man is compelled to be cruel because he faces the necessity of sacrificing one value for another, one good for another good: for example, sacrificing those near and dear for the fatherland, or for the struggle for social justice, sacrificing patriotic or social activity for scientific or artistic creativity, or the reverse. Man either sacrifices his calling in learning or in art for the sake of religious values, ascetic attainment and greater personal perfection, or he sacrifices his personal perfection for the sake of the creative work of a poet or a philosopher. The erotic life, the life of love, is full of such tragic conflicts. And here the most tragic point is reached when it becomes necessary to sacrifice one quality of love for another. Sometimes a man sacrifices a love which he considers of the highest value and good, for the sake of values of another order, for the maintenance of a particular type of freedom, for the sake of family relationships, out of pity for others who suffer from that love. But the reverse may happen: a man may sacrifice the unquestioned values of his freedom and his task in the world, the values of family or of sympathy for others, for the sake of the infinite value of love.

And here it is important to note that no law, no norm, can help solve the resultant conflict. Man is granted enormous freedom in the solution of moral conflicts which are the cause of life's tragedy. Man has freedom, not only to act well or ill, but to decide for himself what is better or worse. The law does not know tragedy: it knows only the categories of good and evil. But the tragic is a category quite other than that of good or evil. . . . Legalistic ethics solves the problem very simply: if a conflict occurs between moral duty and love: although the latter is a superior value, it is necessary to sacrifice love for the sake of moral duty: if there is conflict of purely moral values, with one's creative calling in learning or art, the latter must be sacrificed for the sake of values purely moral. Thus the area of 'the moral' is greatly narrowed, and life is fettered in the clamps of law.

The ethic of creativity, having passed through the ethic of redemption, takes another view of life and its tasks. For the ethic of creativity, life's tragic conflicts are resolved by man's creative freedom; and the area of 'the moral' is broadened: even something that does not ordinarily relate to values of the moral order, or is linked with values of another order, acquires moral significance. . . . Once a man has recognized that he is a free and creative spirit, by this very fact he makes the solution of life's tragic conflicts dependent on his freedom and his creativity, and not on the abstract acceptance of a uniform universally-valid law. Such a man, when a conflict arises, sacrifices one value for the sake of another. But this is not obligatory for another man, who may do just the reverse, sacrificing the other value. In this case one man is no better than the other. The law and the norm, however, are concerned with the elementary and non-tragic events of life: one should not kill, steal, commit adultery, etc., and this applies equally to all people. The law can say that no single person should be cruel, but it has no knowledge of the case where a man is obliged to be cruel, as a result of the necessity of sacrificing one value for the sake of another. 'Thou shalt not kill' is an absolute norm, the same for all men, but man sometimes tragically takes upon himself the guilt of murder, in order that there should be less killing in the world, and that supreme values be preserved and confirmed. . . .

Destiny, pp. 165-7

The Tragedy of Love

Christianity has terribly increased the tragic contradictions of life, for the Christian faith enters into conflict with man's ancient instincts, with old beliefs that have become superstitions. This is the conflict of the consciousness introduced by the new faith, with that instinct which is actually an ancient faith deeply rooted in the unconscious. It is so difficult to carry out Christian truth in daily living because it conflicts not only with our profound instincts, carried over from ancient times, but also with values we find it difficult to give up. But here we do not yet have a revelation of the tragic in its pure and eternal sense. . . . Our moral life is enwrapped in social conditioning in which the tragic element is unclear and confused. When the tragedy in love arises from the conflict of the value of love with social institutions binding a man, with the enslaving will of parents, with the impossibility of divorce, with fear of public opinion, etc., this is still not the pure and eternal element of the tragic. Here the element of tragedy lies only in the eternal conflict of the personal and the social. But the tragic exists in love itself, not only in its conflict with the social milieu, where everything is passing and temporary, and this is pure tragedy. The tragedy of the love of Tristan and Isolde, or of Romeo and Juliet, includes the eternal element of the tragedy of love which consists in the relation between love and death, but it is sullied and complicated by conflict with the social milieu. Love bears in itself an eternal tragic element, which has no connection with social forms, and is mysteriously and inseparably linked with death. The tragedy would be there, even if there were only the two loving hearts in the whole world. Not only unrequited love is tragic, but requited love is perhaps more so. The full tragedy here is manifest when all social hindrances are put aside. Pure tragedy occurs when people are completely free and a conflict of values occurs—the value of love with the value of freedom or creative vocation, or a conflict of the higher values of love for God and for divine perfection, when one has to struggle for man's eternal godlike image, with which love is connected, but with which it may also enter into conflict. *Destiny*, pp. 167-8

This Tragic Conflict is Inevitable

Moral consciousness always faces the almost unbearably tragic conflict between the person and society, the person and the family, the person and the state, between person and person. And there is always the tragic conflict between personal and social morals. A religious value conflicts with a value of the state or the nation, love for a living person conflicts with love for creativity, etc. And here no smooth, normative, rationalized solutions of the conflict are possible. Good is realized by means of contradiction, sacrifice, suffering. Good is paradoxical. Moral life is tragic. For the very origin of good and evil was in itself a terrible tragedy. And the basic contradiction is always that between the ethics of the race, or social ethics, and personalistic ethics, the ethics of creative personality. The contradictions between the means and the ends of life are equally substantial. Means turn out to be contrary to aims and to absorb the whole of life. Man strives for freedom, as his aim, and is so absorbed by the violence he uses as means to this end, that he forgets freedom altogether. . . . For the realization of justice men resort to falsehood, for the aim of salvation they have recourse to the inquisition and the stake. . . . This contradiction is solvable only by grace and creative love for living beings.

Destiny, p. 172

SIN

Original Sin

Original sin is slavery, bondage of the spirit, subjection to diabolic necessity, the incapacity to affirm oneself as a free creative agent; man loses himself by his assertion in the necessity of the world and not in the freedom of God. The way of liberation from 'the world' for the creation of a new life is at the same time the way of liberation from sin, the overcoming of evil, the gathering of spiritual forces for life which is divine. Slavery to the 'given world', to necessity, is not only bondage but it is legitimizing and confirming the hated and divided non-cosmic condition of the world. Freedom is love. Slavery is hatred. But the escape from slavery into freedom, from the hatred of the world into cosmic love, is the way of victory over sin, over our lower nature. And we may not be refused entrance into this way on the ground that human nature is sinful and sunken in a lower sphere. It is a great falsehood, a terrible mistake of religious and moral judgment, to leave man in the lower depths of 'the world', because he must be obedient to the results of his sin. On the soil of such judgment there grows a shameful indifference to good and evil, the refusal of manful resistance to wrong. The depressive concentration on man's own sinfulness gives birth to double thinking: the constant danger of confusing God with the devil, Christ with Antichrist. This fallen state of the spirit, shamefully indifferent to good and evil, has now gone to the length of a mystic fascination with passivity and humility, to play with double-thinking. The fallen soul likes to flirt with Lucifer, likes not knowing which God she serves, enjoys feeling terror and danger everywhere. This fallen state, this palsy and cleavage of man's spirit, is an indirect result of the Christian doctrines of humility and obedience—it is a degeneration of these doctrines. Over against this decadent doubling of thought and this palsied indifference to good and evil we must firmly set the manful liberation of the spirit and creative action.

M.C.A., p. 12

Sin

Too many people on this earth consider their suffering unjust, and do not understand why just upon them should fall tormenting illness, bitter want, failure, betrayal; why they have to suffer more than others who are not better, or even worse, than they are. Explanation of human misfortunes by original sin explains nothing because it is addressed to the 'general' rather than the 'individual'. The more fortunate and successful, those who suffer less, are just as much affected by original sin as the unhappy and those who suffer inordinately. If we try to establish a proportionality between suffering and sinfulness, we are like Job's comforters. It is impossible to rationalize human fate. Any such rationalization is forced to consider everything as just and so in effect to deny the existence of evil. The task facing spiritual life is not to explain and justify life's suffering, but to illuminate it and endure it spiritually. Bearing one's cross means the spiritual, serene endurance of suffering.

Reality, p. 102

There is something slavish in the conception of sin as a crime which contravenes the will of God and calls forth a judicial process on God's part. . . . Sin is cleavage, impairment, lack of fullness, disjunction, enslavement, hatred, rather than disobedience and the formal contravention of God's will. It is impossible and impermissible to construct an ontology of evil. Hence the idea of eternal punishment in hell is absurd and evil. Evil is only a way, a testing, a disruption. The Fall is above all a trial of freedom. Man moves towards the light through darkness.

Divine, pp. 113-14

Why the Fall?

We cannot think of the Kingdom of God in moralistic terms; it is beyond moral distinctions. The fall made us moralists. And we face a great enigma: how is it that man should not have desired paradise, which he remembers and dreams about in this our earthly eon; how could he fall away from paradise? Paradise was a life of blessedness: the cosmos was in man and man was in God. Man's expulsion from Eden meant that he fell away from God, and the cosmos fell away from man. Paradise was a life of blessedness, but was it fullness of life? Were all possibilities revealed in the life of Paradise? The Bible story is exoteric: it presents symbols of the spiritual world. But a more profound interpretation of these symbols is necessary. Not everything was revealed to man in Paradise, and ignorance was a condition of life there. This was the realm of the unconscious. Man's freedom had not yet developed, had not yet tested itself, had not yet participated in the creative act. Meonic freedom, which was in man from non-being, from nothingness, was temporarily hidden in the original act of the world's creation, but it could not be destroyed. This freedom remained in the substructure of life in Paradise, and it had to manifest itself. And in order to experience this freedom to the fullest, to its depths, man turned away from the moment of paradisiac harmony and integrity, and craved the suffering and tragedy of the life of the world. This is the rise of consciousness with its tormenting duality.

And in this fall from the harmony of Paradise, from unity with God, man began to make distinctions and to evaluate: he had tasted the tree of the knowledge of good and evil, had come to this side of good and evil. When man was forbidden to touch it, it was a warning that the fruits of the tree of the knowledge of good and evil were bitter and deadly. Knowledge was born of freedom, out of the dark womb of the irrational. And man preferred the bitterness of distinction and death to life in Paradise in innocence and ignorance. He might have fed from the tree of life, and have lived eternally a life in Paradise, vegetative and unconscious. But in this innocent life in Paradise, where man fed on the tree of life and did not approach the tree of knowledge, the relationship between the Creator and creation was revealed in the aspect of God the Father. The divine Trinity was not revealed in Paradise, and the Son did not appear as boundless love and sacrifice. God was only a nourishing force. The story of Paradise is so expressed as though only God the Father was there, or even not God the Father, for without the Son there is no Father, but God the creative force. It is a paradox of Christian thought that Christ could not have appeared in the life of Paradise. Of course, it may be said that God the Word was present in Paradise, but this was the Word not incarnate, not become man, not making the sacrifice of love. The life of Paradise was altogether in Old Testament categories; it is not in the image of the Holy Trinity. If man had remained in the passivity and innocence of Paradise, in the immediately elemental and unconscious, i.e. in a divine-natural stage of life, he would not have known Christ or attained the possibility of becoming Godlike. *Destiny*, pp. 40-1

HELL

A Postulate of Freedom

Salvation from eternal destruction is not at all the ultimate truth: it is only a utilitarian and vulgarized transcription of the truth about seeking the Kingdom of God, of love toward God and the attainment of perfect life, of theosis. This in no wise eliminates the problem of hell or dulls its tormenting acuity. This is the sound of one of the two voices in the soul's inner dialogue. But immediately the other voice begins to be heard, and it confirms the unsurmountably antinomic attitude toward hell. On one hand we cannot admit the existence of hell, it is inacceptable to moral consciousness; on the other, we cannot simply deny its existence, for such denial means ignoring certain indubitable values. It is very easy to deny the existence of hell, if one denies personality and freedom. There is no hell, if personality does not belong to eternity. There is no hell if man is not free and if he can be compelled to be good and to enter paradise. Ontologically, the idea of hell is linked with freedom and personality rather than with justice and recompense. However paradoxical it may seem, hell is a moral postulate of the freedom of the human spirit. Hell is not necessary that justice may triumph and the wicked receive their just reward, but that man should not be violated by good and forced into paradise. Which is to say that in a sense man has a moral right to hell, the right freely to prefer hell to paradise. Herein lies the whole moral dialectic of hell. . . .

Hell Cannot be Eternal

Eternal hell is a vicious and contradictory combination of words. Hell is a denial of eternity, the impossibility of entering eternal life and of communing with eternity. There can be no such thing as hellish and devilish eternity: there can be only divine eternity, the eternity of the Kingdom of God. But in the subject, in the closed subjective sphere, an evil infinity of torment may be revealed. The experience out of which the idea of eternal punishment was developed, is given in man's experience in the subjective sphere of torment which has no end in time. In this, our life experience, we live through torment which to us seems endless. . . . But this endlessness is not eternity, neither is it objective being. Objectively this endlessness of torment may continue for a moment, an hour or a day, but we call it eternal hellish punishment. The experience of eternal torment is actually the subject's incapacity to tear himself away from his imprisonment in his own tormenting experience. There is no hell, a phantasmagoric, illusory and non-existential sphere. But it may be a supreme psychological subjective reality for man. Hell is a nightmare which cannot be eternal, but may be experienced by man as endless.

Not Evangelical

It cannot be assumed that hell was created by God. Hell was created by the devil. Hell is created by human sin. But the terrible thing about it is that hell is created not alone by 'bad men', by evil, but in a far greater degree by 'good men'; it is created by good itself for 'bad men' and for evil. The 'bad' set up hell for themselves, but the 'good' establish it for others. For centuries the 'good', having known they were saved, affirmed and confirmed the concept hell. This was a powerful movement of Christian thought, penetrated by the unchristian, unevangelical idea of justice. In this construction and eternalizing of hell, the early Greek fathers of the church had very little part. This evil work of 'the good' was chiefly accomplished in western Christian thought, beginning with St Augustine, and it culminated in Thomas Aquinas and Dante. The concept of hell, created by 'good' men for 'bad' men, flourishes in all the catechisms and all the theological schools. It is based on Gospel texts which are accepted literally, with no account taken of the imagery of New Testament language, and no understanding of its symbolism. The Gospel words about hell trouble only the new Christian consciousness: they rejoiced the old Christian thought.

Salvation from Hell is Possible Only Through Christ

Belief in Christ and His resurrection is also belief that hell can be conquered. Belief in eternal hell is really unbelief in the power of Christ and belief in the power of the devil. Herein lies the basic contradiction in Christian theology. . . . Manicheism is a metaphysical fallacy, but it has moral depth: it is agony over the problem of evil, with which rationalistic theology copes all too easily. Men have tried to escape from the tormenting difficulties linked with the problem of evil, by recognizing hell itself as the triumph of God's righteous judgment and hence the triumph of good. But this is a most disturbing consolation. The problem of victory over the dark powers of hell is not at all forgiveness, for these are limitless; it is the problem of how God can conquer the dark freedom of a creature who hates and turns away from Him. The devil's realm is not in being, but in non-being, in the sphere of meonic, dark freedom, in a subjective and illusory sphere. A man who enters this sphere no longer belongs to himself, but is in the power of the dark forces of non-being. Victory over dark freedom is impossible for God, for this freedom was not created by God, and is rooted in non-being. And this victory is impossible for man, since he has become the slave of this dark freedom, and is no longer free in his own freedom. This victory is possible only for the God-man Christ, who descended into hell, into the bottomless darkness of meonic freedom; it is possible for the complete union and reciprocal action of Divinity and humanity. Victory over the terror of hell, as an expression of the freedom of creation, is possible only through Christ the God-man. Aside from Christ, the tragic antinomy of freedom and necessity is insoluble, and by right of freedom, hell remains inevitable. The terror of hell in one's soul is always a departure from Christ, a dimming of His image in the soul. Salvation from hell is open to all, to the whole of creation, in Christ the Savour. *Destiny*, pp. 287-302

The Ultimate Mystery

The problem of hell is the ultimate mystery, incapable of rationalization. But the doctrine of eternal torment in hell as the triumph of divine justice, which occupies an honoured place in sections of dogmatic theology, is a rationalization of the mystery, a denial of the eschatological mystery. Eschatology should be free from both the optimism and pessimism which are born of rationalization. All rationalized eschatologies are nightmarish: the idea of eternal torment in hell, the idea of endless reincarnations, the idea of the personality disappearing in divine being, even the idea of inevitable universal salvation is nightmarish. And all this bears witness to the fact that forced rationalization has transgressed the mystery. We neither can nor should set up any rational ontology of hell, neither optimistic nor pessimistic. But we may and we must believe that the power of hell has been vanquished by Christ, and that the final word belongs to God and to God's meaning. *Destiny*, p. 303

Incompatible With the Idea of Justice

The level of one's mental consciousness may be measured by his attitude toward the idea of eternal punishment. This is one of the chief obstacles in converting the dechristianized world to Christianity. Men prefer not to become imbued with religious beliefs which threaten them with forced labour for life. There is quite enough hell on earth, no need to project it on heaven as well. And a large part of modern Christians to whom a medieval thought is alien, prefer not to think about it. But it should be thought about. The idea of eternal punishment is one of the most terrible offspring of ill and fearful human imagination; here one feels the continuation of ancient sadistic and Mosaic instincts which have always played a large rôle in religious life. True spiritual religion must be completely cleansed of this idea.

It is most shocking that the idea of hell is linked with the idea of justice, which derives from the instinct of revenge. We see this in St Augustine, St Gregory the Great, St Thomas Aquinas and Calvin, although with him the idea of justice played only a minor rôle. All this was the ultimate expression of the legalistic concept of Christianity. But in this theory the justice of the Supreme Judge who passes sentence, is far lower than earthly justice of an earthly judge. The sentence to hell is passed by an all-powerful and all-kind God who created everything, including man's freedom, who has foreseen and consequently predestined everything. Sentence to eternal punishment is passed on a feeble, finite being in a very short space of time, a being completely under the authority of God. . . .

Of Time, Not Eternity

There is such a thing as hell, and only a careless optimist can deny it. However, hell is not of the beyond, but of the here and now; it is phenomenal rather than noumenal: in time rather than in eternity; it relates more to the sphere of magic than to that of mysticism. But it seems to me that hell, if only for me alone (and there are moments when I think myself worthy of it), is a failure of creation as a whole, a fissure in the Kingdom of God. On the other hand, paradise is possible for me only if there is no eternal hell for a single being who has ever lived. We cannot be saved one by one, in isolation. Salvation can only be a collective (soborny), general liberation from torture. The very word 'salvation' is only an exoteric expression for inward illumination and transfiguration. Without this concept, the creation of the world is inacceptable. . . .

Defence of hell by the use of the idea of free will is simply moving the problem to the rear of the stage, but not solving it, for the very idea of free will is seen to be the idea of criminal law, not at all applicable to the divine mystery we are facing. It is very important to understand that the idea of hell deprives man's moral and spiritual life of all meaning, since it places him under the sign of terror. The whole of life passes in terror. And frightened man is willing to accept anything in order to escape eternal punishment. This deprives spiritual life of all dignity. . . .

Truth, pp. 110-12

IMMORTALITY

> Man's eternal destiny is not destiny in endless time: it will be decided by the ending of time. *Beginning*, p. 180

Only Spiritual Life Deserves It

Immortality is a spiritual and religious rather than a naturalistic and metaphysical category. Immortality is not a normal quality of natural man: it is the attainment of spiritual life, a second birth in spirit, birth in Christ, the source of life eternal. Man's immortality is not an infinite extension of his metaphysical nature. It is rebirth to a new and higher life in the spiritual race of the new Adam. This life is life eternal, life which has overcome death. Immortality, eternal life, is the revelation of the Kingdom of God: it is not the metaphysical nature of being. Therefore Christianity does not teach the immortality of the soul, as do various forms of naturalistic metaphysics, but rather it teaches resurrection. Resurrection is an event of the spiritual life, of the spiritual world, which overcomes the corruptibility and mortality of the world of nature. The Christian church detects the falsehood in every form of monophysite doctrine, i.e. the untruth and perversity of that spiritual experience which cannot comprehend the mystery of two natures, divine and human, and expresses itself in teachings about one nature. . . . The mystery of the eternal life of two natures, eternal life not of God alone, but of man as well, is the mystery of Christ the God-man. It cannot be translated into the language of any sort of metaphysical nature, it escapes such definition. The greatest of the scholastics struggled quite hopelessly to express this mystery in the language of substantial metaphysics and theology. . . . Natural man, the natural mental-physical monad, does not have immortality as a natural quality. Only spiritual life deserves immortality; only the spirit possesses the quality of eternal life. And man's immortality is his entry into spiritual life, his acquisition of spiritual life for himself, the return of the spirit that has been wrested away. The source of immortality is in God rather than in nature; it is unthinkable without life in God and the divine. *Freedom* I, pp. 73-5

Immortality Is Creative

Victory over death cannot be evolution, the result of necessity; victory over death is creativity, the result of freedom, of man's creative working together with God. Life's tension and passion lead to death, and are related to death. In the whirlpool of the natural world, life and death are inseparable. . . . The tension of life's passion leads to death because it is part of the finite; it does not extend into the infinite and eternal. Eternal life is not attained by mortification or destruction of life's passionate intensity, but by its spiritual transfiguration, by controlling it through the creative activity of spirit. *Slavery*, p. 210

Immortality: a Basic Problem

The problem of immortality is basic; the chief problem of human life, and man forgets this only because of his superficiality and thoughtlessness. Sometimes he tries to convince himself that he has forgotten, does not permit himself to think of what is most important. The prayer that we be given remembrance of death is a very profound prayer: and the remembrance of death, not only our own, but even more the death of others, determines the seriousness of life itself. All religions, beginning with the elemental religious beliefs of savages, have been built in relation to death. Man is a being who faces death throughout his life, not only in his last hour. Man carries on two struggles: for life and for immortality. Death is a phenomenon of life here, rather than in the beyond; it is a most stunning phenomenon, bordering on the transcendent. . . .

About victory over the horror of death and the attainment of real or illusory immortality, many types of religious and philosophical doctrines have been developed. . . . The spiritualistic doctrine of the immortality of the spirit offers immortality to a part of man only, not the whole. The doctrine of transmigration of souls offers still less. . . . The doctrine of fusion with Divinity means only the immortality of the divine in man, not of his whole personality. . . . Turning away from the theme of immortality by means of what I might call social pantheism, by looking toward the coming happiness of all humanity, shows the insolubility of the problem and hostility to putting the question. Only the Christian doctrine of the resurrection of the integral man answers the question, but as we shall see, this involves many difficulties.

The problem of death and immortality is inseparably linked with consciousness of personality, of personal destiny. Only the death of personality is tragic, the death of an immortal being: there is nothing tragic in the death of something impersonal. . . . If we were to lose the keen sense of personality and forget about its unique and eternal destiny, we might console ourselves with the thought that life in nature, in the race, is reborn and immortal. As a person, man struggles with death for the sake of immortality. The biologists say that death is the price to be paid for highly differentiated development. Zimmel expresses this more philosophically by saying that life takes form because the living thing dies. But this means that what dies is the thing that most needs immortality. . . . So it is from the naturalistic viewpoint, so it is in the objectivized world. . . .

The difficulty in solving the problem of immortality depends on the fact that it is put in the perspective of objectivization, the exteriorization of human existence in the objective world. Externally, the soul depends upon the body, and the body on the objective, physical world. Biologically, death occurs from the decomposition of the complex organism. The cell is immortal, because it is simple. Weissman thought the cell was the virtual incorporation of immortality. Plato defended the possibility of immortality on the basis of the soul's simplicity. . . . The physical energy of the human organism does not perish, but is merely transformed, dispersed through the world. We may be permitted to ask, what becomes of psychic energy after death? The human organism has a multitude of parts: it is colonial and hence easily decomposed. Personality is unity, and unchangeableness within the constant changes of man's multitudinous make-up. The spiritual element is what maintains this unity and unchangingness.

But the paradox lies in this, that the spiritual element itself demands death, for man's infinite striving is not realizable within the bounds of this phenomenal world. Death reigns only in the world of phenomena, subject to cosmic and historic time. In existential time it means only an experience of passage through trial. Death is man's fate, the passage through the most irrational and shattering experience.

The spiritual meaning of death is different from the biological. It is wrong to think that the 'neant' exists in the world of nature. In nature there is no nothingness, non-being: there is only change, decomposition and composition, development. The horror of non-being exists only in relation to the spiritual world. . . . I catch myself in this contradictory judgment: if there is nothing for me after death, I will know about it after death. If I die and there is no life for me afterward, if I disappear finally, then there will be nothing, and there will be no world, for I was the only proof of the world's existence. . . .

Immortality in man is also linked with memory. One of the tormenting things in human life is not only the loss of memory, forgetfulness of things precious and dear, but (still worse), the impossibility of forgetting the evil and difficult things in the past. Immortality is illuminated memory. The most terrible thing in life is the sense of the irreparable, the point of no return, of absolute loss. Human freedom can do nothing about this, even belief in natural immortality will not help: this is the point where divine-human connection is broken off: it is the sense of God-forsaken-ness. Only belief in the power of the race which proceeds from Christ can help us, for in Him is incarnate the divine-human bond. The light may shine out in the deepest dark. . . .

The judicial concept of immortality is just as low as the ancient magic concept. The pedagogical element plays a great part in the traditional doctrines about immortality. Only the spiritual concept of immortality is fitting for a higher consciousness. But this does not mean that only the spiritual side of man is immortal. We must understand the resurrection of the body spiritually, as well. 'There is sown a mortal body, there is raised a spiritual body.' Man is immortal because in him there is an element of the divine. But it is not only the divine element in man that is immortal—the whole of man possessed of his spirit, is immortal. The spiritual element in man is that which resists the total objectivization of human existence, the death-bringing current of time. . . .

Quite independent of man's conscious ideas, the thought of immortality may give him a weighty idea of his calling and mission in the world. Personal eschatology is interlaced with universal and historical eschatology. My immortality cannot be separated from that of other men and of the world. . . . Concern with one's own personal immortality exclusively, is the same transcendent egoism as exclusive concern with one's own salvation. The idea of personal immortality, apart from the general perspective of eschatology, from the destiny of the world, contradicts love. But love is the chief spiritual weapon in the struggle against the kingdom of death. The antipodes of love and death are linked with each other. Love is revealed at its strongest when death is near. And it is impossible that love should not overcome death. He who truly loves, is a victor over death. We should put forth superhuman effort to assure that those we love, not people alone, but animals, should inherit eternal life. Christ conquered death because he was the incarnation of universal divine love. And it is impossible that love should not desire universal salvation from death and universal resurrection. If even one being with an existential centre should not be resurrected for life eternal, the world is a failure and theodicy is impossible. Under these conditions my personal immortality is not only partial, but in reality impossible. I am dependent upon the destiny of my dear ones and of the world, and they are dependent upon me. . . .

Man's death, on this earthly plane, cannot be the final decision as to his fate. If the one-plane transmigration of souls conflicts with the idea of personality, the idea of a many-planed reincarnation is fully cogent with it. If the way of realization of the fullness of life for human life is continued in the spiritual world this does not contradict the idea that man's body, the bodily form, should inherit life eternal, and not merely his soul. For the form of the body, inextricably linked with the image of man's personality does not involve the indissoluble connection with the material of the body, its physical-chemical constitution. And the resurrection of the body is the resurrection of the body spiritual. . . .

Immortality is not an affair solely human or solely divine; it is a divine-human affair, a matter of freedom and grace, an affair that is accomplished both from above and from below. It is just as inexact to think that man is a naturally immortal being, as to think that he receives immortality from above, from divine power. Here the error, as always, is in severing the divine-human relationship, in man's self-assertion, in the degradation of man's humanity. We so often think of immortality, transferring to the world of phenomena what relates only to the noumenal world, and vice-versa. . . . The true view of immortality is divine-human rather than abstractly human. *Divine*, pp. 183-202

Immortality: Victory over Death

I never could be reconciled to anything corruptible or passing: I always thirsted for the eternal and only the eternal seemed to be of value. I have suffered torment at separation, in time, in distance or in space. The problem of immortality and eternal life has always been for me a basic religious question. And I never could understand people who saw the meaning and perspective of their lives outside the solution of that question. There is nothing more pitiable than comfort drawn from the progress of mankind, and the happiness of coming generations. And the comfort of world-harmony, sometimes offered to personality, always revolts me. . . . I never had any special fear about my own death, and really have thought little about it. I am not one of those who are possessed with the fear of death, as was Tolstoy, for example. The question of the death of others, near and dear, has been very painful. But victory over death has always seemed to me to be the basic problem of life. I felt death to be a more profound event than birth. . . . The problem of his eternal destiny faces every living man, and every objectivization of it is falsehood. If there is no God, i.e. if there is not a higher sphere of freedom, of eternal and genuine life, if there is no deliverance from the necessities of the world, then we cannot value the world and this corruptible life within it. *Autobiography*, p. 318 ff

Suffering

There are two kinds of suffering: suffering unto life, and suffering unto death: suffering which exalts and cleanses, and suffering which crushes and demeans. Sympathy should strive first of all to liberate creation from the second type of suffering and to aid those who are being purified and uplifted by their suffering. . . . It is humane to sympathize with and help the suffering, even if it be that of a criminal or a great sinner. For we are all criminals and sinners. . . . We must aid others to bear their cross of suffering, help reveal the meaning of the cross, not lay upon our neighbour a heavy cross supposedly for his soul's salvation. The moral pathos of punishment for crime, the imposition of a cross and suffering as a means of improvement and purification, is false. . . .

There is awakening in the world a new morale of sympathy with men, with animals, with everything which suffers pain. This is a great spiritual achievement. But here, as always, we discover duality. Modern civilized man cannot stand cruelty, suffering or pain, and he is more pitying than men of earlier times, not because he stands above them, morally and spiritually. He has come to be more afraid of pain and suffering, has become softer and less courageous and fearless: he has less endurance. He has weakened, spiritually. This is the reverse side of the increase in sympathy and pity, the lessening of cruelty.

Destiny, pp. 208-9

I suffer, therefore I am. This is truer and more profound than Descartes' 'cogito'. Suffering is related to the very existence of personality and personal consciousness. . . . Suffering is related not only to man's animal condition, i.e. to his lower nature, but also to his spirituality, his freedom, his personality, i.e. his higher nature. . . .

Suffering is the basic theme of all religions of redemption; in general, it is a basic religious theme. In suffering man passes through moments when he feels God has deserted him, and also in suffering he comes into communion with God. Suffering may turn into joy. Man on the earth is terribly unhappy, frightened, lives through horror and agony. And everything that lives is in the same condition. But man has the power to create, to accomplish heroic acts, to experience ecstasy. . . . Misfortune is first of all segmentation, cleavage. The basic and most important question of human existence is how to conquer suffering, how to endure it, how not to be crushed by suffering, how to lessen the quantity of suffering for everyone, and for all of life. Before Christianity there were religions of the suffering god, Osiris, Dionysius and others. God himself suffers and this is salutary. The mystery of Christianity is bound up with this idea. . . . The whole matter, here, is in the union of human with divine suffering, since in it cleavage and alienation, both human and divine, are overcome. . . .

Christ transformed suffering into a way of salvation. In the world truth is crucified. The only sinless, just man hung on the cross. But this does not mean that one should seek suffering, torture oneself, neither does it mean that we should cause others to suffer for their salvation. By the way, the most believing Christians have been very cruel because, and for the sake of, their faith. The Inquisition was founded on this belief in the salutary value of suffering. This is also the case with torture and the justification of cruel or capital punishment. . . . Christians sought suffering, illness, self-torture or the torture of others. . . .

The task man faces is not to explain the suffering in his life, the meaningless incidents, 'the sin which doth so easily beset us', and see in it punishment for wrong-doing. The spiritual task is worthily to bear suffering and to transform incomprehensible suffering which threatens ruin, into enlightened suffering which leads to salvation. . . .

Sympathy (suffering *with*) is an absolute commandment. . . . The tormenting problem of suffering is insoluble, finally, within the limits of this world of phenomena. The contradiction between man's nature and the conditions of his finite existence in this natural world is insoluble: it predicates the necessity of transcendence, of an end to it all. Can good save us from suffering? It cannot, and hence the necessity for redemption and a Redeemer, both human love and God's love. Man is powerless in the face of evil and suffering. But God himself, as Creative Force, is powerless also. Only God becoming man, taking upon himself the suffering of man and of all creation, can conquer the source of evil which engenders suffering. No theological systems, no authorities of any sort, can stop human suffering and torment. Only religious primal realities, only divine-human bonds, only divine-human love can put an end to them. . . . *Divine*, pp. 87-108

LIFE'S MEANING

For everyone with religious feeling and a vision of human personality, man's fate is a mystery, not to be unravelled within the small section of eternal life which we call man's earthly, empirical life. The destiny of every man is immersed in eternity, and in eternity the deciphering of its meaning is to be sought. Within the limits of our brief life, everything appears accidental, meaningless and unjust. But everything takes on meaning and finds justification in eternity. *Inequality*, pp. 42-3

Men have advanced various well-reasoned and optimistic justifications of life. They have justified life either by the traditional theological idea of Divine Providence, everywhere present (God in everything), or by the idealistic-pantheistic idea of world development of spirit or reason (the idea of Hegel, Schilling and other great idealists), or by the positivistic idea of world progress toward a perfect, more reasonable, free and just life in the future. These various justifications actually reflected the irrational element in our world of phenomena, but did not explain the existence of evil, triumphant in the world, did not catch the tragic nature of the world-process, and so it was impossible to construct a theodicy. The least acceptable of these it seems to me, are all forms of historical pantheism, those that have a wider understanding than usual of pantheism, and incline toward the most orthodox theological doctrines. Dualism, not pantheism is true for our world of phenomena: our world is full of the conflict of opposing elements, poles apart. But this dualism is not final. The final word, which has not yet been spoken, belongs to God and His righteousness. This is beyond human optimism and pessimism. And this is our final faith. This will conquer the tragedy born of freedom which has been the way of man and of the world included in him. And we shall not transfer to that world beyond all boundaries, any dualism, any of our all-too-worldly divisions into heaven or hell. *Beginning*, pp. 60-5

GNOSTICISM

We may discover the beginning of an evolutionary doctrine in the gnostics; they recognize historic epochs and periods. This is very valuable, but it is not the Christian dynamism that teaches the transubstantiation, the transfiguration of lower nature into higher. For the gnostics the image of God and that of man were sunk and shattered in cosmic processes. The cosmos in its infinitely complex hierarchical system and its endless eons, oppressed not man alone, but God as well. The Church's consciousness revolted against that sort of gnosticism, revolted for the sake of both man and God: it would not consent to giving man over to torture by cosmic forces. This spiritual liberation from the power of cosmic forces became the mark of church knowledge and church experience. In order to understand the mystery of the transfiguration of the lower into the higher, man must be freed from the oppression of cosmic law. And until man had stood on his own feet, spiritually, until he had increased his independence of the forces of nature, until he had united his spiritual nature with God, church consciousness set a limit for the gnostic penetration by man into the mysteries of cosmic life. . . .

The consequence of church agnosticism in the mental history of mankind was the development of positive science, natural history and technics, the mechanization of nature and a mechanical doctine about nature. Christianity set free in man forces which later rose against Christianity itself. Such is man's tragic destiny. And today churchmen often prefer positive mechanics and physics in which they see no threat to Christianity, to the gnostic cosmology which they consider a competitor to Christianity. But Christianity's connection with the mechanical concept of nature is of no principal importance: it does not follow that Christianity does not admit gnosis in principle, or the knowledge of cosmic mysteries. This is not a part of the Church's dogmatic thought. Clement of Alexandria and Origen were Christian gnostics, as were St Gregory of Nyssa and St Maxim the Confessor. And a Christian gnosis is possible in principle. Christianity cannot permit a return to the pagan concept of nature, to demonolatry, to the power of magic over man's spirit, to the laceration of man's image by the elemental spirits of nature. But nature is alive, not dead, for the Christian mind, as well. . . .

Freedom, I, pp. 143-5

ESCHATOLOGY

I must explain what I understand by the word eschatology. I have in mind not the eschatological part of a theological system: this you may find in any text on catholic or protestant theology. I am thinking of the eschatological concept of Christianity as a whole, in contrast to the historical concept of Christianity. The Christian revelation is eschatological, a revelation about the end of this world, about the Kingdom of God. The whole of early Christianity was eschatological: men awaited the second coming of Christ and the beginning of the Kingdom of God. Christianity in history, the historical church means that the Kingdom of

God did not begin; it indicates the adaptation of the Christian revelation to the kingdom of this world. Hence the messianic hope, the eschatological expectation, remains in Christianity, and this is stronger in Russian than in Western Christianity. The Church is not the Kingdom of God, the Church appeared in history and has been active in history, but it does not mean the transfiguration of the world, the appearance of a new heaven and a new earth. But the Kingdom of God is the transfiguration of the world, the transfiguration of the individual man, but social and cosmic transfiguration as well. This is the end of our world of injustice and deformity, and the beginning of a new world of justice and beauty. When Dostoevsky said that beauty would save the world, he had in mind the transfiguration of the world, the coming of the Kingdom of God. *Idea*, p. 197

The modern Christian mind cannot be morally reconciled to the old eschatology. It is very difficult to accept a metaphysic according to which the eternal fate of the soul is finally decided by its life in time from birth to death. Understood in this way, our short earthly life is a snare, and our worth for eternity is decided by the infinitesimally small experience of time. The Christianity of our time cannot so easily assign a whole life to the torments of hell, as was the case with mediaeval religious thought. This is one of the results of the spiritual process we have lived through. And for us this is more a moral and spiritual, than a dogmatic, question. It is not at all that, like Origen and St Gregory of Nyssa, we want again to construct a theory of apokatastasis. Everything is transferred from the sphere of the theological-metaphysical, resolving the ultimate mystery of human fate by means of rational categories (Origen attempted to give a rational eschatology), into the sphere of our spiritual tendency, our spiritual will. We must strive toward the salvation of everyone. We should be saved together, as a world collectively, rather than individually. . . . *Freedom*, I, pp. 184-6

ATHEISM

Modern Atheism and its Earlier Forms

We are living in a world entirely different from that of the eighteenth or nineteenth centuries. And the atheism of the twentieth century is as different as everything else. In the last two centuries we had atheism of the day, of enlightenment: it was based on the belief in the supremacy of reason. I say 'belief', because there was a faith in reason which now has been gravely shaken. In contrast, modern atheism is best described as atheism of the night, an expression of modern man's yearning, terror and hopelessness. Everything has become more extreme, more naked, . . . and at the same time atheism has become more complex and refined: it is no longer bound, as it once was, to elementary materialism and positivism, to an optimistic faith in endless progress and in the leading rôle of reason. In the past it was reason, conscious of its independence, that rebelled against God: now it is the irrational force of life which rebels against Him. Once it was argued: the world by itself is good and is constantly developing, hence there is no God nor any need of Him. Nowadays they say: 'The world is bad and meaningless, there is no progress, and therefore there is no God.' *Truth*, pp. 74-5

Indifference—the Worst Form of Atheism

We find the most terrible form of atheism, not in the militant and passionate struggle against the idea of God himself, but in the practical atheism of every-day living, in indifference and torpor. We often encounter these forms of atheism among those who are formally Christians. Impassioned concern and struggle against God may lead to enlightenment and a higher religious consciousness. In this way godlessness may even be useful, and may bring about purification of the idea of God and liberation from servile concepts of God which have been distorted by sociomorphism.

Christian indignation against atheism, against the militant godless may often be a good thing, also. Perhaps the Christians' distorted conception of God or their godless lives have been the cause of the very atheism they decry. They have ascribed to God the worst of qualities: self-satisfaction, stubbornness, cruelty, love of obsequiousness. It is not fitting for Christians to be self-satisfied and to scorn those who are tormented by the idea of God, such men as Nietzsche, for example. Some atheists may be better men than those who cry 'Lord, Lord'. Atheism has its own internal dialectic: at first God is denied for the sake of man, his freedom and his creative activity. But it ends with the denial of man himself, but for the sake of something not human, something superhuman which has been substituted for divinity. *Truth*, pp. 76-7

Two Psychological Forms of Atheism

Psychologically, there are two types of atheism. We have a self-satisfied, optimistic atheism, when man feels relief because there is no God: this predicates faith in reason, in man's own powers, in the reasonableness of material itself, faith in endless development. Then there is the suffering, tragic type of atheism, when man says, with Nietzsche, 'God is dead.' The first type of man says, 'Thank God, there is no God, and we are free to make ourselves comfortable on the earth.' The second says, 'What a terrible situation: there is no God, everything is lost, and life for us is without meaning.' Godlessness may be calm, well-intentioned and not at all hostile toward those who believe in God, and it may be angry, stormy and menacing. We have godlessness which results from sympathy, from love of justice and good, and we have godlessness which rebels against that same good, and is ready cruelly to persecute those who believe in God. There is godlessness and there is anti-Godness. In theory atheism does not necessarily have to be stuggle against God, but it may quite easily turn into such struggle. The atheism of the anarchist Bakunin sometimes gives the impression of active struggle against God, and not merely the theoretical denial of God's existence. We must always remember that godlessness may be a protest against false and servile ideas of God. This type of atheism deserves our sympathy. The denial of God's existence has often been understood as liberation from an enslaving idea of God, where God was thought of as master and man as slave. God was transformed into a denial of man's dignity and his creativeness. And struggle against God became struggle for man. Belief in God was thus terribly distorted by the process of objectivization and socialization. God was used to defend evil, untruth and injustice.

Truth, pp. 77-8

Scientific Atheism is Naïve

Godlessness justifies itself on various grounds, scientific-positivistic, moral or social. In the second half of the nineteenth century a heavy stratum of both European and Russian intelligentsia convinced themselves that science had demonstrated that there was no God, that belief in God could not be combined with the existence of science. It must be said that this is the most naïve and the feeblest of all the arguments of atheism. It was based on the belief that science is supreme not only over all knowledge, but over the whole of human life. Men thought that science had the answer to every question. In the twentieth-century positive science, specially physics and chemistry, have made colossal advances, but there is no longer the belief that science can solve all problems. Such a remarkable scholar as Eddington, astronomer and physicist, expresses his recognition of the results of science in these words: 'something unknown does something unknown'. The very existence of material, in which the earlier science believed so firmly, is now subject to doubt, consciously or unconsciously. Everything in the principal basis of science has become doubtful. . . . True science, always conscious of its limitations, can say nothing about God, positive or negative: it can neither prove nor disprove the existence of God. The problem of God's existence belongs in quite another sphere than that of science, which is concerned with the knowledge of the world of nature. The arguments of atheism based on the natural sciences, are just as feeble as the arguments for God's existence, based on these same natural sciences. And Christian apologetics that refute the arguments of natural sciences against faith in God are very feeble and out-moded. We may ignore completely the arguments of natural science. But the Christian consciousness should be freed from all connection with the out-moded natural history with which it was linked in the past. Biblical natural history is the knowledge of humanity in its childhood; we cannot now consider it of serious importance. What is really important, is the possibility of a conflict between Christianity and the science of history. Historical knowledge may offer serious difficulties for the Christian faith in so far as this faith is to be based on the facts of history. . . . And only the worship of God in spirit and in truth rises above the difficulties connected with the science of history. *Truth*, pp. 80-1

Russian Atheism

In conformity with Russian psychology, the Russian soul experienced the crisis of culture very acutely, and was inclined to criticize culture. Hence it rises against religion and the church, in so far as they had become part of culture and subject to culture's norms and laws. Not alone the Russian anti-religious tendencies of the nineteenth and twentieth centuries, but Russian religious tendencies also, rose against 'historical Christianity', i.e. against Christianity as expressed and active in history and hence subject to the injustice, violence, untruth and evil reigning in history. This is a very characteristic Russian attitude, sometimes taking the form of a radical denial of Christianity and religion, sometimes a yearning for some kind of pure Christianity, not yet distorted by history. Russian thought was historo-sophic, but the relativity of history disgusted Russian maximalistic thought. Every earthly city is bad, unjust, relative, subject to the prince of this world. Christians have here no abiding city; they seek a City which is to Come. And those Russian souls who desired God for the sake of the Coming City, in protest against the modern city, full of evil and injustice—these, too, sought the Coming City. Russian atheists seek the Kingdom of God on earth, only without God and against God. In the psychology of Russian atheism we find the old gnostic-anarchistic motives: the Creator of the world is an evil God: he created an evil world, full of injustice and suffering, hence every authority in the world is evil and satanic; it belongs to the prince of this world, and struggle against untruth is struggle against the evil God, who created this world. These motives have already appeared in the radical tendencies of Russian schism and sectarianism. They are active in the Russian revolutionary intelligentsia, but here they are united with the most superficial doctrines of Western materialism. We may express Russian atheism in its most profound forms, in a paradox. We must deny God in order that the Kingdom of God may be realized on earth. There was always a strong prophetic element in Russian religious psychology. Torn loose from its religious roots and distorted, it now remains in Russian socially-based atheism. Atheism is above all forgetting Christ, the suffering and sacrificing God. *Idealism*, pp. 27-9

. . . I should like to formulate the basic motives which actuated anti-religious psychology. Wherein lies the pathos of atheism? This phenomenon may well be studied, precisely in Russian psychology. Anti-religious psychology develops first of all as a consequence of the fact that the mind cannot endure the experience of evil and suffering, personal or social; it cannot endure the temptation and testing bound up in the problem of theodicy, the justification of God. The collision of religious faith with reason and science is a secondary, subordinate moment, often only an excuse for unbelief which the mind uses to convince itself of the truth and purity of its unbelief. When a man says that he would like to believe, but scientific honesty and conscienciousness do not permit it, he is tricking himself. Actually, this means that his faith did not withstand the trials of life which man experiences outside the realm of knowledge. But faith never disappears completely: it is transformed, continues to exist in new forms: it may be directed toward reason or science, both of which are used for the denial of faith. That supreme Russian genius, Dostoevsky, had a brilliant understanding of the psychology and dialectic of atheism, particularly Russian atheism, and he did more than anyone else to analyse it. The prime source of unbelief is to be sought in the experience of suffering, the non-acceptance of the meaning of suffering, which is the meaning of the cross. The basic Christian answer to the atheistic revolt against suffering is that God himself, the Son of God, suffered, and that since then suffering is the bearing of a cross. *Idealism*, pp. 47-8

THE THIRD EPOCH

We are standing on the threshold of a world-epoch of religious creativeness, on a cosmic divide. Up to now all the creativeness of 'culture' has been only a preparatory hint, the sign of the real creativeness of another world. *Just as bloody pagan sacrifice was merely a foreshadowing of the world's true redemption through Christ's sacrifice on Golgotha, a foreshadowing which did not attain true redemption, so man's creative efforts, which have brought into being the values of culture, have been up to now only a foreshadowing of a true religious epoch of creativeness which will realize another sphere of being.* The religious epoch of creativeness will be a transition into another sphere of being, not merely to another 'culture' or to another sphere of 'science and art'. The religious epoch of creativeness is a third revelation, an anthropological revelation following those of the Old and New Testaments. . . . If the religious life is complete with redemption from sin, then a higher creative fullness of being is both unattainable and unnecessary. Being is narrowed and simplified. In the religion of redemption, creative values are not necessary to attain sanctity—neither beauty nor knowledge of any kind. Christian beauty and Christian knowledge are attained only through religious-moral perfection; they have no self-sufficient sources of equal value with the moral. The thirst for beauty or knowledge does not bring salvation. Creative desire is never of saving worth. . . .

From this tragic problem of Christianity there can be only one way out: the religious acceptance of the truth that the religious meaning of life and being is not wholly a matter of redemption from sin, that life and being have positive, creative purposes. *That higher creative, positive being, though unattainable at the time when redemption was begun, when God was still transcendent to man, is attainable in another period of religious life, after the redemption, when God in man is immanent.* Salvation from sin, from perdition, is not the final purpose of religious life: salvation is always *from* something and life should be *for* something. Many things unnecessary for salvation are needed for the very purpose for which salvation is necessary—for the creative upsurge of being. Man's chief end is not to be saved but to mount up, creatively.

M.C.A., pp. 103-5

The Third Epoch Demands Heroism

If redemption concerns only one aspect of Christ, the suffering and sacrificing Son of God, creativeness concerns another, that of Christ the glorified and mighty Son of God. The Christ who was crucified for the sins of the world under Pontius Pilate and the loving Christ, who will appear in glory, are one and the same Christ, Absolute Man, and in Him the mystery of man is revealed. The final mystery of man is revealed not only in the Christ who took the form of a servant but in His kingly aspect; not only in the image of Christ the Sacrifice but in the image of Christ the Victor. The creative mystery of human nature is related to the Coming Christ, to the power and glory of the Absolute Man. This creative mystery could not be revealed in the Gospel image of Christ, since man still had to pass with Christ through the mystery of redemption, through the sacrifice on Golgotha. But can man, oriented as he is solely and completely towards the redemption, and seeing the Absolute Man only under the aspect of the sacrificing Redeemer, glimpse the Absolute Man in the creative image of the mighty King of Glory? The Coming Christ will never appear to him who by his own free effort has not revealed within himself the other, the creative image of man. Only the courage of free creativeness will bring man to the Coming Christ, prepare man for a vision of another image of the Absolute Man. And if great obedience is needed for redemption, for creativeness there is needed great courage. Only by great valour can we envisage the Coming Christ. In the spirit of obedience we shall always see only Christ Crucified, only His aspect as the Redeemer. We need the sacrifice of valour, the heroic courage to cast loose from all safe harbours. We must have the virtue of living dangerously. *The third creative revelation in the Spirit will have no holy scripture; it will be no voice from on high; it will be accomplished in man and in humanity—it is an anthropological revelation, an unveiling of the Christology of man.* *M.C.A.*, pp. 106-7

The Third Epoch Will Create New Being

The dawn of the creative religious epoch also means a most profound crisis in man's creativity. The creative act will create new being rather than values of differentiated culture; in the creative act life will not be quenched. Creativity will continue creation; it will reveal the resemblance of human nature to the Creator. In creativity the way will be found for subject to pass into object, the identity of subject with object will be restored. All the great creators have foreseen this turning-point. Today, in the depths of culture itself and in all its separate spheres, this crisis of creativity is ripening. At its highest, culture arrives at self-abnegation. Creativity in art, in philosophy, in morals, in social life, exceeds the limits of its own sphere, is not to be contained in any classic norm, reveals an impulse towards the transcendental. The creative man of today can no longer create science and art in the classic manner, just as he cannot play politics according to classic norms. In everything he strives to go to the limit, to the end, to pass all boundaries. Literature ceases to be only literature; it would be new being. Within the separate sphere of culture and its values the power to hold itself is lacking; the creative upsurge towards another type of being puts an end to the division of culture into a row of separate fields. At the heights of culture the question is put whether culture is the way to another kind of being or retention in the middle way, without any transcendental way out. Art is transformed into theurgy, philosophy into theosophy, society into theocracy. The norms of classicism are overthrown, according to which beautiful art, true philosophy and a just social order are supposed to be created. Symbolism in art passes beyond the boundaries and norms of classical art, reveals the final limits of the creative artistic act, and leads to theurgy. *M.C.A.*, pp. 120-1

The world is passing through three epochs of divine revelation: the revelation of the law (the Father), the revelation of redemption (the Son) and the revelation of creativity (the Spirit). These epochs correspond to certain signs in the heavens. It is not given us to know the definite chronological limits of these three epochs: they are all co-existent. Today we have not fully lived out the law, and redemption from sin has not yet been completed, although the world is entering a new religious epoch. Even in the epoch of the law the world had a premonition of new religious epochs: not only the prophetic consciousness of the Old Testament but the palpitation of the world-spirit in paganism awaited the advent of Christ the Redeemer. The three epochs of divine revelation in the world are three epochs of the revelation about man. In the first epoch man's sin is brought to light and natural divine force is revealed; in the second epoch man is made a son of God and redemption from sin appears; in the third epoch the divinity of man's creative nature is finally revealed and divine power becomes human power. The revelation about man is the final divine revelation about the Trinity. The final mystery is hidden in this, that the divine mystery and the human mystery are one, that in God there is hidden the mystery of man and in man the mystery of God. God is born in man and man is born in God. The ultimate revelation of man means the revelation of God. Not only is God in man but man is the image of God: in him divine development is realized. Man is a participant in the Divine Trinity. . . . And in its religious depths the anthropological revelation is only the revelation of Christ as Absolute Man. With the appearance of Christ in the world, man's sonship with God, his likeness to God and his participation in the divine nature are all revealed. But Absolute Man is not completely and finally revealed in the appearing of Christ the Redeemer. Man's creative energy is directed towards the Coming Christ, towards His appearing in glory. The creative revelation of man is a continuing and completing revelation of Christ, the Absolute Man. The anthropological revelation of the creative epoch is at once fully human and fully divine: in it humanity is deepened to the point of divinity and divinity is made visible to the point of humanity. The divine-human nature of revelation must become completely evident and this is possible only in the creative act of the revelation of man himself. The whole meaning of our epoch is in the fact that it is passing over to the revelation of man. But this means passing over into suffering, into a temporary perturbation of the human image, into the crisis of humanism. *M.C.A.*, pp. 320-2

Not to be Understood Chronologically

The epoch of the Spirit, or the third revelation, must not be understood in exclusively chronological terms. There have always been men of the Spirit, men preparing the epoch of Spirit; there have always been men of the prophetic Spirit. In the history of Christianity there have always been men with a constant inward fire. There have always been wise men, who received the light, even in the pre-Christian world. There have always been mystics of universal significance. But another mentality has prevailed, a mentality connected with authoritarian organization, built in the image of the realm of Caesar, and in despite of the words of the Gospel. This does not mean that, following the ancient gnostics, we must recognize the existence of various spiritual races, such as the pneumatics, and the psychics, and must feel that each is doomed to remain within its own limits. This would contradict both universal Truth and man's freedom.

But it is most important to understand that in the process of objectivation to which man's social and historical life is subjected, the Spirit is symbolized, rather than realized. The source of this symbolization is in the fact that we are given only signs of a future realization, marks of another world. But once symbolization is considered to be already realization, it fetters us. In a profound sense of the word, cult and culture are both symbolic. But in them is given the way to realization, if this symbolism is not considered as something static, as finished and final. The true epoch of the Spirit will not be symbolic, but reality.

Truth, p. 127 ff

The New Epoch Means a Changed Mentality

I am not at all an optimist. Rather I am inclined to think that we are entering an epoch of darkness and of vast destruction. It is even possible that all our seeming, illusory cosmic order may be blown to bits. And I do not assume a religious-social Utopia, conceivable as realizable within the limits of our eon. I am talking of something quite other, of a new eon and a new revelation within it. But the beginning of a new epoch presupposes a change in human mentality, the liberation of man's consciousness from the power of 'objectness'. This change will not take place in an instant: it presupposes a complex preparatory process. There must be, first of all, a revolution in thinking, a revolution of the spirit which does not want to be alienated and cast out into the object-world. . .

Earthly Categories Are Inapplicable

In the new epoch everything will be changed, and our categories, our distinction between good and evil, will be quite inapplicable. But the new epoch is not simply something beyond the grave, something quite other: it is also our world, enlightened and transfigured, which has become creatively free. Incidentally, we may imagine a multitude of worlds of which our world is a part, and in which man's spiritual way is continued. We must free ourselves from the deadening effect of hardened scholastic dogmatics. It is surprising how the human and the divine-human image of Christ disapppears in idolatrous dogmatics, just as the human image of the saints disappears under the touch of the icon painter. In Jesus Christ there was revealed the ideal relationship between the human and the Divine. This should have been accepted, not dogmatically, but existentially, that is in a way free of all sorts of idolatry. But this will be acceptance in Spirit and in Truth.

Truth, p. 134

CHAPTER IX

The Elder Sister of Philosophy*

'Religion may be defined as the experience of nearness, of kinship with being.' FREEDOM, p. 48

'I have no use for a religion which has no relation to the fullness of life, to the process of history, to the future of human society.'
SUB SPECIE, p. 4

RELIGION

In the objective history of the world there is nothing sacred, only a conditioned symbolization; the sacred obtains only in the world of existence, only in existential subjects. The real depth of the spirit is known existentially in experiencing one's destiny, in suffering, yearning, death, love, creativity, in freedom rather than in objects. Religion is above all existential in its nature, it is rooted in the spirit; it is contact with primal realities. *Reality*, p. 49

Duality in Religion

Religion means connection, and it may be defined as the conquest of loneliness, as an outgoing from self, from self-containment, as the obtention of kinship and communion. Herein is its essence. Religion means union with the mystery of being, with being itself. But loneliness is not overcome because of religion; religion is only a relationship; it is secondary and transient. My loneliness is overcome because God exists. God is the conquest of my loneliness, the obtention of the fullness and meaning of my life. It is often forgotten that God is primary, not religion, which sometimes may even prevent our seeing God. In religion as it has developed in history, in the life of human society, man's relation to God has undergone objectivization and socialization. In such socialized and objectivized religion, loneliness is dulled because the 'I' is cast forth into the objectivized and socialized world, even if that world is called the church; but ontologically, loneliness is not overcome. Loneliness is ontologically overcome only by my relationship to God in the order of inward existence, of primal life, in the church as communion, rather than the church as society. And in the religious life we find repeated the same situation as in knowing, in the life of sex, in everything: the same duality,

* W. S. Landor.

the same two perspectives—spirit and nature, freedom and necessity, objectivization and existence or primal life. Of course, religion is a social phenomenon; it is secondary and objectivized, cast forth in the world. But religion is also revelation, the voice of God, the incarnation of God, and then it is primary, and does not belong to the world of objects, the socialized world....

The Christian Religion

The mystery of Christianity is, of course, the mystery of the conquest of the solitude of the 'I', in Christ the God-man, in Divine-humanity, in the body of Christ. But formal confession of the Christian faith and formal membership in the church do not overcome loneliness. The conquest of loneliness may be apparent or superficial; it may occur at the surface level and mean only a surface phenomenon. In socialized Christianity, love has been of a conditioned and symbolized, rather than a real, nature. But loneliness is truly overcome only by love, the summit-peak of life....

Solitude, pp. 113-15

Of the New Religious Consciousness

We are living in an epoch not only of the depression and shallowness of culture, in a godless epoch of little affairs on the plain, but in an epoch of the beginning of a new religious renaissance, a dawning *new religious consciousness*, which fascinates by its universal significance.

It is characteristic of our new renaissance that it is double, dialectic; the Christian God is resurrected and the pagan gods are reborn. We are experiencing not only a Christian but also a pagan renaissance.... We are fascinated by both Golgotha and Olympus; we are attracted not only by the suffering God dying on a cross, but the god Pan, god of the elements of earth, the god of passionate living, and by the ancient goddess Aphrodite, goddess of beauty and of earthly love....

The man of the new religious consciousness cannot renounce either paganism or Christianity: in both he sees divine revelation: in his views flow two streams of blood and this produces storm: in his head his thoughts are divided. There can be no return to paganism as thesis and Christianity as anti-thesis.... The new religious consciousness thirsts for synthesis, for the conquest of duality for a higher fullness; it would contain what it formerly did not, unite two poles, two opposite abysses.... If religion in general is possible and useful, then we must consider the whole world-historical process as divine revelation, as the intimate mutual action and reaction between humanity and Divinity. The new religious consciousness is a continuing revelation comprehending more fullness of religious truth, since on the former levels of religious revelation truth was revealed only partially....

If up to now there has not been a revelation of Divinity in the world and in history, then there never will be, and the rationalists and the vulgar deists have imagined a distant and unnecessary God. If, however, there has been a revelation, then it is now continuing and will continue, since fullness of religious truth is attained only in the course of the whole process of history, and this process must be divine-human. The question of the relation between a relative and temporary historical revelation and an absolute mystic revelation must be reviewed and reworked by the new philosophy, the mystic and at the same time critical philosophy of the future which is destined to serve the new religious consciousness. Only then will the historic limitations of theological schools be shattered, external authority will be replaced by inward freedom, and the way will be laid toward the fullness of mystical knowledge of God. . . .

Hitherto, religious light has come from the Christ who died on the cross, in whom truth is not yet fully revealed, and that light is fading, but lo, a new religious light begins to shine and it flows from the Coming Christ. It is as though time had begun to move in the opposite direction.

Apocalyptic Christianity will reveal the nature of the Holy Spirit, the Comforter, promised by Christ; that will be included, which was not included in historic Christianity. There will be a new, eternal church, the church of St John, and a new eternal religion, the religion of the Holy Trinity, the full revelation of all the divine hypostases where all duality will be overcome and all the values of world culture will find their place. In the church of St John, in the universal theocracy whose formation will mark the beginning of the apocalyptic process, the truth about 'the earth' will be revealed, the problem of sex will be solved, the problem of bread, of society—everything which has been impossible for the human historical process. . . .

Thus the centre of religious consciousness will be transferred to the *prophetic* sphere, and solidified dogmatism, historical limitations, will be overcome. . . . Free prophecies will be revealed in the new mystic experience: in this there is great joy, but great torment as well. Religious dogma itself must develop under the influence of the new prophecies and free inner revelation, rather than by exerting pressure on them. . . .

Life's Questions No. 9, 1905

PANTHEISM

Orthodox believers of all faiths have always specially condemned and persecuted the pantheistic tendency. . . . But they do not understand that if pantheism is a heresy, it is first of all a heresy concerned with man and his freedom, rather than a heresy concerning God. When I say 'heresy' I am using a language that is not my own. But it is surprising that just the most orthodox dogmatic formulas and the most orthodox theological doctrines include a pantheism that enslaves man. God is all in all. God holds everything in his hands and directs everything; only God is true being, while man and the world are nothing; only God creates, while man is incapable of creativity: everything is of God. That is what the orthodox are constantly saying. This extreme form of degrading man, the recognition of his nothingness, is the same sort of pantheism as the assertion of man's divinity, the recognition of man as an emanation of Divinity. This is monism, as well. To avoid both monism and pantheism we must recognize man's independence, the freedom in him, freedom uncreated and not determined by God; man's capacity for creativeness. ... The idea of all-oneness is only another form of the idea of the absolute, and is open to the same criticism. All-oneness cannot be thought of as the way to overcome the contradiction between the One and the many. The mystery of the union of the One and the many, the universal and the individual, in the person of Christ, cannot be expressed by saying that Christ is all-oneness. *Slavery*, pp. 77-8

PROPHECY

There is a widespread opinion that prophecy was possible only in the Old Testament times, only until the appearance of the Messiah, Christ the Saviour. But men seem to forget that among the canonical books of the New Testament is that prophetic book, the Apocalypse. They forget that Christianity contained prophecy of the second coming of Christ, of the end of the world, of the world's transfiguration and illumination, of a new heaven and a new earth. The priesthood has always tended to deny prophecy. And by its nature prophecy cannot be subject to or depend upon the priesthood. Prophecy is free; it is not bound to the hierarchical element; it is always personal, individual inspiration, a personal, individual human gift. Unlike the priest, the prophet does not belong to the order of angels, but to the order of men. The defence of the prophetic mind and the prophetic function in Christianity, was Vl. Solovieff's central idea: he puts the prophet on the same level as the priest and the king. The prophetic spirit is in opposition to the spirit of legalism in Christianity. And every thought of the Second Coming, of the Coming Christ, of the Resurrection, is fraught with the spirit of prophecy. *Freedom*, p. 93

The Prophet

Unlike the priest, pagan or Christian, the prophet is always alone; he always experiences a phase of sharp separation from the religious collective, from the milieu of the people among whom he lives. By his spiritual type, the prophet is always the bearer of the subjective element in religious life, as compared with the objective element whose bearer is the religious collective. And only later those spiritual elements, first expressed by the prophetic individual, take on objective significance, and religious life enters the objective stage. Religious life is born in propheticism and is precipitated in the priesthood. . . . Always oriented to the future, the prophet is always dissatisfied with the present, denounces the evil in the life about him, and awaits the future triumph of higher spiritual elements which are revealed to him in prophetic visions. . . .

The prophet breathes the air of freedom, he smothers in the hardened world about him, but in his own spiritual world he breathes freely. He always visions a free spiritual world and awaits its penetration into this stifling world. The prophet foresees the fate of man and of the world, and through contemplation of the spiritual he unriddles the events of the empirical world. The prophetic gnosis is always a philosophy of history, and a philosophy of history is possible only as free prophecy. Unlike the saint, the prophet is submerged in the life of the world and of his own people; he shares the fate of both. But he renounces and denounces the life of the world and of his people; he foretells its ruin. . . .

The prophet belongs to the human hierarchy, he is a man inspired by God. The prophet does not strive for personal perfection, saintliness or salvation, although he may rise to the highest degree of spiritual perfection, he may or may not be a saint. . . .

The prophetic is always a spiritually explosive psychology. The prophet does not calm men's spirits, or bring peace to their souls. Hence the prophetic cannot be the sole or even the predominant element in religious life. The world could not bear the ardent and consuming spirit of prophecy and it must guard itself against such domination. But without the spirit of prophecy, spiritual life would die out in this world. . . .

A Christian renaissance will require not only a consecrated, priestly spirit of the sanctification of life, but a prophetic spirit as well, a spirit of transfiguration, the real alteration of life. The Christian movement proceeds not only from the popular collective, but also from the prophetic individuals of various hierarchical ranks. The priestly hierarchy is the necessary foundation of Christianity, but it must not dominate completely and throttle prophecy. Orientation to the Coming Christ is the prophetic side of Christianity, and cannot be eliminated from it. Through long centuries of objectivization, Christianity has become so congealed into a racial, national, collective religion that the spirit of prophecy has dried up and has come to be considered almost as heresy. . . .

At the summit of the spiritual life of humanity are two figures: the image of the prophet and that of the saint. Man has never risen higher than these two images. And both are needed for God's work in the world, for the coming of the Kingdom of God. Both these spiritual ways, the way of sanctity and that of prophecy, are part of the final appearance of Divine-humanity, both are part of the integral life of the Church, of the Church's fulfilment and completion. For the time being, in the mysterious plan of God, prophecy is active outside the visible body of the Church. But the time will come when the prophetic spirit will be recognized as the spirit of the Church, as proceeding out of the Church's depths. So man's religious fate is accomplished in tragedy, in apparent separation, in tormenting conflict. But mankind moves toward fulfilment, toward deification, toward the Kingdom of God. . . .

Christian prophecies are not optimistic; they do not justify the theory of progress; they denounce severely the evil coming into this world. But they are not pessimistic; they are above human pessimism and optimism. They await the coming of Christ in power and in glory.

Freedom I, pp. 230-6

REDEMPTION

Redemption is Negative: Christianity Must Be Positive

For the religious consciousness of the man of the new epoch there is only one way out: the religious realization of the truth that New Testament Christianity is a religion of redemption, the good news of salvation from sin, the revelation of the Son of God, the second hypostasis of the Holy Trinity in the aspect of God suffering from the sins of the world. This is one of the stages on the spiritual road. The second Gospel commandment of God and man has direct relationship only to the redemption from sin through divine love and grace. On the way of the spiritual life this is crucifixion on the cross of the rose of life. But does the mystery of salvation take in the whole of life? Is life's final purpose only salvation from sin? Redemption from sin, salvation from evil, are in themselves negative, and the final aims of being lie far beyond, in a positive creative purpose. Redemption from sin is only one epoch of the mystic life of the world, the core of the world-process. But the process of the world's life cannot be limited to redemption: it must contain other mystical periods. Like its Creator, man's life could not be created by God only for the purpose that, having sinned, he should atone for his sin, and should put into the work of his redemption all his powers, throughout the whole extent of the world-process. Such a conception of human nature would not correspond to the idea of the Creator and would demean the godlike dignity of man. The absolute Christian truth turns on the one hand towards redemption from sin and evil and on the other towards the positive creative calling of man: it reveals a Christology of man. The New Testament truth of the Gospels is only a part of Christological truth, oriented towards redemption and salvation; in it we cannot seek the direct justification of man's creative purposes. The Gospels reveal only one aspect of Christ, the Absolute Man redeeming and saving human nature.

M.C.A., pp. 95-6

Not a Process of Justice

The mystery of redemption, like all other mysteries of divine life, cannot be understood rationally. The juridical, legal doctrine that, beginning with St Anselm of Canterbury, plays such a rôle in catholic theology, and from which even orthodox theology is not entirely free, is a rationalization of the mystery of redemption, its assimilation with relationships existing in the world of nature.... This is transferring the pagan idea of racial life and social revenge to divine life, that is always bottomlessly mysterious. In the pagan, Old Testament concept, God is imagined as a terrible potentate, punishing and revenging for disobedience, demanding sacrifice and bloodshed. God is thought of in the image and likeness of ancient, pagan human nature. For this level of human thought, anger, revenge, ransom, cruel punishment are easily understandable. Men put the stamp of the Roman and feudal idea of rehabilitating honour upon this juridical theory of redemption. For the formal transgression of God's will a lawsuit is begun and God has to be reimbursed: it is necessary to give Him satisfaction on a scale sufficient to propitiate His anger. No human sacrifice is sufficient to satisfy and propitiate the anger of God. Only the sacrifice of the Son of God corresponds to the scale of man's crime and the offence to God this has caused. All this is a completely pagan concept, transferred to Christianity. Such a concept of redemption is external, exoteric....

This idea of blood-sacrifice shows all the limitations of naturalistic religions. Divinity was apprehended and believed in, through nature, and this put upon divinity the seal of relationships and qualities of the world of nature.... 'I came, not to judge the world, but to save it.' The redemption achieved by the Son of God is not judgment, and yet it is salvation. Salvation is not judgment; it is the transfiguration and illumination of nature, the process of endowing it with grace and making it divine. Salvation is not justification, but rather the attainment of perfection. The idea of God as judge is mental rather than spiritual. The juridical conception of redemption has meaning only for the natural man. For the spiritual man, another aspect of God is revealed. We cannot ascribe to God qualities we consider reprehensible in men; pride, egoism, stubbornness, rancour, vengefulness, cruelty. The natural man made an image of God which is monstrous. In its juridical conception of redemption, the religion of Christ is still a religion of the law and in it even grace is understood legalistically instead of ontologically....

The legalistic conception is being eliminated from Christianity with some difficulty. Man needs the law, and he naturally tends to understand everything legally. Christ neither denies nor refuses the law, but He reveals a spiritual world in which really and actually the law is overcome, overcome by abundant love and abundant freedom. But freedom is not of grace; lower freedom cannot deny the law; it is subject to its action....

The sphere of activity of the Old Testament law, and the sphere of activity of New Testament grace, are quite different. And this is why we must not understand New Testament grace in an Old Testament, legal manner. . . . The New Testament reveals that God does not await the formal fulfilment of the law, but rather man's free responsive love. The law is the conviction of sin, the refraction of God's will in sinful nature, but it is not the expression of the basic mystery of God's relation to man. This mystery is revealed in redemption. The legalistic concept of redemption supposes that man's sin may be forgiven, the wrath of God may be appeased by the sacrifice of the Son of God. In this concept of redemption the relationship between God and human nature remains something external, and nothing in human nature itself is altered. But sin cannot and should not be forgiven. God cannot forgive a man his sins, and man cannot forgive himself his sins and his defection from God and His great plan. God does not know wrath and His all-forgiveness is without limit. Man yearns to redeem his sin, feels his own powerlessness, awaits a Redeemer and Saviour who will bring him back to God. Man's spiritual nature demands not the forgiveness of sin, but a real elimination and destruction of sin, i.e. the transfiguration of human nature, its inner illumination. The meaning of redemption is in the appearing of the New Adam, of love which the old Adam did not know, even before the Fall, the transformation of man's lower nature into a higher. The meaning of Christ's coming into the world is in the real transfiguration of human nature, in the founding of a new race of spiritual men, but not at all in the institution of a law for whose fulfilment spiritual life is granted....

Redemption is Not the Result of Evolution

The coming of Christ and redemption can be understood only as the continuation of the creation of the world, as the eighth day of creation, as the appearance of the New Adam, i.e. as a cosmogonic and anthropogonic process, as the disclosure of divine love in creation, as a new stage in man's freedom. The appearance of the new spiritual man cannot be the result only of a natural evolution of human nature, although this is playing a part in the preparation of the new spiritual man. This presupposes a breakthrough from another, spiritual world, from eternity into our natural world, the world of time.... If Christ is not only God, but man as well, then not only God's nature is active in redemption, but man's nature also, heavenly, spiritual, human nature.... The human nature in Christ participates in the work of redemption. Sacrifice is the law of spiritual upsurge. In the Christian race, in the new spiritual race, a new period in the life of creation is opening....

Redemption cannot be understood as the return of human nature to its original condition, that of Adam before the Fall. Such a conception makes the world-process meaningless. It is seen to be pure loss. But the New Adam, the new spiritual man, is higher than the old Adam, not only the fallen Adam, but Adam before the Fall. This mystery was revealed only in Christ. The coming of Christ is not to be explained by negative causes only; it is a positive revelation of a higher stage of the creation of the world....

Christ Makes All Things New

The Old Testament picture of creation does not reveal the plenitude of God's creativity. And the New Testament consciousness must not be narrowed by the Old Testament limits and concepts of creation. The creation of the world continues: the world is entering new eons. And the coming of Christ is a new eon in the world's destiny, a new moment, not only in anthropogony, but in cosmogony as well. Not human nature alone, but the whole world, the whole of cosmic life, was changed after the coming of Christ. When a drop of blood, shed by Christ on Golgotha, fell upon the earth, the earth became something other, something new. And if we do not see this with our eyes of flesh, this is only because of the sinful limitation of our perception.... This can be understood only by theologians who are free of the depressive influence of Old Testament thought. Redemption is the only possible theodicy, the justification of God and God's creation. *Freedom* I, pp. 249-58

The Ethic of Redemption

The thirst for redemption is thirst for reconciliation with God and the only way to the conquest of atheism inspired in man's heart by the evil and suffering in the world. This is meeting with the suffering and sacrificing God, which means that He shares the agonizing fate of the world and of man. Man is a free being; in him there is an element of original, uncreated, pre-existent freedom. But he is powerless to deal with his own irrational freedom, with its bottomless darkness. In this lies his perpetual tragedy. And God Himself must descend to the depths of this freedom, into its bottomless dark, and take upon Himself the consequences of the evil and suffering born of it. Redemption is not at all God's reconciliation with man, as this is perversely conceived by limited human thinking. Redemption is above all man's reconciliation with his God and Creator. Man is never left entirely alone, left to his own strength. But he does not recognize God's participation in his fate. This is the result of the ethic of the law. God gives the law, but takes no part in its realization. And when good is placed under the law it is, in a certain sense, Godless good. For the law means that God has deserted man. Herein is the law's incapacity to alter human nature. In the law, good is split off from being and cannot change it. . . . Redemption tears up the roots of evil and sin, and by this it frees man from the undivided power of the law. Redemption is first of all liberation. The Redeemer is the Liberator. But the law does not liberate man from slavery. Redemption means a revolutionary change in moral evaluation of all values. It removes a countless number of taboos, overcomes the external fear of impurity, transfers everything to the depth of the human heart, overturns all the hierarchies that have been set up in the world. The ethic of redemption of the Gospel is a divine-human ethic. In the moral act not God alone, not man alone, but both, are active; there is none of the separation and contrast set up by the law. And what was for man impossible becomes possible for God.

Christianity Puts Man Above Good

Christianity put man above the idea of good, and in so doing achieved the greatest revolution in the history of mankind, a revolution that Christian man was incapable of fully accepting. The idea of good, like every other idea, must bow and retreat when man comes into the picture. Not the abstract idea of good, but man as God's creature and child. Man inherits eternity, and nothing is left of the law. So the Gospel breaks through from the morality of our fallen world based upon the distinction between good and evil, into the morality of a world beyond, the opposite of the law of this world, heavenly morality, the morality of the Kingdom of God. Man is redeemed from the power of the law....

Destiny, pp. 111-15

REVELATION

Revelation is not an evolution of consciousness, but a revolution. *Freedom*, p. 146

Revelation is Partial

Religion is the revelation of Divinity and of divine life in man and in the world. Religious life is man's discovery of his kinship and nearness to God; it is his escape from a condition of loneliness, forsakenness and alienation from the primal bases of being. But what happens in religious life is not only the revelation but the partial concealment of Divinity. Revelation does not remove the mystery, but rather reveals its bottomless depths, points to its impenetrable profundity. Revelation is something quite opposite to rationalization; it does not mean that Divinity becomes penetrable for reason or for concepts. Hence revelation always leaves some things still mysteries. Religion is a paradoxical union of the hidden and the revealed. The esoteric always remains, along with the exoteric. Religious exoterism strives for the confirmation of the finite. Any naïvely realistic and naturalistic concept of revelation is always a form of exoterism. But in this concept the depths of revelation are neither attained nor divulged. The revelation of Divinity is not an external and transcendental event, taking place in objective natural actuality, in the world of nature; it is not a light which flows into the inward world from without. Revelation is an event which takes place in the inward world, in the world of the spirit, and it proceeds from the most profound depths. Revelation is an event in spiritual life, not at all like the perception of external realities. Revelation is given in spiritual experience, an event which takes place within the person to whom things divine are opened. Revelation does not proceed from the object to the subject, but at the same time it must be said that the nature of revelation is not subjective.... To understand revelation objectively, transcendentally-realistically, is to cast it outward, to project revelation outside; it is naturalism in the understanding of revelation. For revelation does not take place in the objective world. But neither does it take place in the subjective, psychic world, which is only a part of the world of nature. Revelation takes place in spirit. It is a breaking-through into our world from the spiritual world, into our natural life. *Freedom* I, pp. 137-9

Revelation is Progressive

In the first stages of man's religious consciousness, revelation is understood naturalistically, as an event which takes place in the objective world of nature. The Father is revealed in objective nature before He reveals himself through the Son in the depths of the spirit. He reveals himself first as power rather than as justice. Power is a category of nature, while justice is a spiritual category. Only in the Son, only in Christ, is the inner nature of the Heavenly Father revealed. To the naturalistic type of thought about God, He is revealed as master, as monarch, and the traces of that early concept of God have not entirely disappeared even from Christianity. But the Christian revelation of the Holy Trinity is not a revelation of a heavenly monarchy, which is heresy, but rather a revelation of heavenly love, of divine communion (sobornost). In the Son there is revealed an image of the Father different from the image of God who does not know the Son. But to know the Son, who proclaims the Father's will—to come to a knowledge of Christ in the objective, historical, natural events of the Gospels, is possible only if He is revealed in the depths of the spirit, in the events of spiritual experience, and the revelation of Christ in spirit presupposes the action of the Holy Spirit. The world of nature, the natural man, put the stamp of the limited and the finite on this revelation of the Spirit in spirit. But refraction through the limitations of the natural world, through man's frail nature, produces degrees or stages of revelation and this limitation of revelation gives rise to exoterism. Absolute truth and light are refracted in the natural man, and passing through this dark medium, the light is dimmed. No words are completely adequate to express the truths of revelation....

The Old Testament God, Jahwe, was not a revelation of God in his inner, secret nature. It was only an exoteric manifestation of the Divine Visage to the old-testament mind of the Hebrew people. The wrath of the God of the Old Testament is only an exoterism, which expresses the wrath of the Hebrew people, the race of old Adam. Wrath does not express the esoteric life of God: God the Father is revealed in the Son as boundless love.... The esoteric life of God is revealed only exoterically in the religious life of the world of nature and of natural man. And at only one point in the world was there a partial revelation of esoteric, secret life, the life of the Divine Trinity; it was partly revealed in the

Son, as boundless love and freedom. But up to the present, the mystery partly revealed in Christianity remains cramped by the law, by the exoteric conception of Christianity, by the limitation of the infinite in the finite. And the absolute Christian revelation continues to act in the relative, natural world; it is received by the natural man and receives the stamp of his limitedness. And within Christianity itself light is poured out by degrees, and is refracted in the dark milieu which receives it. Therefore Christianity knows its various epochs, its ages, its hierarchic degrees. Christianity is too great to fit into any legalistic system, to be all included in any doctrine or any finite order. Man's spiritual organization is mobile and dynamic, and therefore what only suits the medium, normal spiritual organization, something which corresponds only to a consciousness enslaved by the finite, cannot be recognized as final truth.

Freedom I, pp. 139-42

Religious revelation is an event which happens not only for me, but to me as well: it is an inner spiritual catastrophe. And if this inward spiritual catastrophe has not happened to me, then events about which I am told as being revelations of God have no meaning for me. I can decipher the Gospels only in the light of the spiritual events of my inward experience. Without these inner events, the Gospel means no more than all the other events of history. More, we can understand the meaning of history itself, only in our own spiritual experience, only as a reflection of spiritual phenomena. Without this inner, spiritual comprehension, history becomes only a heap of empirical material, devoid of meaning or relationship. Revelation is always revelation of meaning, and meaning is only in spirit; there is no meaning in external events unless they are interpreted in the spirit.

Freedom I, pp. 142-3

The Revelation of God in the Revelation of Man

The revelation of God is always both a revelation of God and a revelation of man, which is to say that it is divine-human revelation. This divine-human revelation has its final expression in Christianity. In Christ the God-man there is given the revelation not only of God, but of that other-of-God, which is Man. The Second Hypostasis of the Holy Trinity is Absolute Man, and the revelation of the Second Hypostasis is the revelation of Absolute Man, that is the disclosure of the new spiritual man, the eternal man. But the new spiritual man has not been disclosed completely and finally. And in principle a new revelation in Christianity is possible: against this possibility of a new revelation no substantial arguments can be presented. But the creative-dynamic process in the world cannot stop. Stopping the creative-dynamic process would mean ossification and quenching of the Spirit....

Freedom I, pp. 171-2

Christian revelation acted in history and was destroyed by history. *Divine*, p. 31

Revelation and Knowledge

Revelation in itself has no quarrel with knowledge. Revelation is what is revealed to me; knowledge is what I reveal or discover. Is it possible that what I discover in knowing may collide with, or get in the way of, what is revealed to me in religion? This may actually happen and this collision may become tragic for the philosopher, since the philosopher may be a believer and recognize the possibility of revelation. But this is because religion is a complex social phenomenon in which the revelation of God, that is the pure and primal religious phenomenon, is mixed up with the collective human reaction to this revelation, with human utilization of it for various purposes and interests. . . . In its pure and primal form, revelation is not knowledge and contains no perceptual elements. This perceptive element is brought in by man, as the reaction of his thought upon revelation. *Solitude*, p. 7

Revelation is the Action of Spirit on Spirit

The very understanding of revelation becomes subject to objectivization. This is particularly evident in all the authoritarian concepts held by the church. Revelation is conceived as the entrance into man of an objective reality or a system of concepts, which are then endowed with the significance of reality. This is a naïve realism in the understanding of what revelation is, and it does not take into account the activity of the subject. . . .

Revelation is an event within the spiritual life; only within spiritual life can the voice of God be heard. Then it is in a secondary process, where the spirit is exteriorized, that revelation is objectivized, appears to be an external event, proceeding from the object. But the meeting with Christ in faith and love is no meeting with an object, as this is conceived in objectivization, but rather is a meeting with the subject, with Thou, which is to say that it relates to the existential plane. A meeting with God is a meeting with subject, not object. *Reality*, p. 50

Revelation in the Bible

Revelation is an event of the spirit within me, in the subject; it is spiritual experience, spiritual life. The intellectualistic interpretation of revelation which is expressed in dogmatics is at the same time an objectivization of revelation, adapted to average-normal thinking. But the events of the Spirit which are described in Holy Scripture, the appearance of the Spirit in the lives of the apostles or the saints, were not of a purely intellectual nature; here the whole, integral, spiritual nature of man was active. Thus the intellectualistic, rationalistic doctrine of God as pure act, which has played so large a rôle in catholic scholastics, is derived, not from the Bible, not from revelation, but rather from Aristotle.

Divine, p. 26

Revelation: Result of God's and Man's Mutual Longing

The religious phenomenon is two-sided: it is the disclosure of God in man and the disclosure of man in God: in it we discover man's yearning toward God and God's yearning toward man. Traditional rationalistic theology denies this longing of God for man, fearing to introduce passion and emotion into the idea of God, this because the rational concept of perfection does not admit of yearning or the need for completion, and predicates a stony, changeless kind of perfection. *Divine*, p. 27

Revelation is an Inward Experience

The disclosure of the divine in man and the process of lifting the human toward the divine, is not a steady, continuous process, but rather intermittent, transcendent. That there is such a thing as spiritual experience of the transcendental and the transcendent in man, one cannot deny, without doing violence to the reality of experience. Man is a being who transcends himself, passes out beyond his own limits, a being with a tendency toward mystery and the infinite. But the experience of the transcendent, of transcending, is an inward, spiritual experience, and in this sense it may be called immanent. But here immanent does not mean that man remains within his own bounds, but rather that he passes out beyond them. The transcendent comes to man from within, from the depths. God is deeper within me than I, myself, as St Augustine has said. I must transcend myself. The depths within a man may be closed off, and these depths demand a break-through, transcendence. Through this transcendence the secret in man is made manifest: this is revelation.

The revelation of the transcendent is not an evolutionary process: it is a tragic process in the world. Revelation is objectified and socialized, and then it becomes immanent at the level of human consciousness and human society. The prophet, the apostle, the saint, the mystic, move out beyond the limits of this poor sort of immanence. Men speak of the immanence known by the mystics, but this has nothing in common with everyday, social immanence, the immanence of limited consciousness. The revelation of the immanent in the world is not an even, evolutionary process, but rather it presupposes different epochs and stages, both in regard to the individual man and to the history of mankind. And we are standing at the borderline between the old epoch in its death-agony and the opening of a new epoch of revelation, of a new eon. What takes place in the depths of man takes place in God. *Divine*, pp. 62-3

Revelation: a Divine-human Process

If there is a God, he must reveal himself and let himself be known. He reveals himself by word, in what we call the Holy Scriptures, but not only there. God's revelation to man and to the world takes place in many forms: any other viewpoint is inhuman. There can be no knowledge of God unless God himself is active. He comes to meet man. This means that the knowledge of God predicates revelation, that it involves both God and man. We must always remember that revelation is a divine-human process, that it cannot be one-sidedly divine. Revelation is not something dropping upon man from outside, with man himself completely passive. In this case we would have to think of man as like a bit of stone or wood....

Like Truth, revelation predicates the activity of the whole man. The assimilation of revelation, making it our own, demands our thinking also. Revelation is not intellectual truth, although it presupposes man's intellectual activity as well. We must love God with our whole mind, although the basic truth of revelation must be accessible even to children. We cannot think of revelation as something man automatically receives by virtue of a special act of Divinity. *Truth*, pp. 35-7

Revelation Continues

Revelation cannot be something finished, static, requiring only a passive acceptance. The old static concept of revelation, requiring passive obedience, is essentially one of the forms of naturalism so strong in theology. The events revealed to us in the Gospels, which do not resemble ordinary historic events, are understandable only in the case that they are also events of my spiritual life and my spiritual way. The fact that men have always tried to interpret and explain revelation, a process which went on in the development of the church along with traditionalism, means that revelation has always been subject to the judgment of reason and conscience, but of reason and conscience illumined from within by revelation, the judgment of an illumined humanness. There is still much which must be submitted to that kind of judgment, for instance the idea of eternal punishment, of predestination, the juridical concept of Christianity. *Truth*, p. 38

A Critique of Revelation

A critique of revelation presupposes reason inwardly enlightened by true revelation: faith presupposes knowledge by integral spirit. A critique of revelation predicates that God is neither above Truth, nor subject to it, but that He is Truth itself. God is mystery, but he is also Truth, Spirit, freedom, love, conscience....

The critique of revelation about which I am thinking must move in the opposite direction from that which it has followed from the beginning of the modern age, i.e. socialism, natural religion and deism, toward a rationalistic and moralistic interpretation of Christianity, toward the denial of mystery and the mystical side of Christianity. On the contrary, it must move toward mystery and the mystic, toward the elimination of theological rationalism. This is not a critique of reason of the age of enlightenment, but a critique of the spirit. The first movement was toward objectivization; the second must move in the opposite direction, toward primary spiritual experience, toward the existential subject; not toward the 'natural' but rather back toward spirituality. *Truth*, pp. 53-4

SALVATION

Concentration on one's own personal salvation and fear of one's own personal loss is monstrously selfish. Concentration on the crisis of one's own creativeness and the fear of one's own powerlessness is monstrously prideful. Egoistic and self-conceited concentration on oneself indicates a morbid separation between man and the world. Man was made by the Creator with qualities of genius (not always genius in the full sense of the word), and these qualities must express themselves in creative activity, must overcome everything personally-egoistic and personally self-conceited, conquer all fear of one's own loss, all concern for what others may think. In its ultimate base on the Absolute Man-Christ, human nature has already become the nature of the new Adam and is united with divine nature—it no longer has a right to feel itself cast-off and lonely. This sense of isolation and depression is itself a sin against man's divine calling, against the call of God, God's need of man. *M.C.A.*, p. 13

Personal Salvation—'An Ethic of Transcendent Egoism'

A religious ethic based on the idea of personal salvation of the soul is a minimalistic ethic, an ethic of transcendent egoism. It calls the human personality to arrange things happily for himself while other men and the world are unhappy; it denies the general responsibility of all men for all, denies the unity of the created world, of the cosmos. In the spiritual world there are no closed and separate personalities. The ethic of personal salvation leads to distortion and perversion of the idea of heaven and of the Kingdom of God.... Salvation is the reunion of man with man, and of man with the cosmos, then reunion with God. Hence individual salvation, or the salvation of the elect, is impossible. Tragedy, crucifixion and suffering will continue to exist in the world until universal salvation is attained, the enlightenment and transfiguration of all humanity and of the cosmos. And if this cannot be attained in the eon of our world there will be other eons, in which the work of salvation and transfiguration will be continued. And this depends upon my creative effort. Hence the ethic should be cosmic in character. Man is the supreme centre of the world's life: by man this life has fallen, and by man it must be lifted up. Man cannot lift himself, alone. The idea of the Kingdom of God is incompatible with religious or ethical individualism, with concern for personal salvation, exclusively. And the affirmation of the supreme value of personality is not at all concern for personal salvation, but rather the expression of the person's supreme creative calling in the life of the world. The least admissible type of aristocracy is an aristocracy of salvation. *Destiny*, pp. 314-15

Salvation, Personal and Social

The concept of Christianity as a religion of personal salvation has led to the narrowing, the diminution and the weakening of spirituality. . . . Seeking the Kingdom of God and His righteousness means seeking not merely personal but social salvation as well. The symbolization of the sacred in social life (the sacredness of monarchical authority, the sacredness of the nation, of property, of historical tradition) does not save us: only the realization of justice in the relationships of man to man, of 'I' to 'thou' and to 'we', the realization of communion and the brotherhood of men—this only can bring salvation. And from this attitude personal spirituality becomes more free, and its content is widened. . . . Personal salvation is given to those who seek general salvation, i.e. the Kingdom of God. . . . We cannot be saved, one by one: isolated salvation is impossible. We may be saved only with our neighbour, with other people and with the world. . . .

Man's seeking, not personal salvation but social transfiguration, reveals his personal, deeply personal, vocation to the spiritual life. . . . Vocation is always linked with creativity, but creativity is oriented toward the world and toward other people, toward society, toward history.

Reality, pp. 143-6

DOGMA

> Dogmas are only symbols of spiritual experience and the spiritual way, not congealed systems of concepts, not intellectual doctrines which always belong to time and are always changing. *Put* No. 49, p. 79

Dogma: Essential to Christian Living

The dogmatic consciousness of the oecumenical councils was only an objectivized translation of what had been immediately perceived in mystical experience. The dogmas recount in a conditional language the story of mystical encounters. The dogmas stiffen and become deformed into external authority when their mystical sources are closed, when they are received by the outward rather than the inward man, when they are experienced physically and mentally rather than spiritually. Everyday historical faith is the faith of the outward man who has not plunged his spirit into the mystical springs. This is mysticism expressed in adaptation to the physical plane of life. This is involution into the material. Everyday religiosity and everyday dogmatism are of enormous historical importance: they educate man at various stages of his development. Of course, there is such a thing as religious life for those who do not know the mystical sources of the dogmas, those who accept them on external authority. But to turn religion entirely into external living and external authority is to cause it to fade and degenerate. *M.C.A.*, p. 297

Christian Dogma—Dogmas Are Not Doctrines

The dogmas of the church must not be confused or identified with either dogmatic theology or dogmatic doctrine. The dogmas contain absolute and imperishable truth, but this has no connection with any doctrine. The truth of the dogmas is truth of the religious life, of religious experience. The meaning of dogmas is not moral and pragmatic as some modernist catholics think, but rather religious and mystical: it expresses the essence of spiritual life. It is only in theological doctrines that dogmas acquire a rationalistic character and not rarely are they combined with naïve realism and naturalism. The dogmas are necessary and salutary for life, because the confession of one or another doctrine or teaching is necessary for life and salvation. For my life, for my destiny, it is not unimportant whether or not a person near and dear to me exists: in the same way it is not unimportant for my life, my destiny, whether or not Christ my Saviour exists. But Christ my Saviour exists only if Christ is the Son of God, of one substance with the Father (homoousios). The dogma expressing this is the indication of a mystical fact, salutary for my life, but not a precept or a doctrine. Dogmas are mystical facts, facts of spiritual life and experience, the indication of real, religious meeting with the divine world, not theological doctrines. Dogmas are symbols pointing out a spiritual way, and the mystical events which take place along this way.

It cannot be a matter of indifference to me whether or not events took place in the spiritual world, on which my whole life and destiny depend, not alone in time, but in eternity. Whether God exists or not, whether God is a living reality or an abstract idea—for me this is a question of life and death, not the confession of some theological and mystical doctrine. If there is no God, there is no man; I do not exist, and my whole life becomes a meaningless illusion born of moments of the incomprehensible process of nature.... No, a dogma is neither a precept nor a doctrine, but a symbol and a myth expressing events in the spiritual world which are of absolute and central significance. *Freedom* I, pp. 119-20

Dogmas Are Symbols

Dogmas are only symbols of spiritual experience and the spiritual way, not fixed systems of concepts, not intellectual doctrines which always belong to time, and are always changing. Religious truth can be accepted only actively by a man's integral, his illuminated reason and conscience. Only a slave can accept a doctrine forced upon him by authority, if his conscience does not accept it, if freedom does not agree to it. Nothing has meaning for me without my freedom. Freedom takes precedence over authority. Authority exists if you believe in it. And this means that faith takes precedence over authority. In the catholic world, when authority attempts to violate the conscience and the consciousness of catholics, really no one accepts this: they either keep silence and conceal their own opinions, or break away. Religious life belongs to the spiritual plane of being and here nothing has meaning without freedom.

Put No. 49, Oct.-Dec. 1935

The Meaning of Dogma May Develop

The battle against the gnostics was struggle against pagan mythology and demonolatry rather than struggle against myth in general; it was struggle against knowledge falsely so-called, and not against gnosis in general, struggle for a true and pure expression of the events of the world of spirit. But church consciousness always fears defining times and seasons in advance, for the mass of humanity, always strives for a balance, does not permit too great changes, up or down. Church conservatism is democratic; it guards the truth for the average man, for the masses. The creative spirit in religious life is aristocratic; it dares to affirm what is revealed to the elect, to a minority which is qualitatively superior. The first spirit is primarily sacramental, the second primarily prophetic; the first reveals itself through the collective, the second through personality. Creative development in the church is always accomplished by moments of upsetting the balance between minority and majority, by creative personalities set forth from the average church milieu. The clergy is the conservative element in religious life, while the prophetic is the creative element. Prophetic service is always accomplished by the appearance out of the crowd of religious personalities, through individual charism and inspiration. The prophetic spirit is always against a theology and a metaphysic of the final, against the enslavement of spirit to natural flesh, against every absolution of the relative. To deny the possibility of creative development in church life, in dogmatics, is to deny the existence of the prophetic spirit. This would confine religious life to the clergy, alone. The spirit of God acts differently through the priest and through the prophet. In prophetic consciousness and prophetic service there is unfolded the infinity of the spiritual world; all the bounds of this finite natural world are broken down. The dogmas which give adequate symbolic expression to events of the spiritual life which are of absolute and central significance, cannot be reconsidered and altered. The Trinity, the Divine-humanity of Christ, are eternal mystical facts. Christ is the only-begotten son of God to all eternity. But the meaning of a dogmatic formula may be made more profound, may present itself in the light of new gnosis, and other events of the spiritual life may find symbolic expression in new dogmatic formulae. The myth-creating process in religion and ecclesiastical life is a continuous process—it cannot stop. It is a process of life itself. One cannot live at the expense of another life, live entirely on the myth created by earlier generations; one must live his own life. But our life and our myth-making cannot be separated from that of earlier generations, our fathers and grandfathers. It is all one unending, continuous, creative life, both individual and super-individual life, 'soborny' life, in which past and future, conservation and creativeness are joined in eternity. *Freedom*, II, pp. 125-7

Dogma Means Community

We are no longer in that period of history when for their self-protection men had to have a 'double truth': we can affirm a single truth. It is quite naïve to argue that clarifying criticism of revelation by the subject, i.e. by man, makes revelation unstable, arbitrary and 'subjective', while if we consider 'objective' revelation as not subject to any criticism whatever, this means its stability and soundness. But that very 'objective' revelation, which is held to be unshakable and independent of man, also presupposes selection, for instance the canons of Holy Scripture, the decisions of the church councils and papal decrees. That is to say, the actions of men distinguish between what is unshakable, already 'objective' and what is not yet finally confirmed, and hence is only 'subjective'. The 'objective' has only the one advantage of antiquity and of recognition by a large number of people, which is also something 'subjective', and represents the confirmation of human actions. . . .

The objectivization of faith does take place, but it has validity when it is the expression of communality, rather than the external, authoritarian succession of individuals. Khomiakoff called this inner communality 'sobornost'. And it is a great truth that the Christian life is realized not alone individually, but 'soborno' corporately, as well. But sobornost is not at all objectivity in some naïve sense of that word: it is divine-human. Sorbornost, communality, is not collectivism, it does not mean a collective which stands over man. It has no objective rational or juridical signs which could serve as a criterion of truth. Such a criterion is to be found only in the Spirit, the only guide. There is no criterion of Spirit outside Spirit itself: there is no criterion of Truth outside that Truth which is manifested in the Spirit. *Truth*, pp. 47-8

CHAPTER X

What First Was Named at Antioch

Christianity is a religion of freedom.
DOSTOEVSKY, p. 69

CHRISTIANITY

The Dualism in Christianity

In Christianity two elements are always in conflict: the inward-mystical and the outward-everyday; the aristocratic and the democratic; the spiritual and the intellectual; the intimately-secret and that which is adapted to the average level of human society. We must always remember that Christianity, as a historical world-phenomenon, is not only absolute divine relation, but also an adaptation to the humanity which accepts this revelation in the degree of its spiritual growth and development: the Christianity which is the mysticism of the inward man, and the Christianity which is an historical adaptation to the outward man. Only thus can we understand the tragic duality of Christianity in history. . . . Mystically, Christianity has followed the line of greatest resistance, the line of foolishness for the wisdom of this world. Historically, Christianity has followed the line of least resistance, the line of adaptation to reason and the reckoning of this world—adaptation to man's pagan nature, to the physical plane of life. This dualism presents a great temptation and it must be recognized and thought out. Any everyday Christian, a true believer and not devoid of religious experience, be he priest or layman, will tell you that in Christianity there is nothing mystical, that mysticism in Christianity was always a sign of abnormality and heresy, that the gnostics and the sectarians were mystics, and that the church is against mysticism. And along with this no one will attempt to deny that the greatest and most authentic saints were mystics; that the depths of church-consciousness are mystical, that the Gospel of John, the Epistles of the Apostle Paul and the Apocalypse are mystical books, that the religion of Christ is a religion of the mystery of redemption and that there is an Orthodox mysticism and a Catholic mysticism, recognized by the Church. In Christianity there is a profound mystical tradition which goes back to the apostles. The church in its world-historical action and its necessary adaptation to the level of humanity has been pre-eminently the Church of Peter, from whom the priestly succession derives. From

Peter comes the tradition of Judaeo-Christianity. The Catholic Church openly recognizes itself as the Church of Peter, but the Orthodox Church also accepts the succession from Peter. Peter was the apostle of the average level of humanity. In him is the spirit of involution, of condescension. But Christ's beloved disciple was John, and from him comes the mystical tradition. The mystical church, which because of man's low estate has not yet been fully revealed, is the Johannine Church. The saints and the mystics have been the living bearers of the Johannine tradition: St Francis is of the spirit of John rather than Peter. But holy tradition is not Petrine alone, but Johannine as well. The fearful torpidity of the Church of Peter, the decay of its upper ranks, must bring about a revelation of the Church of John, an incarnation of the mystical tradition of Christianity. Here, in the mystical sense, the apostolic succession will not be broken. The Church of Peter and the Church of John are one single Church of Christ, but seen from different sides, directed towards different aims which are subordinate to one sole purpose.

M.C.A., pp. 297-9

Christianity is not Democratic

Christianity recognizes the equal value of all human souls before God, not only the equal value but the absolute value of all souls. But this absolute value of the souls or of the inner man not only has nothing in common with mechanical, levelling-off equality—it is actually profoundly hostile to it, for such mechanical quality denies the existence of the soul and destroys the inner man for the sake of his external social position. In its mystic sense, Christianity is not at all democratic: it is genuinely inwardly hierarchic and aristocratic. Recognition of the inner man and his unique individual qualities, his unique vocation and place in the world predicates the metaphysical recognition of the aristocratic inward structure of the world, its hierarchic organism. This true metaphysical hierarchism and aristocratism has always been the source of all greatness in the world, all heightening of the quality and the values of human life, all movement in the world. The metaphysic of democratism, with all its revolutionary features, is in essence profoundly conservative, inert, and opposed to heightening qualities or values; it is timid and fearful of all greatness. Only genuine aristocratism, aristocratism of the inner man, rather than his external bourgeois situation, can be a dynamic, creative and revolutionary principle. Aristocracy is the only necessary, desirable, normal, cosmic form of authority in the world, since this is the authority of the inner man, the authority of the great and of those called to authority. This is the aristocracy of sacrificial service.

M.C.A., pp. 289-90

Christianity and Socialism: the Failure of Christianity

You bring up again the ancient criticism of Christianity which was first made by the Jews. . . . The Saviour and Redeemer of the world came to this earth, and still evil continues to reign in the world, . . . justice has not triumphed. Christianity has failed to realize itself in history.

But is it just or even logical to argue against the truth of Christianity on the basis that man has not realized that truth, or only poorly realized it? The so-called failure of Christianity in history is a human failure, not God's or Christ's failure.

Truth cannot be blamed if it is distorted, betrayed, not realized in life. In regard to Christianity, Christian men have been guilty of a triple betrayal: first they distorted Christian truth, then they denied it, and finally began to traduce Christianity because it has not succeeded. Why has it not succeeded?

The freedom of the human spirit enters organically into the purpose of God. The Son of God was revealed in the form of the Crucified One because He did not desire to do violence to man, to realize justice on the earth by compulsion. If Christian truth had been realized on earth by compulsion and force as men are trying to realize the truth of socialism, it would have ceased to be Christian truth, and not Christianity would have been realized, but something else. Love cannot be enthroned in the world by violence or compulsion. . . . Every realization of Christian truth by force is just as much a failure as apostasy from Christianity.

In the old theocracies God was affirmed without human freedom . . . in democratic societies man's freedom has been affirmed without God. And in communism man's freedom is denied, but in the name of a godless and inhuman collective. Such is the tragic way of history.

No, Christianity has not failed. It has not realized the Kingdom of God on earth, and it has known very well how difficult this would be, but people have lived, spiritually, by Christianity, from it they have learned to distinguish right from wrong, have gained the capacity to bear life's unbearable burden. Christianity has furnished blessed energy which has prevented the final victory of evil. The old Christian societies were characterized by a consciousness of sin and a capacity for repentance. In this they were boundlessly superior to modern socialist societies which have raised selfishness, hatred and revenge to the rank of virtues.

Days, Berlin, 8-IV-23

Divine-humanity

Christianity is not only faith in God, but faith in man, as well, belief in the possibility of the revelation of the divine in man. There is a commensurability between God and man and only because of this is God's revelation to man possible. Pure, abstract, transcendentism makes revelation impossible; it cannot open the way to God, and it excludes all possibility of communion between man and God. Not even Judaism or Islām are transcendental in this extreme form. In Jesus Christ, the God-man there is given the complete union of two natures, the human and the divine. This must take place collectively in humanity, in human society. For Vladimir Solovieff the very idea of the Church is related to this concept. The Church is a divine-human organism, the history of the Church is a divine-human process, and hence there is development. A free union of Divinity and humanity must take place. Such is the task set before the Christian man, and he has fulfilled it badly. The evil and suffering in the world did not hinder Solovieff in his time from seeing a divine-human process of development. Divine-humanity was being prepared in the pagan world, in pagan religions. Before Christ appeared, history was striving toward God-manhood. Since He came, history strives toward the God-man. . . . The appearance of the God-man and the coming revelation of Divine-humanity signify the continuation of the creation of the world. Russian religious philosophical thought in all its better representatives, struggles against all juridical interpretation of the mysteries of Christianity, and this is a part of the Russian idea. The idea of Divine-humanity is directed toward cosmic transfiguration, something almost completely alien to official Catholicism and Protestantism.

Idea, pp. 174-6

Christianity is Divine-human

Christianity is a religion of the Divine Trinity and a religion of Divine humanity. It predicates belief not only in God, but in man, as well. Humanity is a part of Divine-humanity. A non-human God is not the God of Christianity. Christianity is essentially anthropological and anthroprocentric: it lifts man to an unheard of, dizzying height. The second Person of God is manifested as a human person. This places man in the centre of being: the meaning and the purpose of history are found in him. Man is called to creative work in the world, to participation with God in His work, in the work of world-creation and world-ordering.

Freedom, II, pp. 27-9

> The central idea in Christianity is not justification, but transfiguration.
>
> *Freedom*, p. 254

Christianity Facing Modern Social Actuality

It is Christianity's misfortune, at least in modern history, in the course of recent centuries, that Christians all acted too late; they acted when what should have been done was already done either by non-Christians or by people hostile to Christianity. Christianity acted post-factum, after the new actuality had defined itself, when it was necessary to live in it and it was impossible not to take an attitude toward it. In social questions, for a whole series of centuries, Christians lacked creative initiative. I am speaking here, not of the inner spiritual life of men—here Christianity has always done its work—but of Christians' relations to the cultural process, to those life-problems which history constantly presents. . . .

The processes of improvement, humanization, liberation in human social life became possible only as a result of the gracious action of Christianity on men's souls. . . . Slavery, perhaps, might never have been abolished without Christianity. This is true, but alas, how often it was not Christians who did what had become possible only by the appearance of Christianity in the world! This is a disturbing question for Christian consciousness. Often, even today, and perhaps with more emphasis than ever before, you hear the affirmation that the Christian has no choice but to support the existing order of life, that this has always been so. . . . This is often derived from the doctrine of the sinfulness of human nature and a false idea of humility, or from a view of life's suffering as redemptive for man's soul, or finally from the principle that any government is sacred, as coming from God.

This, of course, terribly demeans the active, transfiguring and creative rôle of Christianity in the world. From the truth of the sinfulness of human nature (and it must be said that this truth has been vastly misused not for conflict with sin, but for submission to it) it does not follow that we are not to struggle against the social projection of sin, any more than that man should not struggle against his personal sin or strive for the transfiguration and betterment of life.

There was a time when the teachers of the Church were abreast of the social actualities of their time and attempted to answer their questions. St John Chrysostom is a good example. This was true in the Middle Ages: the Church's social language corresponded to the social actualities and to what was taking place. But now, in our time, both the social thought and the social language of the Church are quite archaic, out of touch with reality, as though Christians were living in another world than that which surrounds them. Unquestionably, the Church, by its nature turns above all toward eternity and preaches eternal truths which do not grow old with the turning of the centuries, which do not change in the most essential and important, under the influence of the social and cultural processes going on in the world. But we must remember that the Christian Church also exists in time, and in the historic world, in social actuality: the Church is oriented not toward eternity alone, but toward time, and it exists in time quite inescapably. This cannot be denied. This is the dual situation of the Church, the two planes on which it has to act. . . .

We must admit that facing the new capitalist world—and capitalism was a great novelty in the social structure of humanity—Christianity lost its orientation and did not know how to react to it, often turning against it, often adapting itself to capitalism. But a creative reaction, a creative way out of the situation in which life had placed it, was not discovered. . . .

There were times when men with a special calling did the thinking about the social question: the time has now come when this is inevitable for every man if he does not want to become lost in the world. The social question is a spiritual question in the highest degree, and it is the greatest catastrophe for mankind that this is not sufficiently realized. . . .

I think it is the strength of Christianity that it does not have a unique social system, obligatory for all times. And this means that social creativeness is a part of man's freedom. But it must be inwardly spiritualized and Christianized: Christians should participate in the creative social process.

Berdyaev's speech at a meeting of the Religious-Philosophical Academy, Paris, 1932

Christians Must Stand Above Both Capitalism and Communism

Christians are living in this sinful world, and they have to share its burdens; they cannot refuse to participate in the struggle of the opposing forces which rend the world. The Christian religion cannot adopt as its own some economic system which is obligatory for all men and all times. The Church does not teach political or economic truths. . . . But the relation of man to man is liable to Christian judgment and demands an active expression of Christian conscience. The transformation of man into a thing, of labour into a commodity, must be something unbearable for the Christian conscience. The same is true of the heartless egoism of competition. But capitalist society is founded on just this basis. From both the religious and the moral viewpoint Christian conscience should condemn the exploitation of man by man, of class by class; it ought to defend the rights of labourers or those who are exploited. Man, human personality, the human soul—the Christian faith must hold these above all most precious. And it cannot but condemn a system of life in which human personality, the human spirit, are transformed into means to the end of a spiritless and inhuman economic process. . . . More easily and consistently than any other, the Christian mind can recognize that economic and historical categories are not eternal, that these are transistory categories. And the categories of capitalist economy are the least permanent of all.

Class War, pp. 54-5

Christianity is More Important than Class or Social Structure

From the standpoint of absolute Christian values, both capitalism and materialistic communism are to be condemned, and we may discern in both the same element which demands condemnation. Marxist socialism puts class above personality, and considers man as solely a social function. But bourgeois-capitalist ideology looks at man in exactly the same way. Capitalism is exactly the same kind of domination by an impersonal collective as is communism. . . . Christianity must enter upon a solution of the social problem with its own evaluations. It accepts Christian communion which overcomes the isolation of personality, Christian commonality or 'sobornost', a fraternal communism of persons, but it cannot accept the impersonal, inhuman, social collective. It should not deny the fact of class war, or its significance in the solution of the labour problem, but it must rise decisively against the oppression or suffocation of man by this struggle, no matter from which side these evils come. And in the social problem the highest value is man. The social question is to be decided for man. Every class is temporary and passing. . . . Man himself is not eternal, but the human spirit is: it alone will stand before God.

We cannot completely deny the importance of the class struggle in solving the social problems of our time. But the social problem cannot be solved by class struggle alone, as marxism would have it; it is not solely a material-economic problem and it cannot be solved only on the basis of material economic theory. Besides its material economic side, it is a spiritual, religious, moral problem, a problem of culture, of pedagogics and technics, a problem of the spiritual renaissance and education of the masses. . . . The social question of our times has its material, economic and legal phases, but in reality it is in an historiosophic question; it includes an eschatological element; it is the last judgment on civilization, on the old world. *Class War*, pp. 66-9

Christianity and Labour

For the Christian consciousness, the most important thing in economic life should be its real foundation, which is labour. Christianity recognizes labour as something holy, and hence it must take labour under its protection. . . . The labourer is worthy of his food, and St Paul said he that does not work should not eat. The world of antiquity, Greek and Roman, scorned work, considered it the lot of slaves. Christianity brought respect for labour and the labourer. Jesus Christ, the Son of God, in his human form was a carpenter, and belonged to the social class of the workers. And this sanctified the social position of the workers. The apostles, also, were labourers. For Christian economics the basic problem is that of labour, and its attitude toward labour determines both its attitude toward social classes and its attitude toward the class-struggle. . . .

No social system protects the economic rights and interests of the workers, of every human personality. All social systems recognize the priority of society over personality, even the capitalist system which formally affirms personal initiative and the right of private property. But the problem of labour is an inner, spiritual problem and unless it can be solved, the further existence of human society will be impossible: the problem of a religious attitude toward work, one's own work or that of others. The old labour disciplines, always slavish in one way or another are breaking down and can probably never be restored. The social weight and power of the working class is growing and will increase even more in the future. And this class will never want to be slaves in any form, open or disguised. This puts the question of the inward attitude toward work of every single person, of the ethics of labour, inseparably connected with the religious attitude toward life. The social question is also a religious one, a Christian problem of attitude toward labour. Not economics alone, but the whole of society, is built upon labour. And the question of the spiritual bases of labour is a question of the spiritual bases of society. Man is a worker, a labourer, and he has a right to know why he is fated to be a worker and what is the meaning of his work. Improving the condition of labour, shortening the working-day, freedom from unbearably difficult work—this is one question. Another is the question of work itself, of one's inward attitude toward labour. And if the first question may be solved by changing the social order, by social reforms, the second is insoluble by external social measure: in its depths it inevitably becomes a spiritual, a religious question. Outside Christianity this problem is insoluble. . . .

We may and we should strive for the social alleviation of the hardness of labour. . . . But beside the social phase, we have here the individual, personal phase, quite incommensurate with the social. Labour is also man's personal lot. And as personal, labour can be experienced only religiously. In labour, viewed inwardly and not outwardly, there is an eternal element of the ascetic. Man is condemned to work, by the material world, by material necessity. But man is also a free spirit, and he may freely accept labour as his spiritual way, . . . as service to super-personal aims.

The spiritual problem of labour, the free acceptance of work, will be specially acute for a socialist society. In a socialist society not every form of labour will be creative and satisfying—and labour should have an inner motivation. If there is no such motivation, then military discipline will be necessary to compel men to work, and life will become a barracks. Materialist socialism for some reason hopes for a rebirth of human nature as the result of the new organization of society. But in this way we come into a vicious circle. No one has discovered the necessary spiritual fulcrum. It can be found only in the Christian renaissance of human spirits. *Class War*, pp. 56-61

Modern Christianity and the Cosmos

The prevailing Christian thought of our times reflects the loss of a feeling of the cosmos, and of a capacity for cosmic contemplation. The mediaeval world, like the world of antiquity, perceived the cosmos in nature, saw cosmic order, a hierarchical system. The modern man has lost his capacity to contemplate the cosmos: for him nature has become an object of knowledge through mathematical natural history, and through practical action upon it by technics. In our time church consciousness is losing more and more of its cosmic character. Men are beginning to think of the Church as a society of believers, as an institution. They begin to interpret the dogmas moralistically, to see only the psychological and social phases of the sacraments and not to see their cosmic phase. In the consciousness of the Church nominalism has overcome realism. The reality of the cosmos disappears and everything is centred on the reality of psychic and social life. Religion is valued first of all as a force for social organization. The doctrine of the Church as the mystical body of Christ is disappearing from theology.

Solitude, p. 140

The New Christianity

A new Christian piety must be revealed in our world. And upon this new Christian piety depends the fate of the world and that of man. It cannot be an abstract form, retirement from the world and from mankind: it must be a form of spiritual effort exerted over man and the world, labour for man and the world. It cannot permit human slavery to cosmic or social and technical forces. It calls man to a kingly rôle, and to creative work in the world. The new Christian man does not curse the world, neither does he condemn and anathematize the possessed and idolatrous. He shares the suffering of the world, bears in his body the tragedy of man. He strives to bring the liberating, spiritual element into all of human life. A personality which is strengthened and supported spiritually, cannot permit the powers of the world to divide its forces, can never permit itself to be possessed by demonic powers. Such a personality is not isolated and shut in upon itself, it is accessible to all universal meaning and open to all super-personal values.

This presents a very complex spiritual problem of relationship between the personal and the super-personal, a problem of personality entering into communal relationships, which is something quite other than personality becoming non-personal. The new piety is the road not only from the world and man to God, but the reverse, from God to man, descent as well as ascent, that is, the realization of the fullness of Divine-human truth, the truth of the God-man realized in life. In the old forms of Christian piety love of God often meant lack of love for man, repulsion from man, renunciation of the world as of something accursed. The only possible escape from this is in a new piety in which love of God will be love for man as well, and where freedom from the powers of this world will at the same time mean love for all God's creation, a religion in which man's spiritual life will be not merely a process of attaining salvation, but creative in the world, as well. This does not mean a renunciation of asceticism, but only a new understanding of it, where the ascetic will be free from elements hostile to true life, and from what may be called religious nihilism.

Christianity is above all else a religion of love and liberty, but just because of this, the future is not determined by blind fate, either for good or for evil. Hence we move forward toward a tragic conflict. The new Christianity must rehumanize man and society, culture and the world. But for Christianity this process of humanization is something not merely human; it is Divine-human, of the nature of the God-man. Only in Divine-humanity, in the Body of Christ, can man be saved. Otherwise he will be torn to pieces by demonic forces, by the demons of hatred and malice. *Fate*, pp. 123-5

Christianity and History: a Judgment on Christianity

We are witnessing a judgment not on history alone, but upon Christianity in history, upon Christian humanity. Christianity in history has been not only the revelation God, but also a work of man. And this work of man has been both good and bad. The purity of revelation has often been sullied by the human element, the human consciousness through which it has been filtered. The sins of Christians in history are great and numerous. How many have been the false theophanies man has imagined! Too often the human has been passed off for the divine. The history of Christianity, of the Church, is a divine-human process, and in it, as in every life-process, there have been pathological elements, elements of decadence. The postulate of free will offers the possibility for the failure of Christianity in history. Christianity is not God, not Christ Himself, although God and Christ are active in Christianity. Christianity is human history, and in it are represented all the contradictions of human existence.

Christianity, Christian humanity, has passed through all sorts of the temptations of this world, often disguised as holy things. A decadent freedom, presenting itself as the true will of God, has been at work in Christian history. The judgment on Christianity is a judgment upon the natural and the historical. Too much of the merely relative and unworthy has been declared sacrosanct. . . . This judgment upon Christianity is a process of purification—the way to a transfigured life. It places man face to face with pure, naked reality. And that is well. The collapse of many historically sacred shrines may mean that man is approaching the true holy of holies, is nearer to God Himself. God does not need to be sanctified by man: He is holy in Himself alone.

For the world, the holiness of God is a judgment. This judgment extends to Christianity since Christianity is a part of history and has become infected with all of history's temptations and imperfections. Christianity as a human phenomenon, has been found to embody many of those mental and physical complexes which are revealed by modern psychopathology—sadism and masochism, the torture of one's self or of others. Sadism is evident even in Christian doctrine, for instance in that of endless punishment in hell. Here we need a process of spiritual cleansing. . . . The tragic conflict between Christianity and history is nothing new—it is eternal and in the process each judges the other. History's judgment upon Christianity is its revelation of Christianity's failures in history. These failures indicate the points at which history has overcome Christianity instead of the reverse. History judges Christianity for having been conquered by history. But on the other hand this defeat of Christianity turns into a judgment upon history. The failure of Christianity is the failure of history as well. This is more clearly evident now, than ever before.

It is in the social realm, which holds the centre of the stage in our time, that the judgment upon Christianity is passed, first of all. It is undeniable that much of the true progress in social history is due to the open or indirect action of Christianity upon the human spirit: the abolition of slavery and serfdom, the recognition of freedom of conscience and of spiritual life are proofs of this. But instead of realizing these social reforms themselves, Christians have often left them to the hands of others, they have often even done injustice and consented to adapting higher spiritual values in the interests of the ruling class and the established order. They have succeeded in producing a 'bourgeois' Christianity. . . . The religion of love and mercy has been transformed into proclamation of cruel and relentless attitudes toward men. God's very idea of man as His image has been betrayed, as has that of the God-man and Divine-human life.

The judgment upon Christianity goes on in the cultural realm as well. All too often, as the result of a false concept of asceticism, Christianity has been hostile to creativity in culture: in philosophy, science, art, technics. It was only by second-thought, almost too late, that cultural creativity and social reform were sanctioned by Christianity, and hence human creative culture got out of Christian hands. . . .

Fate, pp. 115-19

Christianity in Crisis

The world faces two crises—a crisis in the non-Christian and anti-Christian world, and a crisis of the Christian world, a crisis within Christianity itself. The second crisis is more profound than the first: everything which takes place in the world and gives us the impression of being something external or even coarsely material, has its source in the inward, in the spiritual. In a certain sense we may say that Christianity is ending and that we may expect a renaissance only from the religion of the Holy Spirit, which will revive Christianity itself, since it will be its fulfilment. . . . This eschatological Christianity will be a religion of the Spirit, a religion of the Trinity, fulfilling all promises, hopes and expectations. We find ourselves, as it were, in the entr'acte, and this is why we live in such a tormented age. *Divine*, p. 11

> Every word in the Gospels is only a seed, only the beginning of an endless process of development. *Freedom*, II, p. 160

Can Christianity Stand Scientific Criticism?

Christianity is the revelation of God in history, rather than in nature.

The Bible tells of the revelation of God in history. The mystery of Christianity is connected with the incarnation. It is often said that the Christian revelation is not a revelation of an abstract Spirit, but of the Spirit which is active in history. The appearance of Jesus Christ is an historical phenomenon, this is an historical fact in time. But this produces a very complex problem which is made more acute by biblical criticism, by the scientific-historical exploration of Christianity. Christianity was formed and crystallized at a time when men trustingly accepted myths and legends as realities, a time when there was no such thing as historical criticism or a science of history. Can my faith, on which depends my salvation and life eternal, be dependent on historical facts which are disputable? Can I maintain my faith, if historical research proves scientifically, thanks to new facts and materials, that the facts recounted in the Holy Scriptures never happened, that these are not events in history but myths, legends, theological doctrines, created by the Christian community? Official Church history does not permit the rise of such problems, since it does not permit historical criticism to touch holy things. It is well known how on these grounds history has been falsified. But a spiritual religion must recognize that there is no religion higher than the truth, since God is truth and is known in spirit and in truth.

This means that the concept of historic revelation is contradictory and is the product of a religious materialism; it belongs to a stage of revelation which is already past. There exists only spiritual revelation, revelation in the Spirit. But historic revelation is a symbolization in the phenomenal, historical world, of events which take place in the noumenal, historical world. The whole mystery lies in the fact that noumenal events break through and enter into the phenomenal world; the meta-historical breaks into the world of history. And there is no absolute reparation between these two planes. But when meta-history enters history, it not only reveals itself in history, but also adapts itself to the limitations of historic time and place. Light shines out in a dark milieu. The infinite God speaks with the finite tongue of man, in the limited conditions of a given epoch and a given people.

Divine, pp. 28-9

Christianity Must be Eschatological

Christianity remains something messianic; it awaits the second coming of the Messiah, and the messianic kingdom. But Catholic theology resists all attempts to introduce the messianic idea into Christianity, for fear of prophetism. Primitive Christianity was indisputably eschatologically-minded. But a long perspective was disclosed, of the historical way between the two appearances of Christ the Messiah, during which, instead of the Kingdom of God, the Church was formed; now having become a part of history, Christianity began to adapt itself to this world, to the realm of Caesar. Only a few in 'historical Christianity' have expected a new revelation of the Holy Spirit, and that often in some distorted form. The prophetic side of Christianity became feeble and almost disappeared. Historical Christianity took on an organized-dogmatic and authoritarian character. The historical Church was recognized as the approach of the Kingdom of God. The idea of the Kingdom of God, which permeates the whole Gospel, is a prophetic idea. 'Thy Kingdom come.' That kingdom has not come yet; our world does not resemble the Kingdom of God. We can think of it only eschatologically.

Divine, p. 33

There is no Christian Doctrine of Society

Christianity has repeatedly defined its attitude toward forms of social organization made by others, but has never revealed the truth of society organized from the depths of Christianity, itself. The Christian truth about society has not yet been revealed—the times and seasons for that have not yet come. Hence, for the time being, we have to affirm the dualism of 'God' and 'Caesar', a natural-social dualism, and that of society and the state. This is a source of freedom, but this is not final: this is dualism *en route*, temporary. The final point of orientation must be the Kingdom of God, in which all dualism is overcome. . . .

The chief reason for the crisis of Christianity and of society, and for the decline of faith, lies in the concept of Christianity as exclusively a religion of personal salvation. On the basis of such a concept it is impossible to solve the problems of relationship between man and society. Only a new concept of Christianity, only comprehending it as a religion, not alone of personal, but also of social and cosmic transfiguration, that is by an increased sense of messianism and prophecy in Christianity, can bring a solution to the tormenting problems of relationship between man and society.

Spirit and Caesar, pp. 61-2

HUMILITY

Christian humility is usually understood in a distorted and decadent way. It should be understood ontologically. Humility is the manifestation of spiritual power in the conquest of egoism. The egoistic orientation of life is the chief consequence of original sin. Man is bottled up within himself and views everything within, and for its relation to himself. Man is obsessed with himself and his ego. We all commit the sin of egocentrism, and viewed from without, there is no more comic spectacle. Egocentrism distorts all life's perspectives; everything is seen in a false light, nothing is in its proper place. To see the world in its true light, in its true dimensions, to see the horizon, we must rise to the heights, climb out of the hole of egocentrism. We must discern the centre of being in God, not in ourselves, and then everything falls into its proper place. . . . Humility is not the opposite of freedom, it is an act of freedom. Nothing in the world aside from myself can force me into humility: it comes only by an act of freedom. It always means the discovery of greater freedom. Humility is a profoundly inward and secret phenomenon. And one of the most terrible distortions of Christianity has been a slavish and superficial conception of humility. Man's 'ressentiment', his unhealthy self-love, can be conquered only by the spiritual act of humility. . . .

Of course this does not mean that man should not struggle for the improvement of the external situation, for social change and reform. But he must be spiritually free when these changes do not occur, or are delayed, even if he is in prison. Holiness is a higher spiritual force, victory over the world. Love is power, a merciful emanation which gives life energy. The conquest of passion is power, and to this power Christianity calls us. The whole of moral life is nothing other than obtaining the energy of spiritual life and victory over the weakness and dimness of natural life. Christianity calls us to victory over the world, not to submission to it. Humility is not submission: on the contrary, it is insubmission, movement along the line of the greatest resistance. But together with this, Christian morals and Christian spirituality are extraordinarily simple. Only this simplicity can be power, for complication means division and weakness. Christian morality, so unbearable for the world, is possible only because it is divine-human, the reciprocal action of man and God. *Destiny*, pp. 124-5

RESURRECTION

The Resurrection of the Body

Death is tragic for personality: this tragedy does not exist for anything impersonal. It is natural that every mortal should die. But personality is immortal; it is the only immortal thing; it is created in eternity. And for personality, death is the supreme paradox in its destiny. Personality cannot be transformed into a thing, and the transformation of a man into a thing which we call death can not be extended to personality. Death is a break in the history of personality, cessation of its communication with the world. Death is not a cessation of the inward existence of personality, but cessation for the personality of the existence of the world, of others whom it has met on life's road. It makes no difference whether I disappear for the world, or the world disappears for me. The tragedy of death is above all in separation. But our attitude toward death is dual. It has positive value for personality, as well. In this life, in this objectivized world, personality cannot realize fullness of life; its existence is imperfect, partial. And personality's passage into the fullness of eternity predicates death, catastrophe, a leap across the abyss. Hence anguish is inevitable in the existence of personality, and terror before transcendental eternity is also inevitable. The usual doctrines of the immortality of the soul, propounded by spiritualist metaphysics, fail to understand the tragedy of death, do not even perceive the problem. Immortality can only be integral—the immortality of the integral personality, where the spirit controls both the mental and physical parts of man. The body belongs to the eternal image of the personality and the separation of soul from body in the dissolution of man's physical part, the loss of the form of the body, cannot lead to the immortality of personality, that is of the whole man. Christianity is opposed to the spiritualist doctrine of the immortality of the soul: it believes in the resurrection of the integral man, the resurrection of the body, as well. Through breaking-up and separation, personality passes to integral restoration. There is no such thing as man's natural immortality; there is only resurrection and eternal life through Christ, through man's union with God. Without this there is only man's dissolution into impersonal nature. Therefore the life of personality is constantly accompanied by anguish and terror, but also by hope. When I associate man's immortality with Christ I do not mean to say that immortality exists only for those who consciously believe in Him. The problem is more profound. Christ exists even for those who do not believe in Him. *Slavery*, pp. 46-7

THE KINGDOM OF GOD

Every kingdom is an opposition to the Kingdom of God. And those who seek kingdoms stop seeking the Kingdom of God.
Slavery, p. 129

The Way to the New City

The new city can never be created out of elements of the old social order. The ways to the new city are neither conservative nor evolutionary nor revolutionary. No sort of social evolution can bring us to the coming kingdom of divine-humanity. The state, the law, economics —none of these can be transformed and made Christian, changed into divine humanity, the City of God. You cannot affirm a Christian state or Christian economics by means of maintaining them, because they never were, and you cannot affirm them by evolution or revolution, because they never will be. Every state and every economy is essentially non-Christian and opposed to the Kingdom of God. In order that the City of God should reign in the world, all the old social order must burn up, the state, every law, every economy. *The new social order will not be created from elements of 'the world'; it will be created, in the 'worldy' sense, out of nothing, from other sources which lie outside the world's social evolution, out of Spirit rather than out of the world.* The new social order is vertical movement, rather than horizontal. And we cannot place our hopes on any social force or class, on any historic force, but only on personality reborn in the Spirit. . . . The way to the New Jerusalem is a way of sacrifice. It is written that it will come down from heaven, which means that it will not be created out of elements of 'the world'. We cannot deny the meaning of social order or world civilization, but this meaning is not to be found in their evolutionary transfiguration into the Kingdom of God, into the city which is to come. The new city is the church which is to be created, created in Spirit, outside the evolution of the world. . . . The new creative religious social order is not theocracy, neither is it anarchism nor the order of the state nor socialism: it is inexpressible in the categories of 'the world', untranslatable into the language of the physical plane of life. The Kingdom of God will come unperceived by 'the world', and man will enter it only in the measure of his growth in Spirit. In so far as man is still the higher achievement of Spirit, in so far as he belongs to the physical body of the world, he must participate in the evolution of the world's social order, he must pay tribute to Caesar. . . . But this does not mean that the Kingdom of Christ will not be on the earth, for the earth is not only physical, but metaphysical; our earth belongs to another world, it belongs to eternity. In the same way our delicate transfigured body belongs to another world, to eternity. And the religious social order will be born not of the physical but of the spiritual body. The New Jerusalem will appear catastrophically, not by evolution; out of the creation of the spirit of divine humanity, rather than out of 'the world', or out of the old social order. But the New Jerusalem will be on earth and revealed in the flesh, though not in the physical but rather in transfigured flesh.

M.C.A., pp. 293-5

The Kingdom of God . . . on Earth?

The Christian revelation is above all the tidings of the Kingdom of God. The essence of Christianity is seeking the Kingdom of God. But the idea of the Kingdom of God is extraordinarily difficult to interpret and gives rise to irreconciliable contradictions. We cannot think of the Kingdom of God in time. It is the end of time, of the world, a new heaven and a new earth. But even if the Kingdom of God is outside time, in eternity, still we cannot relate it exclusively to the end of the world, for the end is thought of as within time. The Kingdom of God comes, not only at the end of time, but in every moment, also. In any moment there may be a transition from time into eternity. And between me and eternity, i.e. the attainment of the Kingdom of God, there does not stretch the long space of time which yet remains before the end of the world. There are two ways out into eternity: through the profundity of some moment and through the end of time and of the world.

The Kingdom of God comes unperceived. It is thought of as the Heavenly Kingdom. But the Kingdom of God is possible on earth, as well, for the earth too, may be illuminated and may inherit eternity. And it is not given us to fix the boundaries between that new earth and ours. . . . The eschatological interpretation of the Kingdom of God is the only true one. But it is a paradox of the eschatological consciousness that the end is postponed until some indefinite time in the future, and yet it is near in every moment of our life. . . . *Destiny*, p. 310

Division (of the Church) took place in the realm of Caesar. The Kingdom of God can be only one. *Freedom*, II, p. 217

PARADISE

At the Beginning and the End

The world process began with paradise and it moves toward paradise, rather than toward hell. Man recalls paradise in the past, dreams of paradise in the future, at the end of all things, and at the same time he has a horrible premonition of hell. Paradise at the beginning, paradise and hell at the end. It looks as though all the gain and enrichment of the world-process consisted in the addition of hell to paradise: hell is something new that will appear at the end of worldly life. But paradise is not new, it is a return to something previously known. But how sad is man's return to paradise, after mankind has been divided and one part has gone into hell! This is the way the result of eating the fruit of the tree of knowledge of good and evil is always pictured. Life in paradise was integral—there was nothing but life in paradise, until there came the knowledge of good and evil. After this distinction, paradisical life fell apart and beside it appeared hellish life. This was the price paid for freedom, freedom to know and to choose good or evil. . . .

Hence we cannot speak of a return to the primal, lost, condition of paradise. We not only cannot, but we should not return to that. This would mean that in the last analysis the world-process was without profit or meaning. The paradise at the end of the world-process is quite another thing than the paradise at its beginning. This is paradise after the knowledge of freedom, after all trials and testings. . . .

Paradise as man's original condition, does not yet know the appearance of the God-man, but the paradise which will end the world-process will be the Kingdom of Christ, of Divine-humanity. The first paradise does not know Divine-humanity. Divine-humanity is the positive result of the world-process. But in the midst of the world-process weary man constantly dreams of return to the *lost* paradise, to the pristine innocence and integrity. He is ready to renounce knowledge; knowledge seems to him the result of division and the loss of the wholeness of life. He is ready to flee from the discomforts of 'culture' to the joy and blessedness of 'nature'. And always man experiences a sinful disillusionment in his dreams and yearnings, for he finds that not only 'culture' but 'nature' also, is spoiled by original sin. And there is only one way open to man, the way of faithfulness to the end to the idea of 'man', the way which enters into the realm of the spirit, where transfigured nature enters, as well. . . .

We Imagine Paradise under our own Categories

We live in sinful life, this side of good and evil, and we find it difficult to picture paradise. In our thinking we use the categories of our sinful life, our distinction between good and evil. But paradise lies beyond good and evil, and therefore it is not exclusively the kingdom of good and of good men, in our sense of the word. We have a better approach to the true idea of paradise when we think of it as beauty. The transfiguration and illumination of the world is beauty, not good. Paradise is theosis; it is creation becoming divine. Good relates to the untransfigured and unenlightened world. Only beauty is liberation from worry and burden; good is still worry. . . .

Intimations of paradise are given us in ecstasy when paradise breaks through our time and erases our distinction of good and evil, moments when it is given man to experience a sense of final liberation, when all burdens vanish. The ecstasy of creativeness, of contemplation of divine light, the ecstasy of love, transport us for a moment into paradise, and this moment is no longer in time. But after this moment of eternity, dreary time again comes in, and all is wearisome once more.

Destiny, pp. 305-9

PREDESTINATION

Calvin's Monstrous Doctrine

To test our ideas of God, imagine that the omnipotent God recognized the eternal suffering of creation as the highest good. Could we be reconciled to that? Only man's terrible fearfulness explains why men have been reconciled to Calvin's doctrine of predestination. A higher and liberated consciousness would recognize God's humanness. Otherwise that which men idolatrously call God is the Devil, not God. Like man and the world, God can be known only by man's evaluation, but evaluation is creative destiny. *Divine*, p. 23

The problem of predestination has been central for the whole of western Christianity, both Catholic and even more, Protestant. Western Christian disputations have centred on this: this was the theme of freedom and grace. St Augustine had a dominant influence on western Christian thought, Catholic as well as Protestant. Here the theme of freedom and grace turned into the theme of predestination. This idea attains extreme acuity in its conscience-disturbing expression in Calvin. The problem of predestination never played such a rôle in eastern Christian thought, for Orthodoxy. The Greek doctors of the Church, and Russian Christian thought were not interested in it. And this is very characteristic. The idea of predestination is indisolubly connected with the juridical concept of Christianity, and it loses all meaning under another concept. Predestination means predestination to salvation or destruction. But this is judgment, in the present instance judgment enacted by God before time began. This is an unjust decision of a legal case, before the case arose, and even before the crime was committed. But this predetermines not only the destruction because of crime, but the crime itself. If we think this through to its conclusion, then the coming of Christ the Redeemer means, not improvement and salvation, but deterioration and even worse, destruction. . . .

The whole thing is a consistent system of frightening men. The doctrine of predestination expresses man's fearfulness and degradation. We may be surprised that human conscience could be reconciled to Calvin's monstrous doctrine of predestination. This idea was present in others, also, though in a less radical form. It is to Calvin's credit that he reduced this idea to the absurd, *reductio ad absurdam.*

But it must be said that predestination lies in wait for every doctrine which declares that God endowed man with freedom, knowing in advance that this freedom could bring him to destruction. And admitting freedom of the will in a larger measure than Calvin, or even St Augustine, does not ease the situation in the least. Freedom of the will which overcomes sin turns out to be a snare to trap men into judgment and punishment: this is primarily a doctrine of criminal pedagogy. The results of acts of free-will, which proceed not from man himself, but in the last analysis from God, are foreseen by God in eternity, and hence foreordained by Him. Predestination is the final conclusion drawn from the traditional-orthodox theological system. Only the admission of uncreated freedom avoids this conclusion about predestination. . . .

But the connection of the doctrine of predestination with the judicial concept of Christianity is indubitable. Once this concept is radically swept aside, no place is left for predestination: it is simply meaningless. Predestination is a judgment, monstrous, arbitrary, despotic, but still judgment. But salvation *may* be understood as the attainment of God-like perfection, as movement upward toward fullness Since there is no process of judgment, no sentence, there can be no snares which greatly increase man's difficulties. There is simply a revelation of the divine element in man; the divine-human lien is strengthened. *Truth*, pp. 102-5

THE LAST JUDGMENT

Can Christianity cease awaiting a last judgment? Here, I think, it is not a matter of refusing what is eternal in the idea of the last judgment. The very terminology has a judicial flavour. It is like the end of a criminal trial and the expectation of the final sentence. This is exoteric terminology, which does not go into the mystical depths. In a deeper sense it means awaiting the day of the triumph of God's truth over all unrighteousness. Every man knows the judgment of conscience within himself. But here the word judgment does not have the sense of criminal law. This is again the question of the limitations and 'conditionedness' of human language, evidence of how it is permeated by sociomorphism. But man must rise, spiritually, above these limitations. The mystics have done this. The last judgment that exists both in individual life and in that of the world is, as it were, an immanent conviction of untruth, but this immanent conviction is accomplished through transcendent truth, which surpasses everything human. God will not judge the world and mankind, but a blinding light will pierce the world and man. This will be not only light, but a searing, purifying fire. In this purifying fire it will be evil that burns, not living beings. And that will lead to transfiguration, to a new heaven and a new earth. Toward this man moves through darkness and suffering. The grain of truth in the nightmarish and exoteric idea of predestination is only in fact that man must live out his destiny, but this is only a way (to something other).

Truth, pp. 108-9

CHAPTER XI

God Between Four Walls*

'The Church . . . is a secret spiritual reality.'
BEGINNING, p. 45

THE CHURCH

For me Jesus Christ exists not only in the past: He is our eternal contemporary. The work of Christ continues on the earth and will continue to the end of the world. . . . I do not doubt the unbroken existence of the Church of Christ in the world and its inner significance in the process of history. The question . . . is of the concept of the Church and its limits. Is the sphere of the Church as a mystic organism limited to the visible structure of the church and its appurtenance to one or another confession? And does everything which historically has been recognized as sacramental actually belong to the Church of Christ and is this inseparable from it? The sphere of the Church ought to be at once both widened and narrowed. For a clarified conception of the Church it seems to me important to recognize that the Church has been understood to mean not only the mystical body of Christ, but a social institution. As a social institution, acting in history, the Church is fallible and bears the same limitations as all social phenomena, everything historic: it has served worldly interests, has soiled its hands, has passed off the temporal for the eternal. In this sense one may await and demand from the historical Church repentance, the recognition of its sins, of its partial betrayal of Christ. This the Church can do in its human make-up, in the person of its hierarchy and of the church people. And they must repent of treason toward God, toward Christ and the Holy Spirit. And this does not mean the personal sins of clergy or laymen, but the sins of the Church, the distortion of Christianity. Christians, whether hierarchs or laymen who consider themselves churchmen are very much to blame for the godlessness of our modern world, and it does not become them to take the pose of accusers who are defending the truth. . . .

What troubles me is the question—does the Church save only those who are formally its members, or does the work of salvation extend to those who are apparently outside it, i.e. to a large part of the world? I find it difficult to understand that spiritual attitude by which people protect themselves and their friends from evil, but commit a large part

* Victor Hugo.

of mankind to destruction. I think the parable of the Prodigal Son may have a wider interpretation. The Prodigal is wandering in the world, away from his father's house. But this is true not only of those who are seeking happiness and the pleasures of life, but often those who seek truth and justice. . . . Many have left the visible church with high motives of the love of truth, rather than for low motives. And toward these the phariseeism is out of place, of those who remain within the courts of the Church, guarding themselves from evil. My question is this: should the Christian Church use not merely the old methods of attracting to itself those who have fallen away and are experiencing the suffering and anguish of the world, but give a creative answer to this suffering and anguish, give an answer to the new questionings, and thus draw men to itself? . . . This means the confidence that a new epoch in Christianity is possible. . . . *Put*, No. 48, July-Sept. 1935, pp. 69 ff

The Church and Social Reform

Christians cannot pretend that everything in the world has remained unchanged since patriarchal times, that a new social reality has not appeared in the world. Christian consciousness seems always to lag behind the social and cultural processes going on in the world; Christians do everything too late. This is evidence of the decline which Christianity has suffered in recent centuries, evidence of the absence of creative initiative. As an external and historical entity, the Church seems not to have observed that the world has radically altered, . . . that quite new social relationships have appeared. And the Church must now define its attitude toward this new social reality. Out of the depths of Church consciousness, Christians will have to decide and say which side is right in the struggle now being played out in the new social world. Of course Christianity condemns the hatred in both opponents in the struggle; the malice of the proletariat as well as the malice of the bourgeoisie. But it is impossible any longer to avoid judgment as to which side is right. St John Chrysostom was abreast of the social questions of his time and his preaching was in real conformity with social actuality. He was even quite near communism, although this was communism of a non-capitalist time. The sermons in the churches of our day, calling for the solution of social problems by charity and benevolence may sometimes . . . soften hardened hearts, but they are completely out of touch with social reality, with today's struggle for social justice.

Class War, pp. 125-6

The Nature of the Church

The being of the Church has not yet been so sufficiently revealed and actualized that the construction of an ontology of the Church was possible. For that matter, is it possible to define the nature of the Church? From without it is impossible to perceive and understand the

Church: impossible fully to define it, rationally, to make it penetrable for our understanding. One must live in the Church. It is comprehensible only by experience. It is not given to us as a compulsory external reality. And what is glimpsed from without, as the Church, is not the Church in its hidden nature. The Church is not a temple built of stone, it is not the clergy, the hierarchy, not a society of believers or a parish consisting of people: it is not an institution regulated by legal norms, although all this enters into the being of the Church. . . . The Church has its physical, and psychic and social sides, but none of these actualities permit us to define its nature. The Church is not a visible thing; it does not belong to the world of visible things: it is not an empirical actuality like rocks, plants or animals. The Church . . . belongs to the world of invisible things, disclosed to faith; it is a secret spiritual reality. It is true, the Church exists for everyone as an external empirical reality and men determine their attitude toward it or they battle against it as a reality—enemies who do not believe in the Church. But to them the Church is quite another sort of reality than to those who believe in and live in the Church. . . . The genuine existential reality of the Church is hidden, it abides beyond the limits of its stones, its hierarchy, its rites, its councils. The nature of the Church is spiritual. . . .

'Sobornost' is an ontological quality of the Church. In church experience I am not alone; I am with all my brethren in the spirit who have lived everywhere and in all times. I myself am very narrow and know very little: my experience lacks breadth and does not comprehend the fullness and the variety of being, and I myself have never had many spiritually definitive meetings. Here I have written a book, but in that book I have caught only scattered rays of light, have seen only separate phases of truth. But it is possible for me to go out of myself, mystically to cross the boundaries of self: I can have communion with the experience of spirits akin to mine, with super-personal experiences. In his church experience, in his meeting with Christ, man is not alone, not left to his own narrowness: he is with all those who at any time have had this experience, with the whole Christian world, with the apostles, the saints, with his brethren in Christ, with the living and the dead. Not only the living belong to the Church: all the generations who have died belong to it just as really; they all live in the Church and there is real communion with them. This is an essential mark of the Church. In the 'soborny' spirit of the Church there beats one heart. In the Church there is a recognition of Christ, the meeting of all with the one and the same Christ, and the reception from this same Christ of one unifying power. Christ is in us and we in Him. . . .

The Church is the mystical body of Christ. To belong to the Church means being a member of the body of Christ, a cell in that mystical body, an organ of that mystical organism. Belonging to the mystical body of Christ, we receive the mind of Christ, the love of Christ, the freedom of Christ, which in the world of nature or in our spiritual narrowness we neither have nor know. . . .

The potential Church, the Church as yet unrevealed or actualized, is boundlessly greater than that part of it which is actualized and revealed. The true foundation of the Church is mystical, bottomless and endless. The historical Church does not encompass the fullness of the Church's being. The Church is mystical and potential. Only such concept of potency reveals the infinity of its being, overcomes all the bounds of the finite which oppress us. Christianity was a break through the bounds of the finite, the revelation of the infinite and the bottomless. . . .

The Church is two-sided in its nature: it cannot be understood in a monophysite way. The Church has not only a divine, but a cosmic basis: it bears not only the label of Divinity, but the world's label, as well. The Church is God-world, God-humanity. The Church is not God, alone. And in the cosmic, worldly foundations of the Church there must be achieved in the world purity, innocence, virtue. If there had not been this attainment of purity and virtue in the world, the birth of God and the Incarnation, the appearance of God's Son in the world would have been impossible: there would have been that power which accepts God in oneself and brings Him into the world. God's entrance into the world can not be external compulsion: the world must unveil itself to God. *Freedom,* II, pp. 190-201

The Spirit in the Church

The Spirit is active in the Church, but the Church is not collective spirit. Sobornost means something else. Sobornost is not collectivity, it is a quality of the communion of men, of personalities and We, which is not exterior to those personalities and the collective which acts upon them. The 'soborny' 'We' is immanent to people; it means their penetration by spirituality, their entry upon the spiritual plane of being. If the Holy Spirit is considered in Christian dogmatics as an hypostasis, i.e. as a person, we must say first of all that the Holy Spirit is not a collective person and calling it a person is a symbol to express an inexpressible mystery, the mystery of the conquest of the contrast between the personal and the general. The Spirit is incarnate and symbolized, but does not become objective. . . .

In the Church, as a social institute, there occurs an objectivization of the Holy Spirit. This is at the same time a socialization—that is, an adaptation to the social everydayness of the human mass, to an alienation of spirit in them. Spirituality remains only in the few at the top. But the Church is not only a social institution, which always has to do with the world of the everyday; the Church has existential significance, as well. And in this second concept of the Church freedom is just as dominant as is authority in the first. Conscience, which is man's spiritual depth and the place of his meeting with God, is at the same time freedom, and it cannot be alienated or objectified, or transferred to any part of the collective organ. The spirit is pure, and free from social utility. Social utility appears only under objectivization. As an organized social institution the Church in history is subject to the laws of the objectivized world, is caught in the power of the utilitarian, and the light of truth in it is darkness. . . .

The objectivization of the spirit in the Church as a social institution, is symbolization, rather than realization. Even in the cult which contains a mystically real element, symbolization takes place. Ritualism, belief in rites, is a conditioned symbolization. The covenant of Christ is not realized, but symbolized. Christian love and charity are expressed in conditional signs, but not in realities. The relations between the hierarchs of the Church and the attitudes toward the hierarchs of the Church are full of such conditional symbolization. The Church parish is not a real Christian community, but only a conditional symbol of it. In dogmatics and in the sacraments symbolism overcomes realism. . . .

Kenosis, the incarnation, God's descent into our human world, is spiritual realism rather than symbolism, and the processes in the human world should correspond to that spiritual realism. But symbolic sacralization has substituted itself for the realization of the Gospel commands. In this lies the historic tragedy of Christianity. This happened because Christian spirituality fell on the soil of an objectivized, fallen world. Spirituality was stretched to fit the condition of a world which was in a state of objectivization. . . .

Authority in the Church

Authority is a phenomenon of the Church as a social institution. The search for authority is the search for a criterion that could stand above the relative and deceptive multiplicity of the human world, something which would be super-human. This is a quest for guarantee and security. But guarantee and security are human, all too human. They are related to men's social, rather than to their spiritual life. Spiritual life is perilous, it knows no guarantees: it is freedom and freedom means risk. Authority is determination from without. External society is such a sphere, rather than the sphere of spirit. Hegel was a poor Christian, but he was right when he said that Spirit is a return into oneself, that the Holy Spirit is a subjective spirit. Authority is the extreme of objectivity. Spirit is the extreme of subjectivity, the depth of subjectivity. In religious spiritual authority the Spirit is alienated from itself. Spiritual authority is not spiritual, it is social. . . .

Objectivization of spirit, which leads to recognizing as sacred the structure of the Church as a social institution, of hierarchical authority, national or state or racial order, etc., inevitably moves over into idolatry. The spirit moves further and further away from itself, and hence what happens is not the spiritualization of those spheres where spirit is working, but only a conditioned symbolization. True spiritualization is subjectivation, subjectivation of spirit, i.e. the institution of an order based on subjectivity, on existential subjects, which is personal order. Only the existential can be holy, freedom, creativity, love, not historical formations and structures. *Reality*, pp. 37, 51, 58-9, 63, 158, 162

The Church as Reality

In the general question of collective realities the question of the Church is specially difficult. In what sense is the Church a reality? The Church as objective reality standing above man, is a social institute and in this sense is an objectivization of religious life, an adaptation of spirit to social conditions. But in its depths the Church is life of the spirit, spiritual life not subject to social laws, it is community, the brotherhood of people in Christ, it is the mysterious life of Christ in human communion, the mysterious incorporation into Christ. In this sense the Church is freedom and love: in it there is no exterior authority, no necessity, no compulsion, in the Church is freedom enlightened by grace. This is what Khomiakov calls 'sobornost'. Sobornost is not a collective reality standing above and commanding man, but rather a higher spiritual qualification of a people. It is entrance into communion of the living and the dead. This sobornost cannot be expressed in rational or legal terms. Everyone should take upon himself responsibility for all; no one may separate himself from the world-whole, although he should not consider himself a part of that whole. All the tragedy in the Church's history is in this duality of the nature of the Church. The Church is not a personality, not an ontological reality in relation to which human personality would be a subordinate part. The Church as an ontological reality standing above man, is an objectivization, an exteriorization of inner sobornost. The Church has no existential centre save Christ, Himself. The expression 'church consciousness' is only a metaphysical expression, such as 'national consciousness' or 'class consciousness'. The objectivization of the Church was the source of slavery: it also provoked clericalism, so destructive for spiritual life. The traditional form of putting the question of the visible and invisible church, which is brought up in distinction between Orthodox and Catholics with Protestants, is erroneous. The distinction between 'visible' and 'invisible' is conditional, and the marks of visibility and invisibility change, depending on the will of those who judge. The sacrament of the eucharist has external signs of its fulfilment, visible to the senses. But at the same time it is beyond doubt that the sacrament of the eucharist is invisible and is accomplished in a mysterious sphere hidden from the phenomenal world, accessible only to faith, which is evidence of things not seen. The visible church has a whole series of visible signs: the church building itself, built of stone, the service, expressing itself in human words and gestures, the parish meeting, the hierarchical authority, very similar to hierarchical authority in the state.

But the mysterious presence of Christ in the Church is invisible, not appreciable by the senses, is disclosed only by faith. The Church is a visible reality, but this reality is symbolic: in it only signs are given of another, spiritual reality. The noumenal side of the Church is true spirit, rather than nature or society: it is the Kingdom of God which comes imperceptibly. But the phenomenal side of the Church is an objectivization and symbolization of spirit. *Beginning*, pp. 121-2

CATHOLICISM AND ORTHODOXY

Of the two great Churches, Catholic and Orthodox, east and west, each has its own official mysticism. And the difference between the structure of the mystical experience explains the difference between the ways the Orthodox east and the Catholic west have taken in the world. There is a profound difference in the primary attitudes towards God and Christ. For the Catholic west Christ is object: He is the object of all striving, of love and of imitation. Hence the Catholic religious experience is one of man's stretching up towards God. The Catholic spirit is Gothic. In it coldness is joined with ardent passion. The Catholic spirit is intimately close to the concrete Gospel image of Christ, of Christ's passion. The Catholic soul is passionately in love with Christ, imitates His sufferings, receives in its own body the stigmata. Catholic mysticism is through and through sensual: it is filled with languor and longing. In it the anthropological element is put into harness. Thus it happens that Catholic mysticism goes through the *nuit obscure*. The Catholic soul cries out: 'My Jesus, my beloved!' In the Catholic Church it is cold, just as it is in the Catholic soul—it is as though God had not come into the soul or the Church. And the soul strives passionately upward towards the object of its love. Catholic mysticism is romantic, full of romantic longing. Catholic mysticism is hungry, it is ever unsatisfied, it never knows marriage, but only being in love. The Catholic attitude toward God as object, as the goal for striving, produces the external dynamic of Catholicism. This is not to deny that at the height of Catholic mysticism, for example in St John of the Cross, a *unio mystica* is attained. The Catholic experience creates a culture which bears the stamp of being in love with God, of earnest longing for God. In Catholicism energy is poured out in the way of historic action; it is not within, since God is not received within the heart: the heart strives towards God by the ways of world-dynamic. The Catholic experience gives birth to beauty out of spiritual hunger and unsatisfied religious passion. . . .

For the Orthodox east, Christ is subject: He is within the human soul: the soul receives Christ into itself, into the depths of the heart. Being in love with Christ and imitating his passion is impossible in Orthodox mysticism. Orthodox mysticism is prostration before God, rather than striving up towards him. The Orthodox Church, like the Orthodox soul, is just the opposite of Gothic. Orthodoxy is neither cold nor passionate. Orthodoxy is warm, sometimes even hot. For Orthodox mysticism the concrete Gospel image of Christ is not so close. Orthodox mysticism is not sensual; sensuality is considered an enticement: imagination is refused, as a false way of procedure. In Orthodoxy one cannot say: 'My Jesus, my near and dear.' Christ comes down into the Orthodox Church and the Orthodox soul and gives them warmth. In Orthodox mysticism there is no yearning passion. . . . Orthodoxy is not romantic, it is realistic, sober. Orthodoxy is not hungry—it is spiritually satiated. The mystical experience of Orthodoxy is marriage, not merely being in love. The Orthodox attitude towards God as the subject which is received into the depth of its heart, the inner spirituality of this relationship, does not produce external dynamic: everything is directed towards inward communion with God. The Orthodox mystical experience does not favour culture, does not create beauty. In the Orthodox mystical experience there is a sort of numbness towards the external world. Orthodox energy is not poured out in the ways of history. The satiety of Orthodox experience does not produce outward creativeness: man is neither harnessed nor regimented. In this difference between the ways of Catholicism and of Orthodoxy a great mystery lies hidden. And both ways are genuinely Christian. *M.C.A.*, pp. 307-9

Christianity, Eastern and Western

The East and the West represent two ways of life in the Christian world. And their existence was predestined in God's plan for world history. This difference of spiritual life and experience between East and West was determined long before the separation of the churches. And the difference did not make the separation necessary: different types of Christianity can exist in the One Catholic Church. Eastern patristics were always very different from western. In the east the tradition of platonism was strong: the east was more mystically-minded; its interests were more ontological and speculative. The dogmas of the Church were developed largely by the eastern teachers of the Church. All the gnostics and heretics were in the east, a fact which evidences the intense interest in the east for religious gnosis and religious metaphysics. Neither Origen nor St Gregory of Nyssa could have appeared in the west. . . . If we do not count that genius St Augustine, we may say that western patristics did not produce a single great thinker: there were only remarkable writers, like Tertullian and St Jerome. In eastern Christianity the central question was always of the transfiguration of human nature and the world's nature. The greater cosmic quality of Orthodoxy is linked to this attitude, its greater concern with the Second Coming of Christ, with the Resurrection. The eastern teachers of the Church, Clement of Alexandria, Origen, St Gregory of Nyssa, and others, never by themselves would have developed a concept of Christianity as a religion exclusively of personal salvation, and never would have come to the doctrine of the blessedness of the elect in paradise and the eternal perdition of all others in hell. This is primarily a western rather than an eastern idea. Eastern thought is concerned not so much with justification and salvation from perdition as it is with transfiguration and attaining divinity. . . . In the west, in Catholicism and then in Protestantism, the central question was always that of justification, of salvation by good works or faith, of the varying degrees of participation of freedom or of grace in the work of salvation. *Freedom*, II, pp. 218-20

The East is Platonic, the West Aristotelian

By the very structure of their spirit, eastern Christians are platonists, while western Christians are Aristotelians. And this is not a difference in doctrine and theory: this is a difference of life and experience. In Aristotelian-Thomist conception, the order of nature is not permeated by divine energy; it lives by its own laws and is subject to the action of grace transmitted by the church-organization, only from without. . . . The whole way of the west, not Catholicism alone, but all of western culture and social thought, is based on the Aristotelian concept of relationship between form and material, potence and act. The significance of the material of life and the potence of being is reduced. To a significant degree material (in the Greek sense of the word) and potence are non-being. True being is only material which has been subjected to form. Full life is act; potential life is incompleteness. From this comes the actualization, the formalization, the insistence on complete expression and the organization which characterizes Catholicism and western culture in general. In the east, in Orthodoxy, in Russia, not all spiritual forces are actualized, given complete expression, and form; there is much that remains only potential, hidden, inward. And we do not consider this incompleteness to be non-being. The east is even inclined to think that the inward, the secret, the unexpressed, is being in a greater degree than what is completely expressed and actualized. For eastern religious consciousness, the natural is rooted in the supernatural. God's energy permeates the world and is making it divine. The empirical world is rooted in the world of ideas, and the world of ideas is established in God.

Freedom, II, pp. 221-2

PROTESTANTISM

Of Protestantism

The Church is an ontological reality, not merely a society of believing persons. In Catholicism this realism and objectivism began to be deformed into external formalism and authoritarianism, which were substituted for a living ontologism. Protestantism was the revolt of man's subjective world against compelling authority imposed from without. And the centre of gravity of religious life was transferred to faith, to man's inward relationship with God. There was doubtless some truth in this. But

Protestantism was unable to rise above the antithesis between subject and object: it separated subject from object. Hence the consequence of protestantism was triumph of nominalism and individualism, the dissolution of ontological realities. Religious energy became secularized and was turned toward the triumph of culture. The cultural consequences of the Reformation were very significant, but its religious consequences proportionally small, out of proportion to the religious energy and the religious genius of Luther. Processes of dissolution started in religious life. In liberal Protestantism the Christian religion is warped; it is turned into a religion of the professors, into a science of religion. Protestantism rightly revolted against authoritarianism and heteronomism in religion: this was the right of the free spirit, the free conscience. But this was right for a certain moment. Protestanism went on to break with the Church and with tradition: oppositional protest prevailed over creative reform. But it must be said that individualism is characteristic not of Protestantism alone, but of the whole western Christianity. The idea of the salvation of souls, as well as the idea of the predestination of a few to salvation, is a heavenly, metaphysical individualism. Over against this stands the idea of 'sobornost', collectivity in the very ways of salvation. In the Church we are saved as a community, in a choir, together with all our brethren.

Freedom, II, pp. 225-6

ORTHODOXY

The concepts of orthodoxy and heresy are of a sociological nature. Orthodoxy is the religious consciousness of a collective, and behind it is concealed the domination of the collective over its members. This is the organized lordship of the race over the individual. The nature of orthodoxy and heresy is very clear in Russian communism. The whole of Soviet communist philosophy stands under the sign of discerning orthodoxy from heresy, not discerning truth from error. By means of the orthodoxy of its central organs, the Communist Party lords it over human minds. This, by the way, is a sort of anti-Christian soteriology. Heretics are condemned to destruction. . . . The condemnation of heresy always has ecclesiastical-political motives, and behind it there was always malice.

It is quite wrong to think that the pathos of orthodoxy is the pathos of truth. Orthodoxy and truth are two quite different concepts, and behind them are different motives. The pathos of orthodoxy is the pathos of despotism, of domination and forced unity, not the pathos of truth and knowledge. Orthodox doctrine is not knowledge; it denies knowledge. It is always utilitarian. . . . The falsification of history is a special product of orthodoxy. And here marxist orthodoxy differs not at all from religious orthodoxy. Truth is revealed only through freedom, and not through some authority that would smother thought.

Put, No. 49, 1935, p. 78

CHAPTER XII

An Association of Men, not Men Themselves*

'I have a sober sense of reality and I do not believe in the possibility of getting on without the State . . . but my heart belongs to anarchy.'
BERDYAEV'S NOTEBOOK

AUTHORITY

Authority Always Tends to Become an End in Itself

Authority, power, is a means for realizing the good of a state or a nation, of civilization or of mankind. But authority always has a tendency to be transformed into an end in itself, and to substitute itself for all other ends. Here the rapprochement of means and ends takes place in just the wrong way, that of accepting evil means as an end. Both monarchy and socialism mistake means for ends in the very same way and admit falsehood in the realization of their purposes: at the beginning the original purpose was good and had value, but then the struggle for power becomes the secondary purpose and means are transformed into ends. Every bureaucracy is like this: in reality it is a means, but it has a tendency to transform itself into an end. But both the fanatical pursuit of ends by any sort of means, and the opportunistic substitution of means for ends, in equal measure, create falsehood and transform this falsehood into good, assigning to it a normative character. The Russian communists assign to their falsehoods, that they have elevated to a system, the character of moral obligation and good for the sake of the realization of world-communism's final aim, and for the sake of their struggle for power which has become an end in itself. What is tragic here is that injustice, falsehood, the torture of living man, is practised for the sake of aims which are recognized as high and for the sake of means which are recognized as necessary, but which along the way, have begun to obscure the aim. Thus a fictive atmosphere is created and the hypocrisy accumulates which is no longer considered sin, but duty. And all the horror lies, not in the falsehood which is recognized as sin, but in that which is considered as good. The whole life of the state, of the family, of civilization, of men's personal lives, is filled with this hypocrisy, this falsehood. Monarchy, democracy, aristocracy, the bourgeoisie, the pro-

* Montesquieu.

letariat—all are moved by this hypocrisy and falsehood. And one lie succeeds another. Parties, schools and tendencies in thought are permeated by the same hypocrisy and falsehood. And here the reason is not only the divorce of means from ends. The very theological viewpoint is false which sets up purpose . . . outside of, and transcendental to, man's soul, to his spiritual life. *Destiny*, p. 177

Authority, in the Traditional View of the Church

Authority is a phenomenon of the Church as a social institution. The search for authority is the search for a criterion which would stand above the relative, fickle, multitudinous human world—for a criterion which would be super-human. This is a search for security and guarantee. But guarantee and security are human—all too human. They are linked with the social life of men, and not at all with spiritual life. Spiritual life is perilous; it knows no guarantees: it is freedom, and freedom always involves risk. Authority is determination, and it relates to a sphere where things are determined from without. This kind of sphere is that of external society, rather than the sphere of spirit. Hegel was, naturally, a poor sort of Christian, but he was right when he said that the spirit is a return to oneself, that the Holy Spirit is subjective Spirit. Authority is extreme objectivity, the very pole of objectivity. Spirit, on the other hand, is extreme subjectivity. . . . There can be no criterion for the Spirit: the Spirit is its own criterion. There can never be a lower criterion for something higher; and authority, which is always of a social nature, cannot be a criterion for Spirit. The Spirit itself will direct us into truth. And there is no other means of distinguishing that which is of the Spirit from that which is not: the only criterion is the Spirit itself. It is wrong to seek a criterion: this always means lack of faith and disbelief in the action of the Spirit. But the Church has followed the line: whether or not the Spirit is active, in any case let authority act, let power and those in authority take action with guarantees of security. This is the Church acting in its quality of a social institution, acting in history. . . .

Sovereignty belongs only to God. And God's sovereignty is never incarnate: what is incarnate is God's sacrificial love, but not His sovereignty. In the final analysis, God is not sovereignty, for sovereignty is human and not Divine. God never appeared in the world as rich, but only as poor: He was never incarnate as worldly power, but only as crucified truth. God is not sovereignty, for He is not authority. Authority is something human, rather than Divine. Authority relates to the social relationships of men, rather than to spiritual life. God is power rather than authority. God's power is spiritual and in no way resembles the manifestation of power in this world. Spiritual power is freedom. Spiritual power has no need of the powers of this world. In comparison with the determination of this world, spiritual power is a miracle.

Reality, pp. 158-9

This sinful world, fallen away from God,
cannot exist without some compulsory form
of state government which is always relative,
and subject to historical evolution.

Letter to Metropolitan Antony

ANARCHY

Anarchism versus Anarchy

It is a great mistake to identify anarchism with anarchy. Anarchism is not against order, agreement, harmony, but against authority, violence, the realm of Caesar. Anarchy is chaos and disharmony, i.e. deformity. Anarchism is the ideal of a free harmony, determined from within, i.e. the victory of the Kingdom of God over that of Caesar. Behind a despotic, violent state one usually will find hidden anarchy and disharmony. In principle a spiritually-founded anarchism may be combined with the recognition of the functional importance of the state, with the necessity of state functions, but it cannot be joined with the supremacy of the state, its absoluteness, its encroachment on man's spiritual freedom, its will to power. *Idea*, pp. 154-5

DEMOCRACY

Up to the present time democracy has been formal, rather than real. Here the criticism of marxism and even of communism is just. Political democracy gives man political rights but does not give the real possibility of using them, since this possibility lies in the social-economic sphere, rather than the political. In political democracies, men easily fall into unemployment, need and poverty: their economic rights are not guaranteed in any way. Political and legal equality is joined with the greatest social and economic inequality. And the right to vote does not help at all. There is no formal aristocracy, all citizens are equal, but the division of society into social classes comes to its maximum expression. This is truly a revelation of the error in the myth of equality which was created by the French Revolution. A typical expression of this occurs in France, where we may observe it in a pure form: the nation is organized in a democratic state, based on universal suffrage, with a parliamentary cabinet. But society is not organized, society has fallen apart, any organization of society alongside the government is very difficult. Society was stronger in pre-revolutionary France. Now it is almost impossible to defend oneself against the democratic state, based on the myth of the sovereign people. The only real social organizations are the labour unions. Only a social, industrial, economic democracy would be real, representing the interests and needs of various forms of labour and creativeness. *Class War*, pp. 24-5

Spiritual Democracy and Aristocracy

Two types of mental structures have jostled each other through the whole course of human history, and have had great difficulty in understanding each other. One belongs to the collective, the social majority, and externally it seems to predominate in history: the other belongs to a spiritual individuality, an elect minority, whose significance in history is less evident. We might term them, conditionally, the 'democratic' and the 'aristocratic' spiritual types. The socialists say that down through history of human society a privileged minority has always exploited the majority, living in deprivation. But there is another truth, more profound and less evident to the external view: the collective, the quantitative majority, has always exploited and violated, crowded and persecuted the qualitative minority, the spiritual individuals with the divine eros, with the striving toward a higher world. History was constructed for the average, mass, man, for the collective. For this average man, for the collective, were set up the state, the family, legal institutions, the school, the order of daily living, even the external organization of the Church; knowledge, morals, religious dogmas and the cult were adapted to this average man. This mass-man, this man of the collective, has been the master of history, and he always demanded that everything should be done for him, that everyone should reckon with him, with his level and his interests. . . .

This average, mass-man, the man of the collective, was dominant in the nobility, just as he dominates in the bourgeoisie, the working-class, the peasantry. The state was never set up for the spiritual aristocracy; the forms of daily living were not developed for them, nor were methods of knowing or of creativity. Saints, prophets, geniuses, men of higher spiritual life, of true creativity, have no need whatever for monarchy or republic, for the protection of revolution, social norms or the school. The race of spiritual aristocracy bears the burden of history, not for itself: it submits to states and revolutions, to social order and to reforms, to school and method, to the old and to the new, for the sake of 'the people', the collective, for the good of the average mass-man. Of course both the race of the spiritual aristocracy and certain chosen people, living by the divine eros, belong to the sinful race of Adam, and therefore bear the consequences of sin and have to expiate sin. People of the 'aristocratic' spiritual type cannot get out of 'the world'; they must bear its burdens; they must serve the cause of general liberation and enlightenment. . . . The Church had profound reasons for struggle with the gnostics and for their condemnation. If the gnostics had prevailed, Christianity would never have conquered in history: it would have become an aristocratic sect. But the question relating to gnosis is very troubling and profound; it is an eternal question, of significance for our time. The way in which absolute and true revelation is refracted and received, depends upon the spiritual organization and level of him who receives it. Must one recognize as absolute and unchangeable that form of Christian revelation which is addressed to the average, mass-man, and is accepted by an average, normal mental organization? Must a more spiritual man, a man of more complex and delicate nature who has received greater gifts of gnosis, adapt himself to the average level, lower his spiritual level for the sake of everyone else, for community with all Christian people? May we identify sobornost with the people's collective? Or is the one way of accumulating the gracious gifts of the Holy Spirit and the attainment of spiritual perfection, the way of holiness—is this the sole measure of spiritual levels and the only source of religious gnosis? This is a very tormenting question, that of the religious significance of a man's gifts and talents. . . . Must all the questions of Christian consciousness and knowledge be decided in the spirit of the Christianity of simple people, of 'democratic' Christianity for everyone, for the masses, or is the disclosure possible and permissible, of things more secret, inaccessible and unnecessary for everyone? And is there in Christianity a sphere of the problematic, a region of more profound gnosis? *Freedom*, I, pp. 10-15

DICTATORS

Leaders of the masses always have something of the spiritualistic medium, in a greater or lesser degree. They direct the masses, but are also directed by the masses. Freud quite truly says that the mass has an erotic relationship with the leader, is in love with him. Only because of this, is a dictatorship possible, the dictatorship of a Caesar, a Cromwell, a Napoleon or the little Caesars and Napoleons of today. There was the same sort of erotic relationship with a monarch. But the monarch's authority over the masses was based on more stable, traditional emotions; sanctioned by religion. The leaders discover some symbol which inspires the masses, but at the same time holds and confines them. But the symbol always flatters the mass. The leader cannot do otherwise than flatter the mass. *Solitude*, pp. 176-7

> The temptation to imperialism lies in wait for every state. *M.C.A.*, p. 278

Dictatorships: Their Future

The world evidently must pass through dictatorship which will in its turn vanish, once certain radical reforms of society are accomplished. Escape from dictatorship is possible only by moral rebirth and the application of creative spiritual forces. The old socialist parties are powerless —they have lost their enthusiasm, become bourgeois, they have been bureaucratized and are no longer capable of action. In this connection the fate of the German social-democrats is very revealing. We are entering a period of great difficulty for human personality, for freedom of the spirit, for higher culture. And the question poses itself: can these dictatorships confine themselves only to politics and economics, or is it inevitable that they also become dictatorships of world-view, of ideas, of the spirit, that is to say the denial of all free spiritual life and work and conscience? In principle the first is possible, but what actually happens is the second, because of the decline in Christian faith. And we shall have spiritual war. It is already taking place in German Christianity, and it will spread over the whole world. We must battle against monism, for dualism, for the reality of the distinction between the spiritual and the natural-social, between the world of being and the objectivized world, between the Church and the State, between what is God's and what belongs to Caesar. *Fate*, pp. 66-7

COMMUNISM

Communism is a form of state capitalism. . . . Society is completely transformed into the state. *Class War*, p. 84

Communist Injustice Stems from Bourgeois Injustice

My book, *The Philosophy of Inequality*, was written in the summer of 1918 in an atmosphere of passionate resistance to the triumphant communist revolution. It may be that the book reflects, too much, negative feelings which no longer possess me. I had not yet lived through the spiritual catharsis, nor felt the depth of the spiritual experience of the revolution: I had not yet thought this experience through, to the end, in the light of religion. In 1923 I still hold the basic hierarchic and social-philosophical thoughts I expressed in 1918, but my mood is more cleansed and purified from the power of negative feelings, from all hatred, even if it should be kindled for the sake of a true idea or the true faith. One must live through the revolution, by its nature godless and satanic, spiritually deepened and religiously enlightened. And he has not lived through the revolution spiritually and religiously, who has brought out of it only a feeling of anger and hatred, who longs only for a restoration.

A spiritual experience of the revolution cannot lead to a desire for restoration, i.e. for the rebuilding of the old world with all its injustice. It is evident that the injustice of the old world led to the injustice of the revolution, and a return to the old would be senseless, the condemnation of our people's life to an endless whirlpool. We must get out of this evil, exitless whirl of the revolution and reaction into some sort of new life; we must proceed to creativity. We cannot set the anti-Christian injustice of communism over against 'bourgeois' justice, for Christ is no more in 'bourgeoisity' than in communism, and one godlessness gives birth to another godlessness. Communism is only carrying to the limit the godless injustice of the bourgeois world. *Inequality*, pp. 243-4

Communism

It made me smile to read that you were comparing 'my Christianity' with Marxism, one of the most dogmatic, immobile, congealed doctrines ever invented in the history of human thought. The dynamic of Russian idiotic Marxism is altogether external, ostensible. There is no dynamic of thought, no movement of spirit: it is the absolute suffocation of a dungeon. I have always thought that organized materialism would lead to dynamic immobility. *Letters to Mme. K.*, p. 17

Contradictions in Communism

The ideologists of communism have not recognized the radical contradictions in the very foundations of all their aspirations. They have sought the liberation of personalities, they have declared a revolt against all belief, all norms, all abstract idea, for the sake of this emancipation. For the sake of the liberation of personality they threw down religion, philosophy, art, morals and they denied the existence of spirit and the spiritual life. But in doing so they oppressed personality, deprived it of qualitative content, devastated its inner life, denied personality's right to creativity and spiritual enrichment. The principle of utilitarianism is in the highest degree unfavourable to the principle of personality; it subjects personality to usefulness and usefulness then tyrannically lords it over personality. *Origins*, pp. 46-7

Communism an Exclusive Religion

Communism, not as a social system, but as a religion, is fanatically opposed to all religion, and especially to Christianity. It wants to be a religion itself, replacing Christianity; it claims to answer the religious demands of the human soul, to give meaning to life. Communism is integral; it comprehends the whole of life, does relate itself to the social sphere alone. Hence its collision with other religious faiths is inevitable. Intolerance and fanaticism always come from a religious source: a scientific or purely intellectual theory can never be so intolerant and fanatical. As a religious faith, communism is exclusive. Here the Russian religious temperament, the Russian sectarian psychology, plays a large part. But Marx himself predestined an irreconcilable, militant attitude toward religion. In his introduction to a critique of Hegel's *Philosophy of Law* he wrote 'religion is opium for the people', a phrase which has become so actual in Russia. Marx thought that for the liberation of the working class, and hence of all mankind, religious feelings must be torn out of man's breast. *Origins*, p. 129

> Communism, a religion, is the idolatry of the collective. The idol of the collective is just as repulsive as the idols of state, nation, race or class. *Autobiography*, p. 265

Religion a Personal Matter for a Communist?

Communism wishes above all to be a world-view. It is totalitarian, and hence the religious question is very important. Russian communism ... builds all its programme on a definite world-view. In paragraph 13 of the constitution of the Communist Party, not of the Russian party only, but of the international, we read that every member of the party should be an atheist and carry on anti-religious propaganda. Party members must cease all relations with the church. Lenin clearly defined the principles to govern communists in his interpretation of how to understand that religion is a personal matter. Religion is a personal matter in regard to a bourgeois state. In a bourgeois state communists should stand for freedom of conscience, for the separation of church and state; they should defend the principle that religion is a personal matter. But the whole dialectic changes when the question is put of the attitude toward religion within the Communist Party, and hence within a communist state and society. Within the party, religion is anything but a private matter; here it is the most general, the most social, of concerns; here there must be merciless struggle against religion. A genuine, integral communist cannot be a man with a religious faith; he cannot be a Christian. A definite world-view is obligatory for a member of the Communist Party: he must be a materialist and an atheist, and a militant atheist at that. To be a member of the Communist Party it is not enough to share communism's social programme: communism is the confession of a definite faith, a faith which is the opposite of Christianity. All Soviet literature confirms this concept of communism. The communists love to emphasize the fact that they are opponents of Christian, Gospel morality, a morality of love and pity and sympathy. And this is perhaps the most terrible part of communism. *Origins*, p. 135

By its structure and by the spiritual formation of its adepts, the Communist Party is a sort of religious, atheistic sect, which has taken over the power (of the state). *Origins*, p. 136

Christian Sympathizers are Dangerous

Christians who recognize the truth in communism in so far as it concerns the social sphere, are considered more dangerous than those who are openly in the camp of the restorationists and counter-revolutionaries. A free-thinking, atheistic and materialistic bourgeoisie is better than Christians who sympathize with communism. The bourgeoisie can be used for social reconstruction; it is usually indifferent to 'world-views', while Christian communists spoil the integrity of the communist world-view. *Origins*, p. 136

Communist Dogmatism

Ivan the Terrible, that most remarkable theoretician of autocracy, set up the concept of an Orthodox (Christian) kingdom, in which the Tsar must be concerned for the salvation of his subjects. The function of the church is transferred to the state. The communist state also is concerned for the salvation of its subjects: it wants to bring them up in the one saving truth: it knows the truth, which is dialectic materialism. The communist state, unlimited in its power, is moved by hatred for Christianity, in which they see the source of slavery, exploitation and ignorance. The communists are extraordinarily ill-informed and uneducated in religious questions, but their actions are motivated by their own religious faith. The communist government frequently shows great pliability in its politics, in international politics it is very opportunistic; it makes compromises in economic politics; it will even grant a certain liberty in art and literature. Communism changes, evolves, it is nationalized, becomes more cultured, ... but there is one sphere where communism is unchangeable, merciless, fanatical, where it admits no compromise: this is the sphere of 'world-view', of philosophy, consequently of religion. All the Soviet literature in philosophy or anti-religious propaganda is the dullest, the most fanatical, the most petrified possible. Its dogmatism surpasses anything in Christian theology. It sometimes seems as though the Soviet Government would sooner accept the restoration of capitalism in economic life than freedom of religious conscience, of philosophic thinking, freedom to create spiritual culture. *Origins*, p. 138

Communism's Basic Problem

... The basic problem of communism is that of the relationship between man and society.... Marx was a remarkable sociologist but a feeble anthropologian. Marxism puts the problem of society, but not the problem of man: for Marxism, man is a function of society, a technical function of economics. Society is the basic phenomenon, while man is a epiphenomenon. Such a degradation of man is in striking contradiction to Marx's denunciatory doctrine of the dehumanization and 'Verdinglichung' of human life (making man a thing). The radical ambiguity remains: is making man a function of the economic process a sin and evil of capitalist exploitation in the past, or is this simply man's ontology? In any case, a definite answer is given in the fact that in the first attempt to realize communism on the basis of Marxism, as we see it today in Russia, man is considered a function of economics, and human life is dehumanized, just as it is in a capitalist order. *Origins*, p. 148

Russian communism is a distortion of the
Russian messianic idea. *Idea*, p. 250

Russian Communism Lacks Christian Elements

It was not the traditional Russian humanism, with its Christian sources, which helped form Russian communism, but rather Russian anti-humanism, related to Russian state absolutism, which always considered man as means to an end. Marxism considers evil is the way to good. The new society, the new man, will be born out of ever-increasing evil and darkness; the soul of the new man will be formed out of negative elements such as hatred, revenge or the use of violence. This is the demonic element in Marxism, which the Marxists consider dialectic. Evil will be dialectically transformed into good, darkness into light. Lenin declares that anything is moral which promotes the proletarian revolution: he does not know any other definition of good. From this it results that the end justifies the means—any means whatever. The moral element in human life loses all independent significance. And this is dehumanization, without a doubt. The end, for which all means are justified, is not man, not the new man, not the plenitude of humanness, but only a new organization of society. Man is the means for this new organization rather than vice versa. *Origins*, p. 149

Communism versus Capitalism

Communism is too dependent upon the past, has too much hatred of the past: it is too closely bound to the evil of capitalism and the bourgeoisie. The communists cannot conquer their hatred and this is their chief weakness. Hatred is always directed toward the past, and depends upon the past. A man in the grip of hatred cannot be oriented toward the future or a new life. Only love turns man toward the future, frees him from the heavy chains of the past. Only love can be the source of creativeness of a new and better life. In communists there is a terrible prevalence of hatred over love. But they are not entirely to blame for this: here they are victims of the evil past. The spirit of communism, the religion and the philosophy of communism, are both anti-Christian and anti-humanist.

But in the social-economic system of communism there is a large element of truth which is quite in agreement with Christianity: at least more so than the capitalist system, which is the most anti-Christian of all. Communism is right in criticizing capitalism. And when the defenders of capitalism denounce the injustice of communism, they merely bring out in bolder relief its good elements. Only those Christians who cannot be suspected of defending the interests of the bourgeois-capitalistic system, can denounce the injustice of the communist spirit and its spiritual slavery.... The industrial capitalist period subjected man to the power of economics and money, and it is not for its adepts to teach gospel truths to the communists, to teach that 'man does not live by bread alone'. The question of bread for myself is a material question, but bread for my neighbours, for my dear ones, is a spiritual, religious question. 'Man does not live by bread alone' but he does live by bread, and there must be bread for everyone. Society should be so organized that there is bread for everyone, and just there the spiritual question presents itself before man in all its profundity. It is inadmissible to base a struggle for spiritual interests and spiritual renaissance on a situation where bread is not assured for a considerable part of the human race.... Communism is a great lesson for Christians, a constant reminder of Christ and the Gospels, of the prophetic element in Christianity. *Origins*, pp. 150-1

SOCIALISM

In socialism there is always negative truth
and positive untruth. *M.C.A.*, p. 288

Truth and Untruth in Socialism

In relation to bourgeois-capitalist social theory, there is a great truth in socialism. The bourgeois world will have to give way to the socialist world, both by necessity and by justice. Socialism is the necessary and just development of the bourgeois, of a bourgeois world-order. All the bourgeois arguments against socialism are hypocritical and vicious. Socialism is the final justice and the final truth of the bourgeois. The Old Testament elements of a social order which does not know creativeness will have to move on to a socialistic bourgeoisie. The relative truth of socialism is indubitable. But just as indubitable is the absolute untruth of socialism. Willingness to sacrifice is just as alien to socialism as it is to bourgeois capitalism. But the way to all creativity lies through readiness to sacrifice. And the accounts of socialism against disintegrating bourgeois society, like anarchy's accounts against the disintegrating state, are all the same old accounts, kept in the same old world, of elements warring against each other on the same plane with no way out into another world. Socialism is bourgeois because it belongs wholly to the natural realm of necessity rather than to the supernatural realm of freedom. For this very reason socialism is as devoid of the creative spirit. The seal of over-burdened 'bourgeoisity' lies on all social ideologies and hence none of these ideologies is Christian. *M.C.A.*, pp. 283-4

Socialism Would Replace Christianity

Integral socialism, deciding the fate of human society, is not a matter of one or another economic organization: socialism is a phenomenon of spirit. It presumes to speak of last things, not next-to-the-last. It wants to be a new religion, to respond to man's religious questionings. Socialism is not supposed to replace capitalism: it stands on the same ground as capitalism; socialism is to replace Christianity. It, too, is suffused with messianic pathos and presumes to bring the good news of man's salvation from all distress and suffering. And socialism arose on Judaistic ground. It is a secularized form of the ancient Hebrew chiliasm, the fervent expectation of a real, earthly kingdom and the earthly felicity of Israel. It is not accidental that Marx was a Jew. He maintained the expectation of the appearing of a Coming Messiah, the converse of Christ, whom the Hebrew people had refused. For Marx the chosen people of God, the messianic people, was the proletariat.

Socialism Does Not Believe in God

The inner basis of socialism is unbelief in God, in the immortality and freedom of the human spirit. Hence the religion of socialism accepts all three of the temptations rejected by Christ in the wilderness. It accepts the temptation to turn stones into bread, the temptation to a social miracle, the temptation of the kingdom of this world. The religion of socialism is not a religion of the free sons of God, it abdicates man's spiritual birthright; it is a religion of the slaves of necessity, of the children of sin. Since life is meaningless, and there is no such thing as eternity, the only course left to men is to stick closely to each other....

Socialism Opposes Freedom

The religion of socialism has as its goal the conquest of freedom, the freedom of the human spirit which gives rise to the irrationality and the countless sufferings in life. It wants to rationalize the whole of life, to subject it to collective reason. To do this, it must make an end to freedom. Men may be brought to abandon their freedom, by the temptation of turning stones into bread. Man is unhappy; his is a tragic fate, because he is endowed with freedom of the spirit. Get man to renounce this unhappy freedom, enslave him by the temptation of earthly bread, and you will be able to build the earthly happiness of all . . . of choice, the freedom of good and evil and, consequently, the inevitability of suffering, of the irrationality of life, of life's tragedy.... *The Legend of the Grand Inquisitor* is written equally against socialism and against catholicism. I am even inclined to think that it is more about socialism than about catholicism. *Dostoevsky*, pp. 140-6

Socialism Does Not Create Culture

Socialism does not bring into the world any new type of culture.... The socialists themselves are uneasy when speaking of this topic. And those socialists who would sincerely wish for a new culture do not understand that their case is hopeless, that they have begun at the wrong end.... One cannot make culture an appendix to some other essential, basic affair, something like a Sunday entertainment. Culture may be created only when it is, itself, the essential basic matter. The socialists would direct man's will and thought exclusively toward the material, economic phase of life, and then they act as though they were not against culture.... Democracy has already lowered the qualitative level of culture, and has been able only to distribute, but not to create, cultural values. And socialism has lowered that level still further. The division and distribution of culture does not lead to a situation where a larger number of people begins to live by genuine cultural interest. On the contrary, this distribution simply reduces the number of people who devote their lives to higher culture. *Inequality*, pp. 220-1

Religious Socialism and the Religion of Socialism

Socialism is in a state of profound ideal crisis, and this in a time when the world tendency is toward socialism. Religious socialism, free of Marxist messianic illusions about the proletariat, cannot be reconciled with the basic principles on which the bourgeois capitalistic world rests. It denounces the falsehood of that world, first of all from spiritual, religious motives. It desires a radically new life. And it must perceive the source of 'bourgeoisness' in the exclusive belief in the visible world and incapacity to believe in the world invisible. A way out may be found only in a union of the social movement with a spiritual movement.

Novaya Rossia, Mar. 8, 1936

Socialism Inevitably Becomes Bourgeois

Socialism inevitably becomes bourgeois and winds up by being the party of the status quo. In a social democracy the practical-reformer elements come out on top and the revolutionary-messianic pathos disappears. The communists declaim against this with curses and indignation, but they are themselves only the bourgeois of tomorrow or the day after. Following Marx, they can set over against the bourgeois spirit only the spirit of revolution. But the revolutionary spirit is an unstable, fleeting condition, a brief movement in the battle. This movement passes, everything settles down, becomes calm, life begins to build itself again, and a new bourgeoisie arises. We can already see this in Soviet Russia, where out of the very bosom of the communist revolution a new bourgeoisie is arising, more cruel and hungry for life than was the former. The positive ideals of both socialists and communists are fully bourgeois; these are ideals of a grey, shop-style earthly paradise, ideals of earthly power and earthly satisfaction. This, of course, is not to deny the existence of positive social justice in both socialism and communism, but over against the bourgeois spirit one cannot place any sort of economic system.

For and Against Socialism

The opponents of socialism say that it is a utopia, in contradiction to human nature. Here there is ambiguity. It is not clear whether they do not want socialism because it is unrealizable and utopian, or it is unrealizable because they do not want it, and do everything they can to hinder its realization.... Unquestionably there have been socialist utopias, and there is a utopian element in socialism. There is a socialist myth, just as there is a democratic, liberal or monarchist or theocratic myth. But socialism is not a utopia; socialism is a stern reality. If in the nineteenth century socialism might have represented a utopia, in the twentieth it is rather liberalism that is a utopia. The argument is invalid that socialism is unrealizable because it presupposes a moral level, far above that of actual people. It would be truer to say that socialism will be realized just because men's moral level is not high enough, and therefore an organization of society is needed that will make impossible too great oppression of man by man. . . . Abstract moralism applied to social life is hypocrisy: it supports social injustice and wrong. A society of saints would not need any social actions to protect the weak against the strong, the exploited against the exploiter. A socialist society is not a society of saints; it is just a society of sinful and imperfect people, and we cannot expect from it the manifestation of human perfection. . . .

Freedom or Bread?

There are two problems at the base of social life, and nothing is more difficult than their harmonious solution: the problem of freedom, and the problem of bread. Bread is a great symbol, and with it is linked the world-theme of socialism. Man should not be a slave of 'bread', should not give us his freedom for 'bread'. This is the theme of the duality of socialism, of the two socialisms. Collectivist socialism, based on the primacy of society and the state over personality, the primacy of equality over freedom, offers bread, while taking away from man his freedom, depriving him of freedom of conscience. Personalistic socialism based on the absolute primacy of personality, of every person over society and the state, the primacy of freedom over equality, offers 'bread' to all men, while maintaining their freedom and leaving their conscience untouched. . . .

Slavery, pp. 172-4

Socialism's Most Difficult Problem is That of Freedom

How can one combine the solution of the problem of bread for everyone, a problem on which human life itself depends, with the problem of freedom, on which human dignity depends? On the basis of materialism, the problem is insoluble, it can be solved only on the basis of religious socialism. The tragedy of the situation lies in the fact that human masses are passing through a process of de-Christianization and materialism, for which process Christians themselves are to blame. By itself alone, socialism will never create either the perfect society or social equality. It may be that the sinful forms of the exploitation of man by man will disappear, or that classes in the sense that they have been created by the capitalist system will be no more. But there will be formed a new, privileged ruling class, a new bureaucracy—what we now call the 'organizers'.

Spirit and Caesar, p. 65

Socialism is a Religious Question

People of the West do not understand what is taking place in Soviet Russia. The Russians are an apocalyptic people. This people has made an attempt to realize socialism. But it did not accept humanist civilization, with democracy and a parliament, and in this tragic experiment the limits of socialism have been exposed, its real nature revealed. People in the West should learn much from this experiment. Facts have shown that socialism is not an economic or political question, but a question of God and of immortality. *Letters to Mme. K.*, p. 18

MARX AND MARXISM

Marxism recognizes only the quantity of work, but not its quality. *Class War*, p. 74

For Marx, class is more real than man.
M.C.A., p. 287

The Catechism of the Marxist

We should welcome, at last, a Russian translation of the catechism of Marxist philosophy—Engel's famous *Anti-Düring*. . . . Let people take a look at this, almost the only baggage of dialectic materialism, and the legend of its great theory, upsetting all other philosophies, will be finally shattered. . . .

This book is out of date in all its parts, is not up to the level of modern science and philosophy, and does not correspond to modern social actualities: it is a coarse contradiction of modern moods and searchings. . . . It is very important to indicate the basic contradictions of dialectic materialism. . . . Dialectic materialism is a logically inept combination of concepts, since it involves a simply monstrous 'logicalization' of the material. . . . But rationalistic materialism, the logic of the material, is worse than wooden iron or black whiteness. . . .

It is self-evident that the world process can be recognized as dialectic only through the idealistic doctrine of the identity of being and thought, where being is conceived as idea, as Logos, . . . only then do the laws of being coincide with the laws of dialectic logic, in the world-logos. And this means that . . . one may speak only of dialectic idealism, but not by any means of dialectic materialism. . . . In any case we must choose: either the historic process is dialectic, the self-revelation of ideas, and then in it there is an implacable logic, or else it is a materialistic process, and then there is in it no logic, no reasonableness, but simple chaos.

Actually, who among the partisans of dialectic materialism has tried to prove the unprovable and inept proposition that in material, which creates thinking, creates reason itself, there is an inner logic, a reasonableness in the strength of which the material processes are dialectic, i.e. may be identified with a logical movement of ideas? Looking into Engel's book, I am astonished at his naïveté—he does not even suspect the difficulties and impossibilities of the position on which he tries to stand. And none of the Marxists suspect this. . . . How are you to guarantee the reasonableness of an experiment which makes the world logical? On what do you build your certainty that in experience something will not be given us which surpasses all bounds, something out of the ordinary? 'We need no reasonableness,' say the positivists and materialists. Pardon, messieurs, but reasonableness is more necessary for you than for anyone else, otherwise the devil knows what might happen—a miracle might take place, and this you could not endure....

All the positivists, and still more the materialists, blindly believe in the rationality of experience, in some sort of reason in the world-process, in the logic of things.... The dialectic materialist for some reason considers it possible to believe that 'material productive forces' (some sort of a mass of materials) possess an inner logic, that material social development moves by a rational scheme, in a word that in the stuff of the world there is reason on which we may count, as solid as a rock. The whole Marxist system is purely rationalistic; naïvely and optimistically the Marxist believes in the triumph of reason in man's historic destiny; for him everything takes place in rationalistic scheme of things, everything is consequent, everything is prediscerned.... In this monism there still lives the old Logos....

So much for Engel's theory of knowing which is beneath all criticism, and does not even try seriously to put a base under dialectic materialism....

The catechism contains the famous doctrine of the leap from the realm of necessity into that of freedom.... It may seem strange that all of a sudden necessity gives birth to freedom, and some people have begun to introduce a correction: perhaps some time before, there was a bit of freedom, and perhaps afterward there will be a bit of necessity....

Actually, Engels presents a thoroughly rational theory of freedom.... Freedom is the product of necessity, is recognized necessity. This is again a materialized Hegelianism. Freedom is the product of material social development and at the same time the result of the triumph of consciousness, of reason. How comprehend the mystery of the transformation of necessity into freedom, if there was not previously at least the potential of freedom? By what miracle does material create spirit? They think to prepare freedom by some chemical process in a test-tube, but we refuse to believe in that sort of freedom. Neither Engels, nor the Marxists... have guessed that there might be another doctrine of freedom as a creative, constructive force, without which the long-desired liberation will never come to pass. And the leap into the realm of freedom, a long leap extended throughout the whole process of history—such a leap is admissible only on the supposition that freedom, as a creative force, lies in the nature of the world, in man's nature, that it slumbers even in the pristine stages of world-development, in every one of the monads which make up the world. I would even say that necessity is a product of freedom, that it is only a form of liberty alien to us. In his doctrine of freedom, Engels is coarsely rationalistic: he both fails to suspect the existence of irrational freedom, and finally is in accord with the most vulgar evolutionism.... *Life's Questions*, No. 2, 1905, pp. 369-79

Bread for myself is a material question:
Bread for my neighbour is a spiritual
question. *Fate*, p. 124

His are Ethical, not Material, Judgments

Marx was first astonished by the fact of exploitation and the struggle between exploiters and exploited. But the concept exploitation is not scientific and economic, it is axiological and ethical. Marx tried to explain exploitation by his theory of supplemental value, and he thought this was an economic theory, but in reality it embodies an ethical element that is definitive. Exploitation calls forth indignation and judgment—why? ... Evidently Marx began with the ethical premise that exploitation is evil and sin, even the greatest of these. He could not have received this ethical premise by some scientific means, or discover it in economic theory. The problem of the struggle between classes is inevitably not only a social and an economic, but also an ethical problem. Only we must distinguish between the ethical and the economic viewpoints. Marx confuses these two, in his theory of supplemental value and his theory of class struggle. He 'ethicalizes' economics and 'economicalizes' ethics. But even Marx's moralism is demonic: he thinks evil is the only way to good, thickening darkness the only way to the light. In his thought, brotherhood, equality, co-operation among men, are born of envy, hatred, anger, vengeance, and liberation comes out of violence and compulsion. In Marx, evil changes dialectically into good, darkness into light. *Class War*, pp. 47-8

The Myth of the Proletariat

Over against J. J. Rousseau's democratic myth of the sovereign people, possessed of a common will, Marx sets the socialistic myth of the proletariat, also possessed of a common will, a class-messiah, called to liberate and save mankind. Although Marx's doctrine of the messiah-proletariat is manifestly a matter of myth-making and the result of the ancient Hebrew idea of a chosen people of God which lived in Marx subconsciously, still the Marxist doctrine of class war taking place within even democratic society, is more realistic and nearer actuality than Rousseau's doctrine of an infallible, sovereign, common will of the people in a democracy. Marx transferred infallibility from the sovereign people to the sovereign proletariat. In actuality neither the people-nation nor the proletariat is infallible: both are sinful, just as a monarch or a pope is sinful and not infallible. *Class War*, p. 23

Marxism's logical structure in the theory of class-war is thoroughly contradictory and philosophically naïve. He maintains an extreme, scholastic realism of concepts. And he takes abstractions of thought for realities of being. To characterize any whole society with all its complex culture, as capitalist or bourgeois, is an abstraction of concept. And the proletariat, as a universal class, together with proletarian society and culture, is just the same sort of abstract concept. Lenin himself admitted that there could be no proletarian culture, that there could be only the communication of culture to the proletariat. . . . *Class War*, p. 31

Marxian Totalitarism

The problem of totalitarism, of which so much has been written, is more complex than is ordinarily thought. Totalitarism is a religious tragedy: in it is revealed man's religious instinct, his need for an integral relation to life. But the autonomy of various spheres of human activity, the loss of a spiritual centre, have led to a situation where the partial, the divided, claim totalitarity, integrality. Science and politics long ago began to present such claims. In our day, economics, technics, war have become totalitarian. In regard to these spheres, science takes on a utilitarian aspect. Marxism strives for man's integrality, will not be reconciled with the estrangement of human nature which occurs in the capitalist epoch. But Marx tries to create an integral man out of the divided, autonomous sphere of economics. He himself is caught by the power of economics of the capitalist epoch. For this reason Marxist totalitarism is false: instead of liberating man, it enslaves him. In the depths of his being man is not primarily a creature of economics. *Spirit and Caesar*, p. 53

The Contradictions in Marxism

We may well be surprised at the rôle now being played by Marxism. The Marxist doctrine was founded a hundred years ago. It no longer corresponds to either the social realities of today or to modern philosophical and scientific thought. Much of it is completely out of date. At the same time, this doctrine continues to be dynamic and even to increase in dynamism. Marxism is particularly out of date in its evaluation of the rôle of nationality. Two world wars have demonstrated that the Marxist international proletariat does not exist. The workers of all nations have slaughtered each other. Marxist-communists are an unusual, almost mystical phenonemon. They live in a world of their own creation, fictitious, phantasmagoric, mythical, abstract as geometry. They fail completely to see the complexity and variety of the human individual as he really it. At the same time they are very active, and they have aroused the fear of the whole world; some people even believe the Marxists will conquer. Marxist doctrine has been losing its theoretical and apprehensive value, but it has increased in power as a demagogic instrument of propaganda and agitation. . . . The greatest difficulty in comprehending Marxism is that Marxism is interested so exclusively in class, that it does not see the individual: in every thought and estimation of man, the Marxists see only class, with its special class interests. Thought is only an expression of class, and is of no value by itself. Bourgeois-capitalist reason is a different thing from proletarian, communist reason. And there can be no understanding between these two kinds of reason, only war to the death. I think that Marxism is right in its assertion that reason may be modified, that it depends on the type of man's existence, on the integral direction taken by his consciousness. But this must be understood and interpreted in quite another way than that adopted by communism. . . .

The Marxist concepts of class, the proletariat, the bourgeoisie, and the like, are abstract ideas, which correspond to complex phenomena in the world of social reality. Marxism is characterized by a certain scholastic realism of comprehension, although since they call themselves materialists, Marxists refuse to admit it. The Marxist proletariat is a figment of thought, and only in thought does it exist. In reality there exist only a lot of varied groupings of workmen, and they do not at all possess a unified 'proletarian' consciousness. The working class really exists, it is really exploited, and it is carrying on a struggle for its special interests. But the Marxist 'proletariat' is the product of a myth-creating process. . . . And the Marxists, despite all their a-moral theories, are filled with the moral pathos of hatred for the exploiters. The terrible curses in which communist propaganda is so rich, are really moral judgments, and without this moral judgment, meaningless. This is one side of Marxism, concerned with man's freedom and his moral responsibility. . . .

Perhaps the greatest contradiction in Marxism is that it accepts teleology, the reasonable nature of the historical process, a meaning for history, a purpose to be realized in future society. This, quite clearly, is taken from Hegel, and it was justified by the idea that at the basis of history there is a world-spirit, reason. But this is quite unjustifiable by the materialistic understanding of history. Why should material, in the process that it produces, lead to the triumph of reason, and not of irrationality? On what is based this type of optimism? This is possible for Marxism only because into the material there is introduced reason, meaning, freedom, creative activity. But this means that the Marxist philosophy is not materialism, and that calling it thus is clearly doing violence to terminology. . . . There can be no such thing as dialectic materialism; there can be only a dialectic of the reason, of spirit, of consciousness. By itself, the material does not know meaning: this is revealed by dialectic, which receives it from spirit. Soviet philosophy has even invented the word 'self-movement' to justify their contention that the source of all movement is not a push from outside, but inner freedom inherent in matter. It is laughable to call this materialism. . . .

Marxism-communism is so extraordinarily dynamic and active, because it bears all the traits of a religion. Neither scientific theory nor political practice would ever be able to play this rôle. We may note the following religious features of Marxism: a strict dogmatic system, despite practical flexibility; division into orthodoxy and heresy; the unchangeability of the philosophy of science; the holy scripture of Marx, Engels, Lenin and Stalin, which may only be interpreted, but may never be subject to doubt; the division of the world into two parts: the believers (the faithful) and the unbelievers (the unfaithful); the hierarchically organized Communist Church, with directives from above; the transfer of conscience to the supreme organ of the Communist Party, to a group; a totalitarianism which is characteristic only of religion; the fanaticism of the faithful; the excommunication and execution of heretics; the refusal to admit secularization within the community of believers; the recognition of original sin (exploitation). The doctrine of the leap across from the realm of necessity into that of freedom is also religious. This is really the expectation of the transfiguration of the world and the coming of the Kingdom of God. . . .

The contradiction in Marxism lies also in the fact that the realm of freedom, toward which all aspirations are turned, will be the inevitable result of necessity. Here Hegelian influence is very clear. Marxism thinks of freedom as necessity, known and accepted. This is essentially a denial of freedom, which is always bound up with the existence of a spiritual element, an element which is determined by neither nature nor society. As a religion, Marxism is a secularized form of the idea of predestination. . . . Hence for Marxism the new man, the man of the future social society, will be factory-made. He is the child of cruel necessity and not of freedom. The dialectic of capitalist evil is to give birth to good; the darkness in which man is deformed into a thing, is to generate light. This is a clear denial of the inner, spiritual man.

There is one fundamental difficulty in Marxism, connected with a contradiction in logic. What is, really, the Marxist theory? Is it, like all theories and ideologies, a reflection of the economic facts of its time and the class struggles then going on, that is a 'superstructure' and hence subject to the normal marxist explanation? Or is it the revelation of essential truth? In the second case, a real miracle has taken place: in the middle of the nineteenth century, for the first time the real truth about the process of history has been revealed, a truth which is something other than merely a 'superstructure' and a reflection of economics. Either way you put it, the Marxists cannot easily accept. The first proposition makes Marxism a transient and relative theory, useful in the class-struggle, but unable to pretend that it is true: it puts Marxism on a level with all other theories and ideologies. The second, which would recognize Marxism as the revelation of essential truth, contradicts the Marxist theory itself, which refuses to admit the possibility that such kind of truth may be revealed. The Marxist's answer to this would probably be a dialectic justification of relativism. They would say that the Marxist theory is a relative truth, like all other truths, but a truth which is, all the same, very useful in the social struggle. But aside from the logical weakness of such an answer, it in no way justifies or explains the exclusive importance of Marxism which distinguishes it from all other relative truths. It is quite clear that the idea of the unique rôle of Marxism is based on faith, and cannot pretend to have the least scientific significance. Marxism-communism is the religion of a sect for whom the supreme value is not the well-being of the workers, but the confession of the true faith.

The Marxist moral standard is neither Christian nor humanistic, in the old meaning of that word. Marxism holds that this all-human moral standard is a sly trick of the ruling classes who are using the idea of an absolute moral norm to weaken the revolutionary class-struggle. The Marxist revolutionary (I am not speaking of revolutionary and reforming social-democracy) is convinced that he is living in a world of unbearable evil, and that in his struggle against this world of evil and darkness all means are permitted. You need waste no ceremony on the devil: he is simply to be annihilated. . . . In Soviet Russia, alongside the employment of methods which go counter to Christian or humanist moral standards, we often find an effort to implant virtue by compulsion, the insistence on moralism. . . . The moral contradiction lies in the fact that Marx condemned the capitalist system from the viewpoint of this all-human moral standard, condemned it for its inhumanity, for its making man into a thing. Here Marx uses that very all-human moral standard which he is attempting to deny.

Spirit and Caesar, pp. 126-46

Marxism and Religion

Dialectic materialism is useful only for demagogy, not for philosophy.

Class War, p. 38

Marxism pretends to be a whole world-view, answering all the basic questions of life, giving life a meaning. It is at once politics, morality, science and philosophy. It is a new religion coming to replace Christianity. The true integral Marxists are believing dogmatists . . . they confess a system of dogmas. . . . Christianity does not think that the Kingdom of God can be attained without the participation of human freedom; without man's consent, without his spiritual rebirth. Marxism, on the other hand, thinks that a future perfect social order, the 'Kingdom of God on earth' can be arrived at, not only without God, but without human freedom, by means of applying Marxist dogmas to life. . . . Dialectic materialism which is a quite absurd and inadmissible combination of words, means the discovery of thought, reason, meaning, in lifeless material, which is held to be an accidental and meaningless collision of atoms. . . .

But how discover meaning and reason in dead and unthinking material? Marx naïvely believed in the reasonableness of material and the material process, in reason developing from material. But materialism, which considers material as the collision of atoms, cannot be joined to dialectic. From the collision of atoms reason and meaning can never be developed. . . . Marxist dialectic materialism is a distorted form of idealism. For Marxism, at the base of reality, there is not the collision of the atoms of material, and not the blind and irrational material process, but an *idea* in which actually they believe and a development which inevitably leads to the triumph of that *idea*. The philosophic bases of Marxism are contradictory, naïve and never thought through to the end. The purely mathematical interpretation of Marxism, which Russian communism recognizes as obligatory, is actually absurd and philosophically illiterate. In modern science and philosophy materialism no longer exists. . . .

In the material conception of history there is a trace of truth which even the opponents of Marxism should recognize. Economics is the base of human society, without which it could not exist. The truth of economic materialism is expressed in the Bible. I cannot write a philosophical book, make a scientific discovery, create a work of art, pass a moral judgment, unless I support my life with nourishment, cover my body with clothing, have some sort of a place to live. . . . But from this it is wrong to conclude that my thought and knowledge, my spiritual and moral life are born of the psychological processes of the organism, and are the reflection of the processes of feeding and of the elementary support of life. The indispensable conditions of life are not the cause which give birth to the whole of life's fullness.

If man's spiritual life depends on economics, economics itself depends on man's spiritual life. . . . And we may consider it scientifically established that economics depend on religious life and are by it determined, since without man himself as an integral being, without the participation of all his powers in his work, economics does not exist. . . . In comparison with modern research in this area Marx and Engels are terribly retarded and out-dated men of a past century.

> In its efforts to explain . . . philosophical and spiritual tendencies, . . . economic materialism has produced nothing but laughable results. *Slavery*, pp. 30-1

Whatever the Marxists write about religion, and often they write most laughable things, they always presuppose that the basic and absolutely most real fact of human life is exploitation, oppression. This is the fundamental myth of Marxism, everything proceeds from this and leads to this. Hence the anger and hatred with which Marx and Marxists are filled. They are quite incapable of thinking objectively, dispassionately. . . . What Lenin wrote about religion is specially full of anger. Compared with the coarseness of Lenin, Marx was a delicate, cultured, philosophically profound thinker and writer. . . .

Exploitation is a moral category, a morally despicable attitude of man to man. It is not at all an economic category, but Marx confuses the two, economic and moral, completely. For him exploitation, like all other economic phenomena, is a result of the inevitable economic process. . . . Why is this bad, why condemn exploitation? It is understandable that Christians should be indignant at exploitation, as against something morally wrong, but why should the Marxists, who deny the difference between good and evil? . . . But in the depths, Marx remains a Jew, believing in the messianic idea, in the coming of the Kingdom of God on earth, although without God. He is one of those Jews who rejected Christ, did not recognize Him as the Messiah, and one still waiting for the Messiah in the future, who will realize the reign of justice and happiness on the earth. . . . But for Marx the chosen people is no longer the Jewish people, but the proletariat. The Messiah whom the Jews rejected died the death of a slave, on a cross: He did not realize justice and truth on the earth. His kingdom was not of this world. The new messiah will appear in power and glory, will realize all messianic hopes, and His kingdom will be of this world. Such a messiah will appear in the person of the proletariat, the class of factory workers, and Marx discovered it. . . .

Marx is concerned not with the factual proletariat, but with the *idea* of the proletariat. . . . The situation of the working class may call forth indignation against bourgeois capitalist society. But out of this, can you deduce faith in the *idea* of the proletariat and its world-mission? The factory boiler-room is a poor school of morals. . . .

Marx was not a proletarian, neither was Lenin. Marxism asserts not only that the proletariat is exploited, . . . deprived of all the benefits of cultural life, is oppressed and deprived of its rights, but also that the proletariat is in a privileged position, mentally, morally and spiritually, that it is the coming power, fore-ordained to liberate the world, that truth is revealed to the proletariat. But actually 'truth' was revealed to children of the bourgeoisie, Marx and Engels, and they fastened it on to the proletariat. . . .

For Marxism human personality is only a means, not an end in itself. The human soul is not of unconditional value, as in Christianity. Marxism takes no account of the inner spiritual life of human personality. Personality is the only material for social structure, it is the object, but not the subject. Man is . . . a function of the development of material productive forces which are to lead to the triumph of a socialist society, which is itself divinity. And to this divinity human sacrifice is offered.

The nightmare and terror of Russian Marxism is that it brings with it the death of human personality and freedom. Communism denies not God alone, but man as well, and the two denials are inter-related. Communism conducts not only anti-God, but anti-man propaganda also. This is why communism is the antipode of Christianity, the religion of Divine-humanity, affirming not only God, but man. . . . Man's spiritual life does not belong wholly to society . . . or to the state: it belongs to the Kingdom of God and not to this world. The basis of Christianity is love for one's neighbour, for man. The basis of Marxism is the denial of love both for God and for man. . . .

The source of materialism is spiritual.

Reality, p. 153

Marxism is an outdated doctrine: at its base lies the anti-Christian, false religion of the deification of the proletariat. But there were positive elements in Marxism social realism, the affirmation of the great significance of economics in the life of society, and the struggle of classes, the revelation of the ills of the capitalist order, of the falsehoods in idealist-humanist culture. . . . Christian thought is called to unmask the spiritual emptiness of the communist ideal, the spiritual bourgeoisity of Marxism, the inability of the communist revolution to create new life or a new man. Christianity is more radical than communism: it seeks the Kingdom of God, the real transfiguration of man and of the world, a new heaven and a new earth. To combat and overthrow the anti-religious slogan that 'religion is a tool of exploitation', is possible only under the condition that the defenders and servants of religion never turn religion into a means of defence for any interests, whatsoever. . . . Only a purified spiritualized, more profound Christianity can overcome the anti-Christian spirit, a Christianity which recognizes its creative calling in knowledge, culture and in social life.

Marxism and Religion, Brochure, Paris, 1929

Mass Struggle

Man, not class, will inherit eternal life.

Class War, p. 130

CLASS STRUGGLE

Nobler Under an Aristocratic System

The conflict of warriors and of armies in the old aristocratic societies was cruel, but open and honourable. But struggle in a capitalist society, the struggle of banks and stock exchanges, of parliamentary parties and the Press is behind-the-scenes, it is a struggle behind a mask, almost imperceptible. In capitalist society everything takes on the complex symbolism of some secret economic game, the power of the phantasmagoric realm of money. This sort of rôle is played, above all, by the banks which secretly rule the world. In the course of history, of human societies, there have been conflicts between various kinds of social groups, the struggle of races and nationalities, of families and tribes, of religious cults and confessions, of schools and orders, of aristocratic societies, of professional unions, and finally of social classes, one of the most cruel of them all. *Class War*, pp. 9-10

Class War: A Fact of Nature

All the world's life is under the sign of polarization, attraction and repulsion, and in effect war is always going on. Dialectic is war on the plane of logic. The truth about the war of polar, opposite forces in the world was revealed in different ways to Heraclitus, Jacob Boehme, Hegel, Bachofen, Marx, Nietzsche, Dostoevsky. Class war in the social sphere is only one of the manifestations of cosmic war and the conflict of opposing forces, such as the conflict of the sexes, the conflict of races. . . .

But the widespread opinion that Marx and the socialists invented the class struggle, and that only the revolutionized working class carries it on, is wrong and insincere. In actuality, the bourgeoisie carries on class struggle and the ruling classes have always done so. But when struggle goes on for the preservation of one's dominant position it makes less impression than when it is for changing the social order. This is a usual misconception. The maintenance of the existing order does not seem like violent struggle, while changing it, has that appearance. . . .

Class and Society

The struggle of social classes takes place in society. Society itself is a sort of primary unity and reality, a whole that proceeds the classes which form it. Only if this is true can we imagine any positive, valuable results of class-struggle. If in reality only classes existed, and society did not, then class struggle would lead only to complete disintegration. The dialectic of class struggle on which Marx insists, presupposes the triumph of meaning, of reason, for the whole, for all society, for all humanity. But it is impossible to imagine any whole, especially meaning and reason for that whole, as the result of putting together these differing parts. And this means that society is a larger reality than class, although this does not deny the reality of classes. . . . Not only is there such a thing as the pathology of the class struggle, with its fury, its injustice, its class-distortion of truth, but there is also a physiology of the life of society. If Marx, on some unknown logical basis, asserts the reality of class, on one hand he denies the reality of society, and on the other, the reality of personality. Both society and personality are seen as functions of class. Class is the superior unit and whole, in relation both to society and personality. Personality receives all its being, the whole content of its life, from class. Man has no inner nature of his own; he is through and through a being of class and economics. According to Marx, society, at least in the socialist future, will be a reality, but personality evidently never will be real. . . . *Class War*, pp. 7, 18, 36-7, 39

WAR

All are Responsible for All

You want to show that there are people who are not to blame for the war, and therefore should not bear responsibility for it. Here you come against the riddle of individual fate, which is rationally insoluble. There is much in the fate of every individual which seems to us undeserved and unjust. . . . For me, only one thing is certain: personal fate can not be separated from national fate, the fate of all humanity, of the world. It is a great illusion to think that you are outside mutual responsibility, because you hold to some doctrine, for instance Tolstoyanism, which would separate you from the world. . . . Not he alone, who recognizes the idea of nationality is part of the national organism, but every individual living in it. The anarchist uses the state and is as responsible for it as any statesman. This question is decided not by the feelings of a given person, but by the national and state life-current. Even the saint in the desert cannot escape mutual responsibility. War is terrible: it is hard to be reconciled to it. But it is only an individual instance of the terror of life in general. Life in this world is terrible: it is all violence and constant killing. It is hard to be reconciled to the violence done to human destiny by nature and its laws. . . . The violence of war is only an individual instance of the eternal violence on which life in this body and on this earth is founded. And we may be reconciled to this life only if we accept its terrors inwardly, as the way of redemption. Otherwise we are fated to be eternally protesting slaves. The external denial of war does not liberate us.

From a letter to E. F. Gollerbach, August 17, 1915

War and Eschatology

We are all ready to recognize the fact that war by itself is evil, though it may be the least of possible evils. There is a demonic element in war. But when the war broke out people and nations had to put the question of the meaning of war: as in all significant events of their lives, they tried to give it meaning. But war cannot have a meaning: war is meaningless. War is a violation of meaning: in it irrational and lethal forces are in action. The one aim of war is victory over the enemy. But we may put the question otherwise: we may ask about the causes of war, and the tasks it sets before peoples and nations. War by itself does not create new life: it is destruction. But people who have lived through the horrors of war, who have revealed in themselves creative freedom, may direct their powers toward a new, a better method, they may prepare an end which will be transfiguration. . . .

War resembles revolution. Revolution is destructive and fatal, and at the same time, new, creative forces may rise, and new life may begin, in revolutions. *Put*, No. 61, October 1939-March 1940

War: the Communist Attitude

The world war was unquestionably born of capitalism, of the absurdity and irrationality of the capitalist system, but this does not mean that it was produced by class-economic interests; actually, it was ruinous for bourgeois class-interests. The communists indignantly declaim against the world war which set them up and defined their spiritual structure. And they cry out against a new war being prepared by the world bourgeoisie, at the same time that they earnestly long for it, as it is to bring their final victory. *Class War*, p. 22

War is Satanic, Anti-personal

War and everything connected with it is not only the most extreme, the ultimate form of violence, but the most extreme, the ultimate form of anti-personalism, the denial of personality. Once he has accepted war, man ceases to be a personality, and ceases to consider others as personalities. The military is a sort of hierarchic organism where each man feels himself a part, participates in the whole, and occupies his own definite place. This plunges human personality into a very special atmosphere in which slavery and violence are experienced organically and may even be sweet to the senses. This is a special temptation, the particular seductiveness of enslavement to war, that takes ascendence over the human element. War and the war-makers cannot consider human personalities otherwise than as means, as subordinate parts of a non-human whole. . . .

A band of robbers always makes a sharp distinction between their attitude towards members of their own group and toward those outside, and toward these they employ a different set of morals. And in this respect a state at war very much resembles a band of robbers. But there is this difference: the robber-band has its own idea of honour and of justice, its own character, all of which are lacking in a state possessed by the will to power. . . .

There never was a really 'holy' state; still less can wars be 'holy'. But all this is intensified once we begin to speak in terms of modern times and modern wars, that more nearly resemble cosmic catastrophe. The military ideals of honour were always un-Christian, against the Gospel, but modern war is immeasurably lower than those concepts of honour. They are not like a duel, but rather like assassination. A totalitarian state cannot have any ideas of honour, neither can totalitarian war. The concept of honour is linked with personality: it cannot exist under complete depersonalization. When all men are considered slaves or simple war material, there can be no mention of honour. . . .

From the time of the Renaissance men began to think that thought, science and literature, the printing of books, had great and preponderant importance. In our times a movement in the opposite direction has set in. Again men are thinking that the most important thing is action by the sword—and what a revolting sword! The leading people are soldiers, and war and murder are the principal means of action. But those who take the sword are not limited by any higher element, as was the case even in the Middle Ages. The very distinction between a state of war and a state of peace has become blurred. A state of peace is at the same time a state of war, and war is carried on without any declaration of war. Modern war is so mean a condition that it could not be declared; men are at too low a moral level. The temptation to military heroism and might continues, but this is only propaganda, always false; true heroism is no longer possible, for heroism presupposes the existence of personality....

There is nothing more monstrous than the blessing of war by Christian churches, than that awful combination of words, 'Christ-loving soldiers'. Man should be a warrior; he is called to warfare. But this has nothing to do with a corporation of the military which is an extreme form of the human enslavement. We must clearly distinguish this viewpoint from bourgeois pacifism which is powerless to stop war and may even be a condition lower than war itself. Bourgeois pacificism may signify simply love of a peaceful and secure life, the fear of catastrophe, or even cowardice. There is a peace more shameful than war: peace is not to be purchased at any price. True war against war is truly war, courage and readiness to sacrifice.... Many Christians turn away in horror from revolution because it implies killing and bloodshed, but they accept and even bless war which kills more people and sheds more blood than does revolution. And this is because they define their values differently. The state and the nation are considered such high values, even supreme values, that it is fitting to kill and shed blood for them while, on the other hand, social justice and liberation are not considered values for which it is fitting to shed human blood. But such a sense of values is unbearable for the Christian conscience. Freedom and justice are higher values than the might of a state or a nationality. Most important, killing and bloodshed are evil and sinful, no matter for what cause. Revolution may be a far lesser evil than war. But only a Christianity purified and liberated from historical enslavement may put the question of war and revolution....

The satanic nature of war is unquestionable. Bloodshed in a war is not without results: it poisons minds, consciousness is muddled by it. By its nature, war is irrational, it rests upon irrational instincts, but it presupposes rationalization. Preparation for war is rational in the highest degree, and presupposes the rational arming of states. This is the contradiction of war. The most irrational mental states are injected into the human masses. War predicates the awakening of an erotic state; its nature is erotic rather than ethical.... Hatred is an erotic phenomenon. And the human mass, brought to the irrational state, to the insanity of rational armament, is subjected to rational discipline, to be 'technicized'. The myth about beautiful, heroic war, of the warrior-eros, rising high above ordinary prosaic life, is a manifestation of human slavery. This myth is linked with other myths, of the chosen race, of the grandeur of the state, etc. All these myths are set over against the truth of personalism; they are ever hostile to the humanization of life; they all revolt against the spirit of the Gospel, all legalize man's enslavement.

Slavery, pp. 130-7

Is War Inevitable? Always Evil?

War is the basic phenomenon of our world eon. This is a fact, not merely of human social and historical life, but of cosmic life as well. . . . Brief periods of peace, as for example the last quarter of the nineteenth century, produced the false impression that peace is normal for history, rather than war. . . .

War is going on, war of men, of classes and families, war among social groups and political parties, between nations and states. Essentially peaceful order has never been stabilized—inner war has always existed. . . .

The denunciation of the evil and sin of war should not be permitted to lead to absolute pacificism, to peace at any price. In the evil condition of our world, war may be the lesser of two evils. While a war of conquest or subjugation is absolute evil, protective or liberating war may be not only justified but hallowed. The same may be said of revolution, which is a form of war. . . . Good is active in a concrete world-milieu, complex and indistinct, and the action of good may not always be in a direct line. Good may sometimes be compelled to struggle for the lesser evil. The final abolition of war is linked with a change in the spiritual condition of human society and the social order. The capitalist order inevitably gives rise to war. The elimination of war also means the elimination of state sovereignty and of nationalism. The elimination of wars and revolution demands a radical reform of human society. . . . *Divine*, pp. 123-7

REVOLUTION

The spirit of revolution is hostile to a revolution of the spirit. *Slavery*, p. 160

Revolution is Not Creative

All revolutions, both political and social, are directed towards a mechanical external destruction of the law and the redemption of the state and the church. These revolutions lack the true revolution of the spirit: they are uncreative, reactionary; they look backward instead of forward. Revolutions are hypnotized by a passionate hatred for the old life. Revolution is a reaction against the old, without creating something new.

Revolutions affirm the non-cosmic condition of the world: they do not connect the new life with an organic rebirth of the world in the cosmos, rebirth into cosmic harmony.... There is an unhealthy hysteria in revolutionary psychology: the creative mystery of that which is to come is hidden from it. Revolutionary passion is not creative passion. Revolutions are hostile and suspicious of every form of creativity. Men of a creative spirit are not revolutionaries in the social-mechanical sense of that word. Theirs is another sort of revolution, measurelessly more radical, more organic. Revolutions are still in the epochs of the law and the redemption and do not pass over into the epoch of creativeness. All the thinking and all the psychology of the revolutionaries is thinking and psychology of the world-epoch of the law, thinking and psychology of denouncing unredeemed sin.

The revolutionaries want to separate themselves from sin and evil, superficially and mechanically, and by this very attitude they often merely intensify sin and evil. They are not willing to live out the law and the redemption inwardly and organically, in order then to move over into creativity. The law in the state and redemption in the church cannot be destroyed: they must be mystically lived through.... Reaction and revolution do not reach to the roots of being: these changes remain superficial: they are mechanical and hence unreal. In the unhealthy atmosphere of political reaction and revolutions an illusory being is created, illusory passions and interests grow up. In this illusory 'politics', which is presented as the most genuine life, there is no true reality in the metaphysical sense; the true essential is lacking. *M.C.A.*, pp. 280-1

Sons and Stepsons of God

Ugly and ignoble are the very spiritual bases of your social-revolutionary world-view and your feeling for the word: dark is its most occult source. At the base of this world-view is the psychology of affront, the psychology of stepsons of God, the psychology of slaves. The sons of God, free in their spirits, cannot have such a feeling of life. Free sons of God, conscious of their high origins, cannot experience the feeling of servile offence, cannot consider themselves spiritual proletarians who are raising a rebellion because they have nothing to lose and nothing to hold sacred. For truly there is not only a social but a spiritual category of proletarians, a special spiritual type. This spiritual type makes all the external revolutions, torn away from the depths of life, from the world-whole. The sense of affront, anger, envy—these are the spiritual elements, this is the hidden psychology of the spiritual proletarian type. On such a spiritual foundation, you can never construct a human society, beautiful and free. The free sons of God have a sense not of affront, but of guilt. A consciousness of guilt corresponds to man's imperial dignity: it is the seal of his sonship of God.... A man's nobility of spirit does not depend on his external social position. But when the sense of injury, envy and revenge have poisoned a man's heart, his spirit ceases to be free; he is in slavery; he is not conscious of being a son of God. Hence the true liberation of man must call him to a sense of guilt, rather than a sense of injury; they should rouse in him a sense of the liberty of the sons of God, rather than of the slavery of sons of dust, sons of necessity. This is why one who is free in his soul cannot confess the proletarian-revolutionary world-view. *Inequality*, pp. 50-1

The Redistribution of Evil

Neither revolutionaries nor counter-revolutionaries ever think of beginning by organizing the evil in themselves: they want to conquer and destroy the evil in others, in its secondary and external manifestations. ... Revolutions do not so much conquer evil as make a new distribution of evil, and call new evil into being. *Freedom*, I, pp. 268-9

Revolution is the Result, Not the Cause, of Evil

The form of a state is maintained not by force alone, but by faith as well. And if faith is lacking, force becomes powerless. Revolution is the corrective to the phenomenon of the state in our sinful world. Revolution is also providential; it has its own mission. We are forced to take an ethical stand on revolution, and this is not easy, for revolution is something quite equivocal and dual, where good and evil are thoroughly mixed. Revolution is the inevitable fate of peoples; we cannot take a superficial attitude toward it or explain it by exterior political or economic causes. ... Revolution is a spiritual phenomenon, although it may deny spirit, and often tries to. ... It is both superficial and wrong to think that revolution is the cause of evil—just as wrong and superficial as it is to think that revolution is a phenomenon of good and justice, and will set up a perfect society. The cause of evil is unrealized good. Good is to blame for the appearance of evil. This is one of the paradoxes in ethics. The good has proclaimed its high principles, but has not realized these in life. ... Good does not realize either itself or justice, and then evil takes over the rôle of good and tries to realize justice. Such is the dialectic of good and evil. Then revolution begins. Revolution always means that there have been no positive, creative spiritual forces improving and reforming life, realizing more justice. Revolution is retribution, sent upon men because they have not manifested creative spiritual forces, have not created a better life. ...

The Dialectic of Revolution

The relation of ethics to the phenomenon of revolution can be only very complex. Christian ethics denies the ethic of revolution because the latter is based upon revenge, envy, resentment and violence. Revolution unites and organizes the most vengeful, envious and resentful elements of the people, and only then can revolution win. This is the law of every revolution. By its very nature revolution is without grace, and evinces a moment of God-forsakenness.... Religiously, revolutions are condemned because they are not only without grace, and apparently abandoned by God, but also because in the majority of cases they are Godless and persecute religious faith. But we cannot stop with these judgments.... Religiously, ethically, we must lay upon ourselves the responsibility for the revolution and recognize it as part of our personal fate. No one can consider himself innocent while only the other is guilty. Like everything great and significant in human destiny, revolution takes place with me, with every one of us. It is not something quite exterior to me, although I have been free from both the ideology and the illusions of the revolutionaries.... But revolution does not ask anyone if it is just or not: it is as elemental as a geological catastrophe. It always lets loose the subconscious instincts of the mass which have been restrained by old forms of thought, as long as they were sacred for the mass and conformed with their beliefs. The question of the right or wrong of revolution is raised in the reflexes of moral thinking before or after a revolution, but never while it is in course....

The most terrible thing is that revolution oppresses and destroys personality, that source of moral judgment and acts, and hence free and original moral judgments and acts become impossible. . . . One cannot expect personal, free, original moral judgments out of the depths, from Jacobins or communists. Their personal conscience has been paralysed and replaced by the collective, mass conscience developed by the newly-formed social routine. *Destiny*, pp. 223-7

The future which the revolution undertakes to build is always a rational future, and reason is to triumph in that future. But reason triumphs thanks to the revolt of irrational forces. We see this relation between the rational and the irrational in the two greatest revolutions, the French and the Russian.... Revolution is always fettered by hatred to the past, and it cannot exist or develop without an enemy arising out of the hated past....

There is usually less freedom than anything else in revolutions. *Spirit and Caesar*, p. 105

Revolution Results in Objectivization

Revolution is a great experience that both enriches and impoverishes man. The impoverishment itself is enrichment: some forms of enslavement are destroyed in revolutions.... The whole of Christianity was nothing other than a challenge to new spiritual birth, to the appearance of the new Adam. But instead of the new man, the signs and symbols of a new man were clothes upon the old Adam, the old man. This is the tragedy of all historical realization, which is never realization, but objectivization. *Slavery*, pp. 160-6

You Cannot Quell a Revolution: You Must Outlive It

Revolution, in the life of peoples, is a fatum: its course is not determined by freedom, it partakes of the irrevocable. This is usually not well understood by those who live in a time of revolution. Being a mass movement, revolution cannot but debase quality: it always upsets the established scale of values. Revolution throws away many values because of their wrong use in the past. You cannot put down a revolution: you must outlive it, carefully defending spirit, against which revolution always raises its hand. . . .

Spirit and Caesar, pp. 92

Revolution is of the Past

Revolution sings *du passé faisons table rasé*. The essence of revolution is the radical destruction of the past. But this is an illusion of revolution: the furious destruction of the past is still the past, and not the future. And only the decadent, decaying and evil past can be destroyed: not those elements in it which are true and eternally valuable. Idealizing the past is just as false as idealizing the future. True value is independent of time, it belongs to eternity. And there is a danger that the new man may be an outcast, alien to himself, oriented only toward the material side of life, toward technical civilization. It is astonishing how closely the new Soviet man seems to resemble the new man of such a hostile world as is America. This type of the technical, productive man is just as likely to be born of communism as of capitalism. The most positive traits of the Russian, which revolution has brought forth, his unusual readiness for sacrifice, his endurance of suffering, his communal spirit, are all Christian virtues developed in the Russian people by Christianity, that is by the past.

Spirit and Caesar, p. 168

> Revolution does not mean a break with the old: it is only a change of clothing. The old slavery changes its dress, the old inequality is transformed into a new inequality.
>
> *Slavery*, p. 163

A Successful Revolution is Always a Failure

It may be equally well said of revolutions that they are both realizable and unrealizable. They are so thoroughly realizable that once they are started it is almost impossible to stop them. And they are unrealizable because they never attain that for which the first generation of revolutionaries, who made them, strove. It is always so. . . . A successful revolution is always a failure. All the religious revolutions in history, perhaps most of all Christianity, must be considered failures. Hence we must take a dual attitude toward revolution. We cannot worship it like a divinity. Social utopias always involve falsehood, and at the same time man, in his historic destiny, cannot get on without them: they are his motive forces. The revolutionary myth always involves subconscious deceit; and yet, without a revolutionary myth, you cannot make a revolution. This is why history involves inescapable tragedy. *Spirit and Caesar*, pp. 176-7

The Russian Revolution

In 1917, in the atmosphere of an unsuccessful war, everything was ripe for revolution. The old régime was decaying and found no respectable defenders. The holy Russian empire, against which the intelligentsia had struggled for a whole century, fell. And that religious belief which had been maintained among the people by the autocratic monarchy was weakened. The official phrase 'Orthodoxy, the Autocracy and the people' lost all real meaning and became false and insincere. But a liberal, bourgeois revolution, demanding legal order, was an utopia in Russia; did not correspond to Russian tradition or the predominant Russian revolutionary ideas. A revolution in Russia could only be socialistic. The liberal movement was connected with the Duma and the 'kadet' party, but it had no support among the masses of the people, and lacked inspiring ideas. A revolution in the Russian spirit could be only totalitarian. All Russian ideologies were always totalitarian; theocratic or socialistic. Russians are maximalists and for Russians what seems an utopia is felt to be the most real. As is well known, the word 'bolshevism' originated in the majority (bolshinstvo) at the congress of the Social-Democratic Party in 1903, while the word menshevism arose from the minority (menshinstvo) at the same meeting. The word bolshevism turned out to be an excellent symbol for the Russian revolution, while the word menshevism was unsuitable. For the Russian left-wing intelligentsia the revolution had always been an integral idea, a religion, a philosophy. This the more moderate tendencies failed to understand. It is very easy to demonstrate that Marxism is an ideology quite inapplicable for a revolution in an agricultural country, with a great majority of peasants, with a backward industry and a very small proletariat. But the symbolics of revolution are conditional—they must not be taken too literally. Marxism became adapted to Russian conditions, and Russified. The messianic idea of Marxism, bound up with the mission of the proletariat, was joined to and identified with the Russian messianic idea. In the Russian communist revolution it was not the empirical proletariat which dominated, but the idea, the myth of the proletariat.... While continuing to call themselves Marxists, Russian communists reverted to some of the 'narodnik' ideas which were dominant in the nineteenth century: they felt it was possible for Russia to bypass the capitalist phase of development, and leap directly into socialism. Industrialization was to proceed under the sign of communism, and so it does. The communists turned out to be nearer to Tkachev than to Plechanov, or even to Marx and Engels. They deny democracy, just as did many of the 'narodniks'. At the same time they practise a despotic form of government which was typical of the old Russia. They were introducing changes in Marxism which are necessary in relation to an epoch of proletarian revolutions which Marx himself never knew.

Lenin was remarkable both as a theoretician and a practical leader of revolution. This was characteristic of a Russian with an admixture of Tartar traits. The Leninists exalted revolutionary will and saw the world as plastic, capable of any sort of change by the revolutionary minority. They began to assert a form of dialectic materialism in which that determinism which was so much in evidence in Marxism completely disappears. The material itself almost disappears, to which had been ascribed such spiritual qualities as the possibility of movement from within, inner freedom and reasonableness. A high degree of nationalization has also taken place in Soviet Russia, and a return to many traditions of the Russian past. Leninism-Stalinism is no longer the classic Marxism. Russian communism is a distortion of the Russian messianic idea. It affirms that light from the East which will enlighten the bourgeois darkness of the West: communism has both its truth and falsehood. The truth is social, the revelation of the possibility of the brotherhood of men and peoples, the elimination of classes: the falsehood lies in the spiritual bases which lead to a process of dehumanization, to a denial of the value of every man.... And into the higher sphere which will appear after communism, the truth in communism must enter, but liberated from its falsehood. The Russian revolution aroused and released the vast forces of the Russian people. In this lies its meaning.... A new spiritual type has ripened, with both good and bad features. But human freedom is not yet.

With all the lack of unity in Russian culture and the contrasts between them, the revolutionary movement had something in common with the Russian renaissance. In both the dionysiac element pushed out, though in different forms. I call that creative upsurge in Russia at the turn of the century, the Russian renaissance. It did not resemble the great European Renaissance. It had behind it no middle ages: behind it lay the period of enlightenment experienced by the intelligentsia.... The Russian renaissance was not classic; it was romantic, if we may use that conditional terminology. But that romanticism was different from that of the West; there was a great yearning for religious realism, although that realism was not attained. In Russia there never was that self-satisfied confinement in culture, so characteristic of Western Europe.... The Russian revolutionary movement, the Russian tendency toward new social forms, was revealed as stronger than the movement of the cultural renaissance: it was based on the rising masses and was related to the powerful traditions of the nineteenth century. The cultural renaissance was broken off, its creators shoved off the front plane of history, often compelled to go into emigration. For a time the most superficial materialistic ideas triumphed, and in culture there was a return to the old rationalist enlightenment. The social revolutionary was a cultural reactionary. But all this, which bears witness to the tragic destiny of the Russian people, does not mean that the whole reserve of creative energy and creative ideas was completely lost and will have no significance for the future. Thus history moves. It flowes in various psychic reactions, in which consciousness now widens, now narrows. Much may disappear into the depths, vanishing from the surface, but later reappear and manifest itself. So it will be in Russia. The devastation of culture which is now taking place is only a dialectic moment in the destiny of Russian spiritual culture and witnesses to the fact of how problematic culture is for Russians. All the creative ideas of the past will again have fructifying significance. Spiritual life cannot be quenched: it is immortal. *Idea*, pp. 249-52

The autumn of revolution never resembles its spring. *Spirit and Caesar*, p. 88

The Rights of Man

The declarations of the rights of man and of the citizen in reality paid little attention to man. In them the image of the citizen eclipsed the image of man. The citizen was thought of as a political being and his rights as formal rights. . . . For the Christian consciousness the declaration of the rights of man has essentially another meaning than it has for bourgeois-liberal or bourgeois-democratic ideology. From the Christian point of view, it is not the citizen but the man who has absolute rights, man as a spiritual being, as a free spirit which cannot be made into means to an end. But at the same time man's freedom is indissolubly linked with his obligations. Man's freedom is not a claim, but a duty, not so much what he demands as what is demanded of him. Man must be free. God demands and expects this of him. Man as a mature creature must take upon himself the burden of freedom. And here the centre of gravity is transferred from the citizen to the person. The concept 'citizen' is secondary and subordinate; it belongs to political society which partly conceals reality. . . . But the concept 'man' belongs to the plane of the spiritual. Man is above all a spiritual rather than a political being, and his unconditional and inalienable rights are rooted in the spiritual world. . . .
Class War, pp. 70-1

INTERNATIONALISM

Nationalism is Idolatry

Nationalism turns nationality into a supreme and absolute value to which all life is subordinated. This is idolatry. The nation replaces God. Thus nationalism cannot but come into conflict with Christian universalism, with the Christian revelation that there is neither Greek nor Jew, and that every man has absolute value. Nationalism uses everything as its own instrument, as an instrument of national power and prosperity. For nationalism, religion and the church are purely national-historic categories. A Russian should be Orthodox not because this is the true faith, but because orthodoxy has been an historic-national force, it participated in the development of the Russian state and Russian culture.... Nationalism cannot accept universal religious truth: in its consciousness religion remains at the pre-Christian level, the stage of Judaism, the religion of a tribal god who has not yet become a universal deity. Or it is like paganism before the development of the philosophic idea of one God. Nationalism was foreign to the ideas of the Christian universalism of the Middle Ages: it is a product of modern history which has lost its sense of unity and is moving towards particularism.... But nationalism sets eros over against ethos, and transforms the natural erotic in its attitude into a supreme principle or doctrine. In principle it affirms only the erotic and denies the ethical. Hence its inevitable conflict, not only with Christianity, but with general humanistic morals.... We must have not only eros, but ethos, connected with the dignity of personality.

Nationalism denies this. Nationalism involves not only love of one's own, but hatred of other nations, and hatred is usually a stronger motive than love. Nationalism preaches either seclusion, isolation, blindness to other nations and culture, self-satisfaction and particularism, or else expansion at the expense of others, conquests, subjection, imperialism. And in both cases it denies Christian conscience, contraverts the principle and the habits of the brotherhood of man. Nationalism is in complete contradiction to a personal ethic; it denies the supreme value of human personality. Modern nationalism dehumanizes ethics, it demands of man that he renounce humanity. It is all one and the same process, in communism as in nationalism. Man's inner world is completely at the mercy of collectivism, national or social. *Fate*, pp. 85-9

'Internationalism and the Unity of Mankind'

The creative historic instinct is always lacking in revolutionary maximalism. Genius is never attracted toward it.And every observer having some creative historic instinct and comprehending the fate of peoples, must recognize all the maximalist social tendencies abroad in the present historic hour for Russia as what they are, explosions of reaction. This truth is brilliantly confirmed by the fact that a more penetrating look at what is here taking place reveals neither social movement nor socialistic idea. Socialism is the idea of regulating the social whole. It wants to bring everything into line with the social organism: it is opposed to economic anarchy. But the elemental mass-movement, which here is called socialism, is not now inspired by the idea of the social whole, the idea of regulating and organizing one whole economic life: personal and group interests are evidently prevailing, to the disadvantage of the whole.... This anti-social character of the movement is a heritage of the old régime, the old lack of experience in free citizenship....

Change in the social fabric of society is always a long, molecular process: on the one hand it depends upon the condition of productive forces, on economic creativeness, both industrial and agricultural, and on the other upon invisible psychic changes in men. Man's creative relationship with nature, man's creative relation to man, that is both economic and moral creativity—these are what change the social fabric. And you cannot alter anything in social life by plots, riots, uprising or dictatorships—these are only the froth on the surface. . . .

Russia faces the task of social construction, rather than social revolution. A social revolution here now could be only social disturbance, anarchy of the national economy, which would worsen the national situation of both workers and peasants. And facing the extremely difficult and complex tasks which fate has set before Russia, any rosy optimism would be out of place or even immoral. . . . Russian democracy must first pass through a severe school of self-limitation, self-criticism and self-discipline. Not a social paradise awaits us, but difficult trials in our life. And to stand these tests a tempering of the spirit is needed. All social objectives are spiritual objectives, as well. Every nation is called to bear the consequences of its history, is morally responsible for its history. And our history has been extraordinarily difficult. And those are insane who, instead of appealing for a recognition of our stern responsibility, set afire instincts of evil and self-interest and soothe the masses with sweet dreams of the unheard-of social paradise which our poor, unhappy, long-suffering fatherland is supposed to show the world.

Russkaya Svoboda No. 3, April 29, 1917

FREE SPEECH

(Of the Freedom and the Dignity of the Word)

When men speak pathetically of the conquests of freedom in the revolution they should have in view first of all those rights of man which may not be taken from him in the name of any earthly good. But we seem to be thinking and caring least of all about these holy and inalienable human rights. The Russian revolution lacks the pathos of freedom. There is even good ground for thinking that Russians neither love nor value freedom. Our so-called revolutionary democracy is possessed by a passion for equality, such as the world has never seen: but by freedom it understands the right of violence to one's neighbour for the sake of one's own interest, utter wilfulness in a general process of levelling. Our democracy is willing to destroy any or all freedoms for the sake of equality. And the moral source of this denial of those rights which are the guarantee of freedom must be sought in our feeble sense of responsibility and underdeveloped personal dignity. The rights of man mean, above all, man's responsibilities. Without a consciousness of the obligation to protect the sacred rights of my neighbour, it is impossible to speak seriously of any sort of rights: all rights will be crushed....

The spiritual comprehension of freedom is something quite alien to our revolutionary democracy, and it is willing to sell man's birthright, freedom, for a mess of pottage of interests. And the revolution has not given us any of the real and essential rights and freedoms of man. We have no habeas corpus. On the contrary, the further the revolution 'developed' and 'deepened', the more violence against every human right and freedom has triumphed. And the first to be crushed was that most sacred human right, the most holy of freedoms, the freedom of speech. We are living through a period of the most terrible slavery of word and thought. In these nightmare days few there are who dare to think freely and independently, and freely and independently to express their thoughts in words. Our press is under constraint.... Time was when it had to express many conditional lies about His Imperial Highness the Tsar: now it has to tell no fewer conditional falsehoods about its highness, the revolutionary democracy. And no one, as in the Andersen fable, dares to say that the king is naked....

Many there are among us who criticize the tactics of revolutionary democracy, who appeal for union and coalition, but who morally capitulate before the element which gives rise to tyranny, which is violating both thought and word. Too much is laid to the charge of the bolsheviks ... when the evil is not only in them: they are not the only ones who are destroying freedom in Russia. The evil is more widespread and its sources lie deeper. Our intelligentsia has confessed a slavish world-view—it denied the very source of freedom, man's spiritual nature, man's sonship with God.... It must now be declared that true freedom of speech in Russia would predicate the possibility for everyone to speak, even partisans of the monarchy. If freedom of speech is to be granted only to partisans of a democratic republic, it will be not greater, but less, than under the old régime.... Republicans worthy of the name ought to give everyone more freedom of speech than did the monarchists. They have no moral right to speak of freedom, who recognize freedom only for themselves and their friends.

For half a year, the self-appointed workers' and soldiers' organizations have been carrying on a mockery of the rights of man: they live by the denial of freedom. It cannot be denied that the workers have not only the right, but the duty, to organize for the defence of their interests and the increase of their social significance. But our soviets, from the very outset of the revolution, have taken the line of class-dictatorship, ... and this has turned into the extermination of freedom in Russia....

Every freedom predicates discipline and asceticism and always perishes if these are lacking. The libertine orgies of words which have been indulged in by our revolutionary socialist press in recent months have been preparing the extirpation of all freedom of speech. Libertinism, profligacy and wilfulness destroy freedom. Freedom demands that man maintain his dignity and purity, that he control himself. Vicious use of speech destroys its dignity and enslaves the speaker. There is a regular orgy of verbal depravity in our revolutionary press.... To win the fight for freedom of speech we must struggle against this verbal depravity.

Russian writers who are conscious of their calling, their dignity and their responsibility to the fatherland ought to demand the proclamation of a guarantee of freedom of speech and thought.... Too many Russian writers have been hushed by cries in the street about their being 'bourgeois', together with all educated people, all creators of culture. They lacked strength to resist the raging elements; becoming confused, they began to use words which did not flow from the depths of their being.... There should sound forth in Russia a truly free word about the moral savagery and disorder to which we have come. And this word should sound out above all the struggle of class, groups or parties, above the struggle for interest and for power. It should be a reflection of the Divine Word, on which alone can be founded a shrine of free speech and free thought, now so derided and oppressed. This is no question of politics; this is a question of national ethics, of the religious consciousness of the nation. *Narodopravstvo* No. 11, 1917

CHAPTER XIII

The Making of Civil Persons

'Culture has accomplished great things, but it has not succeeded in ennobling man.' LECTURE IN RIGA, 1927

CULTURE

Culture and Creativity

Culture and cultural values are produced by man's creative act: in this man's genius is revealed. Man has invested enormous values in culture. But here is also revealed the tragedy of man's creativity. There is a difference between the creative idea and the creative act on one hand, and the product on the other. Creativity is fire; culture is the cooling of the flame. The creative act is upflight, victory over the heaviness of the objectivized world and over determinism, the product of creativity in culture is a dragging down, a process of settling. The creative act, the creative fire, belong in the realm of the subjective, while the product of culture belongs in the realm of the objective. In culture the same process of alienation, the exteriorization of human nature, seems always to take place. This is why man falls into slavery to cultural products and values.

Slavery, p. 106

Dehumanization

What is taking place in the world today is not a crisis of humanism (that is a topic of secondary importance), but the crisis of humanity. We face the question, is that being to whom the future belongs to be called man, as previously, or something other? We are witnessing the process of dehumanization in all phases of culture and of social life. Above all, moral consciousness is being dehumanized. Man has ceased to be the supreme value: he has ceased to have any value at all. . . . The machine dehumanizes human life. Man, desiring no longer to be the image of God, becomes the image of the machine. In its process of democratization, beginning with the eighteenth century, humanism goes along the line of subjecting man to society, to social ordinariness, it generalizes man—it is losing itself.

Fate, pp. 26-7

Civilization arose as a means, but man transformed it into an end. . . .

Slavery, p. 109

* Ruskin.

Man's Shaken Image

There may have been a time when the image of man, his truly human nature, was not yet revealed—man was in a sort of potential state. This was the case in the past. But now we face something quite different. The image of man has been shaken and has begun to disintegrate after it was revealed. This is going on now in all spheres. Dehumanization has penetrated into all phases of human creativity. In making himself God, man has unmanned himself. This is, of course, a collapse of the humanistic theory of progress. The fate of man is infinitely more complex than it was thought to be in the nineteenth century. The new world which is taking form is moved by other values than the value of man or of human personality, or the value of truth: it is moved by such values as power, technics, race-purity, nationality, the state, the class, the collective. The will to justice is overcome by the will to power. . . .

In the cultural and ideal tendencies of our epoch, dehumanization moves in two directions, toward naturalism and toward technicism. Man is subject either to cosmic forces or to technical civilization. It is not enough to say that he subjects himself: he is dissolved and disappears either in cosmic life or else in almighty technics; he takes upon himself the image, either of nature or of the machine. But in either case he loses his own image and is dissolved into his component elements. Man as a whole being, as a creature centred within himself, disappears; he ceases to be a being with a spiritual centre, retaining his inner continuity and his unity. To the fractional and partial elements of man there is offered not only the right to autonomy, but to supremacy in life. The self-assertion of these disunited elements in man as, for instance, the non-sublimated elements of the subconscious, sexual desire, or the will to dominance and power, bear witness to the fact that the unified, whole image of man is disappearing and giving place to non-human and natural elements. Man has disappeared; there remain only certain of his functions.

Fate, pp. 30-4

ART

Art is Creative

Artistic creativeness best reveals the meaning of the creative act. . . . The artist is always a creator. Art is always a victory over the heaviness of 'the world'—never adaptation to 'the world'. The act of art is directly opposed to every sort of added burden—in art there is liberation. The essential in artistic creativity is victory over the burden of necessity. In art, man lives outside himself, outside his burdens, the burdens of life. Every creative artistic act is a partial transfiguration of life. In the artistic concept man breaks out through the heaviness of the world. In the creative-artistic attitude towards this world we catch a glimpse of another world. To receive the world unto oneself in beauty is to break through the deformity of 'this world' into another. The world which is forced upon us, 'this world' is deformed, it is not cosmic, beauty is not in it. Accepting the beauty in the world unto oneself is always creativity. In freedom, not in compulsion, we attain to the beauty in the world. In every artistic activity a new world is created, the cosmos, a world enlightened and free. *M.C.A.*, p. 225

Art as Redemption

Art, also, may be redemption from sin. There is redemption in classic, canonic art whose attainments are in contrast to the aims of the creative act; and there is redemption, also, in romantic art, breaking all the canons and surpassing all limits. In art, as everywhere else in the world, the sacrifice of Golgotha is repeated. But the creative artistic act, by its purpose, by its intention, passes beyond the epoch of redemption. *The creative act is hindered in the world by the world by the redemption, and therefore it becomes tragic.* By its very essence creativeness passes out beyond the religious epochs of the law and the redemption, beyond both Old and New Testaments. But in these world-epochs it is forced to adapt itself both to the law and to the redemption. The adaptation of creativeness to the law produces classic art; its adaptation to the redemption produces romantic art. The creative act which gives birth to art cannot be specifically Christian: it is beyond Christianity. But the realizations of that creative act may be carried out in a Christian milieu. In the strict sense of the word, creativity is neither Christian nor pagan: it rises above and beyond them. In the creative artistic act darkness is overcome and transfigured into beauty. The demonic darkness of Leonardo burned up in his creative act and was turned into beauty. Art is pagan-classic or Christian-romantic not because of the nature of the creative act itself, which passes beyond such distinctions.

The Crisis of Art

In the course of its history, art has lived through many a crisis. The transitions from antiquity to the Middle Ages, and from thence into the Renaissance were marked by such profound crises. But what is happening to art in our day is not just one more crisis like the others. We are witnessing a crisis of art in general, with the most profound disturbance of its millenial bases. The old ideal of classic-beautiful art has suffered eclipse and one feels that there can be no return to its imagery. Art is struggling spasmodically to get outside its own limits. The lines which separate one art from another are being broken through, and this is true for the lines separating art in general from what is not art, but something higher or lower than art. Never before has the problem been so keenly felt, of the relationship between art and life, between creativeness and being: never before has there been such a craving to pass over from the creation of works of art to the creation of life itself, of a new life. Men are conscious of the feebleness of man's creative act, the lack of conformity between the creative task and the creative realization: our times have seen both creative daring and creative weakness in hitherto unheard of degrees. The creative man of today wants to create something which has never been, and in his creative ecstasy, he transgresses all limitations and all boundaries. But this latest man does not produce such perfect and beautiful works as did the more modest man of former times.

This crisis of the old art and the search for new ways works in opposite directions. We may discover in modern art both synthetic and analytic tendencies, working in opposite directions. And both the tendency toward a synthesis of the arts, their fusion into one single mystery, and the opposite tendency toward an analytical dismemberment within each art—both are shaking the boundaries of art in equal measure, both are equally symbols of the most profound crisis of art. The synthetic tendency began with Mallarmé, and the brightest adornment of those tendencies was the musical drama of Richard Wagner. The symbolists were the forerunners of these synthetic tendencies. Some of them wanted to take art out of its crisis by a return to the organic artistic epoch. The Arts are the product of differentiation. They had their origin in the temple, the cult: they developed from a certain organic unity in which all parts were subject to a religious centre. Many symbolists of our own and the preceding generation dreamed of giving back to art its liturgical and sacral significance. For them the sacral art of the ancient world and of the Middle Ages, the brightest organic epochs in the history of human culture, remained attractive and fascinating, and for them the call of the past was stronger than the call of the future. We are living through the end of the Renaissance, the last remains of that epoch when human powers were so free and their sparkling play gave birth to beauty. Nowadays this free play of human forces has gone over from renaissance to degeneration: it no longer creates beauty. And we feel very acutely the necessity of a new direction of man's creative powers. Man has become too free, desolated by his empty freedom, too much weakened by the long period of crisis. And man in his creativity has begun to yearn for the organic, for synthesis, for a religious centre, for mystery.

Crisis, pp. 3-5

Modern Art

When the new artists of our day begin to put newspaper clippings and bits of glass into their pictures, they continue the line of material decomposition to the point of complete denial of creativity. At the end of this process the creative act itself begins to fall apart and the audacious denial of creativity is substituted for creative audacity. Man is not a passive instrument of the world-process and of all the decomposition taking place in it: he is an active creator. The splitting apart of the cosmos will not destroy the personal spirit, will not extirpate man's ego, if the human spirit will make heroic efforts to stand firm and create in the new cosmic rhythm. The splitting of the cosmos can only forward the development and confirmation of the true nucleus of the ego. The human spirit is being liberated from the old power of organic material. As though with tongs, the machine is tearing spirit out of the power of material, is breaking the old splice between material and spirit. This is the metaphysical meaning of the appearance of the machine in our world. The futurists do not understand this. They place themselves more in the perishing material, than in the spirit which is in the process of liberation. The new art will create, not in images of physical flesh, but in images of another, finer flesh: it will pass over from material bodies to bodies spiritual. *Crisis*, p. 21

BEAUTY

Beauty is purposefulness without presentation of the purpose. *Beginning*, p. 168

Beauty

Beauty is a characteristic of a higher qualitative condition of being, of a higher attainment of existence, rather than a separate phase of existence. We may say that beauty is not only an aesthetic category, but a metaphysical category, as well. If man receives anything into himself integrally, it is beauty. We say what a beautiful spirit, a beautiful life, a beautiful action, etc. This is not only an aesthetic evaluation, it is integral evaluation. Everything harmonic in our life is beauty. . . . Beauty is the final purpose of human life and the life of the world. Good is a means, a way, and it arose in opposition to evil (the knowledge of good and evil). Beauty lies beyond the knowledge of good and evil. But that good which lies beyond the distinction between good and evil, where evil is forgotten, is also beauty. In beauty there can never be that moral distortion which characterizes evil. The beauty of evil is illusion and deceit. We can think of the Kingdom of God only as the kingdom of beauty. The transfiguration of the world is a phenomenon of beauty. And all the beauty in the world is either a remembrance of paradise or a prophecy of a transfigured world. Every experience of a condition of harmony is an experience of beauty. Beauty is the ultimate ideal from which has been eliminated all disharmony, all abjection, all distortion. . . .

Beauty has its own dialectic, and Dostoevsy has something to say about it. He thought that beauty would save the world. But he also says 'beauty is not only a terrible, but a mysterious thing. Here the devil struggles with God, and the battlefield is the human heart.' How are we to understand this? Of beauty we can also say that it is a pause in the conflict and, as it were, a communion with the divine world. But beauty is created and revealed in this darkened world, caught up in passionate conflict. And in men's souls it may be drawn into the conflict of opposing forces. There can be supreme beauty in tragedy. Dostoevsky himself is a tragic writer. Tragedy is the collision of opposing elements: it does not portray harmonic life. But Aristotle's doctrine of catharsis speaks of experiencing beauty through tragedy. Tragic beauty is deeper than its other forms: in it there is divine light.

Externally, harmonic beauty may be deceptive, actually concealing ugliness: like every other element, if torn away from the source of light, beauty may be transformed into its very opposite. Hence we may say with equal truth, that it is harmony and repose from tormenting conflict, and that it may become 'the battlefield' of God and the devil. The devil wants to use beauty for his own ends. Beauty is a great joy in our troubled world, both beauty of nature and beauty of art. Aesthetic evaluation unquestionably does not involve the difficulties of moral evaluation, and perhaps this is why the devil tries to use beauty for his own purposes. Beauty may become demonic, not because of what it is, essentially, but only because it may be used in the struggle of opposing forces, poles apart.

Beauty may be deceptive—the beauty of some woman or of some work of art. But the demonic element is in neither beauty nor creativeness, but in the inward condition and tendency of men. Men like to speak of the demonic element in Leonardo's creativeness, in his John the Baptist or Giaconda, for instance. But the demonic element which may have been in Leonardo himself, was consumed in his creative act which achieved transfiguration, and through which eternity is attained. The ground on which demonic deviation may easily appear is aestheticism which recognizes only aesthetic values and substitutes them for others, such as truth and good. But the great creators were never aesthetes. Aestheticism is not a creative, but a passive condition. The aesthete lives by his surroundings: he moves in a secondary rather than a primary world. He never loves or seeks the truth: it is an unpleasant reminder. But demonic deviations arising out of this ground are not very deep. I am inclined to think that the aesthetes do not love beauty, either, for they have no yearning toward divine heights. Aestheticism's most poisonous fruits are born in social life, where it distorts all values. . . .

Our intuitive appreciation of the beauty of nature, of a person, of a work of art, is the creative conquest of chaos, disintegration or distortion. The appreciation of beauty is a break through the ugly bark of the world. And the books on aesthetics are putting the question quite wrongly when they ask whether beauty is objective or subjective—when they say that beauty is subjective, rather than objective, what they mean is that beauty is a subjective illusion, merely a person's subjective condition. It is incorrect to say that beauty is objective. But saying that beauty is subjective is to say that it is real, since reality is in subjectivity, in the full flame of pristine existence, rather than in objectivized being where the fire has already cooled.

Thus brings us to the complex problem of the relationship between creativity and objectivization or alienation. Is the embodiment of every creative act objectivization? Is the beauty produced by the creative forces of nature or of man infallibly 'classic', 'objective' beauty? The dispute between classicism and romanticism is tied in with this. It would seem that classicism demands objective finality, i.e. the completion of the phenomena of nature, which may be classic, complete; but nature may also be romantic. Walter Scott's novels are full of this. Classic objectivity is the attainment of perfection in the finite, as it were a victory over formless infinity. It was not by chance that the Greeks connected perfection with the finite and feared the infinite as chaos. But romanticism which really is disclosed only in the Christian period of history, is striving toward the infinite, does not believe that perfection can be attained in the finite.

The classic is an element just as eternal as the romantic. Human creativity can no more not strive for perfection of form than it can be satisfied with anything final or closed in the world. The noumenal, from which creativeness proceeds, must always pass the bounds of the phenomenal: the finite must be shattered by man's striving toward the infinite. Now the relationships between form and the infinite content of life are contradictory and paradoxical. There is no beauty without form. Formlessness is not pretty: may even be hideous. Life's creative force must take form. We see this in the processes of nature, in the formation of the cosmos. But form may stiffen, petrify, quench the creative fire of life, may chill or limit it. And then the creative fire must flame up again, shatter the stiff forms, strive once more for infinite content. This is an eternal conflict, which cannot be ended within the bounds of this world. Beauty is connected with form, but it is also connected with the creative force of life, with the striving for infinity. . . .

But beauty is never objectivization for itself, demanding merely a passive attitude toward it. Even when it is only contemplated, beauty demands the creative activity of the subject. Beauty is not objectivity: it is always transfiguration. And only creative transfiguration is reality. Truly great art never could be exclusively classic or romantic . . . and could never be fully objectivized, for eternal life remains in it. The form of great art is never half-dead in formalism; it is related to infinite meaning, the striving for the infinite. Thus it is with Shakespeare, Goethe, L. Tolstoy, Dostoevsky, Sophocles, Beethoven, Rembrandt, Michel-Angelo, and others. Thus the beauty of the human face must also have form—without form it would not be striving toward eternal life: without this it would be dead beauty. And the beauty of nature must be life and not only form. . . . Beauty is the expression of endless life or finite form.

There was a time when symbolism was the mode in art: that belongs to the past. But there is an eternal symbolism of art. It would be truly realistic, if human life—the life of the world could be transfigured by means of art. But in art we are given only signs which hint at a real transfiguration. The meaning of art is that it anticipates real transfiguration. Art is full of symbols of another world. Every attained beauty is an incipient transfiguration of the world. Within the limits of art this transfiguration is not yet achieved. But art may pass beyond the bounds set for it as a separate sphere of culture. Thus the Russian literature of the nineteenth century, at its height, strove to pass out beyond the boundaries of art and move from the creation of perfect works to the creation of perfect life. Richard Wagner wanted to transfigure the whole of life by a synthesis of music and poetry. . . .

Romanticism, unsatisfied with the finality of classic art and its confinement to a separate sphere of culture, could not attain the goals it had set itself. But there is one art, the most powerful of all in its effect on the human spirit, by its nature more romantic than classic—that is music. Music is a dynamic art: it is in movement, in time rather than in space. It lacks the final form of plastic art, but it above all other arts arouses emotional movement in men, agitating his spirit. It is true that one speaks of classic, as different from romantic music, but this is only a conditional expression. The music of Bach is the most classic: it is trying to express the music of the heavenly spheres, rather than human tragedy, as does the music of Beethoven. But Bach's music leads out of this world into another and does not leave us in an already realized complete form, as does plastic art. It is not by accident that music is the art primarily associated with the Christian period of history, with Christian yearning for . . . the transcendent.

Sculpture is the most typical Greek art. Painting is already a more complex art than sculpture. In literature the most complex but the least pure form is the novel, so characteristic of the nineteenth century. Men began to strive, not so much for beauty as for candor. This in itself was a great conquest. But this did not cause an eclipse of the ideal of beauty. Books on aesthetics ceased to connect aesthetic perception and aesthetic emotion, with beauty. This gives rise to a profound crisis in art. This is evident in tendencies like futurism, cubism, surrealism, etc. Poetry and art are ceasing to be reminders of paradise; rather they speak more of hell. Real hell is one of the themes of modern literature (Kafka for instance). And while once art pictured deformity (Goya, Gogol) still it was deformity transformed by art. Now there is no attempt at such transfiguration. The attempts to return to classicism are powerless and reactionary. The crisis of art is a crisis of man, and reflects the condition of the world. The world is moving into a fluid state: it is losing its forms: there are no more firm bodies in the world. In the theories and discoveries of modern physics the firm shapes of the cosmos are disappearing. Even the solid forms of the human spirit begin to be lost in the discoveries of psychoanalysis, the philosophers of despair, fear and terror. In the disintegration of the old world social life is losing its forms. And in literature and art it is becoming constantly more difficult to attain solid form. . . .

Thirty years ago I gave a lecture on 'The Loss of Beauty'. I defended the pessimistic theory that beauty is decreasing in the world. Beauty is disappearing from man's everyday living, too: life is becoming more and more ugly, devoid of style. This is true of art, as well, which is turning away from beauty. Art wants to express the bitter truth about man and this truth is not beautiful. Here we must recognize the great service of modern art and literature, which help so much in understanding life. But for the contemplation of plastic beauty people have to turn to former epochs. The age of technics, of the mass, of overwhelming quantities, of the accelerated tempo, leave no place for beauty. It seems as though the triumph of greater social justice takes the beauty out of life. In the days of social injustice it was more beautiful. . . . Nietzsche was in rebellion against the lack of beauty in the democratic age, and he turned to the Renaissance, a time of profound a-morality but a time which created beauty.

There is a conflict between beauty and good, and the solution is not at all as simple as it seems to the aesthetes and the moralists. The union of beauty with truth is the integral transfiguration, the illumination of life. But beauty which has become separated from truth and good begins to degenerate and finally become ugliness. There is no progressive growth of beauty in the history of culture, though there is refinement and sharpening of aesthetic consciousness and feeling. Here we must recognize the justice in aesthetic pessimism. Aestheticism is not so much at home in an epoch of creative beauty as in an epoch of the non-beautiful. And the periods of the most powerful creation of beauty never were those of the greater acuity of aesthetic consciousness.

Divine, pp. 171-81

> Every bit of beauty in this world, the beauty of man, of nature, of a work of art, is a partial transfiguration of this world, a creative break-through to another.
>
> *Beginning*, p. 133

POLITICS

From the axiological viewpoint, we may fix this hierarchy of degree and value: first comes the spiritual, next the economic, and third, the political as a means in relation to the economic. Only the conscious subjection of politics to economics, while retaining the seniority of the

spiritual, prevents politics from becoming a fiction, masking and concealing economic interests. Axiologically we must think of society as something spiritual-economic, with the necessary minimum of politics. . . .
Class Struggle, pp. 72-3

It is most difficult to defend and assert human-ness in the life of societies, even when we know that human-ness is the basis of the society we desire and hope to see. We must struggle for a new society that will recognize man as the highest value, rather than the state, society or the nation. Right down to our day the human mass has been directed by the use of bread and the circus, by means of myth, pompous religious rites and festivals, by means of hypnosis and propaganda, and most of all by violence and blood. This is human, all too human, but it is not humane. In politics falsehood plays a great rôle, and small place is left for truth. States have been built on lies and on lies have they been demolished. And it is often said that without lies everything would perish and complete anarchy would cover the world. . . . And there has never been a revolution against the unlimited power of politics, for the sake of man and humaneness. Man should not have to stand the outrage of his human dignity, violence or slavery. Herein is the moral justification of revolution. But not all the means employed by revolution are justified. Revolution itself can commit outrage upon human dignity, it can violate and enslave people. The garment is changed, but the old man remains. And humaneness does not triumph. Humaneness demands a more profound, spiritual revolution.
Divine, pp. 149-50

OPTIMISM

Of Christian Pessimism and Optimism

I am not an optimist, but it would be wrong to characterize me as a pessimist. Final pessimism is not compatible with Christianity; it would mean treason to being, temptation by the spirit of non-being. Least of all am I guilty of passive pessimism, and that portion of pessimism which is part of my character may be called active, the pessimism of struggle. More any anyone I believe in man, in his God-like nature, his supreme worth, his calling to creative effort in the world, as it were continuation of the work of the world's creation. . . .

Man stands before the abyss of being or non-being. And he cannot dominate this abyss by his own powers: he needs help from above. This is a divine-human matter. And if in our time the very existence of man is threatened, if man is being torn apart, this is just because he has depended only on himself and his own powers. Man is passing through what is perhaps the most dangerous period of his whole existence. But I do not think that man's fate is quite hopeless. This hopelessness is only here, not in the beyond. For we believe that the world's history will not go on endlessly, that the world and history will end. But this means that we do not believe in the possibility of a final solution in this world, on this earth, in this our time. . . . But this should not hinder man's creative action, and his realization of justice here and now, for man's creative acts will affect the end itself. The end is a Divine-human matter. And the final word, which belongs to God, will include a word of man, as well.

Hence an absolute and final pessimism cannot stand, since every judgment on the evil and meaninglessness of the world and of human life predicates the existence of a higher meaning: very judgment of life here below predicates the existence of God.

Put, No. 46, January-March 1935

Optimism and Pessimism

The experience and the consciousness of evil and suffering give rise to the discussion of an optimistic or a pessimistic outlook on life. But pure pessimism or pure optimism are not a spiritual condition and are not a spiritual attitude toward life. . . .But the idea is false that man is a being striving for happiness: the very idea of happiness is a fiction quite without content. Of the two, pessimism means a more profound attitude toward life and more sensitivity toward life's evil and suffering. Optimism is more superficial and indicates a lack of sensitiveness to evil and suffering. This is true for example of the optimistic theory of progress, for which every concrete human personality is a means for the future, for some coming day of perfection. Pessimism is more noble than optimism, because it is more sensitive to the evil, sin and suffering involved in the depths of life. Absolute, hopeless pessimism is not permitted in Christianity, but a relative pessimism in regard to this world, is characteristic of Christianity. *Reality*, p. 110

SCIENCE

Science does not know truth, but only truths. *M.C.A.*, p. 27

Science versus Gnosis

We do not climb the stair of knowing in the dark. Scientific knowledge climbs a dark stairway—which it enlightens, step by step. It does not know what awaits it at the top of the stair; in it there is no light of the sun, of meaning, of the Logos, which lightens the path from above. But in the true higher gnosis there is an original revelation of meaning, sunlight falling from above on the stairway of knowledge. Gnosis is an original comprehension of meaning: in it is the manly activity of the

Logos. The modern spirit still suffers from fear of the light. By dark corridors the spirit has passed through lightless science and arrived at lightless mystic. The spirit has not yet reached the sunlight of consciousness. . . . But, in a deeper sense, all modern history with its rationalism, its positivism, its belief in science, has been a period of night, rather than of day—the sun of the world has darkened, the light from above has gone out, all the light that was has been artificial and indirect. And we stand before a new dawn, a new sunrise. *M.C.A.*, pp. 14-15

Science is Man's Adaptation to the World

In its specific essence, science is man's reaction for self-preservation: man, lost in the dark forest of the world's life. In order to live and develop, man must consciously orient himself in the given world which crowds upon him from every side. For this protective orientation man must bring himself into correspondence with the realities of the world, with the world's necessity which surrounds him. Science is a highly perfected means of adaptation to the given world and to the necessity forced upon it. Science is knowledge of necessity by means of adaptation to the given world, and knowledge out of necessity.

M.C.A., pp. 25-6

TRADITION

The Church's life is based on Holy tradition, on succession. Through tradition we enter into the one spiritual world, into the life of the new spiritual race. Tradition is a super-personal, 'sorborny' experience: it is creative spiritual life, passing from generation to generation, uniting the living and the dead, overcoming death. In the world, death reigns. But in the Church there is no death. Tradition is memory which brings resurrection, victory over death and decay: it is the confirmation of eternal life. The Church's tradition is not an external authority, not something imposed upon us. Tradition is a real existential conquest of the tension of time, proceeding from within, the grasping of eternity in the deathbearing current of time, the union of past, present and future in one eternity. Life in the tradition of the Church is life in eternity; it is the acceptance and recognition of realities from within, rather than from without. . . . Tradition is not authority: tradition is creative life of the spirit. Authority is a category applicable only to the world of nature, the world of tensions and enmity. Authority means nothing in the spiritual world, or 'it means only humility' and obedience which comes from within. Authoritative tradition is only a translation from the language of the spiritual world into that of the natural-historical world: it is an adaptation to the old race. *Freedom*, II, pp. 194-5

TECHNICS

> Herein is the dialectic of technical progress, that the machine is man's creation and it works against man; that it is born of spirit and enslaves spirit. *Beginning*, p. 193

Technics of Cosmic Significance

The dizzying successes of technics in the nineteenth and twentieth centuries mark the greatest revolution in the history of mankind, more profound than all political revolutions, a radical change in the whole rhythm of human life, a breaking away from the natural, cosmic rhythm and the appearance of a new rhythm, determined by machines. . . . Man is given terrible power, both for destruction and for construction. And it will depend upon his spiritual condition, whether he directs this force toward construction or destruction. The processes of technics, eliminating the boundaries of time and space, give man a completely new feeling of the planetary position of the earth. . . . Man's world-view and his feeling for life have always been closely bound up with the earth. . . . From the earth man came, and to the earth he should return. This is the ancient, very profound, belief of man. But now technics puts man before a quite other actuality, not at all connected with the earth: it transports him into inter-planetary space, surrounds him with new and hitherto unknown energies, whose action has not yet been studied. This means that technics and the machine have cosmic significance. Man's soul is eternal and does not depend on any sort of discovery, but his flesh does so depend, and the coherence of soul and flesh may change or be destroyed.

Technics Cannot be Neutral

One of the consequences of technics is this, that everything men once considered neutral takes on spiritual and religious importance. Technics is neutral only at a certain stage in its development. On a higher level it loses this neutrality and may return into magic, even black magic, if the spirit does not subject it to its own higher purposes. Technics . . . may lead to the destruction of the greater part of mankind—may even lead to cosmic catastrophe. . . . In the beginning nature was populated by gods, then men began to see in nature only dark forces, and finally they neutralized nature completely, as has been the case in modern times. But technics faces man with a new nature and demands a new attitude toward it, and this attitude can be anything but neutral. Man's power over the elements of nature may serve the cause of God or the cause of the devil, but it can no longer be neutral. *Destiny*, pp. 244-5

Technics: a Test for Man's Spirit

Technics, with its constantly increasing power over man, is of enormous significance for the spiritual life. . . . This 'technization' of human life denotes an extreme form of objectivization, . . . turns man's body into a means, an instrument, into a technical function. But the relationship between spirit and technics is more complex that it is usually thought to be. Technics may be a force which de-spiritualizes, but it may be a spiritualizing force, as well.

The romantics connected spirituality with the organic. This is one concept of the incarnation of spirit. The spirit is incarnate in the organic, not only in the organic human body, but in the organic bodies of history as well, for instance in the organic life of peoples, in tradition, etc. Hence the romantic reaction against technics, as destroying the organic. Technics plunges man into an atmosphere of cold metal, and living warmth disappears. But if spirit were completely dependent on material conditions, positive or negative, on external historic forms, on the organic, this would mean a terrible diminution of the spirit's reality. No changes in the conditions of human life can kill the reality of the spirit. Such changes mean only that spirituality is passing through a crisis. It is as though man were being crucified before his birth into a new life, before the rise of a new spirituality. Technics has turned against man: man has been unable to control technics.

But technics is also one of the human spirit's entrances upon the stage of the world's life. It bears witness to man's creative calling in cosmic life. The machine has a fatal effect on man's emotional life. It subjects man to ever-speeded time, in which each moment is merely the means to the next. It is more and more an obstacle to contemplation. Technics actualizes human life and demands extraordinary activity of man. But this power of technics over human life denotes man's passivity, his subjection to the pressures of the world and the processes going on in it.

Such is one side of technics. But there is another side. For man's salvation technics demands extraordinary spiritual intensity and activity, an extraordinary power of resistance. This is a great test of man's spiritual power. . . . This is a critical moment in the history of the objectivization of spirit. In the process of its objectivization the spirit falls under the power of objects. Technics is the expression of the power of objects over spirit. It is as though the spirit had finally gone over into objectivized spirit. But according to the law of the polarization of human existence, the spirit takes possession of the objectivity of technics and may make it an instrument of the spiritualization and humanization of both cosmic and social life. And as always this transition period is frightful and tormenting, an experience almost like death. The transition from organic incarnation in which man was still in the power of the cosmos, to organized-technical incarnation in which man becomes master of the cosmos, is an inward moment in the history of spirit.

Reality, pp. 63 ff

Man a Prisoner of Civilization

Man is a slave, not alone of nature and society, but of civilization, as well. Here I use the word civilization in the widely accepted sense which links it with the process of the socialization of man. . . . In different periods the man of civilization has been haunted by the thought that as he moved away from nature he lost his integrity and original force, and started to come apart. Besides, man began to question the cost of civilization. Man had joined civilization for the life struggle with the elemental forces of nature and for the organization of civilized society. But very soon man began to oppress man for this purpose, and the relationships of master and slave arose. Robinson Crusoe began to oppress Friday. The development of civilization was accompanied by the oppression of enormous masses of humanity, the working people. But this oppression was justified by the objective values of civilization. Evidently civilization could not arise or develop otherwise than by terrible social inequality and oppression: it was conceived in sin. . . .

The most important thing is that in his relation to culture and technics, man should be master, and not slave. When the principle of force is proclaimed, and force is set above truth and higher values, this means the death of civilization. And then we must await some new and mighty faith which will possess man, and a new spiritual uplift, which will conquer rude force. *Slavery*, pp. 99-100, 110

INDEX

INDEX

GEORGE ALLEN & UNWIN LTD
London: 40 Museum Street, W.C.1

Auckland: 24 Wyndham Street
Bombay: 15 Graham Road, Ballard Estate, Bombay 1
Bridgetown: P.O. Box 222
Buenos Aires: Escritorio 454-459, Florida 165
Calcutta: 17 Chittaranjan Avenue, Calcutta 13
Cape Town: 68 Shortmarket Street
Hong Kong: 44 Mody Road, Kowloon
Ibadan: P.O. Box 62
Karachi: Karachi Chambers, McLeod Road
Madras: Mohan Mansions, 38c Mount Road, Madras 6
Mexico: Villalongin 32-10, Piso, Mexico 5, D.F.
Nairobi: P.O. Box 4536
New Delhi: 13-14 Asaf Ali Road, New Delhi 1
Ontario: 81 Curlew Drive, Don Mills
Philippines: 7 Waling-Waling Street, Roxas District, Quezon City
São Paulo: Caixa Postal 8675
Singapore: 36c Prinsep Street, Singapore 7
Sydney, N.S.W.: Bradbury House, 55 York Street
Tokyo: 10 Kanda-Ogawamachi, 3-Chome, Chiyoda-Ku